Library of
Davidson College

STEFANESTI
Portrait of a Romanian Shtetl

Other titles of interest

BARBER, C. R.
Life Journeys

BOCHNER, S.
Cultures in Contact

HALL, R. L.
Ethnic Autonomy — Comparative Dynamics

KLIBANOV, A. I.
History of Religious Sectarianism in Russia (1860s–1917)

POWER, J.
Amnesty International

SCHOORL, J. W.
Between Basti Dwellers and Bureaucrats

WHITAKER, B.
Minorities: A Question of Human Rights

WIRSING, R. G.
Protection of Ethnic Minorities

Related Journal

INTERNATIONAL JOURNAL OF INTERCULTURAL RELATIONS*
The Official Publication of The Society for Intercultural Education,
Training and Research

Editor: Professor Dan Landis, Purdue University School of Science, Psychology Department, 1201 East 38th Street, Indianapolis, IN 46205, USA

This journal is dedicated to advancing knowledge and understanding of theory, practice, and research in inter- and intra-group relations. The contents encompass theoretical developments, field-based evaluation training techniques, and empirical discussions of cultural similarities and differences. Papers are selected for their contributions to an understanding of inter-group harmony and reduction of tensions. Issue-oriented, interdisciplinary discussion is encouraged and highest priority is given to papers which join theory, practice, and field research design.

*Free specimen copy available on request.

STEFANESTI
Portrait of a Romanian Shtetl

by

GHITTA STERNBERG
Outremont, Canada

PERGAMON PRESS
OXFORD · NEW YORK · TORONTO · SYDNEY · PARIS · FRANKFURT

U.K.	Pergamon Press Ltd., Headington Hill Hall, Oxford OX3 0BW, England
U.S.A.	Pergamon Press Inc., Maxwell House, Fairview Park, Elmsford, New York 10523, U.S.A.
CANADA	Pergamon Press Canada Ltd., Suite 104, 150 Consumers Rd., Willowdale, Ontario M2J 1P9, Canada
AUSTRALIA	Pergamon Press (Aust.) Pty. Ltd., P.O. Box 544, Potts Point, N.S.W. 2011, Australia
FRANCE	Pergamon Press SARL, 24 rue des Ecoles, 75240 Paris, Cedex 05, France
FEDERAL REPUBLIC OF GERMANY	Pergamon Press GmbH, Hammerweg 6, D-6242 Kronberg-Taunus, Federal Republic of Germany

Copyright © 1984 Ghitta Sternberg

All Rights Reserved. No part of this publication may be reproduced, stored in a retrieval system or transmitted in any form or by any means: electronic, electrostatic, magnetic tape, mechanical, photocopying, recording or otherwise, without permission in writing from the publishers.

First edition 1984

Library of Congress Cataloging in Publication Data
Sternberg, Ghitta.
Stefanesti: portrait of a Romanian shtetl.
Bibliography: p.
1. Jews—Romania—Stefanesti—Social life and customs.
2. Stefanesti (Romania)—Social life and customs.
I. Title.
DS135.R72S747   1984   305.8'924'0498   83-23727

British Library Cataloguing in Publication Data
Sternberg, Ghitta
Stefanesti: portrait of a Romanian shtetl.
1. Stefanesti (Romania)
I. Title
949.8'2   DR296.S/
ISBN 0-08-030840-6

Printed in Great Britain by A. Wheaton & Co. Ltd., Exeter

Contents

List of Plates	vii
List of Maps and Graphs	viii
Key to Pronunciation and Spelling	ix
Introduction What is a Shtetl?	**1**
I. Geographic Location	**9**
1. Town Proper	12
2. The Houses	16
3. The Climate	24
II. Historical Background	**26**
1. Brief History of Romania	26
2. History of the Jews in the Region	29
III. Social and Economic Structure	**41**
1. The Romanian Administrative Structure and the Shtetl Committee	41
2. The Professionals	45
3. The Merchants	48
4. The Craftsmen and Artisans	54
5. The Paupers	60
IV. The Family	**62**
1. The Family	62
2. Affinal Relations	68
3. Divorce	73
V. Health	**75**
1. Modern Medicine	75
(a) The Hospital	76
(b) The Doctor	77
(c) Sanatea si Viata Fericita ("Health and the Happy Life")	80

	2. Folk Medicine	80
	(a) The Felcher (Untrained Medical Person)	80
	(b) The Barber	81
	(c) Superstitions	81
	(d) The Midwife	83
VI.	**Religion**	85
	1. God and the Torah	85
	2. Calendar of Festivals	93
	3. The Synagogue	112
VII.	**Stefanesti, a Rabbinic Shtetl**	118
	1. The Rebbé's Court	118
	2. A Glimpse at Hasidism	121
VIII.	**Milestones**	124
	1. Birth	124
	2. Education	132
	3. Youth Clubs	138
	4. Marriage	139
	5. Old Age	146
	6. Death	147
IX.	**Leisure**	152
	1. Adults and Children	152
	2. Games	161
X.	**Songs**	173
XI.	**Ethos**	203
	1. Morality	203
	2. Nicknames	222
	3. Proverbs	223
	4. Curses	248
	Conclusions	250
	Glossary	256
	Appendices	267
	Bibliography	280
	Index	283

List of Plates

Between pp – 118–119

Plate 1. Strada Stefan cel Mare (Main Street).
Plate 2. Raspantie (Center of Town).
Plate 3. Soba de terracota (Ceramic tiled fireplace – stove).
Plate 4. Bedekn die Khalleh (Ceremony prior to wedding).
Plate 5. Bankes – ventuze cupping.
Plate 6. Rebbé's court Stefanesti.
Plate 7. Rebbé and hasidim.
Plate 8. Rebbé.
Plate 9. Hava Nagilla.
Plate 10. In Heyder (small boys studying in Hebrew school) charcoal sketch.
Plate 11. Scoala Israelito-Romana Narcisse Leven.
Plate 12. Hebrew kindergarten class.
Plate 13. Grade I and II class picture (2).
Plate 14. Diploma of Jewish–Romanian school First prize.
Plate 15. Diploma of Jewish–Romanian school.
Plate 16. Front cover of Sanatatea si Viata Fericita (2) (paramedical journal).
Plate 17. The Pumpkin seeds vendor (charcoal sketch).
Plate 18. Keren Hayessod (receipt for Zionist contribution).
Plate 19. Ketubba (Kessibe), marriage contract.
Plate 20. Gypsies setting up camp.

List of Maps and Graphs

Figure 1. Romania compared to "Pale of Settlement". 2
Figure 2. Map of Romania 1919–1939. 3
Figure 3. Jewish Communities in Romania. 10
Figure 4. Map (& key) of shtetl Stefanesti. 13
Figure 5. Floor Plan of House on Main Street. 19
Figure 6. Floor Plan of other houses. 21
Figure 7. Floor Plan of house in newer part of town. 22
Figure 8. Floor Plan of working class house. 23
Figure 9. Graph – occupations according to socio-economic standing 44
Figure 10. Graph – professionals Jews–Gentiles. 46
Figure 11. Graph – craftsmen occupational chart. 50
Figure 12. Floor Plan Synagogue – downstairs (men's section). 113
Figure 13. Floor Plan Synagogue – upstairs (women's section). 114
Figure 14. Saritura – game (hop scotch). 165
Figure 15. Carul – game. 169

Key to Pronunciation and Spelling

Romanian spelling is phonetic. The only sounds expressed with different symbols are "sh" spelled in Romanian ş (comma under the letter) and "tz" spelled in Romanian ţ (comma under the letter) and "tz" such as in "tzar", "sg" such as in "she", "ch" was used as in "each".

The pronunciation of Romanian Yiddish is distinctly different from other Yiddish dialects (Galitzianer, Litvak, Russian). The spelling of Yiddish wórds was, as much as possible, phonetic. "Y" was used as in "Yiddish".

In the case of "rebbe", the accented letter "é" was used to indicate that the final "e" was not silent. (Rather than the conventional addition of the letter "h" at the end of the word). The letter "h" is pronounced hard in the throat in both languages and was used as such.

Vowels	As in	Example
a	farm	balaboos (proprietor)
e	ten	Eretz (land)
i	in	gib (give)
o	more	Got (God)
u	turn	gurnisht (nothing)

Introduction

What is a shtetl? The term shtetl, derived from the diminutive of the German *stadt* ("town"), has been applied to the small Jewish communities of Eastern and Central Europe with populations between five hundred and ten thousand people. The term refers to a specific and unique culture with its own mores, values and language.

So far as it can be ascertained, the term shtetl was first used in this context in the 1940s by the Columbia University Research in Contemporary Cultures group. The group's study, inaugurated by Ruth Benedict, was continued under the leadership of Margaret Mead and published as *Life is With People.** It dealt with the entire Eastern European Jewish cultural complex, particularly Polish and Russian Jewish cultures.

The present study addresses itself to one of the subcultures included in the Columbia Project, namely: the Jewish shtetl of Romania. It is hoped that this study, focusing on one cultural area, will reveal specific differences deserving closer attention.

Although it was undeniably part of a larger cultural complex, the Romanian shtetl between the two world wars differed sufficiently from the image of the shtetl as it emerges in Yiddish literature to warrant attention.

On a continuum between two extremes — one the ultra-traditional shtetl of the Slavic word (described in *Life is With People*) and the other the urban Jewish communities — the Romanian shtetl occupied a unique and well-defined place.

Why has the Romanian shtetl been ignored? Several circumstances may be tentatively offered to explain this. First, Romania was geographically marginal to the mass of Jews of Poland and Russia, and the Romanian shtetl was not as economically depressed as its Slavic counterpart appears to have been. Consequently, Romanian Jews did not emigrate in quite as large numbers and were a minority

---

* Elizabeth Hertzog and Mark Zborowski, *Life is With People*. New York: Schocken Books, 1952.

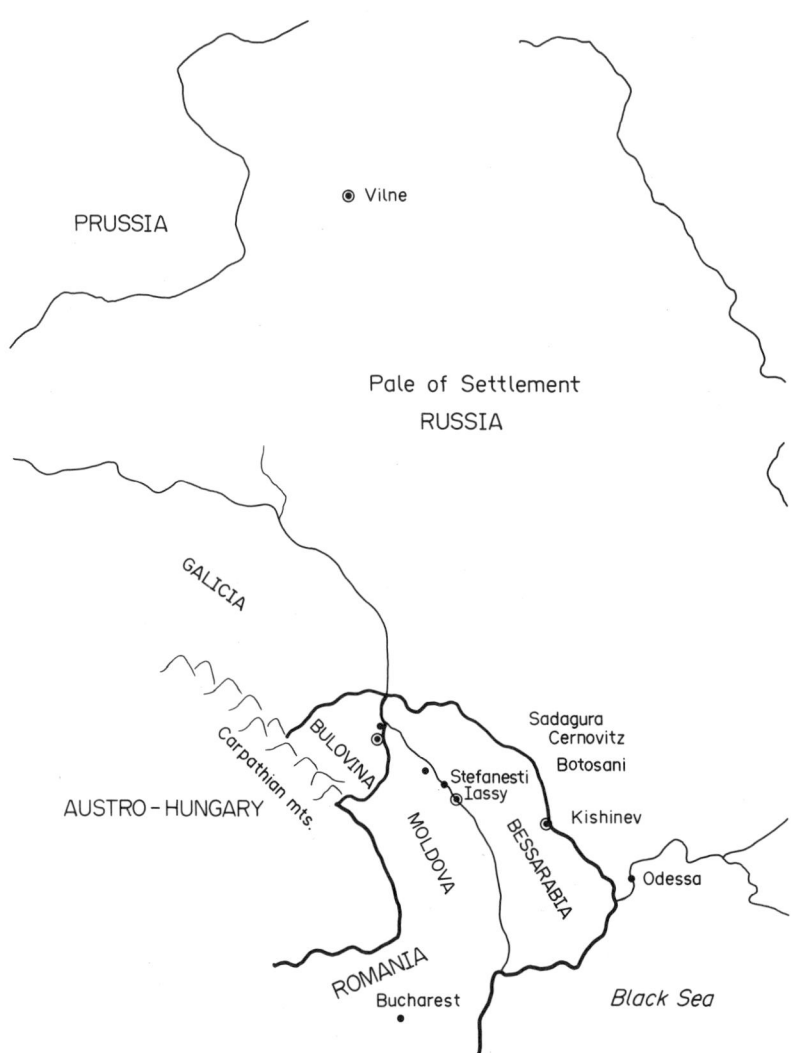

FIG. 1. Romania compared to "Pale of Settlement".

group among immigrants to the United States. Intellectual life in the Romanian shtetl was channelled into Romanian rather than Yiddish. As an open question: to what extent was all this due to the fact that the history of the host country carried with it advantages as well as disadvantages for the Jews in their midst?

History seems to show that geographically marginal cultures remain isolated from the activities at the center of a culture. The

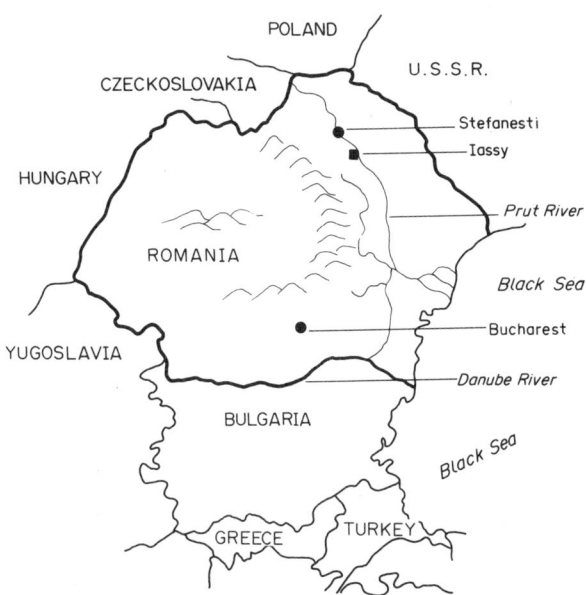

FIG. 2. Map of Romania, 1919–1939.

concentration of Jewish communities in the "Pale of Settlement"* within the Tzarist Empire — the center of Yiddish learning — was in the northwestern area of Russia, and decreased in density as one went farther south. The Romanian shtetl was at the outer limits of this center of Yiddish learning.

Romania, unlike other countries of the region, has been under foreign domination and was established as an independent national state only in the nineteenth century. It was a Latin island within the Slavic world, yet it shared with Russia the Greek Orthodox religion and — what was probably more decisive — the Slavonic or Cyrillic alphabet. The alphabet no doubt functioned as a barrier to the west; it retarded and complicated the cultural and intellectual development of the Romanian provinces. Attracted by language and cultural affinities to the Latin countries of the west, especially France, yet geographically facing east and maintaining religious ties with the Slavic world, a climate of conflicting values was inevitable. This was reflected in the development of the Romanian shtetl.

The Romanian shtetl was relatively less depressed than the shtetl of the Pale. The attitude prevalent among the neighboring peasant

---

* The twenty-five Russian provinces where Jews were allowed to settle.

population (themselves in a perpetual state of economic depression) was "live and let live;" the Jews led a comfortable though by no means luxurious life. And although anti-Semitism was taken for granted, it was not translated into the atrocities of barbaric pogroms, which were common elsewhere. The majority of shtetl inhabitants, therefore, preferred to live in the shtetl rather than launch into the unknown.

Intellectual life in the Romanian shtetl was increasingly channelled into Romanian rather than Yiddish. In a country with a high percentage of functionally illiterate peasants, the Jews who formed the majority of the middle class in the country accepted the Romanian language as a form of self-improvement. They automatically differentiated themselves from their Slavic co-religionists; they evolved differently in a context of a different social reality.

The Romanian Jews found an outlet for their talents in Romanian; the Polish Jews wrote primarily in Yiddish, in spite of the fact that at the time Yiddish was considered a lowly "jargon", a non-language.

This book is about one shtetl, called Stefanesti. Stefanesti was chosen primarily because the writer was born there and spent the 1920s and early 1930s in that town. This coincidence made it possible to contact a large number of former "Stefanester" who were willing and co-operative respondents. The Columbia group of respondents — judging by the report — came from various regions of Eastern Europe, including Romania, which fitted the design of that specific study. In the present case, all respondents came from the same shtetl and had lived there until the shtetl had been bombed out of existence. In socioeconomic status they span the gamut from working-class to professionals, with the majority former merchant families. This was the general profile of the shtetl as well. All of them have succeeded in forging for themselves prosperous new lives in their new homes but still maintain nostalgic memories of their home town.

Stefanesti was used as a model, typical yet different, as any individual differs from yet resembles the species to which it belongs. In discussing the values and attitudes of the Romanian shtetl, it was the "ideal type" that was presented, although in some cases specific examples were given to illustrate a point.

The fact that this town was the seat of the revered Stefanester Rebbé added luster to the town and put it on the map. This, no doubt, influenced the every day life of the people as well as the shtetl ethos. To that extent it differed from most of the small Jewish towns of the region. The infusion of hasidism also resulted in closer ties with the larger fabric of the Eastern European cultural complex.

Inevitably, the contemporary image of the shtetl has been influenced by musical comedies and motion pictures. This resulted in many cases in a distortion beyond recognition.

Fiddler on the Roof, the musical comedy and motion picture based on Shalom Aleichem's *Tevye the Milkman*, is an interesting example of how much cultural content may be lost in translation, and of the difficulty of conveying subtle shades of meaning from one culture to another. The wit and humor is completely lost when equating "milechdiker" with "milkman". "Milechdiker", the term used by Shalom Aleichem, is not a haphazard choice. Its precise translation is "made of milk", or "to be used with milk"; it is therefore not a profession, as suggested by the English translation "milkman" (which, in Yiddish, would be "milechmon"). Not only is there an inference of the ritual hygiene imposed by the separation of meat and milk, but the shtetl's view of Tevye as completely immersed in his profession is thus conveyed with subtle humor.

The description of the shtetl as a collection of ramshackle houses and mud streets that emerges from literature or perhaps from recollections of immigrants who left at the turn of the century is not quite the Romanian shtetl of the period between the two world wars. Differences between the shtetl of the Pale and the Romanian shtetl go deeper than these superficial and obvious ones. For, while the shtetl of the Pale existed in the midst of the repressive Czarist empire, the Romanian shtetl developed and existed within a more placid, certainly less brutal cultural milieu.

Referring to the shtetl as a village is another frequent inaccuracy. The difference between these two well-defined types of community is clearly demarcated in the minds of the respective inhabitants, neither of whom would have appreciated or willingly admitted the confusion of terms.

Nor is the shtetl to be confused with a ghetto, for it was a voluntary rather than an enforced segregation. Unlike the Jews of the Russian empire who were not allowed to settle beyond the well-defined boundaries of the Pale, there were no such overt constraints for the Romanian Jews. They were, however, prevented by law from owning lands outside the confines of a city. Only one or two Jewish families were allowed to live in a peasant village, where they usually owned the sole local general store or the saloon. The fact that in Romania Jews were not farmers may also have played in their favor, since they did not compete with the local peasants and hence were not perceived by them as an immediate threat.

Jews preferred to live in close proximity to one another and the compact shtetl was a form of self-protection and provided much-needed security. Most small towns were founded by special grants and by invitation from the local rulers, who offered the Jews special privileges, aware of their potential asset for the economy of the region.

One other important element often overlooked is the difference between the personality profile of the shtetl inhabitant and the urban-center Jew. This was primarily based on selectivity. Those who left the shtetl eagerly embraced the ways of the impersonal urban centers, while those who chose to remain were by definition tradition-oriented. This resulted in a more rapid assimilation of those who moved to the larger centers, while the shtetl accepted outside influences with great reluctance and under strict control of social approval.

Considered by other Jewish groups as "assimilated", the Romanian shtetl did not regard itself as such. It preferred to view itself as "modern", not fanatical, though it still clung to traditional ways. Outside influences were reluctantly accepted; the selectivity was based primarily on congruence with the shtetl's own core of moral values, and anything that clashed with existing mores was rejected as "goyish", that is, not Jewish, and hence undesirable.

The general outline and design of this study has followed the typical ethnographic structure. This is an attempt at historical reconstruction, based on open-ended interviews, personal recollections and sporadic references to written material. In recent years studies in cultural anthropology are expected to buttress assertions with quantitative evidence. In the present case, precise data were virtually impossible to obtain since the study deals with a society on the verge of disappearing. An effort has been made to obtain detailed information of a quantifiable nature, which is used in the construction of the charts and occupational profile of the shtetl. The emphasis, however, has been on the qualitative aspects of this culture.

Although a little community whose inhabitants shared day-to-day, face-to-face personal interactions, this was not an illiterate or primitive society. We are dealing here with a culture that was heir to thousands of years of literature and historic records, with a highly evolved system of ethical values. Nor was the shtetl culture integrated into the political unit to which it belonged by virtue of its geographic location; instead, it identified with the large Jewish culture, of which it considered itself an integral part.

Fifty respondents were contacted, all former residents of this shtetl; they now reside in Montreal, New York, Tel Aviv, Jerusalem, Nazareth and Bucharest, Romania. Most respondents were initially contacted in person and subsequently contacted by means of correspondence or further interviews. Personal interviews were conducted in an unstructured manner. The reply letters responded to a few general questions.

The diary of a young woman (kept from 1916 to 1919) yielded interesting information, although it pertained to a period prior to the one under discussion. An autograph book (kept from 1912 to 1938) afforded interesting verses and remarks, a chronicle and a look at the emotional structure prevalent during that time in the shtetl. Photographs, letters and postcards provided further firsthand illustrative material. Yiddish literature (read in Romanian and English translations) was used as a standard of comparison.

Since Romanian was beginning to replace Yiddish as the everyday language, surveys of the Romanian journals and reviews – *Magazinul* ("the magazine"), *Dimineata Copiilor* ("Children's Morning") and *Santatea* ("Health") have added another dimension to the study.

In Bucharest, Romania, the Biblioteca Nationala was most helpful in providing archival information. The staff of Revista Cultului Mozaic provided valuable information regarding the Stefanester *Rebbé*.

All the diagrams included here are based on personal recollections, corroborated by the respondents.

That this was not a homogeneous society but one consciously and tenaciously clinging to its social stratification cannot be sufficiently emphasized. It must also be stressed that, in the Romanian shtetl, being a merchant was regarded as a dignified and respectable profession. The shopkeeper was an honorable, upright man who prided himself on his honesty and straightforward manner. (The anecdote was told of one reputable merchant who, when a deal had all but been completed by his assistant, warned the customer that the cloth she was about to buy was not washable. He preferred to lose the sale arrived at with some difficulty, rather than complete it under false pretences.)

Yichus ("status") was vaguely defined but strictly adhered to. It was a family-bestowed prestige, including family reputation and, increasingly, wealth, although the latter was an encroachment accepted with reservations.

The family in the Romanian shtetl differed from the pattern of families in the shtetl of the Pale. No longer did the father study or spend long periods with his favorite *rebbé* while the wife toiled with the family; this was dismissed as sheer fanaticism. The husband

and father was the breadwinner and undisputed master of the household.

The chapter on religion presented the obvious problem of dealing with a vast topic in a limited scope. Yet it would have been inconceivable to speak of the Romanian shtetl without mentioning religion: its core, root and reason for existence. It is hoped that the mood and flavor will have been conveyed.

Most folk songs mentioned by respondents were found in the numerous volumes compiled by musicologists. These songs have been included, sometimes with a few changes, according to the respondents' reports. Two songs, *Die Soche* and *Der Mai Lied* were found in their entirety in a school notebook dating back to 1909. Both are unique in originality of topic, since nature was a subject rarely dealt with in shtetl songs.

It is hoped that this study of one Romanian shtetl will prove of interest, not only to those for whom these descriptions and references evoke a note of nostalgia, but also as a reference book for anyone interested in a closer look at a rarely mentioned culture, in a state of flux, a culture which in the midst of a world in turmoil, succeeded in maintaining a sense of values which served it and its members well.

CHAPTER I
Geographic Location

Staid and placid, as if convinced of its own importance under the sun — for it was the home of the renowned *tzadik*, the Stefanester Rebbé — Stefanesti squatted on the banks of a muddy stream, the Basheu, at the foot of softly rolling hills in northeastern Romania. Three miles east of town meandered the river Prut, which originated in the Northern Carpathians and flowed into the Danube. The Prut has served as a frontier between Moldova (the northern province of Romania) and Bessarabia, a region that throughout recent history, has been volleyed back and forth between Russia and Romania. In the brief span between the two world wars, the period we are examining here, the Prut was part of Romania and Stefanesti had lost some of its bordertown glitter. At the end of the Second World War, Bessarabia was again taken over by the USSR and the Prut again became the frontier. Although it still appears on maps, Stefanesti was bombed out of existence and the Jewish population (the shtetl proper) dispersed; a sort of image of the history of the Jewish people, for wherever former inhabitants have been transported by fate and fortune, they still call themselves *Stefaneshter*, not without some pride and nostalgia for the town as they knew it.

The great majority of the Jewish people of Romania lived in the *shtetlech* (plural for shtetl), which were sprinkled throughout the northern part of Romania as if overflowing the huge cauldron of eastern European Jewry of Poland and Russia. There was a constant network of communication between all these townlets: Sulitza (where the inhabitants of Stefanesti had been evacuated, "chased like cattle", with what they were able to salvage, tied in one bundle); Saveni, Hertza, Bucecea, Frumusica, Bivolari, Podul Iloaiei, Targul Frumos, Harlau and other small towns. A perpetual filigree of friendships, business relations and, of course, a permanent source for a *shiddech* ("a marriage match") existed between these shtetlech. The people of the shtetlech lived a life apart, in their own world.

Stefanesti is found on maps dating as far back as the sixteenth century, under the name of "Stepanutzi", and is referred to in many chronicles and in records of Rabbinic disputations. A Roman

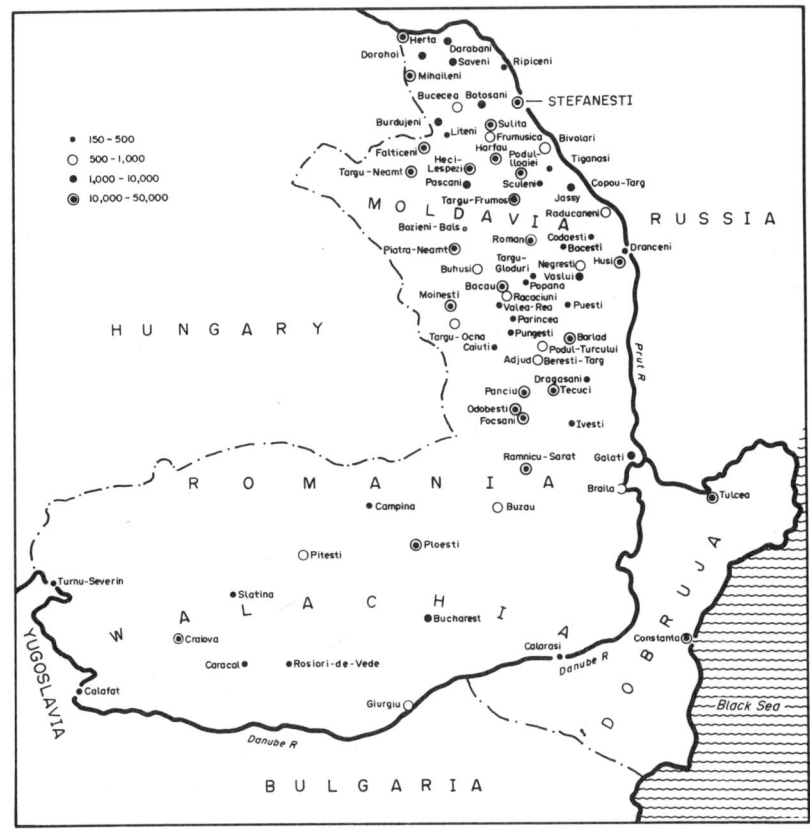

FIG. 3. Jewish communities in Romania on the eve of World War I. Based on *Pinkas ha-Kehillot: Rumanyah* Vol. I, Jerusalem 1969. Courtesy Yad Vashem Archives, Jerusalem.

dictionary lists Stefanesti: "Town in Jud. Botosani, the victory of Tomsa over Movila in 1612".

Like all towns founded during the Middle Ages, Stefanesti was situated at an important crossroads — on the road from Constantinople to Poland. It had developed to fulfill specific needs, which fluctuated with the seesaw of political fortunes, dictated by conditions entirely beyond its own ken.

Located in the district (*judetz*) of Botosani at a distance of forty-two kilometers from the capital city of the same name, Stefanesti was not on any direct railroad line. It was thus left to quietly linger, bypassed by the twentieth century, but evidently not sufficiently insignificant to be ignored by the various belligerent powers who found it worthy of repeated attacks. The closest railroad station linking it to the outside world was in Trusesti, which was sixteen kilometers from town, along a hilly, gravel pitted road that passed through the notorious Guranda forest, a place used as a hideout by outlaws and highway bandits.

At a distance of one hundred and two kilometers was Iassy, the ancient capital of Moldova. During winter months, the bus route stopped entirely and the town was virtually cut off from the outside world. It was not unusual for a trip to Botosani to become a day long affair during the fall or spring rainy seasons. The muddy roads would turn into quagmires and the wheels would sink axle deep into the thick clay. The driver and often the passengers would then be obliged to bodily lift the wagon. During winter months, the sled (or sledge) was the most convenient means of transportation. The only hazards were the several taverns, where drivers had to warm up inside out.

Botosani, the capital of the district, was the seat of the *Prefectura*, and an important center for all the small towns and villages in the region. With a population of about thirty-two thousand, half of whom were Jews, it was one step above the humble shtetl. Its Jewish population maintained friendship and kinship relations with the surrounding shtetlech.

The *cursa*, the daily bus line to Iassy and to Botosani, was an important launch into the twentieth century. The shtetl enjoyed a sort of pride with a twinge of false modesty when the *cursa* was first introduced; it gave the folks a feeling that they had finally arrived. No more old-fashioned horse and wagon. No matter that the bus was old and battered, sputtering evil fumes, shaking at every bump and hump of the road; no matter that the cloud of blue smoke would literally take one's breath away or that the inevitable engine trouble (the *pana de motor*) would often delay the trip, the *cursa* conferred status on the shtetl, for not all small towns could boast of this modernization. Billows of dust on the horizon announced the arrival, at seven o'clock PM, of the daily bus from Iassy and a similar cloud mushrooming at the top of the hill signalled the approach of the *cursa* from Botosani at about the same time. Both stopped at the *Raspantie* "the center of town", in front of the church.

Another means of transportation was provided by the only automobile mechanic in town, owner of a model-T Ford, who, for a fee, would drive those able to afford the luxury, to their destinations. In cases of emergency, he was hired to rush people to the hospital in Iassy. In happier circumstances, he was hired for trips to Vatra Dornei, a mountain resort and spa.

Across the Prut was Bessarabia, part of Romania during the interbellum period. It was still looked upon with some mistrust as somewhat foreign. The Russian-speaking peasants brought their produce to the market and were regular customers in town, though they still spoke only Russian. The Bessarabian shtetlech, such as Beltz, Lipcani and Edinitz, were on friendly relations with the ones on the Romanian side of the Prut, with whom they shared a language and a religion.

At a distance of three kilometers from the River Prut, Stefanesti thus hobbled along the stream Basheau, skirting the vineyard-laden foothills and waiting for *Meshiech* ("the Messiah"). The flatland between the Basheau and the Prut, an area often inundated by spring floods, was partly cultivated vineyards, creeping into thick forest.

1. Town Proper

Four almost parallel streets followed the serpentine contour of the Basheu, joined by several cross lanes. This was Stefanesti. The length from one end of the shtetl to the other was not more than two miles, excluding the *mahala* ("outskirts") or the surrounding peasant villages, Stanca to the north, Baduitz and Bobulesti to the south.

The most unsavory area of town was along the banks of the Basheu. When arriving from Bessarabia across the Prut, one entered the town by the wooden bridge. This was the neighbourhood to which the lowliest strata of society were relegated. Paradoxically, here were located four of the seven synagogues in town, built along a running stream as specified in the *Halakhah* ("the Judaic legal authority"). It was also on this back lane that the *schachthouse* ("slaughterhouse") was to be found, as well as the communal bathhouse with its adjoining *mikveh* ("ritual pool").

During winter storms, the area was deserted and all but swallowed up by snowdrifts mounting higher than most of the surrounding housetops. During the torrid summer months, however, this area in front of the wooden bridge was a virtual beehive of frenetic activity. This was the depot for the embarkation to swim in the river Prut. Each shtetl had its own equivalent stream, pond or swimming hole.

Almost every town had its own *strada mare* ("main street"), usually called *Strada Stefan cel Mare* after the ruler Stefan the Great. Stefanesti, named in honor of this ruler, felt entitled to this prerogative. It was on this street that most of the prosperous merchants had their shops. Four or five central blocks enjoyed the privilege of cement-paved sidewalks; the street, however, was unpaved. Periodically, the street was covered with a load of crudely crushed gravel, which produced a grating noise whenever a vehicle drove in — which happened all day long.

Geographic Location 13

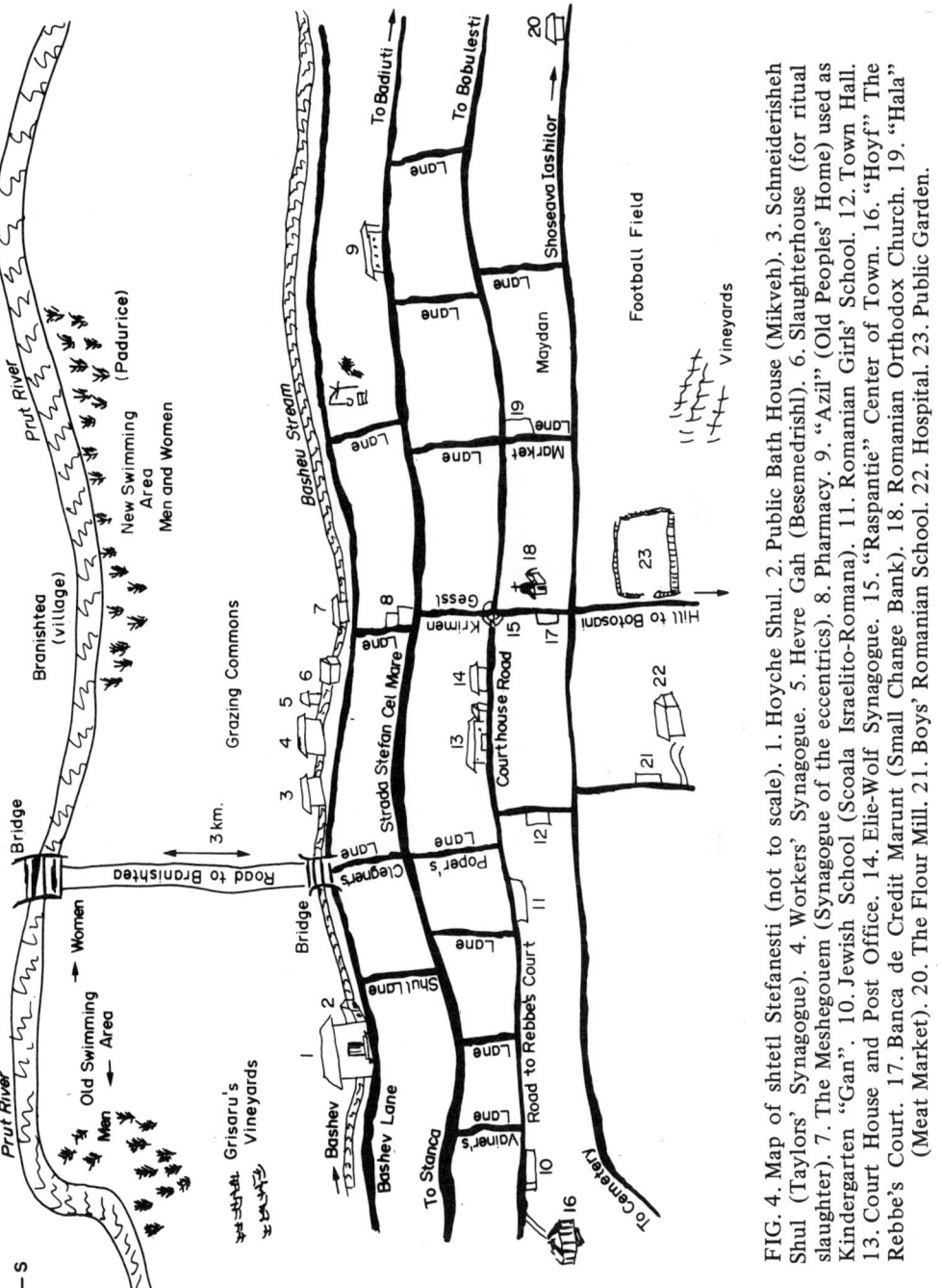

FIG. 4. Map of shtetl Stefanesti (not to scale). 1. Hoyche Shul. 2. Public Bath House (Mikveh). 3. Schneiderisheh Shul (Taylors' Synagogue). 4. Workers' Synagogue. 5. Hevre Gah (Besemedrishl). 6. Slaughterhouse (for ritual slaughter). 7. The Meshegouem (Synagogue of the eccentrics). 8. Pharmacy. 9. "Azil" (Old Peoples' Home) used as Kindergarten "Gan". 10. Jewish School (Scoala Israelito-Romana). 11. Romanian Girls' School. 12. Town Hall. 13. Court House and Post Office. 14. Elie-Wolf Synagogue. 15. "Raspantie" Center of Town. 16. "Hoyf" The Rebbe's Court. 17. Banca de Credit Marunt (Small Change Bank). 18. Romanian Orthodox Church. 19. "Hala" (Meat Market). 20. The Flour Mill. 21. Boys' Romanian School. 22. Hospital. 23. Public Garden.

The alternative, however, during the rainy season, was a mud pond extending between the sidewalks; or, during the dry summer months, a haze of dust hanging like a heavy curtain. In the wintertime the street was ideal for skating or sledding — a fact that did not escape the youngsters, to the chagrin of everyone else.

Beyond the several blocks of paved sidewalks were rudimentary sidewalks symbolically festooned with blocks of stone, ideal for twisting one's ankle. Electricity was acquired in 1933. The few central blocks were lit but this too stopped with the sidewalks.

The row of houses, tall, one-storey buildings, were regular, of equal height, built one against the other. The materials used were brick and stucco. The typical pattern was one door and one or two windows on either side. Several larger establishments had two doors, in which case the windows were omitted and a "galantar" (showcase) was placed between the doors to exhibit the wares. All houses had thick wooden shutters with iron crossbars. Several shops boasted corrugated wrought-iron shutters, called *rollé* and esteemed a status symbol. Whenever these contraptions were pulled up or down, the ominous sound resembled a loud thunderclap, heard clear across town.

On this portion of Main Street were all the merchants' shops: the *manufactura* ("dry-goods shops"); *glanterie* ("haberdashery"); *bacanie* ("grocery") and *coloniale* (which sold foods, olives, canned goods, and so on) and of course the *farmacia* ("drugstore").

As one moved away from the center portion of the shtetl, the houses became less well kept, of uneven height, with unpaved sidewalks. And as one reached the outskirts, sidewalks disappeared entirely. Here lived the craftsmen and artisans. In some parts of town, however, it was not unusual to find, among these lowly dwellings, the homes of some of the wealthiest families.

The *Crimen Gessl* (the little crooked street) ran perpendicular to the main street. It was not as the name would suggest, crooked. It led to the *Raspantie*, the central square, and beyond that, up the hill leading to Botosani. It had been grandiosely renamed *Strada Oituz*, as newly placed street signs proclaimed. Here were several fruit stores, bakeries, ice-cream parlors, a barber shop and the most prestigious dry-goods shop in town, in whose shop window there was a mannikin, in itself a phenomenon in town. This mannikin, a dwarf with an oversized head, displayed fedoras and straw hats, and was a sign of true metropolitan prosperity, envied by all the other shopkeepers.

The claim to fame of the *Crimen Gessl*, however, was the one and only *Salon Binder*, owned and operated by Hayim and Charlotta Binder. It was the acknowledged local hall, where all important

Geographic Location 15

events took place. The itinerant theaters performed here; the more prestigious weddings in town took place at Binder's; and it had the reputation of being the most distinguished restaurant in town. With marble tables, a wall mirror behind the marble bar, plush hangings and chairs, it was elegant. It was there that the occasional famous visitors in town stopped. When, during the First World War, Prince Carol had stopped for one day in Stefanesti, he and his entourage had a memorable (for the town) meal at Binder's. A stereopticon, installed in front of the door, provided a magic glimpse of the great marvels of the world. For two *lei* in the slot, one saw Notre Dame of Paris, St. Peter's in Rome, Trafalgar Square in London – all in three dimensional splendour for people who had probably never heard of these places, much less hoped to see them.

The *Raspantie* ("crossroads") was the officially recognised center of town, often called *Centru* ("center"). It was considered the most prestigious location from the point of view of business. It led past the onion-shaped Orthodox church, which dominated the square, continued along the *Gradina Publica* ("public gardens") and continued up the hill. One favourite landmark was *Yukl's Cofeterie* ("tea shop") where young people met and unofficially courted.

The *cafenea* ("coffeehouse") was another landmark. A few habituées met there daily to transact business and discuss world affairs. Over a demi-tasse of Turkish coffee, they read the daily newspapers, played a hand of *blonch* ("dominoes") or a game of cards. This, however, was not the place for the hard-working shopkeepers, who had no taste or time for such frivolities, especially during working hours.

Along this tree-lined boulevard, one passed the public gardens and, adjoining them, the playing field where all important football matches were played. The sidewalk stopped there, and so did the shtetl. Up the hills there were peasant houses among the vineyards and orchards, and to the right one caught a glimpse of the Municipal Hospital and the old manor house. The Jewish population, however, did not venture beyond the end of the sidewalk.

Parallel to the main street another street stretched from the Rebbé's Court, at the northernmost extremity of town, to the southern end, where the adjoining villages, Bobulesti and Badiuti, began. This street was not honored by any specific name but was known by important landmarks or by the names of families living on it. It was the *Courthouse* street or *Benianovici* or *Vainer's* or the *Rov's* street. Along it were to be found the Romanian Girls' school, the Jewish public school, the bank, the courthouse and one of the synagogues.

From the *Raspantie* going southward one passed the *maidan*, an empty area where, once a week, the farmers brought their produce to market and trade. The *hala* ("meat market"), a drafty brick building, housed eight stalls where the *kosher* ("ritual-hygiene") butchers sold their wares, each to his own faithful clientele. All round the *hala* and the *maidan* were a number of lowly houses where poor widows eked out a meagre living selling produce and various items such as rope, candles, oil and so on.

Shoseaua Yassilor, the highway to Iassy, was a new development. Unlike the uniform aspect of the older parts of town, this area resembled a village, with self-contained houses, each surrounded by a courtyard. Here were the lumberyards and, along the *maidan*, the smiths' shops. The road was unpaved, with weed-grown ditches on either side; rudimentary little bridges or dirt-filled passages provided access to each house. The flour mill was considered the end of town. Beyond it, on the road to Ciur, one entered a region of vineyards and orchards. The Herscovici vineyards had become an important station for the Zionist pioneer training, the *hachsharah*.

This was the shtetl Stefanesti. Four parallel streets, stretching along the Basheu, with several lanes traversing and joining them. This was a typical pattern for a Romanian shtetl. Unlike in a North American town, the business district was also the residential area, esteemed the most prestigious part of town. The gentiles were relegated exclusively to the *mahala* ("periphery"). Jews did not venture beyond the town proper, for safety reasons as well as for status considerations.

2. The Houses

One's socioeconomic level determined the type of house one inhabited. The homes of merchants and shopkeepers were larger, more solidly built, occupying the more prestigious area of town, while the houses of craftsmen and poorer working-class families were smaller, less well-maintained and furnished accordingly.

The very poor lived in one-room dwellings, little more than huts. There they worked, lived and slept. The floor was bare earth, on which jute sacking was used as carpeting. To satisfy an aesthetic need, the sacks were often dyed in stripes of various colors. A large oven served for cooking as well as heating.

These huge ovens, resembling bakery ovens, were a typical architectural feature of the region. The oven, about nine feet by six feet, jutted out into the room. It was built of stone, or of loam mixed with straw, and whitewashed, as was the rest of the house. One interesting characteristic of these ovens was a platform, reached by two or three steps at the rear of the oven where the children slept. In the wintertime, this platform was a cosy, warm little room.

The furniture in these dwellings was usually of the sparsest: a table, some benches, one or two cots or the luxury of a bed on which the feather pillows were piled up, a few shelves on which household utensils were displayed. Paper-cutout lacelike trimmings often adorned the rudimentary shelves. The need for aesthetic expression prompted the homemaker to embellish her home with crocheted window curtains and embroidered tablecloths for the Sabbath or festive occasions.

Lighting was provided by kerosene lamps hanging from the ceiling or from a nail on the wall. Since there was no indoor plumbing, hygiene was often rudimentary. Even outhouses were sometimes a luxury in these neighborhoods.

Many of these houses were built in the style of the peasant huts, with thatched roofs and a *prispa*, a sort of built-in bench surrounding the outside walls. Like the rest of the house, it was built of loam mixed with straw, just high enough to sit on (about eighteen to twenty inches high and about twenty inches wide). People would sit on the *prispa* in front of the house, the men smoking their corncob pipes, the women often knitting socks. The outside walls were white-washed, the *prispa* was left unpainted. This type of architecture was to be found only in the poorer areas, at the outskirts of town.

The somewhat more prosperous craftsmen lived in better built, larger houses, built of wattle and daub or wood slats covered with loam and whitewashed. There were usually two rooms, thus providing a work area and living quarters. Instead of the *prispa* there was an open porch in front of the house. In some cases two families shared one entrance hall with doors on either side of the entrance. Although these houses were not higher than six feet, they had a loft and a shingled roof. There was at least one room with a wooden floor, often covered with rag-plaited rugs or small hand-loomed wool carpets. Depending on the family's financial standing, one would find a large wooden bed, a roughly hewn table, some benches and stools. The walls were whitewashed, as was the omnipresent huge oven. Hand made knick-knacks and other handicrafts decorated the room and simple homemade stencils would sometimes embellish the walls. One respondent said: "There was always a smell of the material, like cloth or leather, and it mixed with the smell of cabbage and fried onions when you walked into a tailor's or cobbler's shop." Some families owned a goat, called "the poor man's cow". This was a ready source of milk and cheese without incurring maintenance expenses. Owing a cow was a sign of supreme prosperity for a working man. "We had a cow and so we never worried about what to eat," explained one respondent.

One permanent feature of the backyard was the rain barrel under the drain pipe. Although water mains existed, they were not within the reach of most working-class families. Water was obtained either from the public well or from more affluent neighbors who enjoyed the luxury of indoor waterpipes, the "robinets".

There was no indoor plumbing in the shtetl. Rich and poor alike depended on the outhouse or privy, built at the far end of the backyard: the *closet* or *latrina*. The condition of this important appurtenance depended entirely on the fastidiousness of the householder. Even the poorest segments of the population complied with government regulations.

The *strada mare*, (the main street), was the enclave of the middle class. Here the structure of the houses as well as the interiors reflected the solid prosperity of the owners, their concern with comfort and their ability to indulge in objects of pure aesthetic value rather than things that were simply utilitarian. These were the *balabatem*, whose families had built the houses and had lived in them, in some cases for several generations. With one exception they were one-storey buildings, all of the same height, built in straight rows, on solid foundations, with deep cellars and high lofts under tin covered roofs. Facing the street were the stores and in the rear the living quarters. The cellar, reached by a trap door in the floor and a ladder, were used as storage for foods and served as pantry all year round, with room for wine barrels, preserves and pickles. The loft provided the ideal temperature during winter months for storing vegetables such as beets, potatoes, carrots, parsley roots and fruit. The *gospodar* ("good provider") saw to it that ample provisions of apples, quince, pears and so on were stored for the winter. Grapes were hung on strings — like on clotheslines — or placed in cases of sawdust in the coolest place in the loft. The loft, too, was reached by a removable ladder and a trap door in the ceiling.

The typical house plan consisted of the store in the front and two or three rooms at the rear, each leading, train style, into the other. A corridor or *sholleh* led from the store or from one of the rooms to a rear porch.

One room, the salon, was always reserved for special occasions. It was the guest room for important visitors. Here were displayed the treasured photographs, crystal and silver used only for festive occasions, as well as the *zestre* ("trousseau"), extra rugs, pillows and comforters that prudent mothers prepared for their daughters.

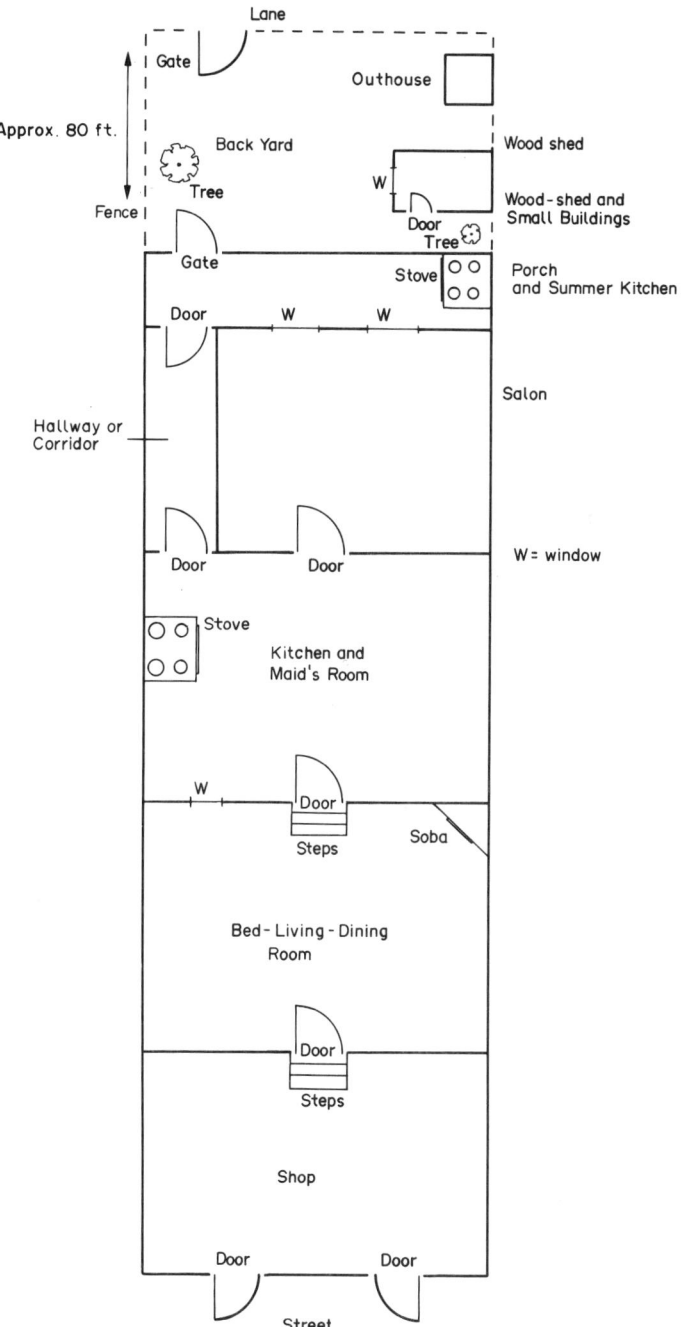

FIG. 5. Typical plan of house on Main Street.

The furniture differed in quality and style according to taste and pocket book. It was either bought from the larger centers or made to order by local craftsmen. The rooms were large and high-ceilinged but often poorly lit, unless they had a *luminator* ("skylight"). A typical room would have a table and chairs, two beds, one or two dressers and one or two large armoires, often with a full-length mirror.

One indispensable feature was the *soba*, a wood-burning hearth, built in one corner of the room and reaching up to the ceiling. The usual size was three feet by three feet. Most houses had the *soba* built of stones or brick, finished in plaster, as was the rest of the interior. Some homes had a ceramic-tile *soba* (plate 3).

The walls were either whitewashed in pale pastel shades or stencilled by professional house painters. Choosing a *tapet* ("pattern of stencil") was a serious enterprise, for it reflected the taste and social standing of the homeowner. The usual patterns were bold flower designs reminiscent of Victorian wallpaper. During the 1930s a new trend reflected a preference for simpler geometric designs and darker backgrounds. Instead of being brushed on the paint was sprayed on; spraying created a mistlike effect around the stencil. Another innovation was the use of metallic paints as accents. The floor was covered with hand-woven wool rugs, brought from the neighboring villages. They were usually multicolored patterns on a black background. The wooden floor was given a coat of oil paint to facilitate upkeep.

One characteristic of these homes was the presence of books, lovingly displayed in a bookcase. This placed the family at a superior level on the social scale.

The kitchen had a built-in cooking stove called a *plita*, (cooking stove) instead of the large, old-fashioned oven. The wrought-iron stovetop was used for cooking, while the *rola* ("baking oven"), built into the stove wall, was used for baking. The *rola* was a tin box, (sixteen by sixteen by thirty-six inches), with several removable racks for the baking pans. Often two such boxes were built on top of one another to provide sufficient baking space.

Cooking and baking were priorities for the middle-class housewife of the Romanian shtetl. Housecleaning chores were relegated to the maid, but feeding one's family was too important a matter to be entrusted to anyone else. Furthermore, keeping a *kosher* home was the undisputed responsibility of the housewife. Two separate countertops with adequate storage space provided separate space for *milechdik* ("pertaining to milk") and *fleishig* ("pertaining to meat"). To distinguish between the two sets of dishes and pans necessary for *kosher* cooking, two colors were used throughout the kitchen.

It was usually in the same room that a washstand was to be

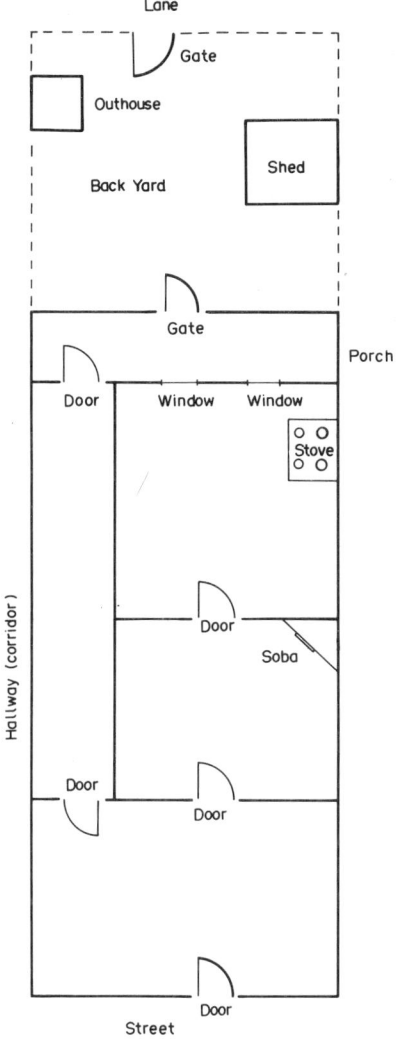

FIG. 6. Floor plan of other houses.

found. A mirror on the wall, the washbasin and pitcher, a comb and brush holder, soap dish and cake of toothpaste, and a toothbrush rack completed the bath room.

Like the rest of the house, the kitchen had a wooden floor. It was however, covered with linoleum. The walls as well as the kitchen stove were whitewashed. Hand-embroidered *tablouri* ("scenes") on linen decorated the walls. Brass and copper pans, polished to a shine, were proof of the housewife's fastidious housekeeping.

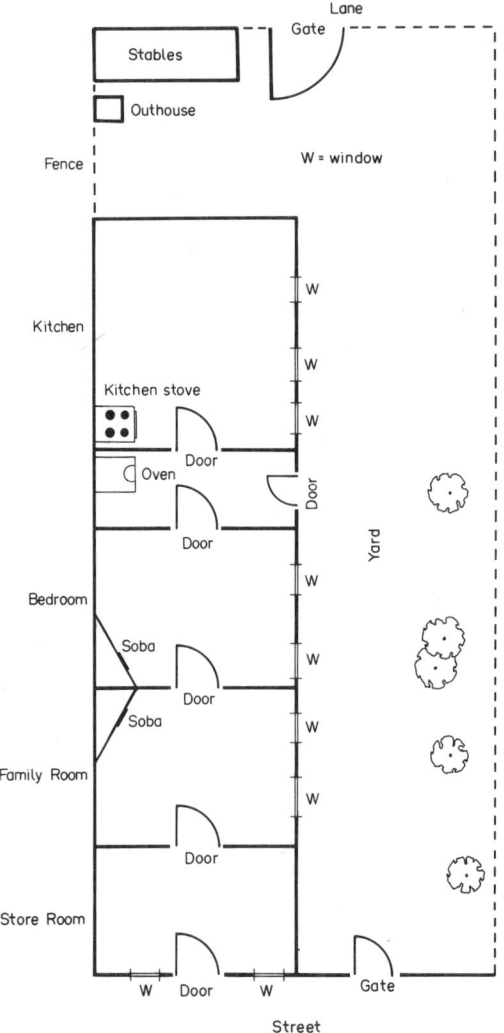

FIG. 7. Floor plan of house in newer part of town.

In most homes, a built-in stove turned the rear porch into a summer kitchen, and often a table and chairs provided a dining area during the summer months.

The backyard, separated from the neighbors by solid-wood board fences, often contained some additional small buildings, which provided storage space. In some cases these small buildings were refurbished to house elderly parents. A woodshed and lean-to

Geographic Location 23

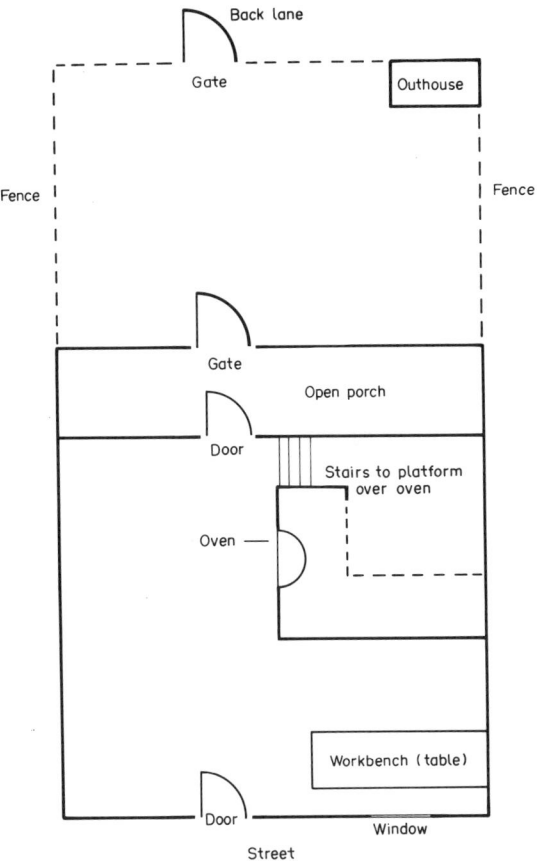

FIG. 8. Floor plan of working class house.

provided the necessary space for the cordwood indispensable for heating and cooking.

The rain barrel and at least one tree (cherry, apricot, locust, plum) were part of every backyard. But no self-respecting household would have neglected the chicken coop, which consisted of one or two wooden cages for the hens, chickens and geese. The turkey, bought young and fattened up for the Purim feast, had his wings clipped and was allowed to promenade freely and scratch for his own food. Protection against prowlers was provided by a mongrel watchdog, kept on a chain.

One of the luxuries that distinguished these houses from the poorer working-class ones was the indoor waterpipe. Although there was no hot water, there were often two faucets. The owners generously allowed their less-favored neighbors to fill their water pails at the faucet. Only a handful of houses had small rooms equipped with wooden or copper bathtubs. The bath water was heated in large copper cauldrons on outdoor fires and brought in by the pailful. During the winter, this was virtually impossible and the communal bath was the only recourse.

Since indoor plumbing did not exist, the outhouse, at the farthest end of the backyard, was the universal means of sanitation. The maintenance of this important appendage was a visible sign of the well-run household. Criteria of comfort, rather than government regulations, determined if the *latrina* was regularly painted and treated with disinfectant, or if it was neglected.

The difference between the middle-class home and that of the professionals and the *negidem* ("rich") was negligible. As in the case of the shopkeepers, professionals had the living quarters together with the place of business. The quality of furniture reflected individual tastes. Better educated than the average shopkeeper or merchant, books were in evidence as a matter of course. There were more signs of affluence, for example, better china, but extravagances were rare.

As previously mentioned, the structure size and interior of houses differed with the socioeconomic status of the family. The better built, larger houses were clustered together. But it was not unusual to find a hovel next door to the rich man's home. The outskirts, or *mahala*, were not a desirable area; the embarkment along the Basheu was considered the most unsavory neighborhood.

3. The Climate

This region of northern Romania has a typically continental climate, with four well-defined seasons, the temperature ranging from ninety degrees Fahrenheit in the summer to minus twenty in winter.

March is considered the beginning of spring. Romanians celebrate the arrival of spring, on March first, with the folk custom of exchanging good-luck charms called *martisori* ("little March"), made with red and white silk thread. These little charms were subsequently hung on fruit trees as a symbol of friendship and to stimulate fertility.

June, July and August were hot and usually dry months, in contrast to the often rainy April. Occasionally, lengthy droughts did damage to grain crops, for which the region was famous.

September was the month of ripening fruits and grains, of pickling and preserving. October and November were gray, rainy, with muddy roads and endless drizzle. The end of November usually saw snow.

The winter months, December, January and February, were snowbound with the *Crivats*, a north wind which blew from the Russian steppes, freezing everything in its wake. Everyone huddled around the soba (hearth) and all activities were confined to the indoors.

CHAPTER II
Historical Background

1. Brief History of Romania

Romania is a small island of Latin culture surrounded by a sea of Slavic peoples. Many Romanian cultural peculiarities have entered the Romian shtetl, just as Romanian words have been incorporated into Yiddish and have displaced those of Slavic origin.

The great majority of the Jewish population of Romania was to be found in the northern province of Moldova. This area, with its rich black earth and temperate climate, has been inhabited continuously since prehistoric times. Cucuteni, a village about forty miles from Stefanesti, is well-known for its archeological discoveries of Neolithic settlements dating from about 3000 BC.

In historic times the inhabitants of this region were the Daci, whose leader, Decebal, was conquered by the Roman Emperor Trajan in 107 AD at which time the entire region became the easternmost outpost of the Roman Empire. Some two hundred years later, the Romans abandoned this region, but not before the Roman legionnaires had settled there, intermarried with the local population and formed the basis for the people we now call Romanians. Vulgar Latin remained the language of the country. A language is a living record of the history of a people. Though the basis of Romanian is decidedly Latin, Slavic, Greek and Turkish words are witness to the various conquering waves. During the 1800s Romania's interest in Latin revived, a result of Romania's close kinship — both spiritually and, until recently, politically — with France and Italy.

Moldova was in the path of the barbarian invasions. The local population usually fled to the mountains or submitted. The town of Botosani owes its name to the Mongol chief Batu-Khan, alleged grandson of the famous Genghis Khan, who occupied the area in the thirteenth century.

Stefanesti is frequently mentioned by early historians.

"In the year 7017 (1500) in the month of July, the Poles burned and looted Stefanesti because Bogdan, ruler of Moldova and the son of Stefan the Great, had invaded Poland with his army in order to revenge himself against King Sigismund who had refused him the hand in marriage of his sister Elysaveta . . . . In the year 7021 (1513) the Tatars with Bet Cherei, son of Khan Meulli, again burned and looted Stefanesti . . . . After the death of Simion Movila there was a battle between his son Constantin who was aided by the Poles and Visnovetski, son of Irimia Movila, helped by the Turks . . . . In the year 1713 the Turks returned from the war with the Poles, built a bridge over the Prut at Stefanesti in order to cross the armies coming from Hotin."*

Moldova was founded in the fourteenth century. The legend, as taught in schools, tells of Dragos Voda, son of Bogdan, who descended from Maramuresh and, with the aid of his loyal bitch Molda, captured a wild boar and took possession of the region, which he named Moldova.

The two principalities, Moldova to the north and Muntenia to the south, developed separately, each with its own local princelings. During the Turkish domination Muntenia was known as Valachia. (The local Yiddish term for gentile was Vulech.)

Stephen the Great (1457–1504) was an ambitious ruler who fought the Turks in numerous battles and, after each success, would build a monastery in pious gratitude for his victory. He is considered the founder of Stefanesti, and is mentioned in local legends. *Stanca Doamnei* ("the lady's rock"), in the village of Stanca at the north of Stefanesti, was named after Stephen's mother, who, legend has it, hid in one of the subterranean caves after one of her son's battles.

During the eighteenth century the Turks instituted the Phanariot regime, whereby wealthy Greeks from Phanar, a district of Constantinople, would bid for the thrones of the Romanian principalities. Some of these rulers were highly educated and well-intentioned. Most, however, exploited the land.

It was not until 1857 that the two principalities were united under the name Romania. In 1864, A. I. Cuza brought about the so-called emancipation of serfs, but within the still-entrenched feudal systems it was not long before the newly freed peasants were again at the mercy of the *boyers* (landowners). To assure stability and through machinations of European royalty, in 1866 Prince Charles of Hohenzollern-Sigmaringen became the ruler of the newly united country.

May tenth, the national day of Romania, celebrates as the National Anthem *Zece Mai* ("Ten May") tells us, the arrival in 1866 of Prince

---

* G. I. Lahovari, C. I. Bratianu, G. C. Tocilescu, *Marele Dictionar Geographic Al Romanie*; Bucuresti, Stab. Grafic J.V. Suceava – 1902.

Carol of Hohenzollern-Sigmaringen, who was to become King Carol the First, and who was the founder of the royal dynasty; independence from the Turks in 1877, and the proclamation of the kingdom of Romania in 1881.

Romania did not enter the First World War until 1916. She started out on the side of the Germans, but then changed allegiance, switching over to the Allies. As a consequence, the "old kingdom" (*vechiul regat*) became, after the treaty of Versailles, "Great Romania" (*Romania Mare*), and gained territories from Austro-Hungary, Russia and Bulgaria. The newly acquired lands brought a series of new problems, since the inhabitants had belonged to various cultural and linguistic groups and had now to be integrated. At the same time, treaties were transacted with the neighboring countries for mutual protection against attacks from Hungary and Russia.

Ferdinand and Queen Marie were crowned in 1922 and it was hoped that the coronation would consolidate the country. But problems abounded. Their son, Crown Prince Carol, lived abroad and renounced his rights to the throne. In 1927 King Ferdinand died; a regency, headed by the Patriarch Miron Cristea, ruled with the six-year-old Michael, son of Carol, as king. In 1930 Prince Carol returned and was crowned King Carol II.

The 1930s were a tumultuous period. The rise of Fascism in the west encouraged the emergence of the Iron Guard, a party fashioned after the Nazis. At the 1937 election, the Iron Guard received one third of the votes. Octavian Goga and A. Cuza received a majority of votes and formed the National Christian Party. Once elected, Goga dissolved parliament. The country was in turmoil.

In 1938 King Carol established a personal dictatorship and a new constitution was accepted by the people in a plebiscite. Romania concluded treaties with Germany and also signed treaties with France and Britain, who promised her territorial integrity, should she be attacked by Germany. With the outbreak of war in 1939 all hopes of reliance on these treaties vanished. Then, with the fall of France in 1940, Carol's pro-French foreign policy became impossible. A new dictator, General Ion Antonescu, initiated closer collaboration with Germany. The king abdicated and his son Michael was again made king, although in name only. With an eye to Romanian oil and wheat, Germany occupied the country. A veritable reign of terror ensued, especially for the Jews, who were treated as Germany treated Jews in all countries she occupied.

On August 23, 1944, the Russian armies "liberated" Romania. King Michael led a plot to overthrow General Antonescu, who was subsequently executed. Petru Groza formed a Communist-controlled government, and in the 1946 elections the Communists won. This placed Romania entirely under Soviet domination. In 1947 King Michael abdicated and Romania was declared the Romanian Popular Democratic Republic.

During World War Two the shtetl, as such, ceased to exist, as the million Romanian Jews either emigrated or were deported.

2. History of the Jews in the Region

In the midst of a people who themselves were in the process of developing a national consciousness, the Jews of Romania struggled to hold on to their culture. In small numbers, Jews were accepted; but as soon as they increased in number and they became a competitive threat, hostility followed. The history of the Jews in Romania is not a pretty story; the topic of harsh anti-Semitism is given front-page treatment. To deny this in the face of overwhelming factual testimony would be presumptuous. Yet, in all the otherwise excellent references, several elements are ignored or are insufficiently stressed. One is the noteworthy difference between the fate of the Jews of the large urban centers and those of the shtetl; another rarely mentioned factor is the marked difference in national character between the Romanian peasant and the neighboring peoples, the Poles, Ukrainians, Hungarians.

The personality profile, and the needs of the Jews who left the shtetl and settled in the big cities, was different from those who preferred to remain in the shtetl. The impersonality dictated by urban living contrasted sharply with the day-to-day relationships that inevitably develop in a small community. At the same time, contact with the gentile world imposed new forms of behavior; tradition was the victim. The shtetl Jew asked only to be permitted to live in peace and *Yiddishkeit* ("Jewishness"); the urban Jew was acquiring new aspirations. Yiddish, still the predominant language of the shtetl, was no longer the *mamme lushn* ("mother tongue") for the urban Jew, who made every possible effort to repudiate his Jewishness.

In urban centers assimilation was rampant as the high rate of inter-faith marriage attests. But in spite of secularization, tradition still predominated in the shtetl, and inter-faith marriage was still considered a calamity and a tragedy for the family.

The shtetl Jew lived among the illiterate or semiliterate peasantry, often poorer than himself. There was some anti-Semitism at this level, but each group learned to accept the other and to appreciate its qualities.

The national character of the Romanian peasant differed substantially from the far more belligerent character of the neighboring peoples. Except when provoked beyond endurance, the peasant preferred to flee rather than to fight. "Fuga'i rusinoasa dar e sanatoasa" ("flight may be shameful but it is healthy") was a common Romanian saying. And in "Mioriza", the beloved popular folk ballad, the young shepherd from Moldova, when learning that his two companions were plotting to murder him, does not seek revenge, but, in resignation, accepts his fate, showing concern only for his mother's sorrow when she will learn the sad news. This, too, is the Romanian national character, especially of the peasant, not only the vile anti-Semite often depicted, who, no doubt, did exist.

Anti-Semitism in Romania percolated downward from the ruling classes, whose interests it served. It was with the help and instigation of the government that pogroms were perpetrated. Students were a handy tool for the politicians. True that "Jidani la Palestina" ("Jews go to Palestine") and "Da'i ca'i Jidan" ("Let him have it, he's a Jew") were familiar enough slogans, which caused shudders, but this was as a rule on an individual level rather than the mass bestiality encountered elsewhere. The church, too, had its own vested interests, and did its share of hate-mongering. Generally speaking, however, Jews knew who was a *fainer Goy* ("a fine Gentile") and who was a *soyne Isroel* ("enemy of Jews"), just as the Romanian peasants distinguished between the honest merchant and the unscrupulous one. The gentile lawyer in town did not hesitate to befriend the rabbi (*rov*) with whom he liked to discuss topics of mutual interest, while the peasant found much in common with his favorite tailor, with whom he may have served in the war. Unlike the horrendous stories of pogroms, which were frequent occurrences in Tsarist Russia, the Romanian shtetl was a haven for those fleeing from such atrocities.

Unjust discriminatory laws passed by various governments and economic and educational restrictions affected the shtetl Jew as much as they did the urbanite, but bloody pogroms were unheard of in the shtetl. As a group, the Jews did not present any competition for the Romanian peasants, since Jews were not farmers and very few Romanians engaged in trade or the crafts.

When did the Jews first settle in this region? References and precise information are sparse and vague. Jews are noted in this area in the year 101 AD, when the Roman legions conquered the ethnic Daci population. Decebalus, king of the Dacians, accorded the Jews of Talmaci special privileges. A decree of the Roman emperor Trajan (conqueror of the Daci) granted protection to the Jews and to their synagogue. Jews often followed the Roman armies of occupation as interpreters, but it is not known whether organized Jewish communities were established at that time.

Many of the small towns of the region were established around the seventeenth century, when Jews were invited to settle and colonize, since they had the reputation of being shrewd in business and industrious. It is probable that they came to settle after being persecuted in Poland and the Ukraine. *Benjamin of Tudela*, the well-known medieval traveler, mentions that a considerable group of Jews settled in the principality of Wallachia as early as the sixth century, during the reign of the Byzantine Emperor Justinian.

The existence of Jews in this region is further confirmed in a voivodal decree of Prince Grigore Ghica in 1717, where the election of a *hahambasha* was decreed. The *hahambasha* was the official representative of the Jewish community in all Ottoman territories: "We name Marco, Haham, over the Jews of Iassy as well as in the towns and villages of the principality such as were the preceeding hahambashas . . . ."*

The most factual proof of the existence of a Jewish community in Stefanesti comes from rabbinical records of the year 5365 (1604). An article by Mr. Manascu Cotter, which appeared in Revista Cultului Mozaic,† is interesting and revealing as a sociological document.

In The *Thirteenth Tribe*‡ Arthur Koestler propounds the theory that the majority of eastern European Jewry are of Khazar-Turkish derivation. He suggests that it was not the immigrants from the west, but rather the Khazars who contributed to the growth of Jewish communities in that region. He writes: "The shtetl . . . was a self-contained country town with an exclusive or predominantly Jewish population. The shtetl's origins probably date back to the thirteenth century and may represent the missing link, as it were, between the market towns of Khazaria and the Jewish settlements in Poland."

The Khazars were a Caucasian people who converted to Judaism and were an important force in the Middle Ages. Koestler speculates about the influence of the Khazars on modern Jewry. He suggests that the social structure of the shtetl resembled too closely that of the Khazars to be a coincidence.

Other historians seem to have toyed with this idea and we read in *The Jewish Encyclopedia* that in the eighth century an armed force of Jews from Southern Russia (presumably the Khazars) entered

---

* *The Universal Jewish Encyclopedia*, Vol. 9, pp. 247–264, 1943.
† Revista Cultului Mozaic, Nov. 1, 1972.
‡ Arthur Koestler, *The Thirteen Tribe* (London: Pan Books, 1976), p. 137.

Moldova and Wallachia and, together with the Jews already settled there, "reigned supreme in the country".*

Another reference to the early existence of Jews in this area is found in *Romania's Scapegoat* by Solomon Bickel, who also states that Jews were living in the region since the beginning of the Middle Ages. It is also known that Stephen the Great had appointed as *logofat* ("chancellor") a Jew named Isaac Benjamin Schor of Yassy.†

N. Yorga, the Romanian historian and politician, mentions the existence of a synagogue in Yassy in 1678 and records the blood accusations of Neamtz in 1726.‡

Where did the Jews of this region come from? Certain expressions and words current in popular usage highlight historic events in the life of a people. In Stefanesti, a common expression used to mean "old-fashioned" or "passé" was *fin Hmilnishke's tzeitn*, ("from the times of Hmilnishke"). The onomatopoeic sound of the word *Hmilnichke* is close enough to *Chmelnicki* to suggest that this sinister period of pogroms and plunder in the Ukraine of 1648 left its imprint in the popular memory of the local Jews, although its transposition did not convey the initial horror of the event. It is most probable that many of those fleeing those atrocities found refuge in the peaceful regions of northern Moldova. A number of respondents remembered hearing from parents and grandparents that they had come to Stefanesti fleeing pogroms, when orphans were literally thrown over to Dniester to be saved. There are no precise records to substantiate these claims, but one may surmise that those orphans, as well as subsequent waves of refugees who fled the pogroms, found a haven in the area and settled there.

We know that in 1745 merchants in Botosani were allowed to own houses; Jews obtained privileges from Prince Alexander Ypsilanti, who granted the Jewish community the status of autonomous corporation in 1799.

The Yiddish spoken in the Romanian shtetl is readily identifiable even among third-generation descendants, by accent, pronunciation and use of a high percentage of typically Romanian terms. There are, however, a large number of Slavic words and expressions, which suggest a common origin. Words such as *chod* ("smoke") or *farchodet* ("suffocated by smoke"), "pomeyented" (to revive from a swoon, used as "it suddenly dawned on me ..." from the Polish for

---

* *The Jewish Encyclopedia*, Vol. X, Funk and Wagnalls, N.Y., pp. 512.
† *Contemporary Jewish Record*, Jan. Feb. 1940, Vol. III, No. 1, pp. 26–38.
‡ N. Yorga; *History of Romania, 1915 and Istoria Evreilor in Romania, 1912*.

"remember") or "krijes" (lower back and haunches) are only a few examples. Kinship terms in particular are significant. There is no Yiddish term for sibling's child — niece or nephew — and the Slavic *plemenek* or *plemenitze* were frequently used; in more recent times, Romanian terms were introduced; *nepot* and *nepoata.*

Nor is the physical type of the local Jews any specific indication regarding their origin. The so-called "racial type" of the Romanian shtetl is mixed. The majority of Romanian Jews are of Mediterranean type, squat and of somewhat swarthy complexion, although blue-eyed blonds were common. The Romanians considered the freckled redheads "typically Jewish". *Fata Jidovului, Ida, cu ochi verzi ca leushteanu, si par rosh ca caramida* — ("The Jew's daughter, Ida, with green eyes like a leaf and hair, red like bricks.")* Most Romanians were dark-complexioned and differences in the "outsiders" were thus easier to establish.

Western ideals of "liberty, equality, fraternity", which swept Europe during the mid 1800s, found eager adepts among the Romanians, still under Turkish domination, but also among the Romanian Jews. Ambitious politicians who had been exiled by the Turkish rulers came in contact with enlightened Western ideas, which they were only too eager to implement when they returned to their homelands. They wrote national hymns and patriotic odes glorifying the newly formed union and "freedom".

In spite of international concern and intervention on behalf of the Jews in Romania, conditions were not improving. The demeaning *more Judaico* oath,† (a public humiliation of Jews), was enacted in courts or outside of synagogues, up to the 1920s, when it was abolished following unfavorable comments in the French press.

The shtetl Jews felt the discriminatory restrictions imposed by the various governments and learned to live with them. The various economic restrictions imposed on them, the special permits required and often denied on the pretext that they were foreigners, and especially the discriminatory laws preventing Jews from education, caused considerable hardships.

The Alliance Israelite Universelle was one of the organizations working at the international level for the improvement of conditions of Jews everywhere. Its slogan was a Talmudic expression, "All Israel is responsible for one another." It was through the auspices of this

---

* A verse which sums up a commonly held view.
† See Encyclopedia Judaica, Vol. 13, p. 1303. Jews made to stand on sow's skin, naked with hair cloth on — swear on Bible.

organization that Jewish schools were founded in many Romanian shtetlech. Narcisse Leven, a French jurist, statesman and philanthropist, was its founder in 1861. He was also its secretary and vice-president, and president from 1898 till his death in 1861. The *Scoala Israelito-Romana Narcisse Leven* of Stefanesti was named after this Jewish benefactor.

The enlightenment of the West reached eastern Jewry. The Haskalah, like its parent, the European Enlightenment movement, accepted reason as the measure for all things. Mendelsohn, who translated the Bible into German and who was its first proponent, believed that there was no conflict between the Jewish faith and reason. Other intellectuals advocated increased secularization and less concern with the Talmud, which they considered outdated.

They called for the removal of Yiddish as the language of instruction in schools, claiming that it was not a true language and that it corrupted the spirit of those who used it. The language of the host country was adopted, and this brought about profound changes in attitudes. French became the language of the élite and Hebrew was advocated as a living language. The education of girls, neglected until then, became a prime concern. The adherents to these ideas of secularization were called *maskillim*. This movement helped erode the Messianic hopes of the Jewish society. It was one of the strongest elements in the current of assimilation in language, dress and manner. The Dreyfus Affair in France shocked the Western Jews who had hoped that through assimilation, anti-semitism would be eradicated. In France, the land of true freedom, it was possible for rabble-rousers to create a subhuman anti-Semitic atmosphere; it became clear that other solutions had to be found.

A new movement arose: the *Hibbad Zion* ("Love of Zion") or *Hovevey Zion* ("Lovers of Zion"), which sought solutions for a people without a homeland. The movement spread to Romania, where more than thirty societies of settlement to Eretz Israel existed at the end of 1881. Groups of Romanian Jews had emigrated to Jerusalem, Tiberias, Safed and Hebron. The cities in Romania that had suffered more from anti-Semitic outbursts were the ones where the current of migration was strongest. In 1882 a conference of Hovevey Zion met in Focsani and elected a central committee with headquarters in Galati, with Samuel Pineles as president. At the time even the Romanian parliament had supported the idea of creating a "Palestinian Kingdom". A delegation was sent to Palestine to buy land and a number of families from Moinesti founded the colony of Rosh Pinnah in Palestine.

These are the early beginnings of Zionism, the nationalistic movement that advocated a return to Zion, the historical homeland. "Zion" was used in the Bible as a synonym for Jerusalem from the time of the Babylonian exile. The hope of returning to the land of Israel had been kept alive through the generations: *L'shanah habba b'Yerushalayim* ("Next year in Jerusalem") a phrase repeated every year at the end of the Passover Seder, dug deep roots.

In 1896 Theodor Herzl, a Viennese journalist of an assimilated Jewish family, wrote *Das Judenstaadt* (*The Jewish State*). It was immediately translated into Romanian and appeared in Botosani the same year. This was Herzl's blueprint for a Jewish homeland in Eretz Israel, the land of the Bible. It was the first time someone actually spelled out boldly and clearly this idea, hitherto thought of only as an unrealistic and unrealizable utopia. Many other countries had been suggested, the Belgian Congo, Uganda, Birobidjean in Russia; all were considered and rejected.

Theodor Herzl is the founder of the Zionist movement. In his brief life — he died at forty-four — this charismatic personality laid the foundations for the return of the Jews to the land of their forefathers. At a time when Jews in Eastern Europe had reached a state of utter despair, discriminated against and persecuted, he was a symbol of new hope. His imposing figure and noble mien had an electrifying effect on the imagination of the humble shtetl Jews, as it had on the rulers and leaders of Europe. He was their prince, their leader of almost messianic proportions, attaining a place generally reserved for heroes of legends. His portrait adorned most shtetl homes. In meeting halls, it was his bust or portrait that was festooned with the white and blue Zionist flag and displayed in the place of honor. (One of my earliest recollections is of "the chocolate man" on my grandmother's sitting-room wall. This was a bas-relief of plaster of Theorod Herzl lacquered in brown varnish, a convincing facsimile of a huge chocolate bar.)

In 1897 Theodor Herzl called the first Zionist Congress at Basle, Switzerland. It was an almost parliamentary gathering of delegates from all countries who listened to his proposals. This was the newly created World Zionist Organization. Its first objective was "to obtain a charter guaranteeing Jews sovereign rights in the territory that they were to settle". In the shtetl, the blue and white *pishké* ("metal box") with the Star of David on it, the *Keren Kayemet* as well as the *Keren Haesod* of the Jewish National Fund, were familiar in every home. Donations to the JNF for the purchase of land in *Eretz* ("The Land"), as Palestine was called, were a willing obligation.

For the Jews of Romania, where political life was a closed door, the cultural life of the country, itself in the early phases of development, was an outlet. Romanian and Yiddish journalism was an open field and the contributions of the Jews were well recognized. Julius Barash, the Galician Jew who brought the Haskalah to Romania, had started the first newspaper, *Israelitul Roman* (the "Romanian Israelite") in Iassy in 1857. This journal, published in French and Romanian, fought for equality and civil rights. In 1879 the weekly *Fraternitatea* ("Brotherhood") was published, representing anti-Zionist feelings and objecting to the establishment of the colonies in Palestine. In 1882 the first Zionist Hebrew newspaper, *Emek Israel*, appeared in Iassy. In 1906 *Curierul Israelit* (the "Israelite Courier"), edited by M. Schweig, became the official organ of the *Uniunea Evreilor Romani*, a political party that attempted to unite the Jewish vote in order to obtain representation in parliament. In 1913, the monthly *Hatikva* ("Hope") appeared. Between 1919 and 1923 a number of dailies appeared in Romanian, among them *Mantuirea* ("Redemption") published by A. L. Zissu and A. Feller. *Renasterea Noastra* ("Our Rebirth") was published between 1923 and 1948, with only a brief interruption during the Second World War. The Zionist Federation published *Stiri din Lumea Evreasca* ("News from the Jewish World"). Between the two world wars, the monthly *Hashmonea*, a student Zionist association organ, was published in Issay. Some of the Jewish journalists became editors of the most important Romanian newspapers. Many distinguished themselves in other fields, such as H. Tiktin in philology and Lazar Shaineanu, who compiled the first Romanian dictionary.

As a result of the Balkan Wars in 1912, Romania acquired new territories with new Jewish populations, whom the Romanian government had promised civil rights that they had previously enjoyed.

On the international scene, in the meantime, Britain, with interests in the Suez Canal, understood the importance of the Middle East area and favored the Zionist aspirations of creating a Jewish state in Palestine. With the groundwork prepared by Herzl and his successors, N. Sokolow and Chaym Weizman, Britain's support was assured.

November second, 1917, marked another milestone on the road to nationhood for the Jewish people, for on that date, Arthur J. Lord Balfour, Secretary of State for Foreign Affairs of Great Britain, formally made what has since been known as the "Balfour Declaration," which read as follows:

> His Majesty's Government view with favour the establishment in Palestine of a national home for the Jewish people and will use their best endeavours to facilitate the achievement of this object, it being clearly understood that nothing shall be done which may prejudice the civil and religious

rights of existing non-Jewish communities in Palestine or the rights and political status enjoyed by Jews in any other country.

In 1920 the Supreme Council of the Allies, meeting at San Remo, included this declaration in the mandate for Palestine, which was to be assigned to Britain by the League of Nations.

In all the shtetlech, the Balfour Declaration was received with jubilation. Lord Balfour entered the roster of legendary benefactors, God's messenger who helped implement the realization of the millennia-old dream. The date was declared a yearly national Jewish holiday. In schools and synagogues, benedictions were offered. The importance this event had in the shtetl is difficult to overemphasize.

At the Versailles Treaty, the western powers agreed to regard the Jews as a "religious or ethnic minority entitled to protection if not autonomy". The newly formed Council for Jewish Minority Rights gave the Jews new rights, in theory if not in practice. The Jews were recognized as a national entity.

The newly created states on the rearranged map of Europe acquired, with their newly found independence, a fresh spirit of nationalism. These feelings were exploited by leaders who turned this fervor against the Jews. In Romania, anti-Semitic propaganda was rampant, especially among students. When one student, Corneliu Zelea Codreanu (who later became leader of the Iron Guard) murdered the chief of police of Issay who was opposed to anti-Semitism), the victim's widow was not able to find one single lawyer to plead her case. The murderer was acquitted.

After the First World War, the Jews in the newly acquired territories were to become automatically Romanian citizens. In February, 1924 the Romanian parliament passed a new law revoking the citizenship of many Jews by the simple ploy of demanding documentary proof of their residence in the new territories. Since Jews of Bessarabia were unable to produce such documents, they were considered aliens and deprived of citizenship rights. To achieve this legerdemain, lists of citizens' names in the annexed lands were supplied to district heads, who had the arbitrary right to strike off any name they pleased. Jewish names were stricken from lists and only *bakshish* ("bribes") – a Romanian institution inherited from the Turks – prevailed.

For the Jews in the Old Kingdom, the problem was of a different nature. They took some pride in being *jet beget Regatzean* ("old timers") whose families had lived in the Old Kingdom for generations. In the shtetl, however, they were submitted to other forms of harassment. There was the problem of the *Besmenari*.

The Romanian authorities circumvented their pledge at Versailles, in the matter of rights of property for the Jews. Jews had not been allowed to own rural lands. Any shtetl that had less than ten thousand inhabitants was considered a rural area, and therefore Jews were barred from owning land, although they were permitted to build houses and to live in them. Stefanesti was a *comuna rurala* ("rural riding") until the surrounding villages were incorporated, when it became a *communa urbana* ("urban riding"). As a rural area, Jews had not been allowed to own land. They were, however, allowed to lease the land for ninety-nine years (not in perpetuity). The contracts they signed with the landowners granted them the right to build on the land. The last landowner was a certain Comartan, who maintained that some of the Jews had not settled directly with him, and he refused to recognize his father's agreements with the Jews. This created a series of court trials and harassments for many families. The trials reached the *curtea de Casatie* ("the supreme court") and the landlord won the case. The Jews who contested the landlords' claims were called *Besmenari*.

The *Uniúnea Evreilor Pamanteni* ("the Union of Native Jews") had tried to obtain representation in parliament, but due to fraudulent election tactics no Jews were elected. In 1926 four Jewish deputies were elected, all from the newly annexed provinces. This in itself is significant, indicating the higher social awareness of Jews, especially those who lived in Bucovina, (previously part of the Austro-Hungarian Empire). In 1930 the Jewish Party (*Partidul Evreesc*) was formed and in 1931 it gained five seats. Life was not easy for these deputies in the Romanian parliament, where their anti-Semitic colleagues did not stop at merely interrupting their speeches with verbal insults; brawls and fisticuffs in the house became a common byline in daily newspapers where they were reported with panache: *Robu da in Fisher — Landau da in Robu*. (Robu was an anti-Semitic bully deputy; Fisher and Landau were two of the Jewish deputies.) ("Robu hits Fisher — Landau hits Robu.")

Student terrorism continued and a new anti-Semitic party was formed; the League of National Christian Defence, the precursor of the Iron Guard, a party structured along Nazi lines with an extreme anti-Semitic program. The success of Nazi Germany was an encouragement for the Iron Guard.

This anti-Semitism worked as a stimulus for Zionism whose ideals became increasingly urgent. *Hachscharah* ("the training stage for a return to working the land") was organized to prepare the young *Halutzim* ("pioneers") to do farming, husbandry and vineyard work. Regardless of ideologies, all Zionists agreed that the only solution was the reclaiming and rebuilding of Palestine as a homeland.

It was in the field of education that the shtetl Jews felt most discriminated against. Upon finishing the four compulsory primary grades, Jewish children had to pass a state examination to enter high school. Jewish schools were maintained by the communities yet were obliged to pay a fee per child, whereas this was not the case in the Romanian schools.

In high schools and higher institutions of learning Jews were accepted only after all Romanian applicants had been admitted. Since the proportion of Jews in the country was five per cent, this was the proportion of students admitted; this was called *numerus clausus*.

This situation, though unjust, was understandable if the logic of the Romanian nationalist government was followed. Disregarding sociological conditions of the two groups involved, the Romanian peasants formed eighty-five per cent of the population, and the Jews formed only five per cent of the population, but consisted of the upper and middle classes, with middle-class values and aspirations, avidly seeking self-improvement. The government would have liked to raise the educational level of the peasants and at the same time prevent the Jews from achieving more education. Every attempt was made to prevent Jewish students from entering the professions, where discrimination was acute. A situation of fierce competition existed between the Romanian students admitted, sight unseen, to the universities and the Jews who were expected to be "twice as good" to obtain the same privileges.

It was this feeling that was stoking the fires of the easily inflammable student anti-Semitism. They envied and hated the ambitious, Jewish students who set high standards of excellence for themselves and at whose level the Romanians were then expected to perform. Furthermore, they regarded the Jewish students as future competitors on the marketplace. The rest was rationalization. The politicians used the students and skilfully exploited their youthful exuberance in the name of nationalism.

In 1937 King Carol, who was increasing his personal control, called on Octavian Goga and A. C. Cuza, both notorious anti-Semites and nationalists (the two terms had somehow become synonymous) to form a new government. The result was a series of laws closely resembling those of the Nazis, who now served as a model. Associations of physicians and lawyers were expelling their Jewish members and "romanization" was being sped up. "Are you ethnic or *sfetnic*?" The quip referred to the laws whereby only "ethnic" Romanians were allowed to own businesses, Jews "sold" their businesses to "ethnics" while remaining *sfetnics* ("advisers"). King Carol declared himself dictator. Early in 1938, in a memorable radio address, he advised the Jews to make serious plans for leaving the country as soon as possible. Octavian Goga said: "A page in history has been turned which cannot be turned back."

Fearing for their lives, the Jews would gladly have taken this advice but for the shut doors they met wherever they turned. Not only small merchants and artisans but the intellectuals lived in constant despair, many reduced to poverty.

In the shtetl, Jews would sit with maps spread on the table, poring over every corner of the globe and pondering where to go — not so much for their own sake as for the sake of their children's future. Few were the countries who would open their doors to emigrating Jews. Pamphlets and books on Bolivia, Uganda, Java and other places indicated that these countries might admit Jews. England's "White Paper" had barred the doors to Palestine, the only place the Jews would gladly have run to. Argentina admitted only Catholics; Canada and America, the *Goldene Medine* (the "Golden Lands") were an unattainable dream.

This was the situation in the shtetl at the outbreak of war in 1939. This was the beginning of the end for most Romanian shtetlech. Shtetl culture, shtetl values and mores, however, have been transplanted in many parts of the world. In some regions of Israel, the Romanian shtetl seems to have picked up where it left off, trying (when not harassed by other problems) to live the life it was accustomed to. No more *Jidani la Palestina*, yet not entirely free of threats. Other problems plague them, but people say "Ein brera" ("There's no alternative"). There, they have suddenly become *die Romanishe* ("the Romanians"), with their own Romanian newspaper, and maintaining the same way of life.

CHAPTER III
Social and Economic Structure

1. The Romanian Administrative Structure and the Shtetl Committee

The shtetl conducted its own affairs autonomously. Its relations with surrounding officialdom were usually amicable, each government aware of its own standing in relation to the other. One of the reasons for survival of Jewish communities was their adaptability to local exigencies. The attitude was one of live and let live, where the Jewish community was grateful for the tolerance shown by the local authorities. Anti-semites often complained that the Jewish shtetl was a state within a state. Since the process of universal suffrage was only approximately enforced, voting was no problem for the Jewish community.

After 1918, Romania was subdivided for administrative purposes into seventy-two districts, called *judetz*, each with its capital or county seat, called *prefectura*. The prefect, or administrator, was the highest authority in the district. Each district consisted of a number of municipalities called *plasa* which were subdivided into communes. Stefanesti was located in the *prefectura* Botosani, the county encompassing the municipality of Stefanesti proper and the villages of Badiuti, Bobulesti and Stanca.

The municipality was governed by a *primar*, (a mayor) and eight councillors. The councillors were elected, and they elected the mayor. The *primarie* ("city hall") was responsible to the *prefectura* for local administrative functions, registrations, records of vital statistics and the inevitable tax collecting. One of the councillors was the representative of the Jewish community, sitting on the local council and acting as liaison between the community and city hall. At one time the councillor acted as *ajutor de primar* ("assistant to the mayor").

The shtetl affairs were run autonomously by a local council called the Jewish *committet*. This executive committee consisted of six councillors, usually elected by acclamation, and a president, nominated by the executive committee.

Unlike most other shtetlech, Stefanesti did not have many volunteers ready to devote their time to the thankless task of looking after the town's affairs. The same individuals remained in the *committet* without interruption, elections being only a formality. The vice-president and secretary-treasurer were similarly nominated. The only paid office was that of the cashier-bookkeeper.

The role of the president of the community was largely honorific. It was usually conferred on the wealthiest and most prestigious member of the community.

The secretary-treasurer was responsible for financial matters. He signed the checks for the community's salaried employees the teachers, *rov, shochet*, school and kindergarten janitors, bath attendants and the cemetery help. He authorized doctors' bills for the needy of the town and various forms of charity within the community. He assigned cemetery plots and assessed the taxes to be paid. The job required a person of impeccable reputation. Few were willing to serve in this capacity.

The cashier-bookkeeper was a paid employee whose task was the actual financial transactions of day-to-day community needs — under the supervision of the secretary.

To cover the expenses required for the functioning of the Jewish community, the *commitet* was empowered to collect taxes from each household. Other sources of revenue were the school tax, tax on slaughter and cemetery-plot sales.

The latter amounted to a form of succession duties. When one wealthy but reputedly miserly man died, the *committet* revenged itself by demanding a hefty sum from his inheritors.

The school tax was paid by every Jewish parent for each child attending the Jewish primary school. This head tax was not imposed on those unable to pay, whose children attended school at the expense of the community.

Ritual slaughtering and killing of fowl by the *schochet* (the "ritual slaughterer") was one of the essential services of the shtetl community and an important source of revenue. The butchers arranged the transactions with the *schochet* and with the *committet*. Housewives bought live fowl, bought a *kvitl* ("a voucher") for a specified sum from the town cashier, then presented the *kvitl* to the *schochet* at the slaughterhouse; this entitled them to have the fowl ritually killed.

The voucher bearing the stamp of the *committet* was a sort of head tax on each fowl consumed. This taxation did not cover the *gabella*, the cattle tax paid by the Jewish community to the municipality for the permission of ritual cattle slaughtering which was a relic of Turkish administration.

Social and Economic Structure 43

There were subcommittees in charge of the school, the bathhouse and *mikveh*, the slaughterhouse and the cemetery. The matzo baking every year before Passover was an important community responsibility and a source of revenue. The *committet* called for tenders from private individuals (and in some cases families) and accepted the lowest bidder. These auctions were often the cause of conflicts and much animosity, especially when nepotism was suspected or preferential treatment was given to individuals.

It must also be recalled that each synagogue had its own structure for fulfilling community needs, especially regarding charitable donations. The *committet* was a superstructure that co-ordinated and collaborated with the other substructures in the running of shtetl affairs. As in all other aspects, the spirit of independence was a strong guiding motive, as was the preference of minimal appeal to the surrounding officialdom.

To the outside world, the shtetl presented a monolithic whole. In truth, however, although differences in wealth were insignificant and group solidarity did not permit exposure of problems to the eyes of the alien world, social stratification was jealously safeguarded and the lines of demarcation difficult to transgress. Not only was this noticeable in the broader brushstrokes of upper-middle- and lower class distinctions, but within these subgroups there existed a well-defined status ranking. In absolute terms the differences were small, so that speaking of "class" in this context may seem incongruous, yet each segment jealously safeguarded its confines, although without any definite internal structure on claims of mutual rights or obligations.

Earning a living, *parnoseh*, was the moving force of the Romanian shtetl. The merchants as well as the artisans worked for themselves. Private enterprise was the only form of economy known and practised. To work for another was considered demeaning, except during the period of apprenticeship. One often heard the comment that it was preferable to deal directly with God than through any intermediary. This spirit of self-reliance is reflected in sayings: "Blessed are the hands that help themselves," or the Romanian farmer's proverb: "The eye of the owner fattens the cattle." The wives were help-meets in the shop; they worked *cot la cot* ("elbow to elbow") to provide for the family. For the storekeeper, his business was his hobby; it was his occupation and preoccupation. There was a saying among the Romanian peasants: "When a Jew has free time, he checks his accounts."

Any form of manual labor was by definition considered inferior. It was taken for granted that the one who worked with his hands

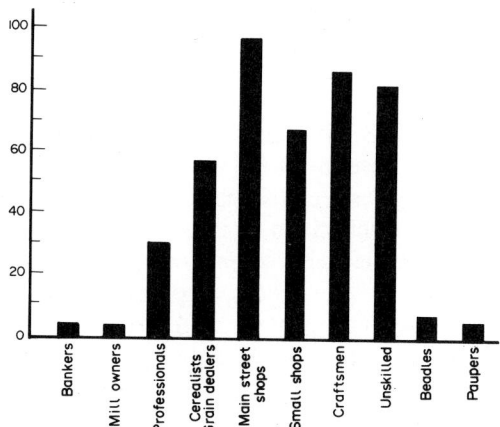

FIG. 9. Occupations according to socio-economic standing.

did not have the required ability for intellectual work and therefore belonged to a lower order. With intellectual ability, one was supposed to possess a series of other qualifications attributed to the *eidler man* ("refined person") in contrast to the *grobber yingh* ("uncouth dolt").

The Romanian shtetl had two parallel criteria for élitism. One was based on money, the other on learning. In both we find a certain dichotomy: the learned élite consisted, on the one hand, of the religious hierarchy, with the *Rebbé* and the *Rov* and, to a lesser extent, the synagogue leadership, and on the other hand, the professionals. The money élite consisted of the wealthy families. The professionals straddled both groups, enjoying prestige accrued from both learning and wealth.

Occupation, material wealth and social status were so closely intertwined that it would be impossible to separate one from the other. They were the ingredients involved in that undefinable term *yichus* ("status").

Yichus, that combination of respectability and refinement one acquired as a family endowment and imperceptibly transmitted with the family name, was still very much a prime mover. One of the respondents, referring to her ancestral origins, was proud of being *neam de Yosupash* ("kin of Yosupash"). The individual's status was decided by the family and in turn the family's *yichus* depended on each and every member of the immediate and extended family. To improve one's social standing was the undisputed aspiration of all. In theory this was achievable by changing one's occupation or by seeking intermarriage with a family of higher standing. In an attempt to advance their social status, working-class parents sent their sons and daughters to apprentice at one of the shops, so that they could subsequently open their own shops. The merchants, in turn, attempted to improve the lot of their children by making often impossible financial efforts, to provide a higher education, the passport to a better life.

Wealth alone was not enough, although it was beginning to matter. Some of the newly rich who had acquired their wealth during the war were only reluctantly accepted into the entourage of the older, established families. A working-class background was still unforgivable. This is illustrated by the reticence with which the town council accepted the principal of the Jewish school, who although well-qualified, had been repeatedly rejected because he was the son of a tailor. Only by dint of sheer perseverance – which in itself had been interpreted as vulgar, pushy, and attributed to his lowly background – was he able to obtain the position of principal of the school. Socially he was accepted by the middle-class merchant group, but not by the intellectuals in town.

This matter of *yichus*, or family standing, acquired dramatic proportions when marriage matches were transacted. For, although young people were beginning to resent excessive parental interference in matters of mate selection, most parents still felt duty bound to arrange their children's marriages. To marry someone of a lower social standing, regardless of the individual's qualities, was a step down the social ladder.

2. The Professionals

The professionals consisted of the lawyers, doctors, dentists, judges, notaries, pharmacists and schoolteachers. The two judges as well as the four notaries and six of the lawyers were gentiles. Only two of the lawyers were Jews. Litigations were not frequent and cases of conflict among Jews were settled by arbitration, by the *rov*, or by one of the local citizens whose integrity and judgment recommended him for the task.

The *Farmacia*, as everywhere in Europe, was a prestigious institution. Any similarity between an American drugstore and the *Farmacia* is indeed purely coincidental. This was the temple of the healing profession. With its impressive shelves of mysterious formulae, porcelain jars and always shiny marble countertops, it was an awe-inspiring place, where the promise of imminent cure floated in the air among the pungent medicinal smells. One spoke in hushed tones and waited respectfully for the white coated pharmacist to

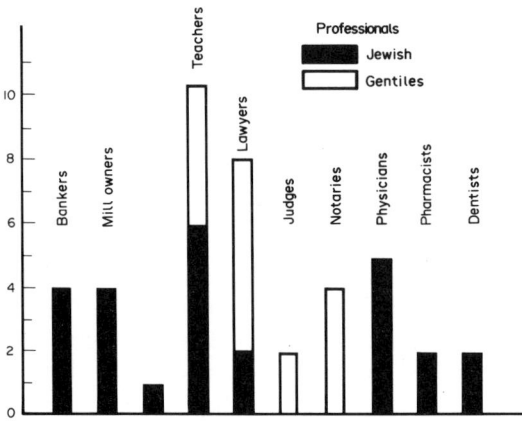

FIG. 10. Professionals, Jews–Gentiles.

prepare the potion of hope, according to the doctor's prescription.

The pharmacist was a *titrat* – he had a diploma and a title – and was part of the local coterie of professionals. Yet, like all other shopkeepers in town, he and his family lived at the rear of the business premises. Most small towns had one pharmacy. When the second pharmacy opened in Stefanesti, it triggered a series of conflicting loyalties among the townspeople. The newcomer instigated the formation of a rival town council and a real *machloyké* ("a warring split") resulted, in a town otherwise notorious for its indifference to local politicking.

Dentistry was considered a branch of medicine. Stomatology and oral surgery were part of medical training. Dentistry was regarded as a profession suitable for women; of the three local dentists, two were women, one of them practising both medicine and dentistry.

Medicine has been, throughout the ages, a field open to Jews and one in which they distinguished themselves, as their frequent presence at royal courts throughout Europe testifies. It is in the tradition of Judaism to revere the healing profession. The Talmud counsels respect for the doctor above all others, since his work is worthy of honor. The shtetl attitude toward the doctor is therefore not surprising. Parents readily made sacrifices in order to provide sons – and often their daughters the possibility of pursuing this profession. For the Romanian shtetl the doctor represented the undisputed epitome of prestige. The doctor enjoyed utter confidence and respect. The fact that medical schools in Romania openly practised numerus clausus, did not stop those who aspired to enter the profession; they pursued their studies *in strainatate* ("abroad"), mainly in France and Italy. Many established themselves there, others returned to practise at home. Their effort and success was understandable since they were highly motivated by the promise of upward mobility and financial rewards.

Of the five doctors in Stefanesti, four were Jews; the one gentile was the director of the municipal hospital. The doctors saw patients at their offices (located in their residences) and on housecalls.

The frequency with which the doctor's services were appealed to was directly proportional to the status of the patient's family. This was not due only to the expenses involved; the more ignorant, poorer segment of the population still clung to other means of dealing with health problems. The healers and soothsayers still played an important role in society. Studies of various ethnic groups of similar socioeconomic levels in New York revealed that, for comparable health problems, Italians and Jews called the doctor more often than other ethnic groups. In this respect, the well-known "Jewish-mother syndrome" was well-grounded in the Romanian shtetl pattern. It was the merchants' wives who kept the doctors in business. One of the doctors had remarked that some of the local ladies ought to take out an *abonament* ("a yearly subscription") with him, considering the frequency with which he was called to the house.

Of the ten teachers, six were Jews. The Romanian teachers, trained at the *scoala normala* ("teachers' school"), taught exclusively at the Romanian public schools; men taught at the boys' school and women at the girls' school. The teachers at the Jewish Public School were often local university students who earned extra money by teaching while completing their studies. This was possible since the Romanian universities did not require daily attendance during the academic year. The Hebrew and kindergarten teachers, on the other hand, were trained in their profession at accredited schools, mainly in Bessarabia.

This group of Jewish professionals formed a small coterie very much aloof from the rest of the community. Their relations with the townsfolk were on a professional basis. They were the trend setters, the accepted leaders in cultural matters. Their mannerisms were openly emulated. Influenced by their sojourns in the large cities and often abroad, they lived a life of comparative luxury by local standards. Their modern ways, imported from abroad, were not always viewed with total approval, nor was the free camaraderie between the sexes much appreciated. Their friendly relationships with some of the gentile intellectuals in town provided gossip for the conservative middle-class shtetl.

3. The Merchants

By far the largest group in Stefanesti, as in other shtetlech, were the merchants and shopkeepers. Being a shopkeeper was an upstanding, prideful occupation and in the Romanian shtetl it enjoyed a high prestige. Shopkeepers were the leaders of synagogues, supporters of charity and of the Zionist movement; in brief, the typical ambitious, conservative core of the community. This was the establishment, the true power élite. Education and hard work, values that make for success in our own society, were drilled into the young from early childhood by example and admonition. Parents sent their children to high school and on to university in the hope of offering them the advantages they felt they had been denied. They had one or more servants and as a status symbol sent their wives and children to a spa at the beach or to a mountain resort. They had aspirations for upward mobility, especially for their children.

Most businesses were run on a minimum capital, buying small stock and subsisting on a five-percent margin of profit, which was considered adequate. Shopkeepers often bought on consignment, returning unsold goods.

This put the small businessman or shopkeeper in a perpetual condition of debt. The sum borrowed to cover a pressing debt was often repaid by incurring another loan from yet another source. "Ma duc la vanatoare" ("I am going hunting") was the somewhat bitterly ironic remark one heard when friends met by chance at an hour unusual for a mere leisurely stroll. It meant that the merchant was in search of a loan to cover an outstanding debt. The alternative was to borrow from the town usurer, at exorbitant interest rates, with usually inextricably disastrous results. Since failing in business was inconceivable, the *gimeless chessed* was the merchant's life line.

The *gimeless chessed* is an ancient institution of Jewish communities everywhere. In the Romanian shtetl there was no formal committee of decision makers or specific association; it was an unstructured arrangement whereby those in temporary straits appealed to the goodwill of friends for help. (The exact translation of the Hebrew term is "an act of loving kindness"). This mutual dependence was one of the many strands in the bonds of camaraderie and understanding. It offered a measure of security to the individual without the humiliation of otherwise asking for help, since the knowledge that he too may be in a position to return the favor prevented the "ego-damaging" relation of patronage sometimes developed in such circumstances.

Within the group of merchants and shopkeepers, fine distinctions of status were discernible, depending on prestige of the family name, size of the business establishment, type of merchandise sold and clientele.

This ranking was intimated rather than overtly expressed, but each family was very much aware of its own status within the *yichus continuum*. One aspired to associate with others at one's own level of preferably one notch above. The touchstone was the choice of in-laws, the *machetonem*. It was of utmost importance to establish kin relationships with families on the same socioeconomic level.

"Tell me with whom you associate and I will tell you who you are," was one Romanian proverb often quoted. Other proverbs illustrate the constant concern with status — "From a dog's tail you can't make a silk sieve" and "If you wallow in chaff you will be eaten by the pigs."

A closer analysis of the occupational structure of the shtetl is relevant. Examining the chart we see that the occupational distribution is a bell shaped curve with few relatively wealthy families at one end, the great majority of merchants and the prosperous working class grouped in the center and very few poor at the other end. This is an interesting contrast to the pyramidal socioeconomic diagram usually associated with the shtetl, where a broad base of poor, supports the few at the apex. (In passing it may be mentioned that it was the middle-class mentality of the Romanian shtetl that contributed to the facility with which the immigrants adapted to their adopted country.)

Since the Jews have traditionally been barred from owning land and from any form of military or administrative participations of the host country, they entered the areas open to them and there attained excellence. It is not surprising to see them succeed in the business and professional world where their talents were not thwarted. The reverence for learning and knowledge, so deeply instilled from early childhood, was easily channelled into secular activities. The aspirations of every family was to educate the sons, and to a lesser extent the daughters. For girls, education was not as important as for boys, although it was taken for granted that an educated girl had a better chance of getting a professional for a husband, since her own education weighed considerably as part of her dowry.

A look at the occupational charts reveals an interesting picture of shtetl life: the number of people attracted to each occupation reflects priorities and values. Northern Romania, where most shtetlech were to be found, was a rich, fertile region. Much of the

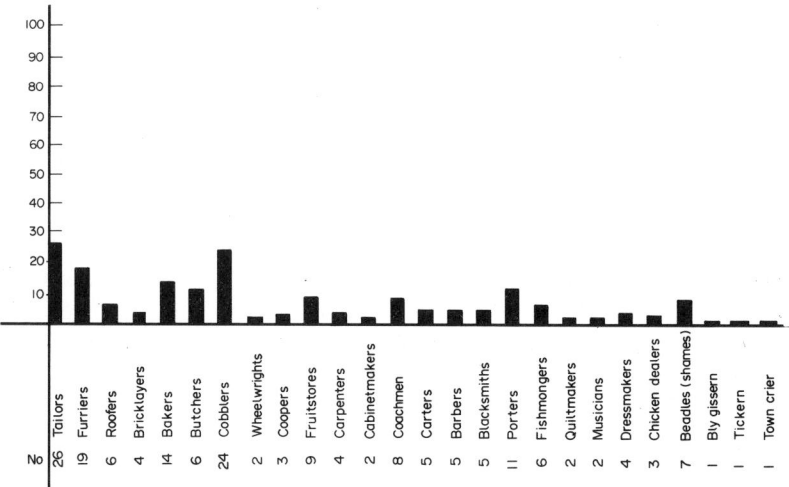

FIG. 11. Craftsmen and marginals (number of households) occupational chart.

commerce and industry that provided a livelihood for the inhabitants consisted in supplying wholesalers with exports. We find five wholesale egg dealers, eight cattle dealers and fifty-seven "cerealists" (grain dealers).

The *cerealist* bought grains from the farmer and sold to the wholesaler, who exported it. The *cerealist* did not own a shop. Like the farmer, he depended for success on fortuitous weather conditions as much as on his own business acumen. The region was known for vineyards, but also for wheat, corn, barley, oats, sunflower seed, rape, beans and buckwheat. The farmer brought his grain in to the *cerealist* in hundred-kilogram jute sacks. A network of friendly relations established over the years facilitated the transaction. The sacks were unloaded in the merchant's shed, or in one of the rooms, temporarily divided into compartments by wooden slats. The individual relied on his business sense and ability to speculate by waiting for the propitious moment to sell.

There were twenty-nine dry-goods shops and twenty-four groceries, which would suggest that food and clothing were of equal importance in the Romanian shtetl. If we add the thirteen haberdasheries and the furriers, we may surmise that this was a more prosperous mode of life than the one emerging from the literature regarding the Polish shtetl, where basic needs were the prime concern. Food was relatively plentiful; comfortable surroundings and especially the children's futures were absorbing problems.

There were few china and hardware shops. Of the six china shops, only one carried imported items, while the others dealt in locally made earthenware pottery, geared mainly to the peasant and working-class clientele. The largest and most prestigious hardware store supplied plows and ironware tools for the farmer.

There were three shoe stores, one of which specialized in the better quality shoes. The peasants' needs were limited. Men and women went barefoot most of the year, or wore *opinci* ("homemade leather sandals"). Only for church and important occasions did the peasants don shoes. They usually bought patent-leather shoes for their dead. In contrast, no respectable shtetl resident would be seen barefoot. It was goyish, not befitting a Jew. Shoe stores relied mainly on shtetl clientele, for both shoes and winter wear — galoshes, rubber boots and snow boots.

In one respect shtetl and peasant women were alike; they preferred to have a small foot and demanded sizes smaller than they needed, regardless of how the shoes fit. The salesman would resort to various subterfuges — by trying on the same shoe several times, thus stretching it, or deftly changing the size inscribed — to make a sale. Haggling over the price, however, was a ritual faithfully followed in all instances.

The two photographers, the printer and the watchmaker have been included with the merchant class by general concensus, mainly due to the prestige these occupations held in the local scale of values. The fact that Stefanesti boasted not one but two photographers denotes a touch of extravagance and would point to some finanical ease in the community. The photographers regarded their profession as an art form and enjoyed suitable recognition.

The printer was classed with the middle class, in spite of his being a manual worker. Since there was no local newspaper, printing was limited to invitations for births, weddings and bar mitzvas, calling cards, and the infrequent announcements for forthcoming theatrical events. Occasionally, political posters and announcements provided work.

The watchmaker, too, was part of the middle class. Wrist watches were rare; pocket watches, the mantel clock and grandfather clocks were once-in-a-lifetime purchases. Servicing was therefore the watchmaker's main occupation. He was also a jeweler, which no doubt augmented his livelihood. His standing in the community was assessed by virtue of his family prestige as well as his intellectual activity.

The high number of taverns (twenty-two, nine of which were owned by gentiles) is unusual in an avowedly non-drinking society, which the shtetl was acknowledged to be. This is the more incongruous, considering the fact that the occupation of tavern keeper did not enjoy inordinate respect in town. The role of the tavern within the Jewish shtetl community was not that of a pub or a bar. Nor was it quite a saloon. It was frequented by peasants who, after a deal, usually went to the saloon to *cinsteasca* ("honor" or "toast") one another with a glass of *rachiu* ("brandy"). Jews rarely went to the *crashma* ("saloon"), nor did they follow the custom of toasting one another after a deal.

The large number of taverns in town is also surprising because many local farmers had their own *alambic* ("stills") and made their own brandy, or *tzuica*. "Am pus la teask" ("I put to ferment") was an often-heard remark. Owning a still was not illegal, though viewed unfavorably by the authorities.

There were five restaurants and six inns in town. For the size of the town this, too, was anomalous. It is explainable by the fact that Stefanesti was a *rabbunish* shtetl, the residence of the Stefanester *rebbé*, who attracted a constant stream of out-of-town visitors.

The flour mill was owned by a wealthy family who considered themselves, and were esteemed by the town, as somewhat aloof and apart from the rest of the community. The flour mill also manufactured sunflower oil and pressed the sunflower husks into cakes used as cattle feed.

It is impossible to discuss the shtetl merchants without mentioning the manner in which a typical sale was transacted. Our own impersonal way of doing business is but a pale image of the complex tournament of wits involved in the buying and selling in the shtetl.

Every store on main street had a *comis*, an apprentice. In the process of learning the art of salesmanship, he was expected to run messages, take the children to school and help the maid with the heavier work, such as shaking out rugs, lifting and shifting furniture and so on. He also looked after customers — and when he was not busy, he was expected to tidy up the store. Sweeping the floor and sidewalk during summer months offered unsuspected opportunities to release hidden artistic talents. For, to avoid the clouds of dust when sweeping, the floor had to be sprinkled with water. A tin can with a hole in the bottom served as sprinkler. As the water dripped onto the floor, it was possible to draw or doodle and obtain a variety of designs, or even write one's name on the floor. It was fun, part of the minutiae invented to make life less tedious of a summer day.

One of the *comis'* tasks was to induce customers into the store. This he did by taking pieces of merchandise out of the store to entice the passerby; if that did not work, he pulled the customer in almost by force. This would have been beneath the dignity of the owner; hence the *comis* did the *shlepping* ("pulling in"). He was the *shlepper*. The term, as well as the feminine *shlepperké* had acquired a rather derogatory connotation of "loafer" or "drifter".

Once inside the store the customer was deluged by a torrent of verbiage in praise of the merchandise. By mutual understanding the price asked was twice the intended sales price. To a protest that the price was too high, the standard reply was "I ask much and give in much". The client would then offer one quarter of the price asked, and they were off. Both the salesman and the customer had to judge with astuteness the propitious moment at which to stop haggling. The shrewd buyer would sense when rock bottom was reached. The salesman had to gauge when the confused customer had had enough. Assured that the best bargain was struck, a vigorous handshake concluded the deal, and for good luck, a spit on the palm. The spit was to ward off evil, since water in any form had a magic preventive power. When large deals were involved, between farmers the handshake was usually reinforced by a few glasses of wine or *rachiu* ("brandy") at the favorite *crashma* ("saloon"). Jews did not follow this custom.

To allow the first customer of the day to walk out without buying something was considered a bad omen, and was to be avoided at any price. This was even more important on Saturday evening or Monday morning. Saturday evening was the beginning of the Jewish week, when the usual greeting was "a good week" or "a full week". As a form of concession to the host country, Monday morning was the beginning of the work week and therefore of similar significance as a starting point. It was important that the first customer on a Saturday evening after the appearance of the first star, or on Monday morning, not be allowed to walk out without buying something; anything. This first sale was called *saftea* or, in Romanian, *pocinog*. *Saftea* is one of the many words of Turkish origin that bespeak the influence of Turkish domination upon the local mores. But the term *pocinog*, of Dacic origin, was also used, suggesting that the concept had existed and was practised by the local population. The haggling, as well as various omens, are to be found in many Oriental lands.

Some people were believed to have a certain magic quality about them and therefore were thought to be *bun la saftea* ("good as a first customer"). The saying accompanying a first sale was *saftea, sa nu mai stea* ("May the merchandise not remain on the shelf too long"). This belief in the ability of influencing or controlling providence by the manner of behaving, also applied to anything used for the first time, or to the beginning of a new package or bolt of cloth.

There was an anecdote told in the shtetl of an anti-Semitic Romanian priest who vowed to "give every Jew in town apoplexy" by walking into a store early in the morning and walking out without buying anything; or, as a variant, to walk into every store and pay whatever price was asked, to give the Jews something to worry about for not having asked a higher price.

4. The Craftsmen and Artisans

The craftsmen were all self-employed, independent artisans, with perhaps one apprentice. The wife and children were expected to pitch in, everyone according to his abilities. At this level conditions were probably closer to the image of the ramshackle, poverty-stricken shtetl often referred to in the literature.

Although not entirely illiterate (as was the case with most Romanian peasants), only a few were functionally literate in Romanian, a language most of them spoke badly, if at all. Yiddish was still the undisputed language of the working class, whereas many of the merchant families were already using Romanian as the mother tongue.

They shared with other shtetl inhabitants their concern for and wish to assure the future of their children and whenever possible provided the opportunity of overcoming the social barriers by facilitating their training as apprentice salesmen. Exceptionally bright sons with obvious academic potential were helped by the family and sometimes by the community to continue their education.

Imbued with the Judaic tenet that a father's duty was to provide his sons with a trade or risk seeing him become a brigand, craftsmen spared no effort in this direction. Many sons followed in the father's footsteps, as there was a tendency to consider one's own métier superior to the others.

In making things, all operations from the planning and measuring stage to the finished product were done by hand, or with the aid of the foot pedalled Singer, as was the case with all preindustrialized societies. For the artisan this provided a source of pride and personal satisfaction in one's work. The latter was also a criterion for determining the socioeconomic standing of the family; the shoemaker who made a pair of boots enjoyed a higher prestige than his neighbor, a cobbler, who was primarily a repair man. The rates they commanded were proportional and considered justifiably so. In general, social status within the working class depended on income, family reputation (for honesty, reliability) and the personality of the individual.

The occupational distribution chart for the craftsmen in Stefanesti illustrates the predominant concern for food and clothing. The twenty-six tailors as well as the other craftsmen involved in the clothing industry served both the shtetl community and the neighboring peasant villages. One respondent explained: "My father was a tailor; there were tailors for the peasants and tailors for the finer people in town. Each had a reputation for a specialty; my father was famous for making *catzaveicas*, or, as they say in Yiddish, *kardikié* – a sort of sleeveless overgarment worn by farmers. He used to buy pure wool cloth of a fine quality and made it nice, with a flaired bottom, lined it with sheep's skins and trimmed with red fox fur around the armholes and the bottom. A farmer wanted a nice *catzeveica*, he came to my father; another wanted a *rand de haine* (men's suit), he went to another tailor, and so on". There were two tailors who specialized in winter coats and suits for the finer people. Others had a peasant clientele.

The same respondent explained that his father often received as payment some product – a sack of flour, some chickens – besides the cash paid. Barter was still a means of commerce in the shtetl. "This way, we always had what to eat, it was a good life," concluded this respondent.

Clothes represented an important fraction of the family budget, and were worn as long as possible. Many of the tailors were kept busy with *ibermachn* ("transforming") clothes to suit one member of the family instead of another.

There were only four dressmakers in town. This was by no means due to an excessive male concern or lack of interest in appearance by the shtetl's female population. The reason for this discrepancy is far more prosaic and easily explainable. The peasant women were not part of the dressmaker's clientele, since their usual garb was the homespun native costume or homesewn dress. The poorer segment of the shtetl population represented a similarly uncertain source of clientele. On the other hand, the well-to-do, who were able to afford it, found it more fashionable to have their clothes made-to-order in the big city. This left only the merchants' wives as a stable and reliable source of customers. Fashion magazines in hand, they kept the four dressmakers busy, demanding the latest Paris styles in new dresses or in the perpetual changes of last year's clothes.

The Romanian shtetl enjoyed a certain level of economic ease: there were nineteen furriers. The continental climate, with at least two months of sub-zero temperature, made warm winter clothing a necessity. Peasants wore the *cojoc* ("sheepskin coats") and people in the shtetl often had the coats fur-lined or added fur collars. The favorite furs were sheepskin, fox, rabbit and, less often, mink, used both for lining and collars and especially for fur hats.

Furriers specialized. The *kushmars* were fur-hat makers; the *cojocars* made coats and vests; others dabbled in a bit of everything. The fur hat worn during the winter months by everyone, and by the peasants all year round, were made of sheep's skins of various qualities. While the peasants wore the usually rougher white, black or gray fur hats, the more refined preferred the black or gray (sometimes brown) hats made of young lambskins called *astrackan*, of a finer grain with a more precise curl, of the Persian lamb variety. The *cojoc* or sheepskin coat worn with the fur inward was the usual peasant garb summer and winter, as was the *bonditza* — the sleeveless vest worn by women as well as men. This was a specialty of some furriers, who embroidered the vests with multicolored wool in bright designs. Mink-trimmed hats were reserved only for the *rebbé*, his *gabouem* ("secretaries") and entourage.

Shoes were bought ready-made. There were twenty-four cobblers in town, including the *richtuitor* and the two deluxe shoemakers. Footwear was an essential item: walking was the sole means of locomotion. And the quality of the merchandise made repairs a frequent necessity. Most cobblers were indeed repair men. Within the métier, too, there were degrees of expertise and each carried a well-defined status. The *richtuitor* cut the leather and prepared the shoes and boots commanding higher prices, while the cobbler put on the soles and heels and did the finishing work considered less important. Consequently most cobblers were poor, and enjoyed a lower status.

As previously mentioned, food was not a problem in the Romanian shtetl. It is not surprising to find fourteen bakers, nine fruit stores and six fishmongers in town. Bread was the staple food, while *mamaliga* ("corn bread") was the bread of the peasant. A slice of bread with butter or with chicken fats, with garlic rubbed on the crust, was a common after-school snack; and a piece of black bread with a slice of onion served as lunch for a harried working man.

The more finely ground the wheat, the whiter the flour and the more expensive it was; consequently, white bread was a sign of prestige. Merchants' families ate only white bread, bought fresh daily, except on the Sabbath, when the egg *challa* was bought or in some cases, home baked. Baking pastries was the Romanian shtetl woman's avocation, and no self-respecting housewife would have considered going out to buy cookies or cakes. Her baking talents represented an important index of pride and accomplishments.

There were six butchers, six fishmongers and three chicken dealers — chickens were usually bought directly from the peddling farmers. Most families had a few chickens in cages, since fowl was a favorite food. Fish was not as popular as it may have been in regions where fish was more plentiful.

Buying a chicken from a peasant woman (a task usually relegated to the housewife) was, like all business transactions, ritualized. The chicken was carefully examined, checked for fat (an important asset) by blowing into the underbelly feathers, to determine by the color of the skin the plumpness of the bird, and trying to guess its weight. Only then would the haggling begin in earnest. There is an amusing vignette ridiculing the manner of the simple shtetl woman and her frequent use of Yiddish words when speaking to the peasant: "Ce vorbesti? Dai un bluz shar'n sus; Mai mult feidern decat gaina!" ("What are you saying? The chicken's so light one blow will blow it away; she's more feathers than chicken.")

Chicken soup was a favorite shtetl fare, with beef second and fish a poor third. Herring, imported in barrels, was not as popular as it would appear from the literature. The fresh fish, caught by local fishermen in the Basheu or the Prut with square nets stretched on pole frames, were carp, pike and trout. The catfish, found in the muddy Basheu, was not edible for the Jews since it has no scales. Although to most shtetl housewives the Friday-evening meal was still inconceivable without the fish dish, many homes were replacing it with vegetable salads and other dishes.

Meat was still something of a luxury, especially for the working-class family. Meat was prepared in stews or brisket: it was used in stuffings or served as hamburgers. Charcoal broiling was not popular in the home. Beef liver was prepared and was a staple *foreshpeis* ("entré").

Milk and milk produce were a most important part of shtetl diet — mainly sour cream, butter, cheese and buttermilk. *Branza*, made of sheep's cheeses and salted in barrels for preservation, was a most popular article, sold in grocery stores rather than by milk dealers. Three milk dealers sufficed.

Although vegetables were very much part of the basic diet, there were only nine fruit and vegetable stores. Fruits and vegetables were usually bought in season from peddlers and farmers, who sold their produce from wagons along the street or at the *maydan* on market days. The better fruit stores were graded according to size of the store, quality of merchandise and class of people they catered to, which in itself conferred a certain prestige.

Although situated next door to prosperous merchants, the fruit stores were placed on a lower social scale. The *merar* ("fruit vendor") did not quite belong. There may not have been any logical reason for this self-styled classification, but that is the way it was in the Romanian shtetl. The stigma of once having been a *merar* clung to families for generations.

The *merar* made rounds of orchards in early spring and leased fruit trees from the farmers, then hoped for adequate weather conditions to obtain a good crop. When the fruit was ripe, the *merar* would pick the fruit and sell it in his fruit store. (The Romanian term *merarie* refers to the apples — *mere* means "apples.")

One staple article sold in the *merarie* were the *kvosnetzes* ("pickled apples"), usually available in early spring when other fruit was scarce. The taste of a *kvosnetze* is undescribable and, for those who have never tasted this delicacy, unimaginable. The apples were pickled in wooden barrels with water and sugar. The *kvass* or juice in which the apples were pickled resembled apple cider.

Another item sold in the *merarie* was pickled watermelon. Small watermelons were pickled in brine seasoned with dill and garlic. Although the prudent homeowner did his own pickling, the *merar* did a brisk business.

There were five barbers in Stefanesti; as one respondent explained, "they didn't make much of a living because only those who could afford went regular to the barber — maybe once in three months was good enough. But clothing and food you need, no matter what. On the other hand, it is a clean work, lots of free time to read the papers, not hard work." During the twenties, when the ladies' hairstyles were *à la garçon* ("boyish"), barbers increased their clientele; they often came to the house to give haircuts to the entire family. Barbers, too, had their own ranking, depending on personality and especially the class of customers they attracted. One of the barbers augmented his income by cupping and placing leeches.

The building trade was not too active in most towns. The four carpenters, four bricklayers and five roofers were busy with repair and maintenance. The carpenters were also cabinetmakers, classified according to the excellence of their work. In general, cabinet making was estimated superior and thus carried more prestige in the community than carpentry. One of the cabinetmakers was a member of the town council (*committeit*). Roofers were also tinsmiths, and supplemented their income by making various household utensils such as funnels, baking trays, cookie shapes and other metal articles.

Wood barrels and kegs were much in use for storing and pickling. It would appear that the three coopers sufficed for local needs.

As previously mentioned, export of locally grown produce (grain, eggs, fruit) was an important industry. The eight wagonners and eleven porters provided essential services. Like most shtetlech, Stefanesti was not on any railroad line; the transportation to Trusesti, the closest railroad station, made it necessary to maintain a network of *cutiugari* ("draymen") and *balegules* ("carters") and also supported the five *birjars* ("coachmen"). The *birjars* subsequently became the owners and bus drivers of the newly formed busline linking the town with the larger centers, Botosani and Iassy.

The five blacksmiths and three wheelwrights provided for local needs. The blacksmiths and wheelwrights depended on the peasants, for whom horsedrawn wagons were lifelines. In the shtetl itself there were a few families who owned a *docar* ("two wheel carriage"); the *birjars* and *balagoles* also relied on the blacksmiths. The smithies were all lined in a row along the *maydan*, the empty lot that served, once a week, as a marketplace. The blacksmiths as well as the draymen and drivers were placed low on the status scale in the shtetl, considered uncouth, ignorant and rough. To swear like a *balagole* evoked an image of unsavory language.

The only quiltmaker and sole upholsterer in town illustrates the prevailing attitude towards what the shtetl considered frills or luxuries. *Colderes* ("quilts"), upholstered furniture, mattresses, were once-in-a-lifetime articles for most families. Those who had acquired more elaborate tastes, and were able to afford it, found the choice for these articles far greater in the larger centers, thus bypassing the talents of the local artisans. The *tobletzirer* (from *tapissier*, which means "upholsterer") eked out an additional few *lei* by making rag and felt slippers.

Ingenuity was not lacking in the shtetl when earning a few *lei* was at stake. The *bly gyssern*, the woman who, as one respondent explained, "was called in when a child was sick and they wanted to know why", poured lead as a form of divining. She melted down old lead spoons or forks, poured the melted lead into a pail of water and then she "read" and prognosticated from the shape which appeared. "For instance, if it looked like a dog, the child was, maybe, frightened by a dog."

Another enterprising woman earned some extra pennies by preparing *borsht* ("sour broth") from *klayen* ("chaff"). She was called the *borshtenitze*. She kept a quantity of chaff mixed with water in a wooden barrel, and sold the ferment. Like the *bly gissern*, she was patronized only by the unsophisticated neighbors.

In a town without a local newspaper, when radios were still a rare wonder, the role of the town crier was not negligible. There were two specialists in this field. One was the Romanian, a local gypsy, who was the official announcer for the municipal authorities. Then there was his Jewish counterpart, the bagel vendor, who, killing two birds with one stone, sold his hot bagels out of a wicker basket while announcing all important news for the Jewish community. One regular announcement was the timetable of the communal bath, especially the hours when it was open to women. He would stop at every street corner and in a nasal tone would sing out his announcement: "Veiber in bud arein" ("Women, to the bath"), while a bunch of ragamuffins taunted him and provided a live audience. When he sold his hot bagels, his singsong was "heyise beiglinolech, heyise: Americaner beigl, heyise" ("Hot bagel, American, hot bagel").

5. The Paupers

Stefanesti, like all shtetlech, had its share of paupers. Within this group there were two distinct categories: there were the few local poor families, and then there were the itinerant beggars.

The local poor consisted of the chronically ill, or those whose poverty was a result of pure bad luck. They did most of the menial work in town, such as plucking chickens at the slaughterhouse or at home, and were the wards of the Jewish community who helped them in all matters financial, paid their doctors' and precription bills, provided them with the free supply of *matzos* for Passover and, as a matter of course, looked after their burial needs.

The itinerant beggars, although not part of the population proper, were a perenial feature on the local scene. They made the rounds of all the small towns on virtual tournées, much like vaudeville one night stands, descending like a swarm of locusts on each town. Some among this group were feeble-minded, some were cripples, lame or blind; but many were shiftless, lazy impostors who had adjusted to this parasitic type of life and thrived on it. Their infirmities were their profession and they elicited pity by exposing their ailments. They travelled in groups of gypsylike caravans, each establishing territorial rights in various shtetlech as their very own hunting grounds. Internal squabbles and fistfights to protect these rights were not uncommon, grotesque as they appeared to the onlookers. With a cloth sack on the shoulder, they would go from door to door asking for alms. They were given pieces of bread, or fruit or cookies and, in some cases, some pennies. In return they would bless the donor, the blessing being proportional to the handout. Both the donor and the recipient were convinced that this blessing was heard and adequately recorded by the Almighty in the proper register.

It was from among this group that the *orchim* ("guests") were brought home by the prosperous householders, from the synagogue, for Sabbath. The paupers would sit at the entrance of the synagogue where, after prayers, the *balabatem* ("householders") would invite them home for the Sabbath meal. Monday morning they departed again, in caravan. *Fiske the Lame*, by the noted Yiddish story teller Mendele Mocher Sforim, describes the life of the vagabond beggars with pathos and understanding.

CHAPTER IV

The Family

1. The Family

Within Judaism, although the family pattern evolved from the patriarchal polygamous tribal type, congruent with the needs of a pastoral society, to the monogamous family of today, it remained the most important single unit. If Judaism survived throughout the millennia it was due to the important role ascribed to the family, for it is within the family that cultural values were transmitted and maturation and socialization of the individual occurred.

A. Kardiner summed it up best: "One of the accidental by-products of the family is that it fostered in man the growth of human emotions and intelligence which greatly hastened social development. Monogamous family creates conditions that are favorable to the development of certain attributes in the child that work best for the society in the long run. It is apparent from comparative studies of cultures with different family patterns that the human infant flourishes best with one parent of each sex. This is the most economically consistent and least confusing pattern".* This concept Judaism understood with infinite perspicacity and translated into every commandment and precept. Every *mitzva* ("good deed"), every prayer instilled from earliest years has as its ultimate aim the maintenance of stability of the family unit and, through it, of the collectivity. *Shalom bayis* ("domestic harmony") held up as a desirable good in itself, resulted in the individual's optimal development.

As an inherent part of Judaic traditions, the Romanian shtetl tried to live by these tenets. Differences between the shtetl of the Pale and the Romanian shtetl existed as a result of different external conditions.

The emphasis was on the nuclear family: the mother, father and offspring, within a strictly monogamous unit. The rules of descent

---

* A. Kardiner, *Sex and Morality*, New York: Charter Books, 1962, p. 195.

and residence were dictated by economic and affective considerations rather than rigidly formulated. In kinship preference, the family was bilateral, emphasizing both the mother's and father's sides equally; it was patrilineal in the sense that the family name was traced through the father, and strong vestiges of the ancient patriarchal authoritarian tendencies persisted. Marriages outside the faith were virtually unheard of in the shtetl. Had such a calamity befallen a family, mourning ritual would have been observed and the person's name never again mentioned. This went so far as to taint the name of the extended family and would have affected marriage alliances with other upstanding families.

It must be reiterated that, as in all other cultural aspects, there were two models pertaining roughly to the two levels of society, based on differences in levels of income, education and social standing. Each group socialized its members to its own value system by inculcating and cultivating these differences. Most obvious was the size of the family: among the more affluent merchant class, two or three children were the norm; the poorer working-class family of eight or ten children was not unusual. Love and devotion within the family were, however, instilled throughout, in theory at least.

The shtetl kinship terminology did not differ from the English one. The "sign-posts", as Radcliffe Brown called them, pointed out the structure underlying realities and expectations of each prescribed role. Terms indicated separation of generations and bilateral descent with which we are familiar. Not surprisingly, the Yiddish kinship terminology was being replaced by equivalent Romanian terms.

The *mishpocha* ("extended family") including the in-laws; the *machetonem* of both sides of the family were *geknipt und gebindn* ("tied together and knotted") with important reciprocal rights and obligations. This was congruent with the internal patterns of the culture and with the social structure. Where social stratification was minutely observed, it is not surprising to find excessive concern for the standing and behavior of future kin.

Yiddish terms of reference for family roles (mother, father, sister and so on) are identical to those in English. In the Romanian shtetl Yiddish was in the process of being superseded by Romanian in every-day usage and this was reflected in the gradual replacement of Yiddish terms with their Romanian equivalents and subsequently with the more stylish French ones. The latter was a sign of sophistication often considered pretentious in the no-nonsense shtetl world. Thus, the siblings of one's parents were called *fetter* ("uncle") and *mymme* ("aunt") in Yiddish. In Romanian this was *nene* ("uncle")

English	Yiddish	Romanian
son	zyin	fiu
daughter	tochter	fica
parents	eltern or tate-mamme	parinti
father	tate or pappa	tata or taticu
mother	momme or mamma	mama or mamica
brother	brieder	frate
sister	shvester	sora
grandfather	zeydeh	bunic or tata-mare
grandmother	bobbeh	bunica or mama-mare
grandchild	einikl	nepot (m)/nepoata (f)
son in law	eidem	ginere
daughter in law	shneer	nora
aunt	myme/tante	tzatza or tanty or matusa
uncle	fetter/oncle	nene or unchiu
brother in law	shvuger	cumnat
sister in law	shveigerin	cumnata
mother in law	shvigger	soacra
father in law	shveer	socru
niece	plemenetze/nepoata	nepoata
nephew	plemenek/nepot	nepot
cousin (m-f)	shvesterkind (m-f)	var (m) vara or (f) verishor verishoara
sponsors	interfirers	nashi (married couple are fini)
godfather	kvotter	nash (no fem. equivalent)
godson		fin
step sister/br	shtif-shvester/brider	sora/frate vitreg/a (vitreg = hostile)
stepmother/fa	shtif-mitter/futter	mama/tata vitreg/a
in law	machetunem	*cuscrii cumatru/a (viz Spanish compadre)
mother in law	macheteinesteh	cuscra (term by which parents of couple call one another)
father in law	machutn	cruscru (term by which parents of couple call one another)
extended fam. incl. in laws	mishpucha	rude or rubedenii

* In Romanian — Cuscrii = relation of wife's parents to husbands's and vice-versa.

and *tzatza* ("aunt"), the latter a peasant term used colloquially. A number of factors determined which language terminology applied to whom. One did not address an unsophisticated, provincial person by the recently introduced French *tanty* and *oncle*; nor did one call a cosmopolitan person *mymme* (or *tzatza*) or *fetter*. The latter terms were reserved for the grandparents' generation. The working class (who continued to use Yiddish in the home) used the Yiddish terms exclusively. Generally speaking, it was a matter of generations, the younger generation adapting themselves and adopting the new ways. French, the prestige language, was used by the better educated, younger group, who looked with some disdain upon Yiddish.

The children of the parents' siblings were cousins to *ego* ("oneself") or *shvesterkinder* ("cousins"). At first glance this term is misleading; it sounds like "the sister's child" (which would have been nephew or niece), for which there was no Yiddish term, and the Romanian *nepot* or *nepoata* ("nephew" or "niece"), were used. (The Russian *plemenek* and *plementze* were sometimes heard). The Yiddish *shvesterkind*, however, derived from the German *geshvesterkind*, which translates as "sibling's child", referring to the parents' siblings.

Parents were referred to as *eltern* ("elders") and were spoken of as *tate-mamme* in one hyphenated word, equally respected and loved, which meant "father-mother". There was a distinct age group difference: parents did not expect to be pals to their children, nor did the children desire it. The parents were regarded as role models, the mother for the girl, the father for the boy. Implicitly and explicitly "Father knew best" fact that parents, being older, had the necessary experience and judgement. Nor were parental motives questioned or doubted. "To whom would one turn for advice and help if not to one's own parents?" The concept of democracy of any sort, least of all in the family, had not yet reached the shtetl.

One of the most obvious differences between the Romanian shtetl and its Pale counterpart was the role of the father in the family. Yiddish literature is replete with references to husbands who spent their time studying the Torah or away on lengthy trips to their favorite *rebbé*, while the wife had to earn a living for the family and bring up a houseful of children at the same time. This was not the case in the Romanian shtetl. Husbands did not pore over sacred tomes all day; they worked hard to earn the daily bread. The husband was the head of the household and the breadwinner. Merchant or craftsman, it was the husband who worried about *parnuseh*. The wife worked with her husband without begrudging the time or feeling enslaved. There were cases where the wife supplemented the family income by sewing or by various other means. One woman, whose husband was a poor wagoner, sold *borsht* ("sour broth"): another opened a store where she sold a variety of articles in minuscule quantities.

Sometimes the wife was the more energetic of the two and was the dominant partner in the family. Since sex roles were largely ignored, the *firma* ("shop sign") went in her name. One went to Tzipoira's to buy a good schmaltz herring and olives, for instance. Similarly some families were known by the mother's or wife's name: Dudl Sheyve's (Dudl, the husband of Sheyve) or Moyshe Bassie's (Moishe, the son of Bassie). This was more frequently the case with widows who continued the husband's businesses in order to maintain their independence.

From the legal point of view as well as by custom, the wife's role was complementary to her husband's. The wife had complete and undisputed responsibility of the home, the *kashrut* (ritual concerning food) her personal ritual responsibilities, such as the *mikveh* bath ("post-menstrual cleansing"), blessing the candles on Friday eve and Holy days, and all that went with making a house a home. Her children's success and happiness were her reward.

An article in the *Journal of Psychiatry** discussing the shtetl family propounds a theory that, in the light of my own humble observations and limited research, appears dubious. It is assumed that the Romanian shtetl was included in the study. Some of the conclusions, in a sense universal, are applicable to the Romanian shtetl. A number of interpretations, however, appear questionable.

The authors present a theory of "tension equilibrium" within the family based on three dynamic relationships: bonds between man and wife, bonds between mother and son, and bonds between father and daughter.

There is no objection to the first hypothesis. In theory, at least, bonds between the spouses were strengthened by a mutual commitment to each other and the love for their children. The sages repeatedly enjoined the husband to honor his wife and the wife to accept the husband's authority and abide by his wishes. *Sholem bayis* ("domestic harmony") was an important concept.

The mother-son bond, however, is distorted. We read: "Romance existed with the son" and "attachment between mother and son . . . caused all other relationships to pale". This is an exaggeration of

---

* Ruth Landes and Mark Zborowski, "Hypothesis Concerning the Eastern European Jewish Family", *Journal of Psychiatry*, 13, 1950, pp. 47–464.

facts, where one important aspect is ignored: the importance of *kaddish* to the parents was inestimable, as only the son may say *kaddish* ("the prayer for the dead"). This adds another dimension to the mother-son relationship. Nor did this attachment preclude the strong affective bond between the mother and the daughter, which seems to be implied. On the contrary, it was well-known that after marriage daughters maintained closer ties with their own families than did the sons who, for the same reasons, usually inclined towards the wife's family.

The article continues: "Mothers were extremely jealous or resentful of their son's interests in another woman even though they wanted him to marry." This, too, must be qualified. Mother-in-law, daughter-in-law conflicts were based not so much on jealousy (implying libidinal attachments) as on the mother's feeling that no woman was quite good enough for her son, especially if he happened to be an only son. Although this may undoubtedly have been the case sometimes, it was abnormal and it would be unjust to attribute these sentiments to the average shtetl mother.

This feeling that no one was quite good enough for her child applied as often to a daughter as to a son. It has not been ascertained to what extent this may have been influenced by the number of children in the family and especially how many of each sex. That is, the mother of a son would have been prone to compare the son's wife to her own daughter, often to the latter's advantage, psychoanalysis notwithstanding.

In the same article we read that mother-daughter hostility was due to rivalry for the father's affections and to the mother's fear of being displaced by her daughter in her role as wife. The article speaks of "her articulated anticipatory refusal to be supplanted in any capacity by her daughter". And, to further substantiate this, the authors quote a shtetl mother who tells her daughter: "get out of my kitchen". When this quote was repeated to some respondents, they laughed in disbelief at the peculiar interpretation of a normal shtetl situation. This ethnocentric world view reveals a lack of understanding of shtetl culture. The shtetl mother's aspirations for her daughter were such as to urge her up the social ladder. Being in the kitchen was considered demeaning; rough hands were not for a lady. The "Jewish-princess" syndrome had its origin well planted in the shtetl. To read fear of jealousy into this, rings warped or, at best, taking the abnormal as the norm.

To what extent the parents (both the mother and the father) unconsciously, used their sons and daughters to vicariously fulfill their own aspirations is a moot question. This is far more plausible than the propounded theory of the shtetl mother's "fear of being displaced by her daughter in her role as wife". This refers to the norm, not the rare exceptions. It would also apply to the father-son relationship, where the father's expectations for vicarious fulfilment were thwarted by the son's failure to measure up to the father's expectations.

Relationships between siblings varied with each family across socioeconomic lines. In spite of rivalries, especially among those closest in age and of the same sex, there were feelings of mutual regard and affection. Relations of siblings of opposite sexes depended on the age-group. At an early stage there was mutual avoidance and quarrels, but as age increased a more permissive attitude of affection and friendship developed. When age differences were sufficiently great, the older girls would do some mothering of the younger children. This was the case mostly in the working-class families with many children. One respondent quoted a younger brother's childish remark: "Mother made me but you grew me." In the absence of the father, the older brother took on the responsibility of the family. He looked after the younger children's education and provided dowries for the sisters.

The youngest child, called *mezinek* ("youngest male") or *mezinkeh* ("youngest girl") usually enjoyed privileged treatment from the parents as well as from the rest of the family.

Step-brothers and step-sisters were considered as blood siblings whether they were born of the same mother or of a common father. In many cases, however, animosities existed.

Siblings married in strict age sequence. No younger brother was permitted to marry before his older brother and under no circumstances, before an older sister. An older sister who did not marry first would automatically be considered a *farzessene* ("one who remained left over"), that is, an old maid, the shame of the entire family.

2. Affinal Relations

Fear of the unknown and suspicion of strangers tend to produce profound feelings of insecurity, which different cultures have attempted to solve in various ingenious ways. By setting up close reciprocal relationships with mutual rights, privileges and responsibilities, the circle of consanguine relatives can be enlarged, trust established and reciprocal assistance assured in time of need. The comparatively short lifespan in the past may have been but one of the factors that prompted this need for reassurance through kinship ties outside one's immediate blood relatives. In view of this, the importance of in-laws and the care and concern with which parents selected the families of their children's spouses is not surprising.

The extended family included the families of siblings of both parents and their descendants as well as those of the grandparents. The entire family of in-laws was called *machetonem*, and the various ramifications together constituted the *mishpocha* ("extended family"). The in-laws addressed one another as *machutn* ("masculine") and *machteinesteh* ("feminine"). There were not simply the in-laws of one's children, with whom one met rarely if at all; they were *true* relatives with rights and obligations incurred as real kin.

A strong consanguine family organization provided its members with a high degree of security, both economic and emotional, but also imposed many obligations, Occasionally the advantages, in terms of security, did not seem to warrant the disadvantages incurred by obligations, in which case the individual would sacrifice the feeling of security rather than pay the price. These were the persons who left town, for within the shtetl network shirking one's obligations would have been impossible.

Kinship connections were further extended by ceremonial ties. One category of affinal relatives for which there is no equivalent in English were the *interfirers* ("sponsors") at a wedding. These were the two couples chosen from among favorite relatives, such as older siblings of the bride and groom or close friends. They attended the couple during the wedding ceremony much as the best man and maid of honor do and were the witnesses at the signing of the marriage contract. Unlike the North American Jewish wedding ceremonies, in a shtetl wedding it was not the father of the bride who gives the bride away; it was the *interfirers* who accompanied the bride and groom, each couple individually, to the canopy ceremony. This subsequently accrued important mutual rights and obligations between the *interfirers* and their charges. This is an interesting example of the adaptability of the marriage ceremony, at least from the point of view of superficial customs. For just as the American Jews have taken over the custom of the father of the bride giving the bride away, the Romanian shtetl Jews have borrowed the Romanian ceremonial customs of sponsorship. The Romanians call the two sponsor couples nashi (interestingly enough, the same term applies to the role of "godfather"), and the bridal couple are the *fini* (again, identical to the term for "godson"). Romanians selected the *nashi* exclusively from friends rather than from among close relatives, which was the case with the Romanian shtetl Jews. Furthermore, the importance given to this relationship by the Romanian culture is such as to forbid these newly established kin any further intermarriage, which would have been considered incestuous. Based on the need for economic as well as emotional security, this device fulfilled a basic need both from the individual's and the community's point of view.

In the same category of affinal ceremonial relatives was the *kvotter* or "godfather", the person who brought the male child from the mother to the *sondek* ("the person holding the baby") during circumcision. The child was his godson, for which there was no specific name in Yiddish, although rights and obligations established were frequently mentioned and scrupulously adhered to. "I am your kvotter" or "I took kvotershoft at your bris" implied "You owe me special consideration" and a special relationship. Girls did not have godparents, since the name-giving for girls required no attendant.

It was not uncommon to select the *interfirers* as well as the *kvotters* with an eye to the potential social and economic advantages to be gained, as the kinship ties were thus reinforced and special rights and obligations accrued.

Stepmothers and stepfathers were considered by law as one's own parents. In reality the adjustments were frequently painful and difficult. The Romanian term for "stepparents" or "siblings" is *vitreg* (meaning "hostile"), which sums up the attitude of these relationships. Siblings, however, maintained normal relationships, differing little from the usual sibling relationships.

There is a contemporary tendency to regard arranged marriages with apprehension, if not with mistrust. Yet in no culture is the selection of marriage partners random. Since marriage is much more than the union of two persons and concerns the community as a whole, there are social and personal restrictions limiting this choice. In the Romanian shtetl (as in Judaism in general) marriage was not taken lightly. Nor was it a matter for the immature to decide. It was the duty of the parents to find adequate life partners for their children and to provide the appropriate dowry for the daughters. The warmest hope and wish cherished by parents was to be worthy, in the eyes of God, of seeing their children under the wedding canopy. (Part of the ritual prayer during circumcision is that the infant reach his wedding canopy.) Selecting a mate concerned as much the family of the prospective partner as it did the individual himself, since the newly established kinship ties were permanent.

The good name of the family, based on a conglomerate of elusive yet ultimately determining factors called *yichus* ("status"), tipped the balance. The health of the family was of utmost importance.

Mental illness, tuberculosis and syphilis were dreaded diseases known to "run in a family" and hence to be avoided. In a small community where little escaped the public eye, it was impossible to keep such things secret; nevertheless, no effort was spared to hide these problems from public knowledge. It was the parents' task to investigate prospective partners.

The attitudes of Judaism towards sex were never ascetic; chastity has never been part of Judaic philosophy, and there are no monasteries or convents. Devotion and dedication to God are enhanced in the partnership of creating life. Bachelorhood and spinsterhood, far from being accepted, were looked upon with mistrust by the community. To avoid promiscuity, marriages were advocated at an early age. Love was not a prerequisite to marriage; commitment was. It was the parents whose judgement prevailed and the *shadchen* ("marriage broker") who still brought the two parties together.

There was no rule for preferential residence, that is where the newlyweds would live. Neo-locality (that is separate household) was desirable whenever possible, based primarily on economic factors and expediency. A widower parent was automatically included in the new household, especially when an only child or the youngest child married.

If the bride came to live in the husband's shtetl, they set up an independent household or lived with the husband's parents at least until the first child was born. (In one family, the eldest son married a girl from another shtetl and went to live there; the second son married out of town and brought his bride to live in a house next door to the parental house; the third son married a local girl and established an independent household; while the fourth son, also married to a local girl – an orphan living in her own house – moved into the bride's house, which was also his as part of his dowry. An only daughter of the same family married a local boy, rented a house close to one of her brothers and subsequently moved in with her widowed mother. This variation within one family indicates the freedom of choice available regarding residential preferences.)

Marriage between relatives followed the usual universally observed incest taboos. First-cousin marriages were not prohibited but were not encouraged. In some families there was more intermarriage with cousins and cross cousins. Marriage was considered a welcome opportunity of enlarging one's network of relatives; hence marriage with strangers was preferred, as long as it was on an equal (or higher) socioeconomic level.

The *kest* – the number of years of room and board offered by the bride's family to the newlyweds – was not known in the

Romanian shtetl. This was due to the fact that in Romania, unlike Tsarist Russia, the marriage age was not as low and the husband was expected to be in a position to support a family when he married. *Kest* was mentioned with derision as part of an unhappy, faraway past.

Expectations from marriage were not extravagant. The assumption was that it was better to fall in love after marriage. Both husband and wife entered into marriage with one commitment: one God and one spouse. This was the ideal type and also the norm, although exceptions were not lacking.

Once established as a separate family unit, the young couple were expected to start a family. In spite of the decided class differences regarding family size, a home was "blessed" with children and "cursed" if there were none. When speaking about a childless family, remarks were prefaced by *nisht do gedacht* ("may it not be mentioned here"). Women went to the *rebbé* to be blessed, especially if they were wishing for a son. Middle-class families, however, influenced by Western values, limited the number of children: *Doi ca la Paris* ("Two like in Paris"). The average middle-class family had three or four children, while among the working class a family of eight was not uncommon.

Children were highly valued and no sacrifice was too great to provide them with all the necessities and even luxuries. The attitude towards child-rearing, too, was contingent upon social class. Middle-class mothers strained the family budget to provide oranges and tangerines (decided luxuries) in the daily diet, often depriving themselves in the knowledge that it was important for the children.

Children were expected to play; they were not, as is sometimes reported, forced to fend for themselves at an early age. Among the working class, children were expected to help and were trained to follow in their father's occupation.

Corporal punishment was taken for granted. This too was concomitant with the educational and socioeconomic level of the family. The *kanchik* ("leather whip") or the *curea* ("belt") were used as disciplinary measures by the lower class, whereas the better informed were more lenient, aware of potential permanent damage physical punishment incurred.

The middle-class parent, literate himself, encouraged the children, especially the sons, in their intellectual pursuits. The children, in turn, eager for approval, were ready to emulate the elders, using the parents as role models.

Exhibitionism of any sort was considered in bad taste. Couples kissed only when leaving or returning from a trip. They usually called each other by their first name in public, or *draga* ("dear") in the home. The common term for husband or wife in Yiddish are *mon* ("man") and *veib* or *frau* ("woman", "lady"). In speaking of one another they used *mein mon* or *mein veib*.

The custom of cutting off the bride's hair at marriage (and wearing a wig) still persisted among the ultra-orthodox Jews, but had disappeared in the Romanian shtetl. The rabbi's wife and several of the old women clung to the custom; most women followed contemporary hairstyles as they followed the style of dress. In general, after marriage, the wife was not supposed to show too much concern for her personal appearance. She was supposed to please her own husband but beyond that she was dressed according to her standing in the community, wearing muted colors and covering most of her body. It was the husband who took pride in his wife's appearance, which was taken as a reflection of his own success and manliness. He saw to it that she possessed jewelry and provided her with adequate domestic help as part of the status that he, as head of the household, brought to the family.

Wife beating, frequently encountered among neighboring peasantry, was all but unknown in the Romanian shtetl. The few *grobbe ingh* ("uncouth") vulgar families, known for their brawls, were considered among the lowest. The expression for any loud squabbling was *pe malul Basheului* ("as in the Basheu slums"); no greater insult was conceivable.

Marital fidelity was the ideal type in spite of the breaches, documented or not, that the wagging tongues in town relished in broadcasting; minor scandals were part of shtetl gossip, and rumor mills provided entertainment in the otherwise monotonous shtetl life. A wife's adultery was a sin and a crime against the husband. He had exclusive rights, important in a society where it was essential to maintain the purity of the genealogical line, since property was inherited through the father. Where for the main infidelity was condoned, a woman who sinned was a social outcast. Men and women suspected of adultery were considered a threat to the healthy functioning of the community, and were ostracized. Adultery went against the tenets of the shtetl and against the Judaic teaching of self-restraint.

3. Divorce

In accordance with Judaic law, divorce was easy to obtain. Yet in the shtetl it was a rare occurrence. It was assumed that, for the children's sake, the parents would sacrifice their personal feelings and not bring disgrace to the entire family. According to Judaic law, a man was entitled to divorce his wife if she did not bear any children after ten years of marriage. That the husband might have had some responsibility in the matter was never envisioned. The safety valve for those cases where discord would have led to divorce was for the husband to "leave for America" or for the family to move to a big city.

To obtain a divorce, the couple went to the rabbi, who, having failed to reconcile them, would grant the divorce. It was not necessary for the couple to be present at the proceedings. Each was able to delegate his or her own agent, who was empowered to act on his or her behalf.

A woman unable to prove that she was divorced or that her spouse was dead could not remarry. She was called an *agunah*, literally, "tied".

The fact that divorce was rare in the Romanian shtetl bespeaks of a stability and cohesive community spirit that worked as a potent deterrent in the form of social sanctions. For a divorce was a spot on the *mishpocha* ("entire extended family") and a virtual tragedy for all concerned, regardless of circumstances.

CHAPTER V
Health

1. Modern Medicine

Illness and epidemics were no strangers in the Romanian shtetl. Coping with illness was a perennial concern, for illness involved the entire household and often the extended family. *M'vaker choyle zein* ("to visit the sick") was a good deed practised assiduously, in the belief that every visitor took away a bit of the illness. The psychological implications are evident.

Except in hopeless cases, illness was coped with in the home; the sick person was surrounded with love and devotion. Even contagious diseases — unless the authorities forbade it — were treated in the home. This applied regardless of socioeconomic level.

In speaking of health in the Romanian shtetl, two factors must be stressed. The old and the new continued to exist side by side, and there was a decided cleavage between the health-care methods of the two socioeconomic groups, though inevitable overlapping existed.

The literate, modern oriented merchant class scoffed at the incantations and superstitions of the ignorant, but on occasion, in despair, were not above appealing to these very methods. *Bobskie mittlen* ("old wives' remedies") had not completely been displaced by the doctor. *Santatea* ("a paramedical journal"), was an important instrument in diffusing contemporary scientific knowledge. Shtetl folklore borrowed and adapted many of the beliefs and practices of neighboring cultures with one qualification: above all else, there was the unswerving faith in God and His mercy. The doctor was ultimately only the *gitter sheliech* ("a good messenger"). Illness was accepted as deserved punishment from above, with inevitable feelings of guilt.

And there was a clear distinction between "white magic", for benign warding off of evil by incantations, and "black magic" or *kishiff,* malicious, invoking alien spirits and hence sinful.

While illness knew no social boundaries, the poor were more often afflicted than the rich. They depended mainly on folk remedies, the prognostications of the *bly gissern* or the *felcher.* Only in desperate situations — often too late — would the doctor be called. In contrast, the literate middle class relied entirely on the doctor.

In Stefanesti, modern medicine was represented by the municipal hospital and its director, the district nurse, also referred to as the "sanitary agent", and four private doctors, serving both the Jewish and surrounding village communities.

(a) *The Hospital*

The hospital, situated on a hill among the parklands of the old manor was removed from the town proper both physically and spiritually. For the shtetl, the local hospital was a place to be avoided. The idea that one went to the hospital to be cured was inconceivable. During epidemics, the government-imposed quarantine compelled some unfortunate families to relinquish the patient to the hands of strangers, but only under duress. It was not unusual to conceal the existence of a person with a contagious disease — for example scarlet fever — for fear that the authorities would take him away to the hospital, which was synonymous with a death certificate, in the minds of the people. In some cases authorities were bribed to allow the family to keep the patient at home. The house was then virtually boarded up, cutting off all contact with the outside.

The hospital served mainly the surrounding peasant population. This attitude resulted as much from a lack of confidence based on hospital conditions and reputation as on the closely knit family ties and conviction that the devotion and loving care in the home could not be expected from the hospital.

The public nurse was the "sanitary agent" for the district. She was a civil servant (and a Romanian, since Jews were not employed in the civil service). Her only contact with the shtetl population was her visits during the frequent epidemics of diphtheria, mumps, chicken pox and scarlet fever. She supervised the enforcement of universal vaccinations against smallpox, especially among the ignorant poor. Smallpox, almost epidemic in the past — as the frequently seen pockmarked faces attested — was disappearing as an epidemic but was still a concern for the authorities.

The nurse was responsible for general hygienic conditions in the shtetl and in the surrounding villages.

From the point of view of individual household hygiene, the shtetl was autonomous since this was under the jurisdiction of the Jewish community, enforced according to religious specifications. The mere presence of a public nurse was a stride forward in the domain of public health.

(b) *The Doctor*

The five doctors in Stefanesti (four of whom were Jews) provided a needed care for the Jewish community as well as for the neighboring villages. Doctors had their offices in their homes and saw patients at all hours, without appointments. They made housecalls or visits regardless of the severity of the sickness and often made subsequent calls, without being asked, to check on the patient and reassure the anxious family. It was not uncommon for a mother to call in the doctor as he passed down the street, to examine the throat of her child or the eye of the grandmother. The only means of reaching the doctor was by message boy or servant girl or a member of the family who would run to the doctor's home and return with the doctor in tow. Thus, everyone knew when there was illness in one of the families.

As was the case with country doctors everywhere at the time, the shtetl doctor was often paid in goods. Most townspeople, however, paid cash. In a discreet, almost embarrassed manner, a neatly folded bill was slipped into the doctor's hand as he edged his way out of the door.

In very severe cases the patient was rushed to Iassy, (the metropolis) to see a "professor", or to a hospital when surgery was imminent. Judging by the reply of one respondent, this was something of a status symbol. She proudly insisted that she did not usually call the local doctors but "always went to see *her* doctor in Iassy". She, however, was unusual; most people in the shtetl had confidence in the local doctors.

Attitudes towards health care differed greatly between the middle class and the working class. We find at one extreme the few snobbish new rich who "went to Iassy to see the professor" and at the other the poor who went to the doctor only for serious illnesses; the merchant families on the other hand called the doctor for the least discomfort, especially when a child's health was concerned. It must be remembered that this was a time when a mild fever or sore throat one day might mean dyphtheria or scarlet fever the next, and there were no antibiotics. People lived in perpetual anxiety. It is not surprising that the doctor was appealed to so often. Most shtetl mothers did not mind at all paying for nothing, and neither did the doctor, who preferred to be called too soon rather than too late.

Infant mortality is often taken as an index of a country's level of development. A 1933 issue of the journal *Sanatatea* shows figures for infant mortality for the previous year, with the various causes of death.

The article mentions that there was a marked decrease in scarlet fever, flu, tuberculosis, pneumonia, septicemia and puerperal fever and that smallpox was disappearing. It also points out that the death rate in the rural areas was higher than in the urban centers. These diseases were still the major killers. During summer months dysentery was difficult to control, especially among the poor, where standards of hygiene were not of the highest. Complications were as dreaded as the diseases themselves, with meningitis, rheumatic fever and kidney disorders most devastating.

Epidemics were difficult to stem; it was sufficient for one child to come down with a disease for an epidemic to be triggered. This, in spite of the rigorous hygienic measures enjoined by the Jewish religion and stressed by the authorities. One measure taken by the authorities to prevent throat infections was the *pensulation* or *badijeonage* ("painting of the throat"). A swab of absorbent cotton, wrapped around a thin stick, was dipped into a solution of iodine and honey and the back of the throat was smeared.

This was a municipally instituted public-health measure. Equipped with as many absorbent cotton sticks as there were children in the school, the public nurse, aided by a teacher, performed this not too agreeable operation. The children lined up in single file, stepped up one by one and presented their throats for the ordeal.

Epidemics also brought out the yearly sachet of camphor and garlic, worn on the neck on a red string. The red string was an added protection to ward off evil. This was harmless, and may have helped preventing too close contact due to the offensive odor of the camphor and garlic.

Another form of *prophylaxis* was gargling with *Apa oxigenata* ("solution of peroxide in water"); it produced a mouthful of foamy saliva. Peroxide, alcohol and iodine were the most commonly used disinfectants. They were used on burns, wounds and cuts, before healing ointments were applied. For outdoor disinfection, formol was favored.

Milk was boiled as a daily routine. Vaccinations against smallpox were imposed by the health department but injections were still rare. In cases of a dog bite, the patient was rushed to Iassy for the series of anti-hydrophobia injections.

Vitamins and their importance were percolating to the Romanian shtetl via the journal *Sanatatea*; rickets, a common scourge in the past, all but disappeared among the merchant class, though it was still common among the poor. Sunshine, known to be a direct source of vitamin D, and cod-liver oil, another known source, were assiduously resorted to by the merchant class. Tight swaddling, which was believed to keep the bones straight, was no longer practised, in view of newly acquired knowledge. Among the poor, however, bow legs and misshapen bodies due to inadequate nutrition were still common. Oranges and mandarines, veritable luxuries, were included in the children's diet by knowledgeable mothers familiar with the importance of vitamin C, anxious to provide the best for their offspring.

A *shtoch* ("a stitch") or *junghiu* ("pain in the back of the chest") called for *bankes*, or ("cupping"), a mechanism whereby blood circulation was stimulated in case of a congestion. Belief in the remedial value of cupping was unquestioned. This was the task of the barber surgeon, who received a fee for the service. Friends and members of the family who were known to possess this talent, were in constant demand, especially during the winter months.

The method of cupping was simple. Deftness and speed were essential. The patient must lie flat on the bed, prone or supine, depending on whether the cups were to be placed on the back or on the chest, which was determined by the location of the pain. In some cases, *bankes* were put both on back and on the chest. On a handy tray close to the patient's bed, the necessary utensils were assembled: a wooden stick with a swab of absorbent cotton twisted at one end, a bowl of alcohol for dipping the cotton, a lighted candle and six or eight cups. The cups were about the size of a small tumbler, fitting into the palm of the hand.

The stick was dipped into the alcohol and lit; the flame was rapidly passed inside the cup, which was immediately placed on the patient's body. A vacuum was thus created in the cup which, when placed on the body, virtually sucked in the flesh and formed a little swelling inside the cup. If the vacuum was not perfect – if the cup was wet or soiled – the cup did not take. The cups were allowed to remain on the body for fifteen to twenty minutes. Gradually the bubble of skin and flesh inside the cup turned red or bright purple as the blood was pulled into the vacuum of the cup. The sensation was painful but not unbearable. The cups were removed by pressing gently on the skin near the rim. A *frictie* ("friction"), (a good rub down with alcohol), completed the task. The more pronounced the marks, the more assured the patient of the treatment's efficacy. During summer months one would often see polka-dotted backs peep out of bathing suits at the beaches.

In spite of the lack of plumbing and other modern amenities, in spite of many difficulties of communication, the shtetl succeeded – against all odds – in keeping up with the big city. In the field of mental health and community cohesion, it evolved its own norms, enviable by contemporary standards.

(c) *Sanatatea si Viata Fericita* ("Health and the Happy Life")

One agent of change and stability was the magazine *Sanatatea si Viata Fericita* ("Health and the Happy Life"). It taught, advised and explained to an eager public the current discoveries in the world of science and medicine, without arrogance and with a remarkable sense of responsibility. The journal aimed to give a sort of blueprint for a wholesome and happy life, with a strong emphasis on the family and especially the woman's role in society.

The publisher, Dr. Sigman Sigma, as well as many of the contributors were Jews, an example of an almost unknown aspect of the life of the Jews in Romania. It offers concrete proof that there existed in Romania a silent majority who did not harbor the kind of anti-Semitic savageries that usually made headlines.

Sanatatea attempted and succeeded in diminishing conflicts between Jews and non-Jews. Its influence on shtetl life was immeasurable. Though the families who subscribed to it were few in number, they were the community leaders. The two-hundred-*lei* yearly subscription was an extravagance in terms of the shtetl budget but the magazine made the rounds of friends and neighbors before being returned to its owner, who treasured each issue. A subscription was unquestionably a status symbol; in true shtetl tradition, status was based on the prestige of learning and knowledge.

2. Folk Medicine

(a) *The Felcher* (*Untrained Medical Person*)

For most working-class families even the minimal doctor's fees were often prohibitive. The *felcher* was an intermediary between the *bobskie mitlen* ("old-wives' remedies") and the medical doctor. The term *felcher* is derived from *feld* ("field") and *scher* ("cutting") – hence, "field surgeon". For, like the barber-surgeon, the *felcher* began his career as an army-doctor's aid on the battlefield. (In the USSR and in many underdeveloped countries the *felcher* functions as an assistant doctor, trained to perform the work a registered nurse does in North America. A *felcher* would visit every factory daily, give injections, take blood pressure, look after minor injuries, while the doctor would only come once a week and be responsible for the more serious medical problems.)

In Stefanesti the *felcher* had no formal training. He learned his skills through observation and experience. He was called to set a sprained ankle or to fix a splint for a broken bone; he knew what to do in case of a swelling or a burn and had a satchel full of elementary first-aid needs such as disinfectant, gauze, absorbent cotton and some ointment (*alifie*). One popular ointment consisted of zinc, lanolin and some disinfectant such as alcohol or iodine. The tube of *Inotyol*, a patent-medicine ointment, was indispensable in the treatment of anything from pimples to a burn or infected cut.

(b) *The Barber*

The barber was the repository of two important remedies, leeches and cupping. The leech is a flat, bloodsucking worm about two inches long. To bleed a patient in case of high blood pressure, dizzy spells or strokes, the doctor prescribed leeches and the barber was called in. In Romania, commerce with leeches was a government monopoly till 1847 when pharmacists and barbers were obliged to have a supply on hand. The barber would arrive with his jarful of leeches and place them wherever the veins protruded visibly. When the leech was sated, it fell off and the barber would pop it back into his jarful of water.

(c) *Superstitions*

The power of the uttered word and the importance of the propitious moment recur like a leitmotif in shtetl beliefs. Euphemisms and circumlocutions were used for dreaded diseases, for fear that the mere pronunciation of the word might trigger evil. Cancer or Tuberculosis were referred to as *die gitte zach* ("that good thing") or *dus gitte pekl* ("that good package"). This may also have been influenced by the belief that the moment at which the word was uttered carried with it the promise of fulfilment, a relic of astrology, for example, "In a gitter shoo" ("May it be in a good hour").

To protect the listener when an unfortunate event was related, one said: "Nisht far dir gezugt gevorn" ("May it not be intended for you") or "Of ale piste velder" ("On all the waste lands"). To this the three spits (*ptiu, ptiu, ptiu*) was added. This was based on the belief that water in any form presented an obstacle for evil spirits, and that the number carried magic powers. The more sophisticated considered the gesture uncouth and unsanitary and regarded it with derision and even with contempt.

One of the antidotes against evil was to preface any remark with an appropriate protective term. Before planning any future event the preface required was: "bli neider un a mascune" ("Without pledge or presumption".)

Belief in omens and the evil eye were common. *A git oigh* ("a good eye") was the euphemism used to avoid possible insult to the evil spirit. Since the evil spirits were jealous of any good fortune, various techniques were used to either deceive them or pronounce the adequate incantations to thwart their evil intentions. Counting persons was forbidden; to circumvent this, the counting would be: "Not one, not two, not three." One witty neighbor of a family blessed with six daughters (in itself almost a calamity), hearing his own little girl say that Hayim-Yidl had "not one, not two, not three, not four, not five, not six daughters," exclaimed: "lucky man, he has not six daughters!" Similarly, sneezing while there was talk of the dead was taken as ominous and the immediate antidote was a good yank upward on the sneezer's right ear.

Stratagems were used to mislead the evil spirits on the premise that demons were not all that clever and that man was able to outwit them. To trick the angel of death — who, it would seem, appeared with a book containing a person's full name and addresss — when someone was very ill, the name was changed or the ill person sold to another family. This applied mostly to children, but was also used with adults. The most frequent names added in these cases were those of a powerful animal: *Leib* ("Lion"), *Beir* ("Bear"), *Velvl* ("Wolf"), in the belief that this would frighten away the demons. Other favored names were those associated with long life: *Haye* or *Ham* ("Life"); *Zeideh* ("Grandfather") or *Bobbeh* ("Grandmother"); *Alte* or *Alter* ("Old one," masculine or feminine).

Based on the belief that evil spirits inhabited dark places and shunned light, candles were used at all ritual occasions, both joyous and sad. This explains the lighting of tapers on the yearly death anniversaries; (by surrounding the soul with light, the soul was protected from evil spirits). At weddings, too, candles were lit to ward off the jealous evil spirits.

One of the most dreaded evil spirits was Lilith, Adam's first wife, who was believed to have a penchant for newborn infants. The *kimpettzetl*, a corrupt form of *kind's bet tzetl* ("a child's bedside amulet"), was a good-luck charm. This consisted of a sheet of paper on which were printed Biblical verses. The paper was placed in the delivery room, at the doors, on the mother's bed and at the baby's cradle.

Amulets and good-luck charms have been known in Jewish folklore throughout the ages. These were among the customs borrowed from the neighboring cultures that remained in the people's mores in spite of admonitions to the contrary from the learned leaders. They usually carried Biblical verses or combinations of letters believed to bring good luck and ward off evil. The *mitbeyeh* was a coin blessed by a *tzadik*, a saintly man. Any coin, not necessarily of precious metal, blessed by the *rebbé*, held magic powers of protection, which gave the person wearing it a feeling of security. It was worn inconspicuously close to the body, usually hanging on a simple string around the neck. Women and children treasured them, while men were usually more skeptical about their efficacy. In Stefanesti, the *rebbé*'s court did a brisk business selling *mitbeyehs* to all those who came to the *rebbé*.

Beads and precious stones had specific significance. Coral beads were considered bearers of good luck and fertility. Jewelry in general was believed to carry magic powers. Since women were considered helpless, they needed more protection against evil, hence more jewelry.

There were also certain individuals who possessed special gifts to ward off evil. They had their own secret spells and were called upon to pronounce them against the evil eye. They did not hold any official position in the community but were known for their talent and called upon in case of need. The Romanian term *a descanta* ("to un-sing") as opposed to *a incanta* ("to put a charm or spell") implies that by uttering the appropriate words, something already existing is being undone, rectified.

It was firmly believed that some individuals possessed an evil eye, that is, that they had the power of bringing about evil. Hence, the use of such expressions as "Kein ein nehore, kein beiz oyigh" ("no evil spell, no angry eye") accompanied by the three spits, when paying a compliment or admiring one another. One respondent related: "When my daughter was a baby everyone remarked about her beautiful eyes. Once a woman came in and admired the baby's beautiful big black eyes without saying 'Kein nehore' ('No evil eye') and as soon as the woman left, the baby began to cry, for no reason. We took the baby's bonnet to the *upshprachern* ('the woman who said incantations') and then put the bonnet on the baby, and she stopped crying right away."

(d) *The Midwife*

In Stefanesti the old midwife, the *bubbeh*, was also the unofficial *upshprachern*. Her secret spells had acquired a reputation of excellent efficacy for which she was greatly in demand. All these spells were closely guarded secrets, not to be divulged for fear of destroying their potency. There were a number of persons known to have inherited incantations, which they presumably transmitted to their descendants. One respondent offered the following incantation:

Drei vaiber steyen of ein shtein
Eine Zugt yo, eine zugt nein
Eine zugt, fin vonet s'is gekimen
Aintzys zol dus geyen

"Three women stand on one stone
One says yes, one says no,
One says wherever it came from
There may it return."

The precise content of the spell was not as important as the faith one had in the spell's efficacy. The recurring theme seems to be the magic number three and the spitting three times to ward off evil by means of the power of water.

Another spell, offered by a respondent, was a Romanian one:

Pasarica pasarea,
Pica ici pica colea,
Pica'n piatra nestimata,
Care a fost
.... (Name of Person) deochiata.

"Birdie, little bird,
Drop here, drop there
Drop on the unesteemed stone, which
.... (Name of Person) was spellbound".

CHAPTER VI
Religion

1. God and the Torah

The social phenomenon we call religion may be defined as man's relation to the unknown expressed through ritual. Whether considered a social phenomenon or as a personal experience, there is no doubt that it fulfills basic needs, regardless of the level of development of the individual or of the culture to which he belongs. Our own term "religion" derives from the Latin *lego*, to bind together. It is indeed one of the most potent social forces binding a group of individuals into a unified whole.

The topic of religion in the Romanian shtetl is approached here with some apprehension; this is not an illiterate, underdeveloped culture, but a complex system of ethic and moral values and beliefs, evolved, documented and discussed from every possible aspect, throughout the millennia. This is not only a literate society, but a society where literacy is a badge of honor and the most sacred symbol was a book, or rather "the Book", which happens to be the basis of our western civilization. Yet it would be inconceivable to discuss the Romanian shtetl without mention of so integral a cultural aspect. The intention here is to set down for the record some of the most pertinent facts, aiming at recreating the general mood and atmosphere of a culture steeped in religious observance, at a stage when this was being eroded by the forces of change.

To speak of "shtetl religion" is somewhat redundant. Religious observance was a way of life, if not its *raison d'être*. It permeated shtetl life in every detail. In this respect the Romanian shtetl of the period between the two world wars did not differ from the rest of the eastern European Jewish complex. It existed for the purpose of maintaining and perpetuating the glory of God, whose chosen People it considered itself to be. Families living in non-Jewish areas moved into town as soon as the children were old enough to go to school or make friends. To have asked a Romanian shtetl Jew what his religion was would have elicited an incredulous stare: "Whatever do you mean? I'm a Jew, of course." Judaism was a religion, a nationhood, a way of life.

God was real, although not corporeally imaged. He was perceived as a personal God, available to all who sought Him, wherever and whenever they needed Him. There were specific times for prayer; there were prayers to meet every conceivable occasion. The synagogue was the place to worship, but where ten adult male Jews (any Jew older than thirteen was considered an adult) – constituting a quorum (*a minyan*) – gathered, a communal service was possible. Praying together intensified the feeling of belonging but it was understood that prayer was not relegated only to the synagogue.

Daily language abounded with expressions substantiating this. "Im Got is viln" ("For God's sake") or the endearing term "Gotinyiu" ("Dearest little God") were sprinkled after almost every phrase. A startled or frightened child was calmed with the soothing; "Got is mit dir" ("God is with you", "Don't be afraid"). The confidence of the adult was thus transmitted to the child who would be convinced that no evil could befall him, since God was always there to protect him.

There was no intermediary between the individual and God. In the synagogue as well as in private each man spoke for himself, directly to his God. There are no priests in Judaism, nor is there a hierarchy. Nor are there any saints in Heaven. Although the rabbi is called "ordained", he is not a priest; his role is more that of a teacher or judge or, depending on his personality, a leader of the community, the latter by virtue of his learning and wisdom, not by divine command. The only divergence is the appeal to the souls of departed ancestors who may intercede on one's behalf. The Biblical patriarchs Abraham, Isaac and Jacob and matriarchs Sarah, Rebecca, Rachel and Leah were invoked in prayers when God was petitioned in the name of their piety and exemplary lives. This was as close as the shtetl came to ancestor worship.

The concept of a harsh, vengeful God was unknown and unheard of in the Romanian shtetl. God was conceived as a father image, righteous and just, demanding but giving and merciful. Speaking to Him as to a trusting, loving parent relieved much of the anxiety of an often bleak existence. Nothing was beyond God's power: "Az Got vill, shyist a beyzem" ("If God wishes, even a broom can shoot"), or "Got git dus kelt noch die kleider" ("God gives the cold according to the clothes"), implying that God takes care of all needs. This attitude, however, did not prevent a realistic acceptance of the existence of pain and suffering. It was the community as a whole that was entrusted by God to provide for the needy (though not without the expectation that their good deeds will be repaid by the Heavenly Father, if not with dividends, at least in kind). With the reliance on personal responsibility there was a blend of fatalism, controllable, to a certain extent. The expression "Fin dain moul in Got's oyrn" ("From your mouth into God's ears") conveys the belief that the problem was one of reaching the ears of God; His mercy being taken for granted. The trusting-parent concept recurs in "Loz zich Got zorgn" ("Let God worry for the future"), or "Got is a futer" ("God is a father"), ringing an optimistic note. Even more precise is the saying "Got zitzt oyvn un purt hintn" ("God sits up on high and matches couples down below"). This reflects both the belief that marriages were made in Heaven and the assumption of God's concern.

Doubting God's righteousness was blasphemous, and to be avoided. His wisdom and above all His justice were NOT questionable. Doubt was a reflection of one's own behavior, and therefore any expression of protest was prefaced with "Ich zol nisht zindign" ("May I not sin").

The concept of evil was not as clearly delineated. Evil spirits were acknowledged and dreaded. But there was a distinction between suffering as divine retribution and therefore to be accepted and evil caused by malevolent spirits, eventually controllable by magic. The latter was a pagan custom, borrowed from neighboring cultures, practised with apprehension as sinful.

It is interesting to compare the notion of the Romanian devil, *dracul* (a term derived from "dragon" depicted in full form with horns, tail and a three pronged fork, and the vague image of *der shvartzer riech* ("the black devil"). The term *riech* is derived from *rauch*, "breath" or "spirit". The only distinctive attribute of *der shvartzer riech* in his blackness, a color associated with evil, with mourning and with dark places. He had no specific bodily shape. The parallel with the deity is thus congruently carried through.

Regarding life after death and the concept of heaven and hell, there was a similar vagueness. "Oylem ha ba" ("the world to come") was an expression, which, however, had acquired the meaning of kindness or compassion, as in "Have oylemobe" ("Do me a favor"). Although not defined, the existence of a future life was inferred throughout. Prayers for the dead were considered of utmost importance; witness the endearing "kaddishl", a term the shtetl parents, but especially the mother, often reserved for her son, who, by saying "kaddish" ("prayer for the dead"), presumably made life in the world to come more agreeable.

Death in general was a taboo subject, discussed with apprehension. Some doubts may be suggested in the expression "Geshtorbn, bagrubn, of yener velt vi geffinen" ("Dead, buried, on the other world, as if found"), sometimes used to maintain that one had better forget and begin anew.

Prayer, the outpouring of the soul to the divine, was a matter of daily concern. One lived and hoped. Prayer was a safety valve; whether in the form of psalms as adoration, thanks for favors obtained or the usual petitioning for specific requests, it was cathartic. From the moment one opened one's eyes in the morning to the time one went to sleep, every act entailed a specific prayer. Many of the younger generation, however, regarded the rote repetition of these formulae with scorn and even ridicule. This was true especially of the sophisticated high school students.

On waking, before doing anything else, one washed the hands with fresh water and poured the water out. A special two-handled pitcher was often reserved for this act, to avoid touching a utensil with a washed hand while the other hand was still unwashed. While pouring water three times on each fist, one said "Modé ani" ("I stand before Thee"), the morning prayer. This prayer caused quite a stir when it was picked up by the women's liberation movement. It was pointed out that this prayer was differently worded for men and for women; men said, "Thank you, Lord, that you did not create me a woman," while women said, "Thank you, Lord, who created me in Your image." Like most prayers in Judaism, this is basically a hymn for the glorification of God, in praise of His wisdom, the excellence with which the Universe and especially man, has been designed as an exquisite work of art, enumerating the minutest details and perfection of functions. Whether this daily bolstering of the male ego contributed to the feeling of male superiority — which undoubtedly existed and was fostered in the Romanian shtetl — is a moot question. Most women who pronounced this daily prayer did not seem to be aware of the discrepancy and the ones who were aware did not seem to mind it. Thanking God for having been created "in His image", that is, able to bring forth life, was no doubt the greatest affirmation of one's self worth. One cannot help wondering to what extent this particular boosting of the male ego was institutionalized in a society where, although not a typical matriarchy, the woman's role and importance as wife and mother was sufficiently secure. Women did not need artifical reassurances; it was the men who were in unfair competition with them. The attitude of most women regarding men's supremacy was one of tolerance. While taking for granted man's superiority in some areas, women felt sufficiently self-confident to give their men all the support and self-confidence they needed to confront the outside alien world. Women did not feel downtrodden or enslaved. This is no doubt due to the perspicacity of those who understood the underpinnings of interpersonal relations and provided for balanced compensations. Men were enjoined to respect their wives, to appreciate their efforts in maintaining a *kosher* home, to be considerate and attentive. For instance, men were expected to prolong the Sabbath meals by singing the *zemirot* ("grace") in deference to the wife and not hurry away immediately after meals. Treating women with respect and deference was a sign of a refined individual.

There were prayers of thanks and blessings appropriate for every conceivable occasion: upon witnessing lightning or thunder; when one survived some life threatening danger, as well as the usual catalogue of prayers associated with specific rituals. For a society such as ours where fresh fruits are available throughout the year, the importance of eating the first fruit of the season may be lost, but in the shtetl, where each fruit or vegetable season was short, a "trufanda" (first fruit) was an event. The first cherries or the first tomatoes or radishes of the season brought special delight, since except for citrus fruits and olives, all fruits and vegetables were locally grown and available fresh only in the brief ripening season. Classified according to the growth habit, each fruit and vegetable was blessed accordingly. For tree growing fruit the blessing was: "blessed art Thou Lord of the Universe, Creator of the fruit of the trees"; for rooty vegetables such as potatoes, the blessing was the same, but replacing the "trees" with "fruit of the earth". A brief prayer was appended to be worthy to survive to enjoy the following year's new crop. It was considered incumbent on the recipient of these favors, to pay homage and to thank the Creator. These sentiments and observances were instilled from earliest childhood. It all reinforced the belief in the benevolence of an all powerful God, while the added element of self restraint, brought another dimension of awareness of the world around.

Prayers, especially in the synagogue were primarily men's responsibility; women's responsibilities pertained mainly to the home. It was the women who performed all rites required to keep a "kosher" home, observance of strict dietary laws essential for the health and well-being of the family and the most important responsibility, which was not taken lightly, that of instilling in the children all important traditional values. Men were supposed to have access to eternal paradise only through their wives' observance of good deeds. It was the woman's privilege to light and bless the candles on the Sabbath and Holy days. At least two candles were lit customarily and at the birth of each child in the family, one additional candle was added.

The daily morning prayer, for men only, "leyign tefillen" ("putting on the phylacteries"), was becoming something of an obligation, a chore rather than a willing offering and prayer. One respondent admitted that it was "only around the weeks before the Day of Atonement" that he assiduously observed the practice "because that is when you pray to be inscribed in the Book of Life and who knows? Better to be sure." Though it was spoken of as a positive quality and considered proper behavior, the number of those who found the ritual an encroachment upon their wordly routine was on the increase. It was more frequently the wife and mother who insisted and prodded the husband and sons in this endeavor. Fathers, who did not themselves observe the practice, were more lenient with their sons. Young boys away from home at high school were admonished to remember to "put on tefillen" every morning. Some did, most did not. (One respondent remarked that although as a young man he resented this task, he now finds solace in it and in observing and fulfilling parental wishes).

The phylacteries are two small leather rectangular boxes containing verses from the Scripture, which are affixed, by means of leather thongs, on the forehead and on the left arm, while reciting the prescribed prayers.

Men attended Friday eve and Saturday morning services at the synagogue. The *talles* ("prayer shawl") folded in its velvet pocketbook, men and boys would be seen wending their way to *shul*. This was the men's world. The husband awaited the break in the weekly chase for *parnusseh* ("earning a living") and welcomed the *Shabbes* as much as did his wife. Going to synagogue was not only a religious obligation, it gave an opportunity to participate in the community spirit. Little boys accompanied the father to *shul* until they reached adolescence, when they began to question the need to attend services, especially if they were high school students.

At the synagogue, men prayed wrapped in the prayer shawl. The *tallit kattan* ("a small prayer garment") was worn only by the very pious.

Covering the head was a sign of respect and very orthodox men wore the *kopl* or *yarmulkè* ("skull cap") at all times and especially during meals. Most men, however, had discarded this habit, except during meals. "He eats bareheaded" was said with disapproval. One did not pronounce a prayer or blessing without covering the head.

Rosh chodesh ("the first day of the lunar month") was considered a special day for women. It was believed to have been dedicated by God to women as a reward for their devotion and for their refusal to worship the golden calf. On the Saturday preceding the first day of the Jewish lunar month, women prayed at home, reading the *tchinah* ("women's prayer book"). This book contained supplications for the health and welfare of the family, with detailed enumerations of all possible misfortunes and afflictions from which they hoped to be spared by the grace of God and in the name of all the meritorious ancestors.

All week was a prelude to the festive Friday evening meal, when the much awaited Sabbath (referred to as the queen, the bride) was celebrated with a copious meal. Rich and poor alike made every effort to do the honors.

The menu varied little: fish, boiled and seasoned, or *gefilté fish* (fish dumplings); chicken soup (prepared with dill, parsley and carrots) served with noodles; roast meat, and chicken with a side dish of *moyna* ("potato or rice pudding"), stewed prunes or apricots and *kygl* ("a sweet-noodle pudding with raisins and cinnamon"). The *kygl* was so important a part of the *Shabbés* ("Sabbath") meal that one of the less-sophisticated older local women was known for her own version of blessing the oven for the preparation of Sabbath cooking:

> *Yerutzn Lefunecho Yerutzn Lefunoy*
> *Burech Yi burech Shemoy*
> *Oyvn zolst mir zein getray*
> *Zolst nisht brennen, zolst nisht bruth*
> *Loz mein kyigl gerutn.*

> "I stand before Thee
> Blessed be the Name, Blessed be He
> Oven, be kind to me
> Please don't burn, don't scorch
> Let my *kygl* be successful."

After dinner the family, regardless of musical talents, joined in the singing of *zemirot* ("songs of grace"). This custom varied with the individual family. These hymns, some dating from the Middle Ages, were instituted to create a warm family ambiance, to keep the family around the table and as a compliment to the housewife for her efforts in preparing the meal. It set the Sabbath meal above the usual rush of the weekday meals, when the merchant gulped his food between serving customers and the craftsman ate his piece of bread with *shmaltz* (chicken fat) and an onion at his workbench.

Since touching fire on the Sabbath was forbidden, the Saturday noon meal presented some technical problems. The *shabbes goy* ("a gentile who performed tasks forbidden to Jews on Sabbath") was a well-known institution in the shtetl. The most pious, however, maintained the traditional *chollent* (or Tchollent).

Chollent was prepared by filling a crock with meat, vegetables, seasoning and water and placing it in the heated oven on Friday eve, before lighting the candles. It remained there overnight, simmering and ready for the Saturday meal. The alternative, especially during the summer, was to have a cold meal, such as *pcea* or *racituri* ("a garlicky jellied leg of veal"), gefilté fish ("fish dumplings"), chopped liver or chopped hard-boiled eggs, *icre* ("caviar") and, in season, fresh-vegetable salads and egg plant salad. One traditional dish served before the Saturday noon meal was the *tzimes nehit* ("chickpeas in honey") or *tzimes bombes* ("kidney beans in honey"), prepared with tons of chicken fat and smothered in honey. After a goodly portion of either of these delicacies, the rest was trimmings. Another favorite Saturday lunch entrée was grated raddish with chicken fat. And always the egg *challah*, compote and sponge cake. Hot drinks were not part of a meal.

The Sabbath day was passed in quiet relaxation, a nap for the parents and quiet play for the children. It was the time for leisurely walks and for visiting friends and relatives. The custom of studying the Torah, often mentioned in literature, was observed only by the very pious and by the *hasidim* of the Rabbinic Court.

Sabbath ended at sunset. The *havdalah* was the ceremony indicating the separation of the Sabbath from the week beginning. It was not practised by many otherwise observant families. It consisted of three blessings: the light and fire, the spices — usually kept in an ornate silver container — and the wine. The *havdalah* was performed with a braided candle, which was extinguished with a few drops of wine, signifying the fact that it had been kindled for the specific purpose of this ceremony.

This ended the Sabbath and indicated the beginning of the new work week with the greeting "A gitte voch" ("A good week") and again the hustle and bustle. The Saturday evening meal was frugal by comparison, often consisting of leftovers or improvised dishes. Visiting relatives often stayed for a *mamaliga* with *branza* ("cornmeal bread, served with cheese, sour cream and butter"). In the summer, an occasional outing to the restaurant for a *mushchiu la gratar* ("charcoal-broiled steak") and *mititei* ("broiled, highly spiced sausage") and a cool beer were indulged in by those able to afford this luxury.

There is some confusion regarding the terms *rebbé*, *rov*, *rabbi* and *rebbeh*. Regardless of spelling, the term means "teacher" in Hebrew. *Rebbé* applies to a Hasidic leader, called a *tzadik* ("a saintly man"); *rebbeh* was used only when referring to the teacher of small children in a *heider* ("first level of Hebrew school"). *Rov* (pronounced "roof") is synonymous with *rabbi*, the spiritual leader of a congregation and, in the shtetl, a salaried employee of the Jewish community. Each shtetl had only one *rov*. Few shtetlech had a *rebbé*.

In a *rabbunish* shtetl, such as was Stefanesti, where the *rebbé* held a uniquely exalted position, the role of the *rov* was eclipsed. In Stefanesti, the *rov* himself was a Hasid and part of the intimate coterie of the *rebbé*.

The *rov* is not, as is often believed, a priest, nor is he "called" or ordained to a pulpit. A *rov*'s ordination is an academic degree, which he obtains upon graduating from a *Yeshiva*, a school of highest Judaic studies.

In the shtetl, the *rov* was more a judge, an authority on tradition and a spiritual leader. He was occasionally invited to deliver a sermon at one of the congregations. His learning and studies gave him a broad background in law and medicine, and especially in veterinary medicine as it pertained to the consumption of meat. He performed religious rites at births, weddings and burials. He was empowered to grant divorces after attempting to reconcile the couple. He was called to arbitrate altercations and quarrels arising from breach of promise or from business deals. His judgment was binding.

Should a housewife, upon opening a chicken for cooking, find some abnormality such as a deformed organ, say an enlarged or spotted liver, she would take the fowl to the *rov* for a *shalle* ("a question") and the *rov* interpreted — decreed whether the chicken was *kosher*, that is, adequate for human consumption, or *treyf* ("unclean") and to be discarded. Similarly, problems arising from inadvertently mixing meat with milk called for the *rov*'s judgment.

2. Calendar of Festivals

Unlike our solar calendar, the Jewish year is lunar. Scrupulously noted in Jerusalem, the appearance of the new moon used to be celebrated throughout the land as *Rosh Chodesh*, the first of the month. All seasonal festivals were subsequently established according to this criterion. However, due to the accumulated discrepancies between the solar and lunar reckonings, adjustments were necessary in order not to displace the seasonal festivals. Otherwise, over a period of time, Passover, for instance, a spring festival, might conceivably have fallen in mid-winter. To avoid this, one extra month was periodically added at the end of the year, a second month of Adar, called ve-Adar, much as we add one day to February in leap years.

For the Romanian shtetl, the entire period of High Holy Days in the autumn was beyond doubt the most important period of the year. The three weeks were spoken of simply as The *Yomtoyvn* ("The Festivals"). It was a time when the relationship between man and his Creator was at its most intense. The emphasis, however, was on the first week, *Rosheshune* and *Yom Kippur*, spoken of as one single entity. Emotionally, it was like a movement in a symphony creating its peak of intensity at Yom Kippur ("The Day of Atonement"), with a gradual denouement during the *Succoth* ("festival of the Booths") and, in complete contrast of mood, *Simchas Torah* ("the Rejoicing of the Torah").

Although falling in the autumn, a season usually associated with endings rather than beginnings, the *Yomtovyn* heralded a new calendar year. For every shtetl Jew, this was a period of introspection, of stocktaking and making resolutions for the future. It was also a time when one remembered departed loved ones, thus establishing the continuity between the generations.

It was believed that, on New Year, God opened three books: one with the names of the virtuous, who were inscribed in the book of life; one with the names of the wicked, inscribed for punishment and even death; and a third for those whose fate was still in doubt and who, during this period of penitence, had the opportunity to repent and be forgiven. In view of this, it was customary to make up any quarrels among friends and ask forgiveness for hurts, be they deliberate or unintentional.

One prepared for *Rosh Hashanah* by a complete renovation and getting ready for the oncoming winter. The Sabbath falling between New Year and the day of Atonement, called *Shabbat Shuvah* ("Sabbath of the Return"), was based on the theme of the prayer "Return O Israel unto the Lord, thy God". The weird sounding of the ram's horn, the *shofar*, is presumed to recall the sounding of trumpets before the arrival of a king. It may also be a reminder of the primitive way of calling the people in the desert on Mount Sinai. At the sound of the ram's horn (blown in a specific ritualized manner) the Gates of Heaven were believed to open wide to receive all the wishes and prayers rushing up to Heaven like a blowing wind.

On *Shabbat Shuvah* each synagogue auctioned off the honorific *allias* ("being called to the *Torah*") to the highest bidder. It was the touchstone for the true social standing within each congregation, with much jockeying for position by the parishioners. After the Sabbath services, standing on the *bimmah* in the center of the synagogue, the *shammas*, gavel in hand, announced that auctions would begin for the forthcoming *allias*. The day's reading was divided into sections and each section carried an assigned honorific value; the last one, called *mafter*, being the most honorific and most coveted. It was customary for the first *alliah* to go to a *cohen* ("priestly tribe"), the second to a levite and the others to the rest of the congregation. There was an unspoken custom not to challenge the most prosperous members of the congregation, who also happened to be the most generous donors. Bidding was most fervent among the middle group, where counter-bidding was often ebullient.

One respondent related with amusement the excitement of these occasions and recounted one particular incident when a near riot broke out in their synagogue. In that synagogue there was only one *cohen* and one *levite* who, every year, were automatically awarded the first and second *allias*. Both were well-known and respected members of the congregation. One year a new *cohen* joined the congregation. When the time came for the *allias*, the old-timer called out his usual bid of one hundred *lei* (not a negligible sum at that time). To everyone's dismay, the new member began to outbid, intent on obtaining the honor. Flabbergasted, the older gentleman kept up the bidding which, however, did not faze the newcomer, unfamiliar with the pecking order of the synagogue. The bidding reached unheard-of proportions but the newcomer won, to everyone's amusement and the glee of the administration. Such scenes were repeated in all synagogues, resulting in many a frayed ego, which the *gabbè* had to diplomatically patch up.

The entire week between New Year and the Day of Atonement was spent in penitential prayer. One respondent wrote, "Just before the Holy Days and especially during *Rosh Hashannah* and *Yom Kippur* I always became much more careful about religious observances; no fooling around with not putting on philacteries every morning." This was corroborated by many other respondents.

"May you merit many years and be inscribed for a good year" was the greeting during the week and especially on *Yom Kippur*. It became customary to exchange well-wishing cards in the fashion of Christmas greetings. Most cards, however, were small, about the size of calling cards, with simple inscription.

One custom observed in the Romanian shtetl but discarded as "superstition" by contemporary Jews was the ceremony of *Tashlich* ("Thou shall cast ... sins"). On the afternoon of the first day of *Rosh Hashannah*, everyone went to the Basheu and across the bridge to say *tashlich* ("pray"). All the pockets were turned inside out and crumbs well shaken into the river, and with them all one's sins. The prayers read were Psalms and recitation from Micah (7:19). Thus, one started afresh in the new year. (*Tash* means "purse" in Yiddish, which gave the erroneous impression to the ignorant that this was a purse ceremony.)

The evening before the eve of *Yom Kippur* was reserved for a ritual that has now disappeared among American Jews: *shlugn kappures*. This is now considered a relic of pagan times. In the Romanian shtétl, *shlugn kappures* was accepted and practised with the same fervor as all other rites in the firm belief that transgression was sinful.

The approximate translation of *shlugn kappures* is "ransom" or "choosing a scapegoat to expiate one's sins". Fowl were sacrificed instead of a person and this act was believed to expiate the sins and guilt of the individual concerned. This no doubt relieved much of the anxiety from accumulated guilt, inevitable under the circumstances.

One bird was purchased for each member of the family, hens or chicks for the females and roosters for the males. Since this ritual was dedicated to life, it was preferable that the birds be white or at least of light color, since black was associated with mourning.

Holding the hen or rooster by its legs, which had been previously tied up with a string, one twirled the *kappura* three times over and around one's head while reciting:

> *Ze halifosi, ze timorosi, ze kaparosi*
> *Ze hatarnagol (or fem. tarnagolet) t'eilech le misa . . .* etc

("This is my charge, this is my compensation, this is my redemption, this rooster or hen should go to its death while I shall enter a long, happy and peaceful life, Amen.") After the prayer was said, the fowl was unceremoniously thrown under the table. There was a genuine belief that this act would transfer any potential evil from the human to the bird.

Part of the *kappures* was kept for family consumption, the rest was distributed as charity to needy families. Each family had its own poor to whom they gave this contribution, each year, with wishes and hopes to live till next year and, in good health, again perform this rite.

We have here a ritual in which the individual's emotional needs are translated to serve the community needs, thus assuring all members of the community adequate food for the holy days. Its disappearance reflects the change in the social structure of contemporary communities, which rendered this rite obsolete.

Yom Kippur ("The Day of Atonement") was the most awesome of days. The day, called the Sabbath of Sabbaths, was solemnized by rigorous fastings from sunset to sunset. Not one swallow of liquid or food was allowed. Fasting is a universal way of preparing oneself for any sacred ritual and is found in many cultures. It is conceived as a purification and abnegation before a ritual feast.

The evening before and the entire day of *Yom Kippur* was spent in the synagogue "clamoring at the Gates of Heaven", literally pleading for one's life. On this day both men and women went to synagogue. It was a day fraught with emotions. *Kol Nidrey*, the liturgy that begins this day of prayers, is "the first movement of a devotional symphony, increasing in momentum from minute to minute throughout the day".* From *Kol Nidrey* to the very last prayer, called *Ne'Ilah* ("closing of the Gate of Heaven"), there was a surge of supplications to God to "inscribe us in the Book of Life". The expression *tzu Ne'Ilah* is ironically used to mean that one arrived just before the very end. Throughout, God was implored for mercy and forgiveness.

In the Romanian shtetl, even the most hardened skeptics did not dare flaunt their disbelief or challenge the solemnity of the day. Young rebels sometimes bragged to one another that they had actually eaten, but under pressure would admit the bluff. The very young were left with maids, siblings or neighbor's children. It was the only day when parents were away the entire day and left children in the care of others. For children it was a long day. Armed with a brown-paper bag in which the mother had prepared a slice of challah, a hard-boiled egg, some chicken and a bunch of grapes, they wandered aimlessly between the synagogue and home. The bread was soggy from the crushed grapes, the crumb-covered grapes were gritty; the whole, one unspeakable mush, was endured or fed to the dog. Older children vied with one another to withstand hunger pangs, feeling grown-up enough to be permitted to fast. They hung around the synagogue, especially awaiting the solemn moments of the *shofar bluzn*, when one's fervent prayers would float up to Heaven to be heard and fulfilled.

After a long, exhausting day, the fast was ended, one hour after dark, amid wishes of *L'shanna Tovah t'kouseva* ("May you be inscribed for a good year"). The fast was broken by taking a small glass of cherry brandy (homemade) and some honey cake, and a light meal of cold fish or chicken. Many families maintained the tradition of breaking the fast together at the home of one of the clan, wishing one another a good year.

The emotional tension of these days was great. *Succot* ("the Feast of Booths") served as a denouement. The pastoral and agricultural past is best perceived in this celebration of the autumn gathering of the crops and the beginnings of a new agricultural season. The Biblical command to live in tents or booths for seven days and nights is

---

* Theodor Gaster, *Op Cit.*, p. 159.

understandable since workers lived in huts in the fields during this time. Historically, it commemorates the wandering in the desert during the Exodus, when the Hebrews lived in tents. The continuity with the historic past, and thus with the God of Israel is constantly reinforced.

In Stefanesti, as in other Romanian shtetlech, building the *succah* was observed, though with some reservations. Neighbors joined forces and prepared the *succah* together, combining their meals, for at least the first two days. Though the spirit was observed, it was far from the letter of the law. In most cases, already existing small buildings were converted, transgressing the Biblical specification of having a roof through which stars would be visible. A tentlike mood was achieved by hanging hand-woven rugs on the walls. The ceiling was covered with reeds and rushes, and bunches of grapes, apples, quince and pears were hung from plaited garlands. This created a festive atmosphere, enhanced by the fragrance of the fruit. In spite of all efforts, eating there was not the pleasant experience one hoped for. In the often damp, cold fall weather, eating dressed up in fall coats was anything but comfortable. After *kiddush* ("blessing the wine") and the fish, the family gleefully repaired to the house for a comfortable, warm meal, with few regrets.

As part of the agricultural past this was the time for blessing "the four species", *benchn essrig*. The *essrig* is a citron, a lemon-like fruit, but larger than a lemon, with a stem-like protrusion at one end (where it was attached to the tree branch). The four species were: a palm branch, a willow branch, a sprig of myrtle (all tied together and encased in a plait of palm leaves) and a citron. Every member of the family was supposed to bless *essirg*, during *Succot*. Since these plants were all imported from Jerusalem it was beyond the financial possibilities of individual families to obtain them. Each synagogue bought one set for the use of its parishioners. The *shamas* ("beadle") of each synagogue made the rounds in the morning, giving everyone a chance to perform this rite. Men often went to the synagogue for this ceremony.

Holding the citron, with the stemlike protrusion downward, in the left hand and the palm branch in the right hand, the blessing was said while pointing the palm and myrtle up, down to the left and to the right, and ending with *Hosanna* ("O, Save us"). This, too, is a rather transparent relic of the pastoral rite of symbolically inviting the winds at the appropriate time. By sympathetic magic (so often observed in primitive societies), one hoped to obtain the co-operation or control of natural phenomena. In Stefanesti, the *rebetzn* ("the *rov*'s wife") prepared marmalade from the citrons she obtained from several synagogues – a rare delicacy indeed – and traditionally offered a *kisea* ("jam bowl") to some of the more prominent parishioners.

According to Theodor Gaster* the use of willows would suggest a re-enactment of the ancient fertility rites, since the willow was a symbol of fertility, believed to induce potency. This motif is repeated in the "beating hosannas" during the litanies of the seven days of the festival. Each day, one prayer was added, until seven prayers were said on the seventh day, while the willow branches were "beaten" until the leaves fell off. On the day called *Hosanna Raba*, or "the great Hosanna", the procession walked around the synagogue seven times. It was done in the belief that the Gates of Judgment were closing and that this was the last chance one had to intercede, hence "Hosanna". The picturesque expression *upgeshmissene oyshannes* ("like beaten hosannas") evoked the beaten look of dejection or referred to people past their prime.

The eighth day, called *Shemini-Atzeret* or the feast of *Atzeret* (meaning "restraint") was dedicated to prayer for rain. Once again, the agricultural motif appears, again through sympathetic magic. During the Second Temple period this rite was performed by pouring water from a silver jug onto the altar to invoke rain. One respondent related with amusement an incident she remembered when, during dinner in the *succah*, on the Feast of *Azeret*, the teenage sons of the neighbors (with whom they shared the booth) decided to play a youthful prank, inspired by this prayer. While the families were gathered around the table and the father was pronouncing the prayers for rain, the boys climbed onto the roof and poured down a bucketful of water through the slats of the roof. They guilelessly explained that the prayer for rain was being instantly fulfilled. While the father reprimanded them mildly, the mother, beholding the dripping tablecloth, was not amused. This sort of lighthearted detachment to some of the ancient rites suggest a lack of identification on the part of the shtetl Jew with the agricultural past. Traditions were observed as a means of identification with *Yiddishkeit*, with the collectivity. "Everyone else was doing it." Continuity was a side effect.

Simchas Torah, ("Rejoicing of the Torah") was a special festival in the Romanian shtetl, as it was among all Jewish communities. It was one of the few joyous occasions in an otherwise gloomy calendar. It was anticipated by young and old alike. Children awaited this day

---

* *Festivals of the Jewish Year*, Theodor Gaster, Wm. Sloane Assoc., New York, 1953.

with impatience. They made paper flags or bought the flags with inscriptions: "Flag of the Camp of Judah." They picked shiny red apples, which they impaled on the flag stick, and placed a small white candle in the scooped-out core of the apple. With these flags, and with the candles lit, they marched home from the synagogue after the big celebration on the eve of the festival, the *hakkufos* ("procession with the Torah scrolls in the synagogue"). Everyone went to *shul* for this celebration.

After the reading of the *Torah*, (the only time the *Torah* was read in the evening), the *Torah* scrolls were removed from the Ark and parishioners took turns in parading, in procession, around the bimmah, with the scrolls in their arms, while the congregation, men, women, and children, crowded around each *hakkufah* and stretched to touch and kiss the scroll with reverence. Most succeeded only in touching the velvet or satin slipcover and piously kiss the two fingers thus privileged. There was dancing with the *hakkufos* and with each other in a mood of exhilaration and occasionally Dionisian abandon, a rare occurrence in the synagogue. At the tables, the *gobbé* and his assistants offered honey cake and schnapps to all, as it was considered a good deed to drink on *Simchas Torah* and rejoice at the receiving of the *Torah*, the greatest gift of all.

The following morning the *hakkufos* were again paraded in the synagogue and the same mood elicited.

This ceremony, evidently part of Judaic tradition, was re-enacted in every synagogue in the shtetl. An additional shtetl tradition was the distribution of slices of honey cake, sponge cake and *ponchiklech* ("cookies") to the children, on *Simchas Torah* day, after the service. A huge wicker laundry basket was filled with slices of honey cake and *ponchiklech*, which the *gobbé* distributed to the melée of stretched-out hands at the synagogue door. The *ponchikl* was a local delicacy (or at least the term seems to be local). It was made of a honey-based dough, twisted in the shape of the letter *S* and sprinkled with sugar. One respondent wrote that he remembered with mouth-watering fondness the unique taste of these cookies. Again, we see here the deliberate involvement of children, and association with agreeable memories, at every possible religious festival.

According to Theodor Gaster,* the *Simchas Torah* ceremony is a mystical imitation of the wedding service, symbolizing the marriage of Israel to the Law. The bridegroom is attended by counterparts of the modern "best man" and the procession with the scrolls,

---

* Theodor Gaster, *Op. Cit.*

recalling the *sheva bruchas*, the walking seven times around the bridegroom under the canopy. This is frequently found in many cultures, as is the imaginary magic circle, protection against evil spirits.

With this last outburst of joy and gratitude to God for His unique gift; the *Torah*, the *yomtoyvn*, ("holy days") were ended and the shtetl began the new year and settled in for the winter months.

Hanukah, "the feast of lights", came along at about the same time as Christmas. It no doubt originated in the celebration of the winter solstice, with the short days and long nights. It is therefore not surprising that the motif is lighting of candles.

The legend explains the lighting of candles in remembrance of a miracle that occurred when the Jews resisted enemy attacks and remained faithful to their true and only God. This is one festival that is not mentioned in the Bible, but is believed to commemorate a well-authenticated historical event: Judah the Maccabee, son of the Jewish priest Matathias Hashmonean, openly resisted the Hellenization to which the Jews were being subjected by Antiochus, the Syrian king. After chasing the Syrians out, Judah Maccabee found only one cruse of sacramental oil for the rededication of the Temple. Miraculously, this oil, sufficient only for one day, lasted eight days. Hanukah is celebrated in memory of this miracle and of the Maccabeans' bravery in refusing to worship other gods. Candles are lit for eight days, beginning with one candle and adding one candle each day, with eight candles lit on the last day.

In the shtetl, this was one more occasion for breaking the monotony of the long winter nights and gray drizzly days.

Good food and *a gleizele vein* ("a little glass of wine") within the comfort of the extended family were welcomed by all at this time of year. The traditional dishes associated with *Hanukah* in the Romanian shtetl were *knishes* and *varenekes* rather than the oft-mentioned *latkes* of the Russian-Polish shtetl. The ingredients are the same, mashed potatoes or *kasha* ("groats") with *grivn* ("cracklings") and *shmaltz* ("chicken or goose fat"). All these festive dishes with only a taste of meat are proof of the ingenuity of cultures where meat of any kind was a comparatively rare luxury. To satisfy all, small quantities were resourcefully camouflaged into holiday fare.

Grivn ("cracklings") are the bits of fried fat and onions obtained when fat is rendered. Chickens were the usual weekly diet, whereas turkey and geese were delicacies reserved for special occasions. Geese were bought in the autumn and force-fed. This not only gave the enlarged liver (*foie gras*) but resulted in deposits of excessive fat, a favorite cooking ingredient of shtetl cuisine. Goose liver and chicken livers were chopped with onions and chicken or goose fat. The expression "A gedile mit grivn" ("A joy with grivn") summed up the epitome of enjoyment and gladness.

Varenekes are a ravioli-like dish made with a potato dough and filled with a mixture of mashed potatoes and *grivn*, or *kasha*, mixed with the same, boiled in water and served with chicken or goose fat. *Knishes*, on the other hand, prepared from a different type of dough, but with the same fillings, were baked, hence giving a different flavor to the same ingredients. The term *"knish"* comes from *"farknishevet"* ("rumpled, bunched up"), picturesquely describing the manner of encasing the filling into the *knish* dough. When smaller in size, they were called *knishiklech*, preferred in some families. Regardless of shape or size, the fragrance of these delicacies wafting through the house was part of the warm conviviality of holy day atmosphere.

Family gatherings usually took place on the last day of *Hanukah* when the eight candles were lit. The children were then given their much-awaited *Honeke gelt* ("Hanukah money") by all the members of the family. Adults did not exchange gifts. *Hanukah gelt* was the children's exclusive prerogative.

With *Hanukah gelt* safely tucked away, the *dreydl* ("spinning top") was brought out and every member of the family participated in the traditional game of chance. The *dreydl* is a small top made of brass or wood, with the Hebrew letters for *N, G, H, S* on its four sides, standing for the phrase *Nes Gadol Hayah Sham* ("a great miracle occurred there"). By coincidence or design, these initials also represent the Yiddish for "take, give, half, put" ("nem, gib, halb, shtel"). Each player put a coin into the kitty and took turns at spinning the top. Winners and losers enjoyed this good fun, with occasional attempts at sleight of hand and hilarious teasing when discovered.

Like most festivals, *Hanukah*, too, was geared primarily to the children. The food, the festive atmosphere, gifts, all put the child on center stage and, his attention once won, the essence of tradition was emphasized.

Although *Hanukah* coincided with Christmas, this did not present any problems in the Romanian shtetl, not only because contact between the two cultural groups was almost non-existent at this level, but the attitude of the parents towards all the customs of the goyim was one of derision if not contempt. Few Jewish children had the opportunity to see the glittering Christmas trees; those who did were admonished that it was not for them, without any further explanation. *Mosh Craciun* ("Santa Claus"), the kindly, old, white-bearded man, was not as important in the peasant lore and was dismissed by the Jewish parent with the same "us-them" argument and by pointing out the superiority of "our ways". The shtetl child had no problems regarding the reality of Santa Claus. The *Hanukah gelt* he received gave him immediate freedom of choice and a form of independence regarding the manner of spending his booty. Furthermore, since most shtetl children attended the Jewish school, there was no conflict between the home values and those they were presented with at school.

Hamishuser B'Shevat. The concern for involving children in some aspect of the ritual and of making the event as appealing as possible to the child recurs in the celebration of *hamishuser* ("fifteenth"), the "New Year of the Trees". Although considered by adults a minor festival, it was an event in the lives of the children. The need for early imprint on the child's mind and the importance of association with pleasant situations was well understood, deliberately planned and assiduously put into practice at every occasion. Parents often performed certain rituals "so that the children will know and remember". And, once again, we see the effort to forge links between generations, links that made it possible for shtetl culture to survive against all odds.

No shtetl child could forget the little blue-and-white crêpe-paper bags, filled with a variety of nuts and dried fruits "from Eretz Israel", that were distributed in school or kindergarten compliments of the community. At home, there was more of the same: almonds, filberts, peanuts (called *Americaner nislech* – "American nuts" – in contrast to the filberts, called "Turkish nuts"), and a variety of dried fruit – dates, figs, raisins and that peculiar fruit, the carob pod, or Saint John's bread, the "boxer". This brown, podlike fruit, which, like all other *Hamishuser* treats, was imported from Israel, was the symbol of *Hamishuser*. All these goodies were to be enjoyed simply because, in a far-off land called Eretz Israel, it was the New Year of the trees, when in the shtetl snow still covered the ground. This in itself was enough to evoke in the child's mind a feeling of warm kinship with the unknown land and with the dim past.

Reverence for the Creator and His noble handiwork, "the tree" whose New Year was being celebrated, was inculcated effortlessly while the foundation was laid for a lasting bond with the ancestral homeland. The leitmotif is repeated.

Come February, the shtetl began to count the weeks to *Purim*, one of the few festivals commemorating a happy event. Briefly, the story of *Purim* tells of a Persian king called Ahaswerosh, whose evil prime minister, called Hamman, decreed that all Jews in the land be hanged. Distressed at the news, Mordechai, a Jew, and his niece, the beautiful Esther — who happened to be the king's favorite — succeeded in thwarting Hamman's plans. The king reversed the decree and ordered that Hamman be hanged and the Jews be saved. Theodor Gaster refers to this as a "romantic fiction" and suggests that the ritual pantomime was borrowed from the Babylonians, and that Mordechai and Esther were none other than the Babylonian gods Marduck and Ishtar. There is no historical evidence regarding this legend, although the court of Ahaswerosh, as described in the Book of Esther, resembles the one discovered at Persepolis.

This romantic legend is told in the scroll called *Megilas Esther* ("the Scroll of Esther"), which is read the day before *Purim*, at the end of a minor fast day called *Esther Tannes* ("the fast of Esther"). Esther is the only Biblical book in which the name of God is not mentioned at all. While the fast day was only sporadically observed, all other customs and traditions associated with this festival were looked forward to by all, and especially by children, who joined in the events with abandon.

Many of the traditions and customs that grew up around this festival are reminiscent of similar customs in other cultures, although integrated in a different context. Masquerading and the *guisers* recall Mardi Gras or Hallow'een. Children dressed up, covered their faces with a mask made of a white rag in which three holes had been cut out for the eyes and mouth, and made the rounds from door to door singing ditties.

> *Haint is Pirem, morgn is oys*
> *Gits mir a para und shtipts mich aroys.*
>
> *Purim* lasts only a day at a time
> Throw me right out, but spare me a dime.

The traditional pastry associated with *Purim* was the *humentash*, a triangular cookie filled with walnuts and honey or with prune marmalade. The *humentash* commemorates the three-cornered hat that Hamman, the evil one, was supposed to have worn. Before *Purim*, the housewives were busy baking not only the usual supply for the household, but enough provisions for the exchange with friends and relatives. It was customary to send a platterful of various baked goods, called *shalchemones*. The correct pronunciation is Mishloach Monos — sending food gifts to friends. This custom was gladly embraced by the shtetl housewives, who took advantage of this opportunity to display their culinary talents. *Hammantashn* baked by the dozens were not the only pastries of this season. There was also the entire array of *strudls*, pastries made of paper-thin dough or of honey based dough, with ground walnuts, jams and *rahat*

("Turkish delight") centers. Various fruitcakes, *pandishpan* ("pain d'Espagne") *fludn*, *honik leikech* and *tziker leikech* ("honey cake" and "sponge cake") and countless other cakes and pastries were piled up on a platter, to which were often added one or two Jaffa oranges or *mandarines* ("tangerines").

The traditional family meal resembled, in many respects, the Thanksgiving turkey dinners we know. Turkeys, like other fowl, were bought live, fattened and used for the *Purim* feast. The gobble of the turkey, translated into Yiddish as *Uder-uder-oo*, sounded almost like the month of Adar. Children jokingly asked "Hindig, hindig, ven is Pyrem?" ("Turkey, turkey, when is *Purim*?"). To which, oddly enough, the clever turkey replied: "Uder-uder oo", the Yiddish rendition of his "gobble, gobble" meaning, "In the month of Adar."

What better excuse than *Purim* for a festive dinner with all the trimmings and with wine and brandy to lubricate spirits? Immediately after the copious meal, the *maskierteh* or *mascattii* ("masked") began arriving. The children made their rounds singing their ditties and collecting their loot in the afternoon. All evening it was the young and not-so-young adults who, disguised with ingenuity, came. The game consisted in guessing the identity of the disguised person. Some were friends or neighbors who gave themselves away by peculiar mannerisms or by familiar items of clothing. They came in twos or threes, never alone. When identified, they would burst out in guffaws of laughter and run out; others resisted any attempt at being recognized and would leave everyone bursting with curiosity. For some, this was a unique opportunity to see how the other half lived, for it was the only time they would have had access to some of the better homes. Gowns of another era, silks, taffetas, with bustles and jet trimmings, were rescued out of naphtalene coffers. Sometimes these old-fashioned clothes were a clue, when, by Holmsean deduction, the identity was guessed, for the shtetl memory was alive and such items were well remembered. "That green taffeta gown, didn't Esther Bassie wear it at your mother's wedding forty years ago?" or "only Blima dem Schoichet's had such an embroidered collar," were whispered together, in an attempt at identifying the *maskierte*. It was a *mitzva* ("a good deed") to make merry on *Purim*, and the shtetl entered into this *mitzva* wholeheartedly.

The important social event of the season was the *Purim* Ball or *Bal Mascat*. For the young, it was a much-awaited opportunity to dance and flirt. It was also an opportunity for fund raising for the Zionist cause. Everyone in town was expected to participate. It is not difficult to see why this festival acquired such popularity in the

Romanian shtetl, addicted as it was to good food and drink and avid for opportunities for amusement.

Close on the heels of *Purim* came the week of Passover. "Ot is Pyrem, ot is shoyn Peisach" ("Here it's *Purim* and before you know it, it's already Passover") was the amazed remark, every year, as if it had never happened before. The New Year was celebrated in the autumn, but the month of *Nissan*, in the spring, is the first month of the Jewish calendar. Passover is celebrated in the middle of the month of *Nissan*. In Israel, it was the beginning of the new agricultural cycle, the awakening of spring, when barley was planted. It was thus a celebration of a new agricultural season. As is the case with all festivals, there is a historical and implicitly a religious dimension: the commemoration of the Exodus from Egypt. The emphasis is on freedom: freedom from slavery and the beginning of Israel as a people and of their covenant with God.

Passover is celebrated for eight days. The first two days, the *seder* is observed in the evening, followed by four days called *holemoyd* ("half holy days"), considered working days in every respect except for the maintenance of dietary observances. The last two days are called *die tzveite tog yomtov* (the "second set of holy days"). "Die tzveiteh tog yomtov" ("Another county heard from") was one of those pithy Yiddish expressions, used with some irony, when greeting some uncalled for remark or when an unexpected, unwelcome guest appeared.

Preparing for Passover began weeks in advance. It was a busy time, both for the individual households and for the Jewish community, whose responsibility it was to provide the community with *matzos* and to assure every member of the community with all necessities. *Moos-chittn* ("charity for the poor") had to be collected and distributed. For the baking of the *matzos*, which every community did on their own, tenders were bid and contractors delegated. In Stefanesti, there was a community-owned oven, used exclusively for the baking of *matzos* for Passover. In smaller towns, one of the bakeries was *kashered* ("ritually cleansed") for the purpose.

Politicking was at its height during the crucial decision-making period since, for many, baking *matzos* represented an important source of income.

Factions supporting one or another of the applicants, accusations of nepotism and favoritism would fly back and forth. Should the same individual happen to obtain the tender more than one year in a row, rumors would start: "Azoy?" ("Is that so?") "He thinks he has *hazukah* (right by precedent) already?" The entire activity of the shtetl was in the grips of these preparations.

Preparing the home for Passover was the housewife's responsibility, with only marginal assistance from the husband. A thorough spring cleaning was not only necessary after the grime of winter, it was a religious duty, since no trace of *chumetz* ("anything leavened or fermented") was permitted within the home for the duration of Passover. "Have a kushern peysach" summed it all up. From floor to ceiling and more, everything in the home had to be rubbed and scrubbed and spruced up. The poorer houses were whitewashed inside and out by slaked lime. The more prosperous homes were renovated for Passover. Furniture was revarnished with *brondolin and turpentin* ("a mixture of turpentine and varnish") and even retouched with bronze lacquer. Every bit of flour, every crumb of bread, every drop of alcohol (except the Passover wine) were packed up and symbolically "sold" to a gentile neighbor. This was another little pantomime, religiously (though lightheartedly) performed. These *chumetz* foods were subsequently bought back after the holy days, at a profit to the gentile buyer.

A complete new set of utensils, for both milk and meat, was unpacked for the specific use of the Passover week. After Passover, these dishes were again packed up and stored in the loft, for use the following year.

Dishes and pots made of metal, as well as cutlery, were *kashered* (cleansed). This primitive but effective means of sterilizing was performed the day before Passover. A deep, crater-like hole was dug in the backyard and lined with rocks, and a fire was lit within. The metal utensils were then placed on the fire and allowed to reach a red-hot temperature, at which time boiling water was poured over them. When cool, they were scrubbed with sand or ashes. Only after this operation, were they deemed clean for use during the Passover week. Not only was visible soil thus removed, but invisible bacteria were eliminated, in an environment where elementary hygiene was otherwise difficult to impose.

Burning the *chumetz* was performed the day before Passover. Equipped with a wooden spoon, a candle, a small rag and a feather, the husband, followed by his wife, would search the house for any "forgotten" unleavened stuff. The wife who, after having thoroughly cleaned the home, had carefully placed some pieces of bread on windowsills and other places, would inadvertently point these out to the husband. Using the feather, he brushed the crumbs into the rag and wooden spoon and burned the little parcel, thus finishing the cleaning for Passover. This was performed — not without a tinge of mockery — "to sit down at the *seder* with a clear conscience".

After weeks of toiling, everyone was ready for the first *seder* (meaning, literally, "order of service") as commanded. Everyone had to *banayen far Pesach* ("put on something new for Passover") even if it meant a made over garment. The traditional season dishes — such as *latkes* ("pancakes") made with *matzo* flour (flour made with finely crushed unleavened bread, *matzos*), or with potatoes; dumplings (also made with *matzo* flour); *chremzlech* ("sweet dumplings fried in honey and chicken fat) — all were prepared and the *seder* table set in strict accordance with prescribed tradition. The father's chair was prepared with cushions so that he could recline during the meal, since he was the king. The ancient Roman custom of reclining during a feast, while the slaves served the masters, was taken as a symbol of being truly free men, freed from slavery, as the occasion dictated. The fact that for the shtetl *king* this particular luxury was somewhat uncomfortable did not stop its observance.

The entire ceremony, lasting throughout the evening, was celebrated privately, by the head of every household, with his own family around him. As soon as the menfolk returned from the synagogue, the family sat down to commence the ritual. It was part of the tradition to invite an *oyrech* for *seder*, so that, as commanded, every needy person should partake of a meal. During the 1930s when *chalutzim* ("pioneers") were stationed in town for *hachsharah* ("pioneer agricultural training"), these young people were billetted to the homes of the townspeople for the Passover feast.

Details referring to the ceremony of the *seder* are still very much a part of any contemporary Jewish community. The young were involved and given opportunities to be in the spotlight, and not merely tolerated. After the preliminary hand-washing and after blessing the first cup of wine, it was the youngest child who asked the four questions:

> Why is this night different from all other nights?
>
> On all other nights we eat leavened bread and *matza*; on this night, only *matza*.
>
> On all other nights we eat all kinds of herbs; on this night only bitter herbs.
>
> On all nights we do not dip even once; on this night, we dip twice.
>
> On all nights we eat either sitting up or reclining; on this night, all recline.

To these four questions, asked by the youngest, the father replies by reading the story of the Exodus, the *Haggada*, with commentaries by sages throughout the centuries.

Theodor Gaster* points out that the Biblical narrative is a "saga, not a factual report and the legendary details are drawn from popular lore". (The same author mentions that historical records confirm the existence, in Egypt, of a special class of persons known as Hebrews who did not enjoy full civic rights; that they lived as mercenaries and freebooters and raided the pastures of Egypt in the land of Goshen.)

Immediately before the end of the first part of the *seder*, when preparations for dinner began, the children would watch the father's every move carefully, for it was at that time that the father stealthily hid the *aphicomen* (half of the middle *matza* and part of the earlier ceremony). It was the task of the children to search and find this valuable piece of ceremonial *matza* and demand ransom for its return. This little farce, played in all seriousness, was also regarded with some skepticism. The child who found the *aphicomen* was entitled to the bounty and bargained the price with the father who was honor-bound to pay before the *seder* could be continued. The copious meal followed, after which the second part of the Haggadah was read.

Depending on the degree of piety of the family, the second part was stretched out for hours, or rapidly dispensed with. One respondent said that his father used to "take the express and rattle off page after page and finish the whole business in twenty minutes, much to mother's distress".

Upon finishing the *Haggadah*, "Next Year in Jerusalem!" was fervently wished by all around the table. The *seder* ended with the singing of ballads in the style of many folk ballads: "Ehad mi iodea?" ("Who knows one?"). "Chad Gadya" ("One kid"), and the other songs. Regardless of musical talents, everyone would join in singing these ancient melodies.

In Romanian shtetl, Passover was taken for granted. There was no philosophical reasoning or justification for its observance. Like all other red-letter days on the yearly calendar, it was part of the yearly cycle, a landmark. Since many "blood libels", Passover plots and other *bilbls* ("false accusations") occupy so important a part in the history of the Jews, it must be mentioned here that in the Romanian shtetl of the twenties and thirties this was not the case. As previously stated, the local Romanian peasantry, although not friendly to the shtetl, did not harbor feelings of hatred, nor did their mistrust go so far as to make false accusations regarding the Passover

---

* Theodor Gaster, *op. cit.*

rituals of the Jews. The Romanian shtetl Jews knew many hardships and had many problems; this was not one of them.

Leg boymer was one of the minor festivals in the shtetl. *S'fires* ("counting") referred to the counting of days begun on the second day of Passover. In Hebrew, each letter also carries a numerical value. The letters *lamed* (L) and *gymel* (G) together form the value of thirty-three. Pronouncing the two letters LG referred to the thirty-third day of counting, the date when *leg boymer* was celebrated. This, too, may be traced to the agricultural past. It resembles the oft encountered period of lent, with abstentions and bans on marriages and banquets, reminiscent of many other cultures. The Romans, too, believed it was bad luck to celebrate marriages in May. The Romanian peasants' festival called "Rusaliile", celebrated at about the same time of year, is similar in spirit. The Rusaliiles were supposed to have been three princesses who were forced to remain spinsters. They revenged themselves by coming back to earth and wreaking havoc with the harvest and homes. As protection against their spirit, pieces of bitter wormwood were worn in the belt.

In the shtetl, *Leg boymer* was geared mainly to the children. Schools and kindergartens used to organize *excursii* ("excursions") into the woods. With bows and arrows constructed with ingenuity out of twigs and strings, children enjoyed the rare treat of romping through the woods in early spring, singing songs, picking flowers and listening to the brave deeds of *Bar Kohbah*, (the hero associated with this festival), and his men.

Shavout, or the Feast of Weeks, also known as Pentecost, was celebrated at the end of the *sfires*, that is forty-nine days, or seven weeks, from the second day of Passover. This was the time in the agricultural cycle when the barley was ready for harvest and when the Israelites would bring the first fruit to the Temple. On the historico-religious plane, it was the Festival of the Covenant. Theodor Gaster points out that there are two important underlying ideas combined here. The first is the Oriental concept that the land does not belong to any one individual but rather to the one who cultivates it; therefore, the farmer must share the bounty with God. It follows that the relationship between God and man is not one of master and servant but rather one of equal partnership, since both participate in the act of creation.

The second idea suggested by Gaster to explain the offering of the first fruit is also ingenious: the fear of the unknown (and the possibility of harmful repercussions) prompted the offering of the first fruit as a sort of safety measure. Since to the Eternal Being nothing is new (eternity has no beginning) it is not dangerous. It follows that by offering the first fruit to God, fear of the unknown is eliminated. Viewed in this light, the relationship between man and God was close to the one envisaged by the Romanian shtetl.

The traditional food associated with *Shvies* in the Romanian shtetl was a delicacy specific to local cuisine called *beigealech*. These cheese-filled pastry rolls were served to fulfill the command to eat cheese, for which various explanations exist. Depending on preference, *beighealech* may be seasoned with salt and pepper and chopped dill, or with sugar, cinnamon and raisins. They were served with sour cream and beet soup (borsht).

On the second day of *Shavuot*, memorial services were held. The story of Ruth and her devotion to her mother-in-law, Naomi, was read in the synagogue. "In uniting these concepts, not all time was telescoped into a single moment, but rather that a single moment was projected into all of time."*

Tishe B'av, the ninth day of the month of Av, was a day of fasting, almost as rigorously observed as the Day of Atonement. It was a day of general mourning, commemorating the destruction of the first and second Temples. In the synagogue, the Book of Lamentations, the *Kinnos* ("elegies"), were recited. Falling at the end of summer, it was a reminder of the forthcoming fall holy days. Jews were no strangers to persecutions and had little difficulty identifying with the ancestral plight.

How were children to be made aware of these tragic events? How to convey to a child the suffering of long ago and the feelings of pain, without resorting to direct physical assault? *Berlach*, that's how. *Berlach* are the thistlelike burrs of the burdock weed, which grew abundantly in shtetl ditches. On *Tishebav*, it was dangerous for any little girl to be caught bareheaded. Even with a kerchief on, she was not safe from the gangs of young boys who sneaked up and rubbed handfuls of *berlach* into her hair. To dislodge these burrs from the hair without pulling the scalp was impossible. The other alternative often resorted to was to snip off the burrs, hair and all. This undoubtedly sadistic streak was indulgently accepted as part of the suffering for the memory of the destruction of the Temple. Suffering for the girls. As for the boys? Well, boys will be boys!

The month of *Elul*, preceding the high holy days, was traditionally the month of prayer and repentance. The *shofar* was blown daily during the morning services and it was customary to visit

---

* Theodor Gaster, *Op. cit.*, p. 63.

the graves of the deceased and to pray to them for intercession. It was the preparation for the *yomtoyvn*. The cycle was closed.

3. The Synagogue

The names by which places of worship have been known at various times and in various places reflect their function and the attitude of the community toward the institution. In the Romanian shtetl, the synagogue was referred to by its generic name: the *shyll* (in Romanian: *synagoga*). *Shyll* is derived from the Greek *scuola* ("school"). The term *shtibl* ("little house"), often encountered in Poland, was unknown in the Romanian shtetl. Nor was the prefix *shaar* ("gate"), often used in North America with reference to a synagogue, known in the shtetl. Whether one went to the *shyllhoyf* ("the synagogue at the *rebbé*'s court"), the *hoyche shyll* ("the tall synagogue") or any of the other houses of prayer, one simply went *in shyll arein* ("to synagogue"). The *beth ha midrash*, or *besemedrish* as it was called colloquially, implied a much humbler structure, and, for emphasis, it was often called *bessemedrishl*.

In Stefanesti, and in most small towns, there were seven congregations. The *syillhoyf* was at the *rebbe*'s court; the *hoyche shyll* was a comparatively impressive "tall building; the *Meshegouem* was the synagogue of the eccentrics, so nicknamed for some long-forgotten reason, which boasted, however, the *negydem* ("wealthy family") among its parishioners; the *Hevre Gah*; the *Elie Wolf*, named after its founder; the *arbeturers*' ("workers'") synagogue; and the *shnayderishe shyll* ("tailors' synagogue").

For, as in all other matters, the community was neatly divided along socioeconomic lines. A few of the more prosperous craftsmen were tolerated in other synagogues.

Within each congregation the membership was ranked on a well-defined pecking order, expressed in the rigid seating arrangement within each synagogue. The *faine Yidn*, the *balabotem*, the pillars of the community, occupied the seats along the *mizrach vant* the Eastern wall, near the Holy Ark, while the other rows of pews were assigned according to the family status; at the door were the poor, the ignorant and the itinerant beggars.

Each synagogue had its own independent internal structure with a *gobbé* or "president" and a council chosen by and from the ranks of the congregation. In perusing the pertinent literature there appears to be some confusion regarding the term *gobbé*. It seems that in the Polish shtetl, the term for "president" was *parnass*, while *gobbé* or *"gabbay"* represented a lesser position, closer to that of the

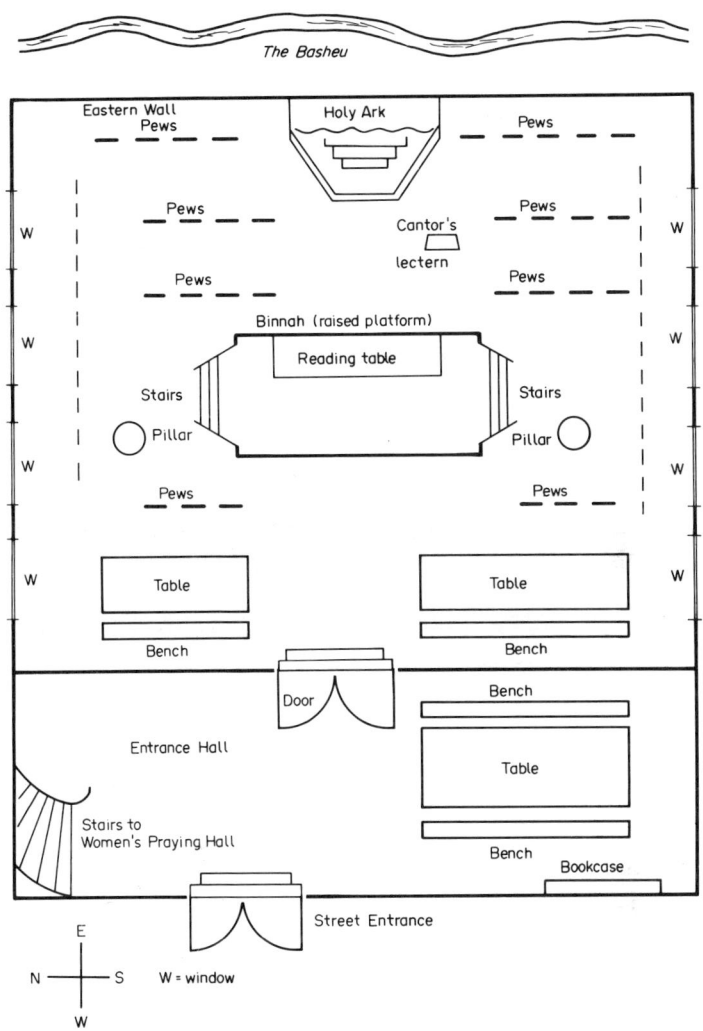

FIG. 12. Floor plan of Hoyché Shyll (Stefanesti) (downstairs) (men's section).

beadle. This was not the case in the Romanian shtetl, where the title "parnass", although known, was not used. Instead, it was the *gobbé* who was the president and the *shammes*, or "beadle", was the janitor or caretaker of the synagogue. The role of the *gobbé* was an honorific one; it carried high prestige and was conferred on a prominent member of the congregation. He was the administration head and also presided at the reading of the *Torah*. Usually he was well versed

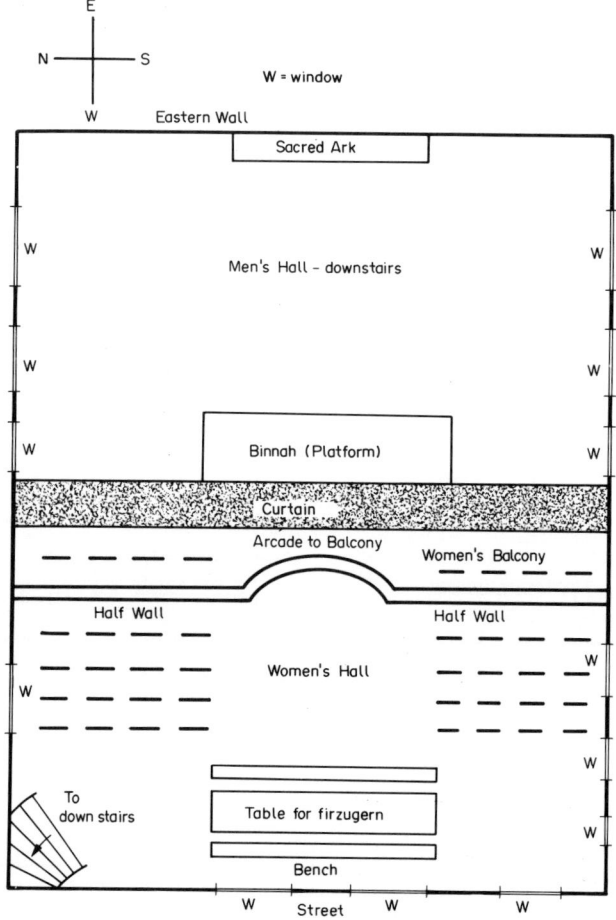

FIG. 13. Floor plan of Women's Hall, Hoyché Schyll (Stefanesti) second floor.

and able to read the *Torah* himself. It was his task to distribute the portions to be read to those called to the *Torah*.

The person so honored was then expected to make a monetary contribution commensurate with his financial ability and social standing. This was a source of revenue for the synagogue and an important prestige lever.

Religion was the *raison d'être* of the shtetl and the synagogue was its stronghold. The vagaries and vicissitudes of life amid an alien environment were endured only due to the binding forces inherent in Judaism, and the synagogue represented the focal point. During the twenties and thirties this role began to be eroded by constant contact with the outside world, especially among the youth and much more so among the young students; for the shtetl, however, it remained an important part of community life.

There is no synod and no national center or secular power to enforce religious decrees in Judaism. The spectacle of a hall full of men wrapped in their prayer shawls, each saying his own piece independently, may appear bizarre to anyone accustomed to the hush of a church. The individualistic shtetl Jew took for granted his prerogative of praying directly to his God, without intermediary.

The *chazn* ("cantor") was a paid member of the clergy. Each synagogue had its own cantor; some acquired a high reputation for their talents. For the high holy days the cantor had his *meshures* ("assistant"), who chanted the prayers along with him. One enterprising "part-time" cantor in town attempted to introduce his own three young sons as assistants. His innovative spirit, however, went too far when he tried to include his twelve-year-old daughter into the family choir. This, the conservative parishioners found too much, in spite of the man's insistence that there was no proof to be found anywhere, prohibiting young girls from singing in a synagogue. This was a male's precinct.

The *shammes* ("beadle") was a paid caretaker-watchman who performed the more menial tasks around the synagogue. Every synagogue had a *shammes*.

Compared to other synagogues, and compared to its lowly surroundings, the *hoyché shyll* ("the tall synagogue") in Stefanesti was an impressive building indeed. The synagogue had been rebuilt after a fire, in the 1880s, had destroyed the building, and it had the architectural imprint of that period. It was built on the banks of the Stream Basheu, where four of the other seven synagogues in town were to be found. (This was in accordance with the *Hallachik* law stipulating that a synagogue be built on an elevation or near a river.) Since medieval laws prohibited a synagogue from being taller than the local church building, to comply with Hallachik law, a synagogue was usually built along a river.

The *hoyché shyll* was a two-storey structure, built of bricks, plastered and painted with oil paint. The doors and windows were varnished. Adjoining the *shyll* there was the communal bathhouse and *mikveh* ("ritual pool"), built, according to regulations, near a running stream.

The entrance to the synagogue was on the west side of the building. From the street, one entered a vestibule from whence a curved staircase led to the women's section upstairs. The heavy, shiny bannister of the staircase was well-polished by the backsides of many a youngster who, slid down when the beadle was not looking. In the vestibule there was a long wooden table with benches and a glass-encased bookcase full of well worn tomes. Here were held the weekly Saturday evening *sholeshydes* or *seudah shelishit* (a communal meal of herring, bread and schnapps). This custom was disappearing as fewer of the *balabatem* ("the community leaders") attended. In this hall, during the high holy days, were placed large sandboxes where the beeswax *yartzeit* ("yearly anniversaries of deaths") tapers were inserted, each lit in memory of the departed by members of the family. It was like a marching army aflame, symbolically embodying for one brief moment, those long gone.

From the vestibule one entered the main hall of worship with its tall, vaulted ceiling. Eight tall and narrow windows, four in each of the north and south walls, were built high above eye level but with good visibility of the sky. Below the windows, the walls were pannelled in polished brown oak. The ceiling simulated the heavenly firmament with a cresent moon, the radiating sun and various constellations, all made of gold, encrusted in the azure sky. This may have been inspired by the sentiment that the sight of the heavens would arouse reverence and devotion in prayer. On the walls between ceiling and windows were twelve panels depicting, in bright colors, the twelve symbols of the zodiac.

The interior was built according to the traditional plan. In the center of the eastern wall was the Holy Ark, the *Aron-Kodesh*, where reposed the sacred scrolls.

The Holy Ark was approached by four steps enclosed by a wrought-iron grille with a gate. Above the Ark burned the *ner tamid* ("the eternal light"), recalling the light of the Temple. When the doors of the Ark were closed, a maroon-velvet curtain was drawn over it; it was decorated with the star of David flanked by two lions of Judah, embroidered in gold thread.

To the right and immediately in front of the enclosed area of the Ark was the *chazn*'s lectern, where the officiating cantor chanted the prayers while facing the east wall.

The *bimmah* ("elevated platform") was at the center of the hall, surrounded by a wrought-iron railing and reached by three steps at each end. A long reader's table, covered with a gold-fringed velvet cloth, occupied half the area of the platform. On this table, facing the Ark, the scrolls were unrolled and the service conducted under the gobbé's baton.

The pews were individual mobile reading lecterns in front of long immobile benches, which lined the walls, and were placed in rows on both sides of the platform. The most coveted seats were on the eastern wall on either side of the Ark, facing the rest of the congregation. Near the door were two long tables, with benches, for the poor mendicants, who sat there through the service and waited for the *balabatem* to invite them for the Sabbath meal.

The curved staircase in the vestibule led to the upstairs hall, the women's section, which was half the size of the men's hall. It was filled with rows of stationary benches and individual, mobile pews. In the Romanian shtetl, women did not go to *shyll* every Saturday. They attended only during high holy days and on special festivals, for certain rituals and to say *yisker* ("the prayer for the dead").

The women's hall had two windows along two of the walls; a half wall and arched portal separated the hall from the balcony overlooking the men's section downstairs. The half wall was necessary to allow the women to hear and follow the prayers.

The most prestigious women's seats were on the balcony facing the Ark and along the eastern half wall. The balcony seats were most coveted.

It had been ascertained that the ladies' "hats" sometimes created a rather irresistible attraction and interfered with the undivided attention of some of the parishioners. To solve this embarrassment, a curtain was put up in front of the balcony.. Thus, while the women were still able to look down and keep up with the prayers, the curtain discouraged the excessive interest shown by some of the gentlemen for the ladies' headgear.

Near the entrance staircase sat the poor, ignorant old women who were not able to read even the Yiddish alphabet. Nodding their heads in unison, they would listen attentively as the *firzugern* (the woman who read out loud and translated for them) read the prayers, and, rocking back and forth, they repeated the last word, like a Greek chorus.

The other synagogues were one-storey rooms, less elaborate in style and décor but with the same floor plan. The women's section was on the same floor with the men's section, with a separate entrance and a half wall divider to enable the women to follow the prayer, yet assure the segregation of the sexes.

CHAPTER VII

Stefanesti, a Rabbinic Shtetl

1. The Rebbé's Court

Stefanesti was a *rabunnish* shtetl, the seat of the Stefanester *rebbé*, Abraham Matathias Friedman, affectionately called "Motitiuye". Being a *rabbunish* shtetl had put the town on the map and the townsfolk were very much aware of it. More than anything else, this had contributed to positive feelings about themselves; their hearts swelled with pride to remarks such as "Stefanesti? noch azoy, nu!" ("And how!").

In spite of this, the majority of the townspeople were not followers of the *rebbé*, whom they respected and revered. They tended to regard the *Hasidim* ("his followers"), and especially those of the *rebbé*'s immediate entourage, either as simpletons or as hypocritic knaves. Hero-worship and exaggerated piousness or extravagant mannerisms went against the grain of the independent spirit of the town. The *rebbé*'s "court" flourished, due to the constant stream of enthusiastic devotees who flocked around him. The merchants were not indifferent to the potential source of income provided by the *rebbé*'s court.

Rabbinic hereditary lineages were the closest claim to an élite among eastern European Jewry. Rabbinic families intermarried only among themselves, very much like royalty; they lived at "courts", where the *tzadik* ("saintly one") was surrounded by an inner circle of admiring disciples and a broad following, who used to come at least once a year to spend some festival at the court of their favorite *rebbé*.

Menahem Nahum of Stefanesti (1827–1869) was the third son of Israel of Ruzhin, who traced his lineage to the Ba'al Shem Tov, the founder of Hasidism, in the eighteenth century. The only son of Menahem Nahum was Abraham Matathias (1848–1933), who was seventeen-years-old when he inherited the court of Stefanesti, where he "reigned" for close to seventy years. His grandfather, Israel of Ruzhin, had established a magnificient court at Sadagora (Cernauti), in Bucovina, where he led an opulent life in the grand manner.

PLATE 1. Strada Stefan cel Mare (Main Street).

PLATE 2. Raspantie (Center of Town).

PLATE 3. Soba de terracota (Ceramic tiled fireplace — stove).

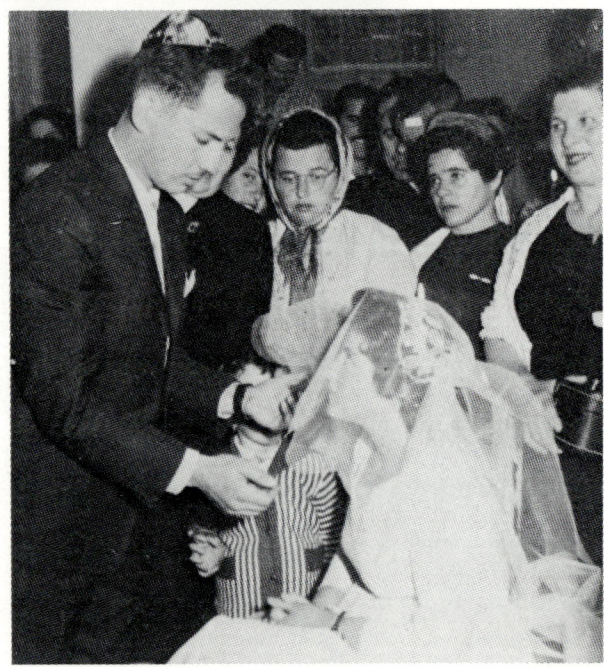

PLATE 4. Bedekn die Khalleh (Ceremony prior to wedding).

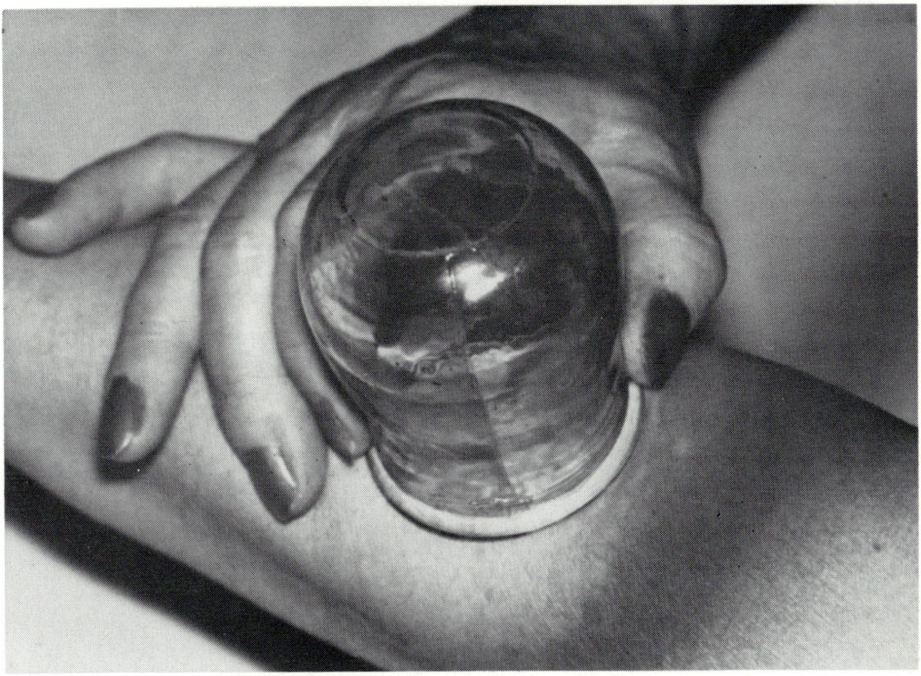

PLATE 5. Bankes — ventuze cupping.

PLATE 6. Rebbé's court Stefanesti.

PLATE 7. Rebbé and hasidim.

PLATE 8. Stefanester Rebbé.

PLATE 9. Hava Nagila.

PLATE 10. In Heyder (small boys studying in Hebrew school) charcoal sketch (G. Sternberg).

PLATE 11. Scoala Israelito Romana Narcisse Leven.

PLATE 12. Hebrew kindergarten class.

PLATE 13. Grade I and II class picture.

PLATE 13 (2)

PLATE 14. Diploma of Jewish–Romanian school First prize.

PLATE 15. Diploma of Jewish–Romanian school.

PLATE 16. Front cover of Sanatatea si Viata Fericita (paramedical journal).

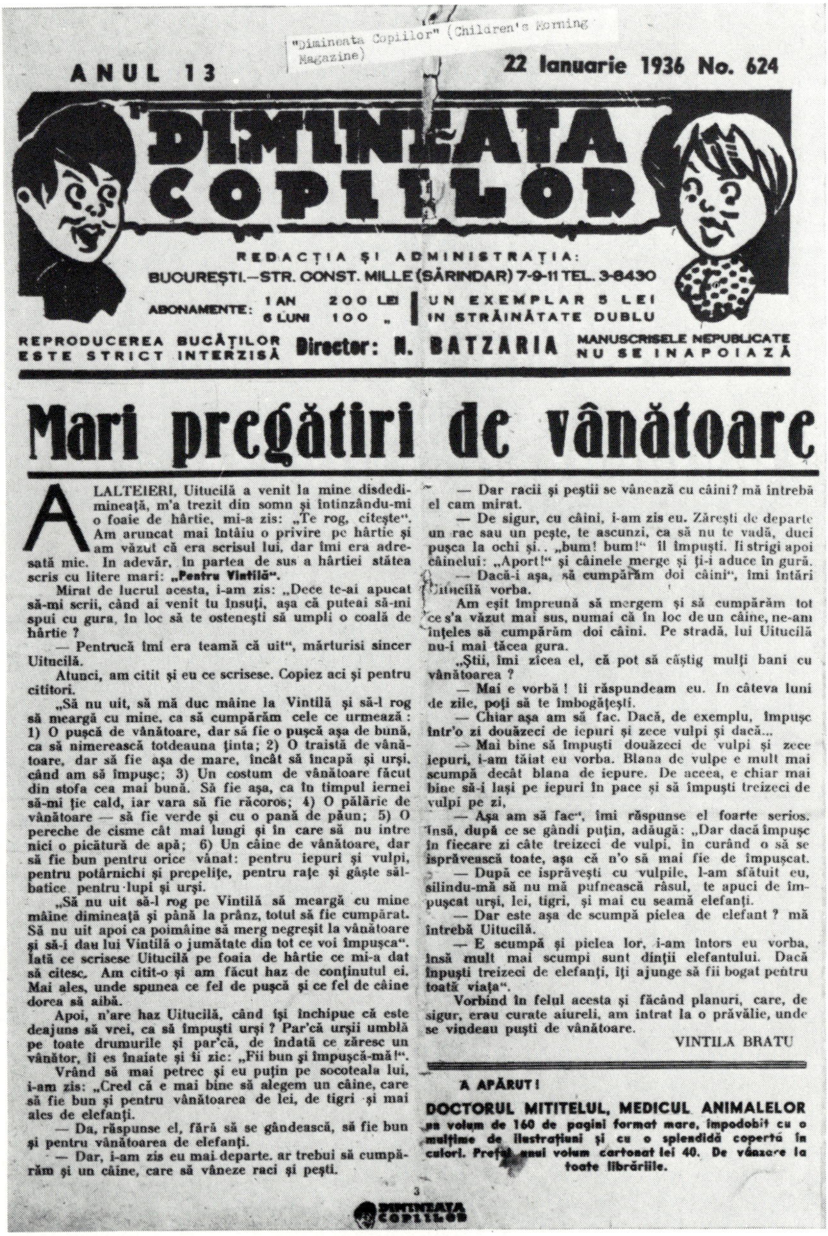

PLATE 16 (2). Children's Weekly.

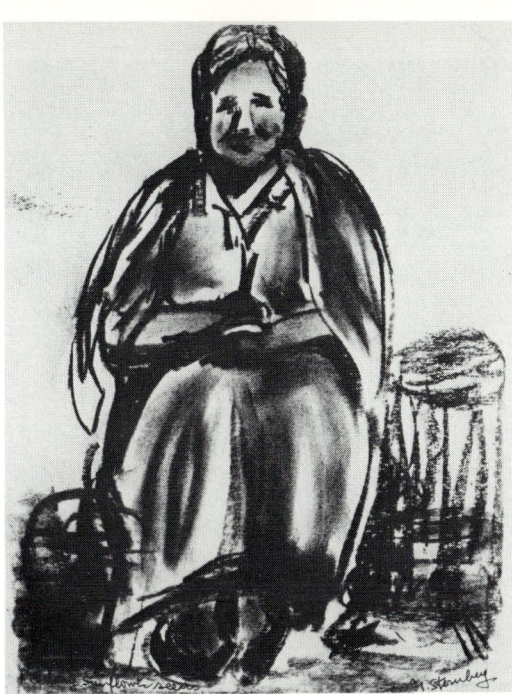

PLATE 17. The Pumpkin seeds vendor (charcoal sketch). (G. Sternberg)

קרן היסוד

KEREN - HAYESSOD

FONDUL DE RECLĂDIRE A PALESTINEI

No. 04945/15 Bucureşti 31 Decembrie 1925

D-lui Froim Wechsler, Ştefăneşti

Cu referire la chitanţa provizorie No. ...., ce v'a eliberat-o delegaţia n/

vă informăm că suma de Lei 1200 (Una mie două sute), ce aţi binevoit a o remite în contul contribuţiei d-voastre la KEREN-HAYESSOD pe anul 5685 (1924/1925), a intrat la noi.

Exprimându-vă mulţumirile noastre, vă rugăm să primiţi asigurarea deosebitei noastre stime,

COMITETUL CENTRAL KEREN HAYESSOD DIN ROMÂNIA

Secretar,

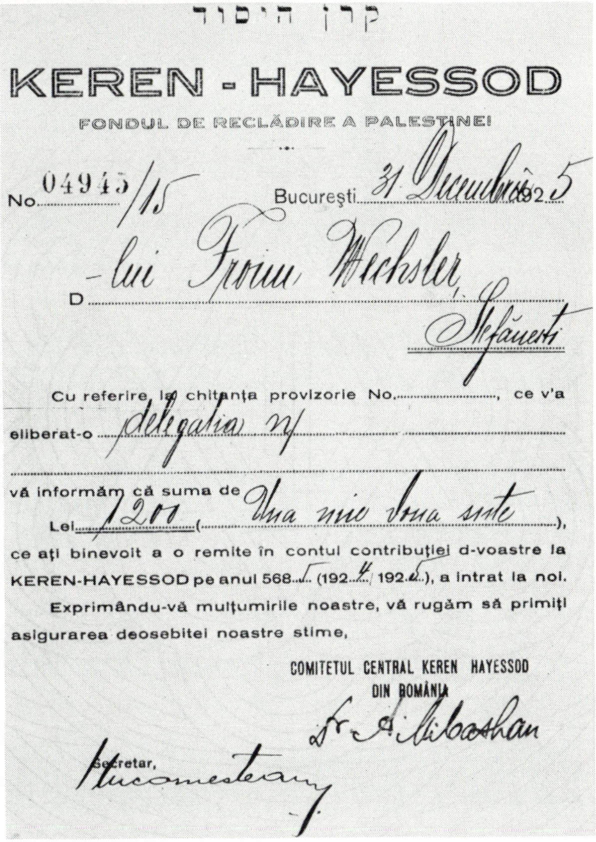

PLATE 18. Keren Hayessod (receipt for Zionist contribution).

PLATE 19.
Ketubba
(Kessibe),
marriage
contract.

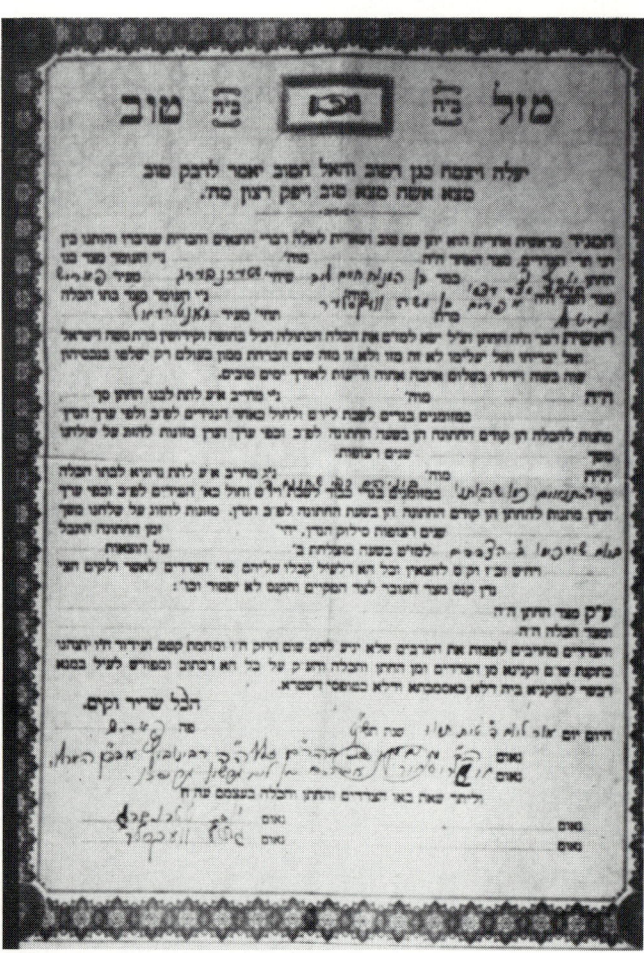

PLATE 20.
Gypsies setting
up camp.

In spite of his own inate modesty and ascetic life style, the Stefanester *rebbé* maintained the splendor into which he had been born, a virtual courtly baronial lifestyle, surrounded by a coterie of admirers.

The *hoyf* ("court") was situated in a small park, in itself a unique feature in the shtetl. The main building, in the neo-classic style, had a portico with six white columns. It was the most outstanding building of the rectangular inner court; other adjoining smaller buildings were the *kloys* or *shylhoyf* ("the synagogue"); three kitchens — one for milk, one for meat and one for passover; the stables for the four horses and elegant carriage; a private bath with a *mikveh*; and the *rebbetzin*'s quarters.

The interior of the main building was as impressive as the outside was imposing. From the portico, one entered a huge hall with painted frescoes and large brass-framed mirrors. To the right there was a door leading to the *rebbé*'s room where the *rebbé provet* ("granted audiences").

This, too, was a large room with elegant furniture, the walls lined with ancient leather-bound tomes, in glass-encased bookcases. Near the door, on a small table, one could leave a donation. Behind a large table, on a raised platform, there was the *rebbé*, seated on his "throne".

From this room a door led to the *rebbé*'s private *succah*, a greenhouse with various tropical plants growing all year; another door led to "the Messiah's room", where, on a round table in the center of the room, reposed a pipe and a silver-handled walking cane. These items were there, ready for the time when the Messiah would appear, which time the *rebbé* fervently awaited. So convinced was he of the imminent arrival of the Messiah that he held himself in constant readiness, and, when falling asleep, he would tell his servant to wake him up if by any chance he was asleep when the event occurred.

In the large hall, the *hasidim* were always milling about, awaiting their turn to see the *rebbé*. This was under the strict control of the *gabouem* ("secretaries and retainers"). At the door to the *rebbé*'s chamber, a gobbé ("secretary") sat at the desk supervising all activities. It was known that one had to *shmier* ("bribe") the secretary to obtain admittance to the rebbé. For a fee, the *gobbé* wrote a *kvitl* ("note") to be handed to the *rebbé*. The secretaries were consumate public-relations experts.

Some of the most lucrative items sought after at the *rebbé*'s court were the *mitbeyes* ("charms"), coins. The *rebbé* blessed the coins, which were subsequently cherished as good-luck charms. Many visitors to the *rebbé* brought valuable gifts from distant lands, fruit bowls carved of Carara marble, silver platters, crystal decanters, all exhibited in the rooms.

Seated behind the large table, the *rebbé*'s small charismatic figure was, from all accounts, awe-inspiring. His long, white beard, kindly look and ascetic mien gave him the appearance of an overgrown child. "Huge eyes, sheer kindness and wisdom of the famous *rebbé*," says Victor Rusu in his description of this saintly man.*

His modesty and simplicity were renowned as was his sincerity. He never looked into a mirror. He was not what was called a "miracle *rebbé*" but rather a wise, saintly man, to whom the simple poor as well as the wealthy businessmen, Jews as well as Gentiles, flocked for counsel and advice.

They came with problems, some serious, some impossible to solve and some bordering on the absurd. One American lady visiting the town went to the *rebbé* because "she had two sons and wanted a girl more than anything else". The respondent who accompanied the lady to the audience related that a fleeting smile appeared on the *rebbé*'s face as he read the *kvitl* with the unusual request. Throughout the audience, she kept pinching her companion's arm and whispering to her, "Tell him, I want a girl, tell him." The women stood near the door at a respectful distance awaiting the blessing. Her wish was fulfilled when she returned to America. (Wasn't that a miracle?).

Though the *rebbé* contented himself with living a pious life, devoting himself to prayer, the members of his coterie were concerned with more worldly matters and manipulated his life in spite of his own modest preferences.

It was this gang that engineered the *rebbé*'s divorce from his first wife. They were distressed that, after more than ten years of married life, their *rebbé* had not produced a son and heir, and began machinations to instigate a divorce. He refused, although, according to Judaic law, the husband had this right. Quoting one of the respondents: "They tricked the *rebbetzn* ("*rebbe*'s wife") into an impossible situation."

The *rebbé* used to go every year to visit his father's grave in Iassy on the twenty-eighth of *Kislev*, in mid-winter. His wife would accompany him, and usually remained in the big city to buy new clothes. One year, a few days after the return of the *rebbé*, the inner clique locked the gates of the court and would not allow the *rebbetzn*'s carriage to enter, much as the coachman banged and

---

* *Alef Bet*, Publisher Federatia Comunitatilor Evreesti din Romania Bucharest 1976, p. 134.

Stefanesti, a Rabbinic Shtetl 121

begged. A kindly gentile neighbor allowed her to sit up all night in his house, and on this manufactured pretext the *rebbé* was forced to "put her aside". Having "spent the night in a gentile's house", she was no longer considered worthy of the *rebbé*. The *rebbé* married a widow with two children. He never had any children of his own.

Wishing to assure himself of an heir, he brought to his court and informally adopted a nephew, "Nuhemunie", a brilliant man who had obtained a degree in philosophy from one of the western universities and who tried to become involved in community affairs. He was at one time the president of *Keren Hayesod*, the Zionist organization collecting funds for Palestine, and was much respected in town. He unfortunately contracted tuberculosis and died.

2. A Glimpse at Hasidism

The religious festivals were special events at the *rebbé*'s court, attended by his followers, who used to spend the holy days with their *rebbé*. Passover and the fall holy days were especially memorable. The *seder* was celebrated with great pomp: "The table was set with crystals, gold and silver, and with a gold and silver crown, placed at the center of the table, said to be prepared for the Messiah," said one respondent. It was, however, a quiet and dignified affair.

Simchas Torah was a happening at the *rebbé*'s court. Everyone took turns with the hakkufes (hakkafot), the ceremonial procession with the Torahs. The *rebbé* used a special miniature *Torah* to fit his frail figure, for the normal scrolls were deemed too heavy for him. After a few glasses of wine, the *hasidim* began to dance and sing and hop on the tables in frenetic abandon. The *rebbé*, however, did not partake in these antics, satisfied to be much more moderate in his own communion with God.

After the meals, the *rebbé* blessed the food and the fun began when everyone rushed to grab some of the *shirayim*, which were leftovers from the *rebbé*'s plate that had been blessed by the *rebbé*. They would stretch over one another's heads, knock off hats, fight, like women in a bargain basement, to grab a morsel of the blessed food. The *rebbé* did not eat much. Grabbing *shirayim* was one of the most coveted events of a visit to the *rebbé* at this time. (The expression "Don't leave me any *shirayim*" was used by mothers when children left food on the plate.)

The *hasidim* and the *rebbé*'s entourage followed him whenever he travelled anywhere in town. Any small trip was an expedition, with the *rebbé* in his carriage, drawn by four handsome horses, followed by other carriages and often escorted by soldiers on horseback. One respondent, whose father owned a mill, recalled the *rebbé*'s yearly visit to the mill, accompanied by his entire entourage. No one but the *rebbé*'s own servants were allowed to touch the wheat or the flour the *rebbé* bought, and only with their very own utensils and sacks. The respondent, a small child at the time, was blessed by the *rebbé*, who put his hands on the child's head and rewarded him with a silver five-*lei* coin. For the child, this was a memorable event.

The *hasidim*'s garb was reminiscent of the dress of the eighteenth-century Russian nobility. They wore long beards and side curls, unlike most of the men in town, who were clean-shaven. They wore *shtramls* ("mink-trimmed hats") and long, black-satin kaftans.

The women were very much in the background, for this was exclusively a man's world. Married women wore wigs over their clean-shaven heads. They always wore somber colored dresses with long sleeves and high necklines of the best silks and velvets and wore gold and silver jewelry.

The Stefanester *rebbé*'s court was reputed for the certification given to the ritual slaughterers. As one respondent put it: "Like a Harvard degree in the field." These diplomas were granted after meticulous training under the supervision of one very much respected local *schoyched* ("ritual slaughterer") whose skills were renowned.

The *hasidic* movement began in the eighteenth century in southeast Poland. Its founder was the Ba'al Shem Tov. It was said to be a revolt against the excessive intellectualism of the current learned leadership. It gained momentum as a reaction to the various Messianic currents of that period, when false Messiahs had convulsed the masses of eastern European Jews who, in a state of despair, were searching for answers. The term *hasid* had originally implied a pious Jew who rigorously maintained all religious commandments. The Ba'al Shem Tov had taught that prayer was to be offered only with a joyous heart. He rejected the elitist concept. Not everyone can be a scholar — one can aspire to a better life in song and joy. One does not chase away morbidity with a stick in the dark but with light and dance. This prompted the outpouring of one's innermost feelings in song and dance, often inducing a state of ecstasy.

According to Martin Buber, the basic philosophy of *hasidism* was "a worship through corporeality".* One was able to express his emotions through singing and especially through swaying body movements while praying. "The dialectical relationship between matter

---

* *Hasidism*, Martin Buber, Philosophical Library, N.Y., 1949.

and spirit was the relationship between the *tzadik* and his followers,"*
and this ecstasy was only possible when worshipping in common. By
means of a communion with God and devotions, man may be able
to uplift himself.

The image the shtetl had of the *hasid*, however, was one of fanaticism leading to excesses. This fanaticism was also believed to be prone to charlatanry, attracting the gullible, who were also the most vulnerable. The excessive claims made by some of the *hasidim* about their *rebbés* who worked miracles or claimed supernatural healing powers were encouraged by certain *rebbés* who attracted flocks of gullible followers.

The Yiddish sense of humor recognized its people's shortcomings and laughed at its people's foibles. This resulted in countless rebbé anecdotes. Respect for the *rebbé*, and admonition for anyone attempting to abuse this respect, was expressed in the saying that one must stand up when the *rebbé* passed by — but the *rebbé* must not pass by too often.

One anecdote illustrating the often absurd claims made by *hasidim* tells of two devotees who were bragging to each other about the miraculous powers of their own *rebbé*. One said that, should his *rebbé* be caught in a rain, he could perform a miracle whereby it would rain in front of him, it would rain behind him, but it would not rain where he happened to be walking. Unimpressed, the other hasid replied: "That's nothing, when my *rebbé* is caught on the road on a Friday eve and Sabbath is approaching, he makes it be Sabbath on one side, Sabbath on the other side, but where the *rebbé* rides, it is still Friday."

The Stefanester *rebbé* was known to discourage improbable claims. His most frequent remark was, "May Gold help." One of his *hasidim* insisted that the *rebbé* never said "God will help" but "May God help." He did not pose as a miracle healer nor a supreme scholar, but had gained renown through his piety and sincerity.

In Israel, where his remains were transported after the Second World War, there is a yearly celebration of his *yartzeit* ("the anniversary of his death"), when *hasidim* and former Stefanester gather to pay homage to this saintly man's memory.

---

* *Hasidism*, Arieh Rubinstein: Leon Amiel Publishers, N.Y., 1975.

CHAPTER VIII

Milestones

Birth, marriage and death, the three major signposts in a person's life, were the highlights, not only in the life span of the individual concerned, but to their family and to the community at large.

1. Birth

The child came into a world ready to receive it with love and great hopes. Regardless of family status, pregnancy was considered a blessing, a sign of God's grace. Barrenness was a curse. After ten years of a childless marriage it was a sufficiently valid reason for a husband to divorce his wife. Women went to the *rebbé* to petition for a child.

The prenatal period was fraught with dangers for mother and infant each with its own counteracting antidote. The pregnant woman, responsible for another human life, was pampered, her every whim catered to. Her cravings, no matter how outlandish, were fulfilled for fear of a *mopl* ("miscarriage"), deemed a tragedy. Her dreams, taken as omens, became guiding precepts. Unlike neighboring peasant women who worked in the field till the last moment, the pregnant shtetl woman was not allowed to lift heavy weights or exert herself in any way. She was treated like a raw egg. In spite of advice in such journals as *Sanatatea*, superstitions were taken for granted. Throwing anything at or after a pregnant woman would mark the child; the same repercussions were the result of unfulfilled cravings. Cherries and strawberries were seen as culprits, since red birthmarks were common. (*angiomas*) A cherry-like mark on the lip of a baby was supposedly the result of the mother's craving for cherries.

It was also inadvisable for a pregnant woman to look upon a misshapen or very ugly person for fear of the defect being imprinted on the foetus. Should this inadvertently have happened, to counteract the potential harm, she was supposed to spit three times. A brown mark on the leg of one young woman was believed to have been caused by the mother's being frightened by a rat. Music and pleasant surroundings, however, though a luxury in the shtetl, were advised. It was believed that if the mother listened to music during pregnancy (regardless of the quality of music) the baby, too, would hear it and would presumably be musical.

There is no doubt that a son was deemed more important than a daughter, as evinced by the elaborate ritual at the birth of a boy, compared with the simple name giving for a girl. For the father, the birth of a son represented the perpetuation of the family name and, it was hoped, the opportunity for vicarious personal fulfilments. For both parents a son was the *kaddish* the one who, by pronouncing the prayer for the deceased, was to enhance their future life. This, girls were not able to do. Pragmatically, too, and fitting in with the cultural patterns, finding a dowry for a daughter was a worry, while a son was a trump card.

Births took place exclusively in the home. During the first week after birth, the room where the mother was lying-in had to be protected from evil spirits, especially from Lillit, envious of mothers and known to be a baby snatcher. *Kimpet-tzetls*, ("amulets") sheets of paper, about four inches by six inches, with Hebrew inscriptions, were pinned at doors and windows as well as at the mother's bed and the baby's cradle, to ward off evil.

The birth of a boy immediately started a series of preparations for the forthcoming celebration, the *bris* ("circumcision"). This was an event in the family. Invitations were sent announcing the birth of a son and the date of the celebration. The *bris* took place on the eighth day after birth, in the home. This was the ritual that ushered the child into the congregation. It was performed by the *mohel*, the circumciser, in most shtetlech the ritual slaughterer, who had elaborate training in this field.

The mother was not allowed at the circumcision ceremony. The *kvottern* ("godmother") took the baby from the mother, and brought it to the *kvotter* ("godfather"), who handed it to the *sondek* ("the person holding the baby during the operation"), usually a grandfather or uncle. A piece of cotton dipped in brandy was put in the baby's mouth. The father pronounced the blessing and the name of the child. After the operation, the *mohel* bandaged the cut area with gauze dipped in alcohol and a drop of wine was placed on the baby's lips. The *mohel's* (or rabbi's) prayer was: "May the baby grow in vigor of mind and body to a love of Torah, the marriage canopy and to a life of good deeds." *Mazeltov* ("good luck") was wished all around and the baby was returned to the mother. This was followed by feasting and merriment and pledges of charity donations.

For childbirth, the poor families relied entirely on the *bubbeh* ("midwife"); the middle class called the doctor, who delivered the baby, assisted by the *bubbeh*. The *bubbeh* used to come in daily during the first two or three weeks after birth. She knew all the proper foods the post-partum mother had to eat to produce a healthy supply of milk; she reassured the young mother if anything seemed to worry her, bathed the baby and was an expert at swaddling the infant. "*Bubbeh* Hayeh took pride in swaddling a baby so tight, you could throw it in the air like a tightly wrapped parcel," one respondent wrote. For bathing the infant the *bubbeh* twisted the cloth diaper around her thumb and unceremoniously scrubbed the baby's mouth, to the horror of the younger mothers, whose concepts of hygiene she ignored. In case of a baby girl, she had one additional task to perform: she pierced the baby's ears. Without much ado, with an ordinary needle and some red thread (to ward off evil), she pierced the ears on the first day. There did not seem to be any problems with infections.

The mother remained in bed for two or three weeks after giving birth, pampered and not permitted to do household chores. She abstained from sexual intercourse for six weeks, since Judaic law prohibits the woman from having intercourse after the menses until she has cleansed herself at the *mikva* ("the ritual bath pool"), at which time she is considered *kosher* for her husband. This ablution is part of all ritual cleansing. The ritual consists of bathing before submerging herself in the *mikva* adjoining the public bathhouse. The attendant, pouring three bucketsfull of water over her head, pronounced her *kosher*.

The *krishma-leinen* ("reading of the prayer *Kriat-Shema*") is one rite associated with the birth of a boy that has not been preserved by contemporary Jewish communities. During the week before circumcision the newborn child was considered exposed to dangers of evil spirits, and as protection, Psalms were read, especially on the day and night before the *bris*. On the day before, the *rebbeh* and his *heider* ("Jewish school for boys") students went to the home of the newborn and read *krishma* at the baby's cradle to ward off evil and bring good luck to the infant. After the reading of the prayers the father distributed to each little boy a slice of honey cake and a *ponchekl* ("S-shaped honey-dough cookie"). The more prosperous the family, the more lavish the give-away of sweets, and the more children gathered. Children appeared in droves; they seemed to smell a *krishma-leinen* from the other end of town. Girls were excluded from the ritual but used to sneak into the crowd to get the sweets, since a piece of cake was a rare luxury, especially among the poorer working class. They would stuff their pockets and stretch out the hand for more, asking for "one for my little brother at home." To prevent unequal distribution, one of the family children was posted near the father to chalk mark the sleeves of those who had already received their loot.

This illustrates how the functional importance of a ritual within a community survives only as long as the need is there. In American Jewish communities, the underlying assumptions as well as the community needs have rendered this, formerly important custom, obsolete.

In contrast to the festivities associated with the birth of a boy, the birth of a girl was passed over with little fanfare. On the Sabbath following the birth, the father was called to the *Torah* in the synagogue, where he stated the name of the baby as well as the names of the mother and father. It was customary to offer a *gleizl schnaps* ("brandy and honey cake or sponge cake") to the congregation. and that was that.

According to Judaic tradition, children were named after deceased persons, to honor and remember them. It was forbidden to name a child after a living person. There was a tacit belief that the name carried with it the potential attributes of the namesake. The tendency was to name after immediate family. In exceptional cases, when strangers were honored, a special bond was established between the two families, with specific mutual responsibilities. In one reported case, a pregnant mother saw a recently deceased neighbor in a dream. This was taken as an omen to name the child after this person, with the family's permission.

In Stefanesti, as elsewhere in Romanian towns, Hebrew names underwent metamorphoses. The Hebrew name was given in the synagogue but on the birth certificate the name was modernized beyond recognition. The name by which the child was called often retained but a remote resemblance to the original, and sometimes only the first letter remained. Thus, "Moshe" became "Maurice" or "Marcel"; "Pearl" became "Pauline"; "Gytl" became "Ghizella", and so forth. French and German names enjoyed special vogue: Charlotte, Betina, Adolph, Freidrich. Typical peasant names, however, usually associated with the names of maids or janitors, were unacceptable: Gheorghe, Maria, Marghioala, Costache, were frowned upon as too *goyish* ("gentile") and, hence too lowly.

A further metamorphosis was the tendency of both Yiddish and Romanian for diminutives by adding a suffix, which was ultimately retained. "Moshe" became "Moyshelica", called "Lica" for short; "Anna" became "Anutza", shortened to "Nutza".

In many societies the first born enjoyed special privileges. Although this was not the case in the Romanian shtetl, the first born son, in accordance with ancient Judaic rites, incurred some obligations, but also enjoyed some rights. The ceremony of *Pidyon Haben* ("redemption of the first born"), performed four weeks after the birth of a first born son, harked back to the Temple days in Jerusalem, when the first born son was dedicated to serve in the Temple, unless the father redeemed him. This ceremony was performed with great satisfaction and pride by the father of a first born son. For this occasion a *cohen* ("a descendant of the priestly tribe") was invited to stand in for the priests of yore. The baby was placed on a silver tray alongside a bowl containing a sum equivalent to five *shekels*, which was about twenty *lei* in Romanian currency. In the presence of friends and relatives, the father was asked whether he wanted the son or the money. The ceremony of redemption of the first born was followed by eating and drinking and merrymaking.

Infant mortality as well as some congenital diseases seemed to run in families. One way to deceive the angel of death was to "sell" the child of such an unfortunate family to one where children were healthy and thrived. This did not change the status of the child thus sold, who continued to live in the parental home. As modern medicine was advancing, this custom was becoming obsolete even among the more ignorant levels of society.

Babies were breast-fed; the concept of bottle feeding was alien to shtetl mentality. A *biberon* ("baby's bottle") was perceived as artificial. In cases where the mother did not have enough milk or was unable to breast feed, a wet nurse was hired. She lived in the home and was fed well to insure a high quality of milk for the baby. In some cases another mother whose baby was being weaned at the time would nurse the baby; the children were then referred to as *frate de cruce* ("cross brothers").

It was firmly believed that babies did not cry without reason, and whatever the cause of the crying, the breast was used as a pacifier. Rocking babies was a constant chore and either an older child or the mother would be busy rocking while they slept. The least cry would elicit the solicitude of an adult, always within earshot and always ready to cuddle and love the baby. Babies slept in the cradle until there was a new baby in the family or until the cradle was too small.

Considering the high rate of infant mortality, it is not surprising that mothers lived in perpetual anxiety; the slightest fever or intestinal disorder was dreaded as a sign of serious illness.

Up to the 1930s, babies were swaddled, in the belief that this would assure straight bones. With better scientific information and as the importance of sunshine and good nutrition were learned, swaddling slowly disappeared. It has been suggested that the early restraint imposed by tight swaddling resulted in a more submissive personality, one more willing to accept authority.

At about six months, babies were fed cream of wheat, and gradually bread dunked in warm milk. Mothers of the lower class were known to masticate bits of food, which they fed to the babies. This the middle-class mothers considered unhygienic and even revolting.

Breast-feeding continued till about one year of age or when the baby's teeth created technical problems for the mother. Weaning was avoided during summer months, since lack of refrigeration made cow's milk or other foods much riskier than breast-feeding. The older the child, the more attached it became, and the more difficult to wean. To repulse the baby, quinine was smeared around the nipple, or a black brush placed in the mother's bosom to frighten the baby away.

Small-pox vaccinations were given at the end of the first year, usually before or after weaning, to avoid the two traumatic experiences from occurring simultaneously.

Hygienic methods of child-rearing were being introduced and gradually filtered down to all levels of society. It was known, for instance, that kissing, especially on the lips, was a potential bacteria-transmitting factor. Strangers would sometimes, lovingly and with best intentions, try to kiss babies. As a gentle hint to these well-meaning strangers, mothers embroidered babies' bibs with the inscription *Nu Ma Sarutati* ("Do not kiss me"). This did not always work.

Corporal punishment was the accepted method of discipline from earliest years. Children were slapped, paddled or had their ears yanked for the least disobedience. In some families it was the mother's heavy hand that delivered the lesson and in some it was the father's, depending on circumstances. Since most fathers were present at all times, they shared equally in disciplining the children. Thoughtful parents refrained from disciplining in public, to avoid embarrassment for the child; others were not so discriminating.

Among the working class, battered children were not uncommon, as frustrated parents would *oys lozn dus hartz* ("let out their hearts") by hitting the child indiscriminately. Mothers were known to regret the hurt they caused the child and tried to compensate by caresses and kisses. To the child, these inconsistencies were bewildering and diminished the value of the punishment. A

Romanian poem based on this theme described the mother's anguish and regret as she finds the little one sobbing uncontrollably in bed. Full of remorse, she picks up the child and, "enfolded by the candle's soft glow mother and child fall asleep in a hugging embrace".

The loss of baby teeth was looked upon as the end of early childhood. Children were assured that this was a sign of growing up and that the new teeth, brought by a little mouse, would be much better and never fall out. The old tooth was placed under the pillow and the child repeated three times:

Maizole, maizole, gib mir an eizern tzoon,
Na dir a beinern tzoon.

"Little mousie, give me an iron tooth,
Here, you have a bone tooth."

From an early age, girls helped their mothers with house chores even in homes where there were servants. Little girls liked to busy themselves in the kitchen and help with the younger children. In middle-class homes this amounted to "playing grown up" and transition from play to work was imperceptible. In working-class homes, the burden of responsibility thrown on children at too young an age resulted in an early maturity beyond their age. In many cases young women looked forward to marriage as an escape from the *ol* ("yoke", "duty") imposed by the responsibilities of the parental home.

An even more pronounced difference existed between the lot of a middle-class boy and his working-class analogue. For most middle-class boys, education and eventually a professional career were part of parental aspirations. Consequently, an interest in intellectual pursuits was deliberately fostered. Reading, debating, sports and involvement in youth clubs occupied most of their free time. Card playing was frowned upon but enjoyed popularity. At this age, preoccupation with girls and incipient pairing off was common. All youth in the shtetl swam in the summer and went sledding in winter.

In contrast, working-class boys were put to work at an early age, either apprenticing for some craft or working in stores as salesmen. During weekdays there was no loitering or idling in the streets; everyone was busy working.

While the major preoccupation of the teenage girl was courtship and eventual marriage, the boy was usually concerned with plans for his future occupation. Boys followed sports scores, played on the football team and developed a team spirit. Girls spent most of their time at home or in small groups, gossiping and confiding in one another. They formed cliques strictly according to age group.

They met in each others' homes where they knitted, sewed, embroidered. Those who did not study were automatically ostracized from the group as unworthy.

Dating was unknown. Social activities were group- rather than couple-oriented, although coupling off was common at this stage, often against parental consent. Couples known to be "in love" were teased and were the butt of gossip. As a rule, boys and girls met in groups at the youth clubs.

The *Bar Mitzvah* is the ceremony whereby, at the age of thirteen, a boy is officially admitted into the congregation as an adult. In the Romanian shtetl, this was not considered a momentous event, for the boy or for the family. (The custom was not mentioned in the Bible, and therefore was not deemed too important. It only appears in passing in the *Talmud*).

Customs and mores were weighed depending on how they fitted in with existing needs within the community as well as the needs of the individual. Conferring adult status on a thirteen-year-old did not correspond to the reality of community needs. It did not compare in significance with the birth of a son, marriage or the loss of a member of the community.

During the 1930s an increased interest was shown in this event. Printed invitations were sent out to family and friends and parties were arranged. The *Bar Mitzvah* boy received gifts (fountain pens and books were favorites) and his parents gave him his first prayer shawl and set of philacteries. The event, however, was not the extravaganza it has become in America.

On the Sabbath, the Monday or the Thursday after his date of birth, the boy was called to the *Torah* at the synagogue. He recited the passage he had learned at *heyder* and was subsequently counted as an adult in the *minyan*, which was the quorum of ten Jews required for public prayer. He was expected to put on *tefillen* ("philacteries") every morning and observe all commandments. These observances were inversely proportional to the level of secular education of the boy and of the family. The *Bar Mitzvah* symbolized the beginning of maturity for the boy, who henceforth was responsible for his own deeds. (Until this turning point, the father was accountable for his son's behavior.)

There was no equivalent rite of passage for girls entering puberty. Information about the menses (which usually occurred when the girl was between twelve- and fourteen-years-old) were haphazard. Girls were informed only at the time it occurred, without any ceremony; mothers instructed them in the hygienic techniques.

Adolescence was not associated with any problems such as

delinquency or with any forms of debauchery. Within the authoritarian framework of shtetl society, young people did not think that they knew everything. They acknowledged parental superiority and decision-making prerogatives. Parents did not abdicate their responsibilities. They sacrificed everything for their children's welfare but did not fail to point this out to the children at all times. Parents and children had one aim: to prepare for the future, to earn a living.

Within the working-class milieu, there was no adolescence as such, since children were channelled early into working. Earning a living, still synonymous with covering the bare necessities of life, did not permit the luxury of much else.

Attitudes towards sex were puritanical. Information on the subject was left entirely to chance. Boys learned from older boys; girls were expected to be pure and remained virtually ignorant. This in spite of the available information in journals and magazines, since articles usually described the bodily functions but did not spell out the basics of sex. Books such as *Lady Chatterley's Lover* were available in translation, the titillating passages marked and avidly read. A perusal of the journal *Sanatatea* shows that the subject of sex was treated rationally in terms of mental hygiene and physiologically, with explicit diagrams. In polite society, however, the topic was taboo.

Among the respondents (all in their forties and fifties), only oblique allusions were made to the topic, which, even in retrospect, seemed too embarrassing to broach. Salacious jokes or bawdy language were relegated to the lowest classes, the *malul Basheului* ("on the banks of the Basheu").

2. Education

With the building of the Jewish schools at the end of the nineteenth century, conditions in the Romanian shtetlech were radically changed. Schools were no doubt the most potent factor of acculturation. Before the first World War, little boys were still going to *chedder* from early morning to late at night, until they entered first grade at the age of seven. The education of girls was much more secular and depended entirely on the socioeconomic level of the family. During the 1920s two nursery schools were founded in Stefanesti. One was the Romanian *gradinita* ("little garden"); the other was the *gan a yeladim* ("children's garden"), which was organized by the Jewish community. Most parents sent both boys and girls between the ages of four and six to one of these two nursery schools.

The *chedder*, where little boys were taught by a *rebbeh* the *alef-bet* ("alphabet"), existed concurrently. Some parents preferred to have the *rebbeh* come to the house for an hour of lessons. When they entered public school, boys continued to go to *chedder* after school for an hour of Yivre ("Hebrew") or Bible studies with the *rebbeh*, although Hebrew was taught to both boys and girls in the Jewish school.

The *gan* was housed in the building owned by the Jewish community; the community was also responsible for the hiring and salaries of the teacher, one assistant and the janitor. Hebrew was the language of communication, in what amounted to a virtual immersion course, for children who had never before been exposed to this language. *Sfardit*, the modern Hebrew pronunciation, was used instead of the older *Ashkenazi-Lushn Koydesh* ("sacred tongue") of the parents. With charts depicting the Hebrew alphabet and pictures of familiar objects on the walls, the child adsorbed the language as well as the alphabet. All songs, poems and games were in Hebrew. A dolls house, building blocks ("*kubiot*"), crayons, plasticine were part of daily activities. The grand finale of the year was a *serbare* ("celebration") when plays, dances and recitations by children (all in Hebrew) provided entertainment for parents and relatives. This was the basis for fresh roots and profound ties with a new culture. This is where Zionism was planted.

The Jewish school, *Scoala Israelito-Romana-Narcisse-Level* had been built in Stefanesti in 1893 under the auspices of the Alliance Israelite Universelle, whose efforts were directed to the fostering of the emancipation and moral progress of the Jews. It was subsequently taken over by the local Jewish community. Its well-intended aim — to improve the conditions and status of the shtetl Jews — posed an indirect danger to Jewish life. It was the most potent agent of acculturation in the Romanian shtetl, for by elevating the Romanian language to a prestiguous level it did not previously enjoy, it also encouraged the replacement of Yiddish with Romanian as the daily language.

Compulsory education as enforced by the Romanian government consisted of four primary grades; students started school at the age of seven. There were two Romanian primary schools, one for boys and one for girls, supported by the state. Most Jewish parents, however, sent their children to the Jewish school, which was mixed.

In school, emphasis was placed on rote memory; understanding was secondary. This was based on the conviction that the brain "was improved by exercise" (provided by memorizing). The basis of the curriculum was memorization of long poems. At the end of each school year, a commission consisting of teachers from the Romanian schools tested the children for promotion to the next grade. At the end of the four years, a final examination granted the student a certificate that enabled him to apply for high-school entrance.

School hours were from 8:00 am to 4:00 pm with two hours for midday lunch, taken at home. The first two hours of the morning were for Hebrew, and the second for Romanian. In the afternoon, one hour was devoted to each. The two fifteen-minute recreation periods were devoted to play in the school yard. Since Romanian schools were closed on Sundays and open on Saturday mornings till one, the procedure was reversed in the Jewish schools (closed on Saturdays) where children attended school Sunday mornings. Children were urged to speak Hebrew during recess, to play games and sing Hebrew songs. Nationalistic sentiments were overtly emphasized. With parent approval, prestige for Hebrew and Romanian were built up while disdain for Yiddish grew.

Holidays were observed according to both the Romanian and Jewish calendars, and homework was amply provided to keep students busy during any free time away from school.

No opportunity was lost in maintaining an awareness of Jewish life, and emphasizing the Zionist, nationalistic concepts rather than the religious traditions, which were considered fully looked after in the home. Personalities such as Theodor Hertzl or Lord Balfour were revered, their anniversaries religiously commemorated. All the well-known Yiddish poets and writers, such as H. N. Bialik, I. L. Peretz, were presented as national heroes to be emulated. Children were urged to excel in learning according to Judaic tradition.

The Romanian curriculum, on the other hand, tugged away from this deliberate identification with Judaism. Confusion for the child, if not a split personality were often the result. This sentiment was not helped by the almost blind admiration for all that came from *strainatate* ("foreign lands," that is the west), a feeling shared by the neighboring Romanian culture.

The curriculum consisted of the usual three Rs both in Romanian and in Hebrew. The Romanian program included reading skills, history, geography and a strong emphasis on memorizing long poems; Hebrew reading and writing skills as well as spelling and grammar; and readings in Hebrew of the Torah, the blessings for the various festivals, were drilled in.

School enrolment was highest in the first grade and gradually diminished through the four years. It was not unusual to cram one hundred children in one classroom for the first grade; by the fourth grade, only forty children graduated. There was a high rate of dropouts among the working-class children due to parental indifference and the demands on the child's time by chores in the home.

Classroom discipline and respect for authority were strictly enforced. Boys were seated on one side of the center isle, girls on the other side. All stood up smartly when the teacher entered the classroom. Corporal punishment was meted out by the teachers according to the severity of the offence. A minor offence earned a slap of the ruler on the outstretched palm. Disrupting order was a much more serious matter; the pupil was sent to stand in the corner, facing the wall. The embarrassment seemed sufficient to prevent further disruptions. Strapping with leather belts or being made to stand on the knees on sacks of dried corncorbs were things of the past.

Athletics were neglected, although there were some attempts to have periods of calisthenics for five minutes every morning. Recess was the only time children had the opportunity to run, play games and engage in any form of socializing.

Caligraphy and drawing were painstakingly taught and highly prized. In both cases the emphasis was on copying skills rather than on originality. Girls were taught sewing and embroidery, which were exhibited at the end of the year. Boys did not receive any manual training since, not surprisingly, the merchant regarded any manual labor with disdain, and the working-class parents transmitted their own skills to the sons as a matter of necessity.

One innovation implemented by the Jewish community during the 1930s was the distribution of free milk to all children during recess. The bagel vendor would appear at recess with his wicker basket full of hot bagels, which children bought with their pocket money.

At the end of the school year, the distribution of diplomas and prizes was cause for bickering and animosities among ambitious parents, each claiming that their child deserved the highest honor.

Compulsory education ended with the four primary grades. Only about five per cent of those finishing the primary grades (at age eleven) continued on to high school, which consisted of seven or eight years (depending on the whims of the department of education, for it must be remembered that, like France, Romania had a rigid, highly centralized educational system.) Of those who reached the baccalaureat (high-school matriculations), most continued their studies in one of the faculties at the university. The point of selectivity was at the end of the primary school, with high-school entrance examinations. Girls, few of whom reached the baccalaureat, rarely pursued university studies.

Parents wishing to provide high-school education for their children faced a serious financial burden. In the shtetlech there were no high schools and many parents found the expense for yearly lodgings beyond their means. Some considered children of eleven and twelve — especially girls — too young to be sent away from parental care and supervision. The problem was facilitated for those fortunate to have relatives in the larger centers. The alternative was for the children to study *"in particular"* (privately) at home with tutors, to pass examinations at the high schools in the larger centers, either in Botosani or in Iassy. In Botosani there was the boys' *Liceul Laurean* and the girls' *Luceul Carmen Sylva.* There was also a commercial high school and an equivalent training school for girls.

Studying "in particular" was not unlike a tutorial system whereby a few students were taught by one or two private tutors. Students were grouped according to grade, never more than six to eight students per year. In contrast to the rigid segregation at the high schools, boys and girls attended these courses together.

The teachers were themselves university students. This was possible since Romanian universities did not require daily attendance at courses and enrolled students needed only present themselves at examination time. By tutoring, they were able to support themselves and frequently, their families.

In the lower grades one tutor sufficed for all subjects; as the courses became more complex, tutors specialized in different areas of study. Thus, there would be one tutor for maths, physics, chemistry and French, and another for literature, history, zoology, botany and Latin. Students went to the homes of the tutors for one or two hours per day, alternating courses. There was no possibility for laboratory work; a few sessions of demonstrations at the high school, prior to exams, was the only contact shtetl students had with experiments.

The curriculum consisted to literature, history, geography, French, Latin, zoology, botany, religion, to which were added Greek, German, psychology, ethics and philosophy in the last two years of high school. Drawing, music and gym were considered ancillary subjects, although the marks counted and influenced significantly the final average, which was a determining factor in admission to university. Fear of lowering the average, prompted many parents to obtain medical certificates forbidding exertion, which reflected unfavorably on "the weakling Jews" using subterfuges.

High-school students wore uniforms while at school but not at home in the shtetl. Each high school had its own uniform; khaki or blue suits with peaked caps to match for the boys, and black dresses with white festooned collars and felt or straw cloche hats for the girls. All bore the school initials and an identification number on their sleeve and cap. Discipline was strict at all times. Wearing a uniform was a status symbol for the student who did not object or resent this. It fostered a sentiment of elitism which set the students apart from others of their age group, whom they came to consider less fortunate and somehow inferior.

In spite of the well-known "need to achieve" and parental admonitions that "a Jew had to be twice as good to succeed", the drop-out rate during high-school years was considerable. Having failed one year, some students continued taking the tutorial courses together with their successful friends without presenting themselves at the examinations. To prevent feelings of inferiority and bruised egos, parents continued to provide these lessons. This was true especially of girls, who often stopped their studies at the age of fifteen or sixteen.

Although the attitude towards education for girls was changing rapidly, most parents still considered matrimony the ultimate goal for their daughters. But whereas, in the past, girls were taught skills deemed necessary for a *domnisoara de salon* ("parlor lady") such as literature, French, German, needlepoint and embroidery, during the twenties and thirties there was an increased awareness of the advantages of formal education for girls as well as for boys. Education became an asset as part of the dowry and commanded a *titrat* ("professional") or at least a well-established young businessman as a husband. It therefore carried a practical value, which the pragmatic shtetl parents did not fail to appreciate. Girls with superior academic talents went onto university and the professions. They rarely returned to the shtetl.

The Romanian educational system was modelled along the French one, although not quite as strictly centralized. The baccalaureat, of which our own high-school diploma is but a pale imitation, was a Draconian hurdle to pass. Young people looked forward to it, with justified dread and apprehension. The Romanian authorities were notorious for their attempts and efforts to prevent Jews from entering universities. The baccalaureat was deliberately made almost impossible for Jewish students. There were known sadistic professors who delighted in inventing torments aimed at belittling if not devastating Jewish students during oral examinations by asking absurd questions. One example was a question in zoology asking how many steps a sparrow took during one year. The answer was "none", since a sparrow hops around and does not take any steps. Or a geography question — how many rocks are there in Romania? The answer was based on the names of towns with the word "rock" included, such as Little Rock, Grey Rock, and so on. These were not riddles or amusing games but deliberately planted, misleading questions, intended to fluster the already intimidated student. In despair, students conscious of the parental sacrifices and with their future at stake sometimes committed suicide.

Fortunately these were rare cases. Most students repeated the examinations two or three times, learning to deal with the stress. Those who passed, unless their marks were at the top, found the doors of the universities closed. In spite of these obstacles, or perhaps because of them, Jewish students entered universities and excelled in the professions. It was the standards they set and their success that elicited the virulent anti-Semitic student riots.

3. Youth Clubs

Each shtetl had several youth clubs, part of larger international networks. There were Zionist and non-Zionist organizations, both political and apolitical. *Maccabi* was entirely apolitical, while the politically oriented were *Gordonia*, left of center and *Betar*, the revisionist. Communists were making inroads.

The latter were a loosely organized group of youths, students and a few self taught workers. Some young adults, recently arrived from Bessarabia, infiltrated the various youth groups and were winning converts. The term "agent" may sound too strong for these individuals, though they were used by the larger political machine for its own ends. In 1937, this group succeeded in smuggling into town communist propaganda pamphlets, originating from the USSR. In typical totalitarian fashion, the local police rounded up some twenty youths, among whom there were two young women. In the early hours of the morning they were jailed until the appalled parents bailed them out. The shtetl was stunned to learn of these subversive activities. The matter was hushed up but infiltration did not stop.

This was not a typical youth group. It functioned only marginally and was violently rejected by the shtetl who regarded communism as the antithesis of everything shtetl values upheld. "Communists" were non-believers, capable of crime, anti traditionalists, of loose morals; they believed in "free love". No accusation was more acerbic than to call someone a communist. This only provoked rebellion among some of the youth, who rejected parental values.

Diametrically opposed were the Zionist clubs: Maccabi, the

apolitical sports association, Gordonia and Betar, the political Zionist clubs. The two latter clubs did not fare too successfully in Stefanesti. In other small towns, they were popular.

Gordonia, the socialist Zionist organization was a pioneering youth movement whose principles were "building up the homeland, educating members in humanistic values, creation of a working nation, the renaissance of Hebrew culture and self labor". In Stefanesti it found few adepts.

Betar was the revisionist Zionist organization. It attracted middle class young people. Founded in Poland by Vladimir Jabotinsky, it was a politically rightist association who believed in the power of the military. In their oath of allegiance, they "upheld beauty, respect, self esteem, politeness and faithfulness".

Maccabi was the nonpolitical sports club with the largest membership and the wholehearted support of the community, who allowed them the use of the community-owned meeting hall. There, they established a lending library, met at regular *sichot* ("meetings"), held group discussions and singsongs and danced. Their major activities were football and gymnastics. The Maccabi football team played other small-town teams at matches, which became heated inter-shtetl events. The girls participated only as avid spectators, each cheering for her hero. There were no cheerleaders as such; this would have been regarded as too daring for the demure girls and too artificial in an environment where spontaneity was valued.

Maccabi gymnastics teams performed elegantly on the horse, rings, *parallelles* and various other *aparate*, as the equipment was called. They put on shows of professional caliber and competed at national and international levels.

Whether politically oriented or not, the youth clubs served an important function in shtetl social life. The usual motivation for belonging to these clubs were group participation, social activities and above all the opportunity to meet members of the opposite sex. These clubs were testing grounds for the young people. Groups were segregated according to age, each age group remaining apart from the group older or younger than themselves. Even within the politically oriented clubs, there was little political commitment on the part of most of the young people; they joined and resigned from the clubs not on the basis of their political convictions but on the acceptance or rejection of their friends.

4. Marriage

Study and socializing were part of adolescence but *tachles* ("the ultimate aim") was to find the right mate and marriage. This was the goal and expectation. Young people looked forward to and geared their lives to this end. For the parents, to see the son or daughter under the marriage canopy was a cherished wish and fervent hope. Increasingly, young people chose or participated in the choosing of their future mates, although it was still the parents who had the last word.

Lest one imagine that this manner of arranging marriages rode roughshod over the wishes of the young, it must be emphasized that in most cases, the young people accepted this situation willingly. They gladly relinquished the responsibility to the parents, whose judgement they trusted. Among the educated youth, voices of rebellion were heard as they considered the "bargaining" humiliating and embarrassing. One Romanian expression — "If the girl wants, the father may burst" — suggests that the authoritarian parental decisions were being questioned. Elopements or marriage without parental consent were virtually unknown.

The feeling of security, derived from knowing that the parents were responsible, should not be underestimated. One young woman, having met a young man whom she wanted to marry, had to appeal to an uncle to act on her behalf; she resented her father's failure to fulfill his obligation. In another case, a professional woman related with bitterness her father's failure to find a suitor, for what she had considered unrealistic *yichus* pretentions.

Although deliberately "engineered" by the parents, often with the aid of a matchmaker, it was believed that marriages were forged in Heaven. It was said that forty days before the child's birth a "zyivig" a mate, was decided for him in heaven.

Free will, in this respect, was rather loosely interpreted. Nor were parental good intentions questioned. Echoes of resentment were occasionally heard against parents whose judgement was considered below expectations.

As previously mentioned, the *shadchan* still played an important role in the Romanian shtetl, although there were no professional matchmakers. Everyone was prone to play Cupid. There were, however, several known persons who were paid for these services. Older women, especially, were amateur *shadchentes*, skilfully bringing together families known to be in the market.

The *shadchen*, having staked out the prospective clients, collected all the information regarding family background and individual qualities. He subsequently approached each set of parents to propose a *shiddech* ("to make a match"). This was referred to in Romanian as a *partida* ("a match"), when accomplished, the *partida* was *transhat* ("settled"). In some cases parents approach the *shadchen* with a specific query or suggestion, which he was expected to pursue.

Girls were marrying older than their mothers due to longer periods of schooling, especially among the middle class. Working-class girls married younger, had lower expectations and less parental pressure regarding *yichus*. As girls reached their midtwenties, parents became anxious and the search intensified. For parents of sons, this was not a problem since men were expected to marry older, the late twenties being esteemed the proper age.

For the *shadchen*, once the proposals were accepted by both parties, the next step was to arrange the *unkickechts*, ("the viewing"), called in Romanian the *intrevedere*, where each set of parents measured the other up and down. This was necessary only when the two families resided in different towns, in which case the meeting took place at a midway point easily accessible to both parties, or at the bride's home. If preliminaries were mutually satisfactory the two parties began talking *yicker* – getting down to brass tacks – the bottom line being the *nodn* ("the dowry").

The dowry was essential and no girl would be considered without one. A sum of money and often furniture for the couple's home were part of the deal. Taking a son-in-law into the business was an important asset. The size of the dowry reflected on the prestige of the family, and only poor families or orphans could not provide an adequate dowry. A *titrat* ("a professional") was worth more than a mere *fainer* "a young man without a specific occupation". The bride's looks, family *yichus* and increasingly her education carried weighted points. The *kest* ("upkeep of the young couple for a specific number of years") was not practised in the Romanian shtetl, where couples married later and where the husband was expected to support his wife and family.

It was a *mitzvah* ("good deed") to provide a dowry for poor orphan girls. Societies called *Hachnasat Kallah* fulfilled this need in the community by collecting funds for the purpose of enabling these girls to find husbands.

Having arrived at a mutual agreement, the two parties decided on a date for the *tenoym* ("engagement"), at which time a contract was drawn up and, according to custom, a plate was broken. The ceremony was often referred to as "breaking the plate". As at all joyous occasions, some sadness was deliberately caused, to appease the supposedly envious evil spirits lurking in the shadows. It was also customary to mount a small chip of the broken plate into a ring for the bride, supposed to be a good luck charm.

Bride and groom exchanged gifts and parents offered gifts to the bride and groom. The bride's parents gave the groom a gold watch. The bridegroom gave the bride earrings or a brooch, and the bride gave the bridegroom cufflinks or other jewelry.

The engagement period usually lasted several months to one year. This was a time of trial when the couple were able to become acquainted with one another. Certain intimacies such as kissing (though never in public) were permitted. Where the engagement was contracted before the bridegroom's military service or before he had finished his studies, the wedding was delayed to give him a chance "to stand on his own feet."

The families began to visit back and forth and closer ties were established. It was also a time when families learned more about one another and sometimes, taking a second look had second thoughts. Broken engagements were rare but known to occur. One reported broken engagement resulted when the bride's father discovered that one of the groom's close relatives was a cobbler, a fact previously withheld by the *shadchen*. Since the *yiches* was not up to par, the engagement was broken.

Every girl brought along a trousseau when she married. The trousseau comprised not only the bride's personal clothing and underwear but also household linens. Mothers lovingly prepared the *kiffert* ("hope chest") for each daughter. It was customary for the girls to embroider their own tablecloths, napkins, towels and bed linen with their monograms and fancy stitching. The more affluent employed seamstresses for this purpose, or had the work done by the nuns. Goose feather or down pillows, comforters made of satin and hand woven wool rugs were set aside as part of the trousseau.

The dowry system did not please everyone. Poor young women resented this discriminating practise, as the following couplet suggests:

> Your mother may believe that you will take dowry
> And with the dowry, you will become rich, Oy, Oy,
> God may help you, the dowry you shall lose,
> And to a pauper you'll become akin.

Similarly, Eliakum Zumser, the well-known Yiddish folk poet, touched on the dowry qeustion in the ballad *Die Soche* ("The Plow"), where the father sings:

> For my daughter, I buy a plain dress,
> And make a match with her, without jewels or money
> See in town the brides, they're almost destitute, yet
> They clean out the parental house of everything, whatever is inside;

For me it is easy to find a local bridegroom,
Dowry I give two goats, and she lives happily with her
husband.

People entered into matrimony with a feeling of genuine commitment. It was the commitment that spelled the difference between success or failure in marriage.

In all societies marriage is the point that establishes the change of status for everyone concerned. In the Romanian shtetl, the bride took on the husband's name and, with it, newly achieved status. The parents acquired a new set of relatives and new titles as the family circle widened. Everyone acquired new rights but also new obligations. Marriage raised the individual man and woman to adult status. As bride or groom, even the humblest member of the community enjoyed a moment of glory. The bride was said to be beautiful because the *schechinna* ("the divine presence") rested upon her, and the bridegroom was king for a day.

The wedding date was agreed upon several months in advance to give the families time for the necessary arrangements; printing invitations, guest lists, buying food in readiness for the wedding, hiring the *sarverns* ("caterers"), the *birjars* ("cab drivers"), the hall, and especially the bride's gown, all were part of the feverish excitement.

On the Sabbath before the wedding day, the groom had his *oyfrifechts* ("call to the *Torah*") at the synagogue. It was customary to throw rice, raisins and candies at him so that his new life would be fruitful and sweet.

The day before the wedding, the bride was taken by her mother and *interfirer* to the *mikveh* ("ritual bath") for purification. This ritual was subsequently a required procedure after each menses, prior to the re-establishing of conjugal relations with her husband.

The wedding ceremony usually took place in the late afternoon, with festivities stretching into the night. The bride and groom refrained from seeing each other on that day and fasted in preparation for the new life they were to begin together.

As in any small community, a wedding was a happening; an event everyone looked forward to, although not everyone was invited to every wedding in town. The higher the families on the social ladder, the more interest was aroused. The ceremony was always followed by a dinner and dance, held in a large hall.

Whether one was invited to the wedding or not, the bridal procession attracted everyone's attention. First came the bridegroom's coach with his entourage, his parents and his set of *interfirers*. There followed the out-of-town guests, friends and lesser relatives, all in hired carriages. The last to arrive was the bride's carriage, with the bedecked horses and tinkling bells. Everyone ran out to catch a glimpse.

With her parents or *interfirers*, the bride sat in all her splendor in the *birja* ("coach") with one or two little girls holding two large white candles, trimmed with white-satin ribbons and with *peteala* ("metal filament in gold or silver shades"). In Hollywood-first-night style, the crowd of curious ran alongside the carriage to the hall to watch the bride and the guests.

At the hall, the guests were received by the *machetonem* from both the *husn sot* ("groom's side") and *kalles' sot* ("bride's side"). *Fondante* ("pastel-colored confectionery candies") were passed around to the arriving guests.

The bride wore white, the long veil fixed in place with a diadem of wax flowers (orange blossoms or lilies of the valley). The bridegroom wore a dark suit, usually black or navy blue, white shirt, felt hat and patent-leather shoes.

The groom with his *interfirers* were the first to arrive. He signed the *kesibba* ("marriage contract") as did his witnesses. In another room, the bride and her witnesses signed the marriage contract and the bride prepared herself for the ceremony of *bedekn die kalleh* ("covering the bride's face with the veil").

She sat in the center of the room awaiting the arrival of the groom who lifted the veil and uncovered her face. This was to assure himself that the bride was indeed the one he was promised. The bride remained veiled to the end of the *chuppa* ("wedding ceremony"). Escorted by his *interfirers*, the groom proceeded to *chuppa*, followed by the bride with her own *interfirers*. The bride took her place under the canopy to the right of the groom.

According to Judaic laws, there were two rings, each a simple gold band with the names of the couple engraved inside. The double ring ceremony was observed, although men were not obliged to wear the wedding band. Women did not always wear the ring on the third finger left hand. Taking off the wedding band was considered a bad omen.

The *chuppa* ceremony usually took place in the middle of the street, outside the hall, as it was written that the stars should witness the ceremony so that the marriage would be as fertile as the number of stars in the heavens. In inclement weather, the *chuppa* took place in the hall. The portable *chuppa* was made of velvet trimmed with gold fringes and decorated with a star of David. The four posts were upheld by members of the wedding party.

The ceremony under the canopy was identical with the orthodox

Judaic wedding ceremony everywhere. The rabbi pronounced the blessing on the wine and handed the glass of wine first to the groom; then the bride's *interfirers* gave the glass to the bride. The groom then placed the wedding band on the forefinger of the bride's right hand, pronouncing the ancient formula: "Harray at m'kudeshes lee b'tabaas zu k'das Moseh v'Yisrael" ("Behold, thou art consecrated unto me with this ring, according to the laws of Moses and of Israel").

This was followed by the cantor's chanting the seven benedictions, as the bride and her *interfirers* circled around the groom seven times. This was a symbol of the protective magic circle. The rabbi again blessed the wine and offered a sip to the groom; the bride's *interfirers* did likewise to the bride. The groom then placed the empty glass on the floor and crushed it with his right foot. Everyone kissed, wishing one another *mazeltov* ("good luck").

The bride and groom were then escorted to a room where they broke the fast together and returned to the wedding party. Sitting on a raised dais on thronelike armchairs, they were ready to receive congratulations.

One custom that disappeared from the shtetl wedding was the *badchen* ("jester"), often mentioned in songs, who used to entertain the guests with spontaneous verses. The antics of some famous performers were missed by those who remembered and who deplored the passing of this custom.

The *ketubba* ("marriage contract") stipulated the exact conditions to which both parties had consented. This was the bride's protection; the contract remained in her possession. The two parties to the contract were the bride's parents and the groom. Cases were known where recalcitrant groom's parents stubbornly insisted on gaining some extra benefit on the threat of not signing the contract at the very last minute. These remained part of the shtetl lore. Following is a sample of a *ketubba*:

EXAMPLE

THE KETUBBA *(Marriage Contract)*

"On ..... (day of the week) the ..... (day of the month) ....., in the year ..... according to the Jewish reckoning, here, in the city of ......, son of ..... said to ..... daughter of .....
'Be thou my wife, in accordance with the laws of Moses and Israel, and I will work for thee, and I will hold thee in honor and will support and maintain thee, in accordance with the customs of Jewish husbands, who work for their wives, hold them in honor and support and maintain them. I will furthermore set aside the sum of two hundred silver denari to be thy dowry, according to the law and besides, provide for thy food,

clothing and necessities, and cohabit with thee according to the universal custom.' "

" '. . . . . , on her part, consented to become his wife. The marriage portion which she brought from her father's house, in silver, gold, valuables, clothes, etc. amounts to the value of . . . . . ; the bridegroom, consented to increase this amount from his property, with the sum of . . . . . making, in all . . . . .' — He furthermore declared: 'I take upon myself and my heirs the responsibility for the amount due according to this Ketubah and of the marriage portion, and of the additional sum (by which I promised to increase it), so that all this shall be paid from the best of my property, real and personal, such as I now possess or may hereafter acquire. All my property, even the mantle on my shoulders, shall be mortgaged for the security of the claims above stated, until paid, now and forever.' "

"Thus . . . . . , the bridegroom has taken upon himself the fullest responbility for all the obligations of this Ketubah as is customary with the daughters of Israel and in accordance with the strict ordinances of our sages of blessed memory; so that this document is not to be regarded as an illusory obligation or as a mere form.

"In order to render the above declaration and assurances of the said bridegroom . . . . . to the said bride . . . . . , perfectly valid and binding, we have applied the legal formality of symbolic delivery."

. . . . witness
. . . . witness

Honeymoon — *luna de miere* or ("the month of honey") — plans depended on whether the newlyweds were to live alone or with the in-laws and on their socioeconomic level. Among the working class, this was a perfunctory arrangement. The well-to-do spent a few days in another town or took a longer trip to a big city.

From the individual's point of view, of the three major events of his life — birth, marriage and death — marriage was the only one where he was an active participant, where his role commanded center stage. The other two, at his entrance and exit, are passive roles, the significance of which pertain to the community at large.

5. Old Age

Living in a society where youth is idolized and the least telltale sign of advancing age is dreaded, it is interesting to examine the attitude of the Romanian shtetl toward old age. Far from being feared or disdained, the maturity and equilibrium acquired with age were considered an asset. Older people were respected for their wisdom and judgement and their advice was sought in preference to the *yinger tzutzik* ("young whippersnapper"). "To one hundred and twenty years" was the wish, with the hope that reasonably good health would be enjoyed. Artificially maintained life or lingering death was impossible under local conditions.

If one had been fortunate to see the children married off and living in their own homes, one enjoyed tranquillity and respect. There was a sense of security in knowing that, in case of need, the children were there to rely on. Parents, however, hoped and prayed not to "fall burden" on their children or have to depend on them. Sayings such as "one parent can support a houseful of children but all the children cannot support one parent" expressed sentiments of apprehension gleaned from popular wisdom. Widowed parents usually resided with one of the married children or with a single son or daughter. There were also cases where married children were forced to move back to the parental home.

Adjustment to old age was gradual. Being self-employed, men continued to work as long as their strength lasted. Upon loss of a spouse, few remarried; most continued life alone. Widows eked out a meager living from little stores to earn enough for their modest needs and maintain their independence.

The *azil* ("home for the aged") in Stefanesti is an interesting example of attitudes toward the aged. At the turn of the century the community had built an old-people's home, which, however, was never used for its intended purpose. Instead, it ultimately housed the kindergarten, since most elderly preferred to live with their families and no child would have "put away" a parent in an institution to be cared for by strangers. This demonstrates how shtetl culture selected only those outside influences that fitted with its own avowed way of life and rejected anything that clashed with or threatened accepted values.

Attitudes towards the elderly and especially towards aged parents would be difficult to standardize since it depended on a number of factors, not the least of which were the previously existing interpersonal relations of family members. In some families where a warm relationship had been established throughout the years, the elderly were treated with affection and respect; in other cases, there was overt resentment. Three generations under one roof was not unusual. Whether or not it was a mutually enriching experience, as most respondents avowed, depended on the personalities of the individual family members. This interpersonal family relationship was one of the yardsticks of *balabotishe* ("fine upstanding") families as compared to the *prosteh* ("lower-class") families where bickering was the norm.

6. Death

In spite of the inevitability of death and the fact that it was a common occurrence, the loss of loved ones was always received with resentment and lingering grief. Where the Romanian peasant would say "God Hath given, God Hath taken away", the shtetl Jew considered the hurt a personal punishment and retribution for his sins. A deeply instilled fear of death and an ambiguous attitude towards the entire mystery rendered the subject taboo. Children were protected and kept away from the house where a death had occurred. Mention of the word, as of any misfortune, was prefaced with the usual formula of protection: "May it not happen here" or "On all wastelands", and, among unsophisticated the *ptiu, ptiu, ptiu* ("three spits to ward off evil").

The closing hours of life and death itself were traumatic times for the entire family. Rituals associated with this trying period were observed in the strictest accordance with Judaic laws. For good measure, many superstitions borrowed from other cultures throughout the ages were observed assiduously. There were many ambiguities between the feelings of love and longing for the departed one on the one hand, and, on the other, the soul, suddenly transformed and presumably become dangerous through death.

Horace Miner* states that in St. Denis, Quebec, the relative importance of the deceased determined the period of mourning. He gives the example of the husband-wife relationship as being the most socially important; a widow mourned her husband for two years. An infant, considered of no social value as yet, was mourned for a short time. This was not the case within the shtetl scale of values, where mourning was not a function of the person's social importance to the community. There was no correlation between the mourning period and relations to the living or to the community. The period of mourning was prescribed by Judaic laws and so enacted. Reconciliation to the loss and especially the feeling of grief did not adapt to regulations; rather, mourning was the only positive means of reacting to the loss of a member of the family.

Funeral rites reflect the fear of the supernatural. Water, used as libation for the spirits and as cleansing from contact with death, prayers, all were protective devices, separating the living from the danger of death.

There were no funeral parlors in the shtetl. The body was cleansed, washed and prepared for burial by members of the *Chevre Kadisha* ("the sacred burial society"). The body was lain on the floor, with the feet to the door. It was wrapped in a simple white shroud, the

---

* Horace Miner, *St. Denis A French Canadian Village*, University of Chicago Press, 1939, p. 231.

tachrichen, made of cotton or linen and sewn with white thread without a knot. (This specification, "without a knot" was to assure easy disrobing when the Messiah would come and all would arise). Interment took place as soon as possible after death. The body was not allowed to remain alone in a room and pious men remained to guard and say the ninety-first Psalm, the anti-demonic psalm, throughout the time it remained in the house.

The secretary of the community was immediately informed and arrangements were made at the cemetery. The community taxed the family, a form of succession duties, according to their means, usually well-known in the shtetl. The poor were exempt, while the well-to-do were expected to make generous donations.

The *levayeh* ("the funeral procession") commenced at the house, then proceeded on foot, taking the longest road to the cemetery and increasing in size as people joined. The body, in a simple wooden coffin covered with a black cloth on which a star of David was embroidered, was carried on a stretcher, on the shoulder of the pallbearers, who took turns on the way to the cemetery. The mourners returned by another route from the cemetery. This was done in the belief that the soul, still hovering around the body, would follow and return to haunt the living. Piercing cries, wailings and lamentations, the women enumerating all the qualities of the deceased, accompanied the body as it was taken out of the house. The *bocitoare* ("professional bewailers"), still customary at peasant funerals, were unknown and would have been superfluous.

Women members of the family did not go to the cemetery. After the body was removed, the house was swept, "to sweep away all sorrow". The sweepings were not picked up, but instead strewn outdoors with the broom. Mirrors were covered or smeared with soap suds.

At the cemetery, a small bag with soil from Israel was placed in the grave. This, the deceased person had prepared, in accordance with the oft-repeated hope of being lain to rest in the sacred soil of Jerusalem. (Old peddlers used to sell these little bags and sometimes they were bought more for the sake of the poor peddler than anything else.)

After interment, the male blood relatives said *kaddish* ("prayer for the dead"). This prayer does not mention death, but, like all prayers, glorifies the name of God. "It affirms faith in the establishment of His kingdom and expresses hope for peace within Israel."*

---

* L. Rosten, *The Joys of Yiddish*, Pocketbook, New York, 1970, p. 164.

The *kaddish*, (said in the belief that it would help the soul of the dead to find lasting peace), was recited at the grave and subsequently every day to the end of the mourning year, as well as at every anniversary of the death.

During interment, the rabbi chanted the prayers. Where there were no direct descendants, pious men were paid to say the prayer as an homage for the dead. Upon leaving the gravesite, mourners picked up a handful of earth and threw it behind them to symbolically put a barrier between the soul and the living. The mourners were greeted with the formula: "May the Almighty comfort you, together with all the mourners of Zion and Jerusalem." Repeatedly, we find the bond created between the past and the present by reminding those concerned of the broader canvas on which they are but a speck.

Upon return from the cemetery, a glass of water and a towel were prepared at the entrance of the home, used to wash hands, thus cleansing oneself from any contact with death. Water as well as the power of prayers were relied upon to act as protective agents.

The mourners were served eggs, a symbol of life, and immediately after their return from the cemetery they "sat down shiva" ("the seven days of mourning ritual"). A part of the garment worn by the immediate mourners was torn as a sign of grief and the mourners* sat on the bare floor, in stockinged feet. Throughout the seven days they were not allowed to sit on a chair. The custom of women wearing a black apron as a sign of mourning, for the entire year, had been discarded by all but the very old women. During the *shiva*, except on the Sabbath, the male mourners, in company with a *minyan* ("the ten adult males"), said *kaddish* in the house.

After *shiva*, there followed a period of thirty days (shloshim) of less stringent mourning. Men were still not allowed to shave, though allowed to leave the house. By command and preference they abstained from all pleasures — they did not listen to music or attend joyous events in deference to the deceased.

In the case of a death of one of the parents, the wedding of a son or daughter, impossible to postpone (since once decided, to change the date would have been a bad omen) was observed without music or dancing; it was called "a still wedding". For those stricken with grief, these restraints were not difficult. Should a child learn of a parent's death thirty days after it occurred, one hour of *shiva* was prescribed.

---

* Immediate mourners — spouses, parents, children. A tie, shirt or dress were cut into strips as a sign of mourning.

Tombstones were made of stone, concrete or in some cases of wood covered with tin and periodically repainted with oil paint. Maintenance of the tomb was considered a *mitzva* ("good deed"). Flowers were not associated with funerals, nor were there flowers planted on graves. The *rebbé*'s tomb was a small mausoleum, standing out in the surrounding simple slabs engraved with the name of the deceased and the dates of birth and death. Childless people sometimes made their own burial arrangements in spite of the superstition associated with anticipation of the event.

One bizarre incident was related by a respondent about an old eccentric, Moyshe-Yosl, who bought his own plot and tombstone and had it engraved with all details except the final date, to be added at the proper time. A former shtetl resident visiting in town had gone to the cemetery and noticed the tomb. That same evening, returning to his brother's house, he heard steps behind him in the dark, and was petrified to see Moyshe-Yosl walking a few paces behind him. Breathless, he rushed into his brother's house as if he'd seen a ghost, which he was sure he had, only to find out that the old man was very much alive but that he had prepared his own place of rest.

Visiting cemeteries on special fast days and on the month of Elul to pray and beg for intercession was still a common practice.

The cycle of life in the shtetl was ended on a note of sobriety. All rituals, regardless of status, were simple as commanded, so as not to belittle the humblest members of the community or their kin. From a functional point of view, all ceremonials served to maintain family traditions, provide continuity and strengthen ties with the community. For the family it functioned as a catharsis, observances helping in expiating feelings of guilt or any regrets they may have harbored against the departed.

CHAPTER IX
Leisure

1. Adults and Children

To speak of leisure within the context of shtetl culture would only reveal our own ethnocentrism. It would be misleading to apply our concept of leisure to a culture where work was synonymous with survival. The purpose of life as conceived in the shtetl was to make a living and to worship God. Work itself was seen as a form of worship, since it was the weekly prelude to the full enjoyment of the Holy Sabbath. Work was a boon; it was the absence of work that was dreaded. Nor did the idea occur that one had to like one's work. The emphasis was on the satisfaction derived from the opportunity to work and especially from a job well done. Shtetl vocabulary had no term for "hobby", since the concept itself did not exist.

For adults the mere notion of leisure was a luxury. This was a society of self-employed small merchants, shopkeepers and craftsmen; time was their own. There was no punching a clock, or "time is money". The line between leisure and work was often blurred, if not nonexistent. A merchant transacted a deal over a game of dominoes; a craftsman exchanged a joke with his customer, without anyone looking over his shoulder. It is interesting to note that the Romanian term for merchant, *negustor*, derives from the Latin *nec otio*, "one who is not free", consequently one who is busy at all times. That was the concept of the shtetl. Leisure was any free time when one was not occupied with the observance of religious rituals or working.

In Stefanesti, as in all shtetlach, recreational activities varied with age, sex and socioeconomic status and depended largely on the weather. The generation of the grandparents still derived their sole enjoyment of leisure from celebrations of the traditional festivals. As in other respects, contact with large urban centers brought currents of re-evaluation of attitudes towards leisure. Except for the teenage group, influenced mainly by the students back from high schools and universities in the big cities, structured leisure was almost nonexistent. The only free time for leisure for adults was Saturday afternoon and religious holy days, and these periods were hemmed in by strict prohibitions.

Leisure was dictated, to a large extent, by socioeconomic status. The shopkeeper was busy in his store from early morning to as late as a customer wished to come in. Regardless of his preoccupation at the moment, a customer was always a welcome intrusion; even mealtimes were gladly interrupted to make a sale. Any free time during the day was spent reading the daily newspapers, socializing with neighbors and friends who dropped in for a glass of tea and a chat. Sometimes a game of chess, backgammon or cards was played on the store counter, while hoping to be disturbed by a customer.

Women who worked side by side with their husbands in the store had little free time after dispensing with the endless household chores. Any free time they had was spent reading and doing needlework.

For the grain merchant, the *cerealist*, part of the daily routine was his visit to the *cafenea*, the coffee house, euphemistically referred to as the *bursa* ("stock exchange"). In some ways it served as an unofficial men's club. Men came there to transact business, read the daily newspapers while dawdling over a demi-tasse of Turkish coffee. Shopkeepers called these activities *luftsgesheftn* ("air-business") and the merchants were known as *luftsmench* ("one who lived on flimsy business"). For the shopkeepers, too busy to indulge in what they considered a frivolous waste of time, this was not serious business.

The craftsman, tailor, cobbler or carpenter was only too happy to be overworked. Spending time away from the workbench was a virtual calamity, and leisure outside of the Sabbath was synonymous with hunger for the family. When time permitted, an afternoon nap was esteemed ample leisure.

Unstructured visiting back and forth, dropping in unannounced was the primary manner of spending leisure time. At these gatherings, friends and relatives exchanged news of mutual interest and gossiped. The hostess served a glass of ice-cold water with Turkish delight or a teaspoonful of her own jam. (She would proudly point out the perfection of flavor and color.)

Entertaining at home and a leisurely promenade in the center of town and up the hill, or a tour through the public gardens, were considered a pleasant way of spending a few leisure hours in the summertime. In the winter, Saturday afternoons were spent quietly at home or visiting family and friends. Gathered around the crackling fire in the *soba*, one of the more talented members would read Yiddish or Romanian short stories. Shalom Aleichem, I. L. Peretz,

Mendole Mocher Sforim were among the favorites. Everyone listened, engrossed in the well-known story, while eating roasted peanuts, filberts or the ubiquitous roasted pumpkin and sunflower seeds. The hostess served hot tea with lemon and honey cake or *strudl*, with some *visinata* ("homemade cherry brandy with brandied cherries"). Cards and other games were played only in the evening, never on Sabbath.

One significant distinction between the socioeconomic levels was their reading habit. The working class had neither the inclination nor the possibility to spend leisure time reading. Perenially exhausted from caring for large families, the women considered the luxury of sitting with their hands in their laps sufficient. The men often went to the synagogue, where they listened to a dissertation on a passage from the holy books and remained at the synagogue for the *sholeshydes** ("the communal meal of herring with bread") and a glass of *schnapps* ("brandy"). Some attended study sessions at the *Rebbé*'s court. Few of the merchants participated in these communal synagogue meals, preferring to spend the time at home with their families.

Among the merchant class, reading was a popular way of spending leisure hours. Women read avidly the classics, often in the original German or French as well as translations from English. This applied to the more affluent, younger group. *Lectura* was a monthly publication of short stories that enjoyed wide popularity. Many paperback publications, such as *Biblioteca Pentru Toti* ("Everyone's Library") were readily available and affordable. A few of the more prosperous matrons received regularly the latest published books, which they shared with friends.

Eating roasted pumpkin or sunflower seeds, *knackn kern* as it was called, was a custom that was part of the Saturday-afternoon or any free leisure time. It is worth explaining, if only for its peculiarity. It was what amounted to a virtual obsession, not unlike smoking (forbidden on the Sabbath) or, a habit better known to us, chewing gum, with similar connotations of couthness. For the uninitiated, the procedure must be minutely described. *Knackn* means breaking or splitting, there is an onomatopoeic sound to it. Sunflower or pumpkin seeds, roasted and salted, were bought from the corner vendors in small paper cornets, or by the tumblerful, straight into a pocket. (This was the only commerce condoned in the shtetl on the Sabbath.)

---

* Literally shalosh — seudah — the third meal.

The unique act of extracting the kernel from its pod took consummate skill to perform. One held each seed between the forefinger and the thumb then placed it between the front teeth in a vertical position, gently pressing the teeth to crack it open. With a deft twist of the tongue, the kernel was then extracted, intact (very important), and the husk unceremoniously discarded – in most cases, on the sidewalk. The streets, especially where groups of people usually gathered, were littered with discarded sunflower and pumpkin husks, the badge of *Shabbes* ("Saturday") in the shtetl. It looked like a patchwork of gray and beige carpet. Those with any claim to refinement considered *knackn kern* an uncouth habit, especially when eaten on the street.

Men did not read fiction; they read the daily newspapers, the Romanian *Lumea* ("The World") published in Iassy, *Dimineata* ("The Morning") and *Adevarul* ("Truth") published in Bucharest; Zionist periodicals, *Hatikva, Hasmonaea,* and the weekly *Renasterea Noastra* ("Our Revival"), published in Romanian, were the usual fare. They followed with interest national and international political events and enjoyed heated discussions of local politics.

Surrounded by a superabundance of music, and when with the turn of a knob we conjure the pleasure of listening to the greatest virtuosos, it may be difficult to imagine the significance of music of any quality in the shtetl. Music was a decided luxury associated with festive occasions. Even the military brass band was listened to with pleasure. Singsongs were part of informal entertainment at gatherings when those with good voices sang the well-known repertory of popular ballads while everyone chimed in or intoned the refrain. Several young men and women played the violin, a favorite instrument. It was considered chic to give young boys violin lessons. The sole piano teacher in town provided piano lessons for the few fortunate little girls of the well-to-do families. This was esteemed the utmost of refinement.

A few of the affluent families owned a *patéfon* or ("funnelled gramophone"). Listening to records of favorite singers of operatic arias, popular ballads or cantorial pieces was an exciting way to spend an evening. The younger set preferred dancing music. Not until the early thirties did radios appear in Stefanesti, and then only four to five homes were able to afford the luxury. Being invited to listen to the radio, regardless of program content, was an event.

So far as adults were concerned, sports were virtually nonexistent. Young men and boys played football and excelled in gymnastics. If the term "hobby" could be applied to any endeavor, it was in the area of gymnastics where the young men, and sometimes young women, reached high levels of proficiency. Men enjoyed football only as spectators when the Maccabi team played on the *shes* ("playing field"). To pay for the privilege of watching these games would have been unheard of; the players derived satisfaction from playing; the idea of paying them would have appeared absurd to shtetl thinking.

The *gradina publica* ("public garden") was fenced-in and the gates were open only during summer months and only till eleven p.m. Always in need of funds, the municipality instituted a five *lei* entrance fee on Saturday afternoons, the time when the shtetl enjoyed a stroll. The gravel paths were lined with benches. In the spring, the air was suffused with the fragrances of the flowering locusts (*salcam*) and linden trees (*tei*). An open air stage was built in the park where concerts were held on Sundays. Promenading in the park was one of the acceptable pleasures for a Sabbath afternoon. For the young boys and girls, a secluded park bench was an ideal spot for a secret rendezvous or for holding hands, a taboo in public.

Yukl's Cofeteria (a tea room) and *Potop's* ice-cream parlor were important landmarks where one stopped for a pastry or an ice cream. In the summer, one enjoyed a dish of ice cream sold by the street vendor from his pushcart.

As late as the mid 1920s, Vasile Tziganer (the local gypsy) provided sidewalk entertainment when he brought his dancing brown bear to parade down the main street. The bear was a head taller than his producer-director. For a slice of bread with honey, the bear hopped around the gypsy, who held the chain around the bear's neck and provided the music by hissing a tune through a comb covered with tissue paper. The urchins, clapping their hands would sing:

> *Joaca bine mai Martine,*
> *Ca-ti dau paine cu masline.*
>
> "Dance well, Martin my pet,
> Bread and olives you will get."

Eating out was not part of shtetl lifestyle. There was one *bodega* ("restaurant") serving charcoal-broiled steaks and *mititei* ("charcoal-broiled sausages") washed down with a *shpritz* or a foaming *tzap* of beer. This was a luxury indulged in by the bons vivants. Most townfolk regarded eating out with some ambiguity; they considered any restaurant a poor alternative to home cooking and questioned the reliability of their *kashrut*, (dietary laws).

During winter months young people went sledding on the hill.

Up the serpentine hill they trudged, taking turns at pulling the sled and piling up on top of each other's backs, they enjoyed the flight downhill. For the small fry, the smaller hills in town were as enticing.

One pastime indulged in during the hot summer afternoons, available to all, regardless of social standing or age, was a swim in the Prut, some three miles away. For the local farmers this was a slight windfall; they provided the transportation to and from the river for a few pennies a ride. They stationed themselves at the bridge on the Basheu, where everyone came to embark for the expedition to the Prut. A towel and bathing suit rolled up under the arm or in a reed basket, and armed with the little brown bag of refreshments, youngsters could barely contain their excitement. They came with one of the parents – since someone had to mind the store – or chaperoned by a neighbor. For two *lei* one made the trip one way and, if willing to haggle, the return trip was obtained for three *lei*. A few rough boards in a wagon provided seating arrangement for as many people as were able to pile into the wagon; several youngsters tossed in on the knees of adults squashed in with their feet dangling out of the wagon completed the equipage. There were always those fortunate few who disdainfully passed through the mêlée in their own *docar* ("two-wheelers") or those who hired a *birja* and travelled in luxurious comfort.

Perhaps one of the most spectacular changes in the mores of this otherwise staid and proper shtetl was the apparently innocent phenomenon of changing the location of the bathing area at the Prut. The repercussions were devastating, although there were those who would have shaken a warning finger and said "I told you so". For generations the dip in the Prut was part of the summer way of life in Stefanesti, as it was in most other shtetlech along the Prut or other such streams. The men bathed in the nude behind a clump of silver maple bushes, down a loamy ravine, carved by the river. Around a bend of the river, and descending the steep ravine a few hundred yards away in the other direction, the women and children enjoyed their own bathing spot. Occasionally some young rascal dared invade the women's area, wreaking havoc among the women, who, thrown into a panic, submerged themselves up to the neck. The cotton underslips they wore, usually red or black, would suddenly balloon around them like floating umbrellas.

This had been the way for as long as anyone remembered until the early 1930s when the young students returning from the larger urban centers discovered that, downstream, on the same bank but on the other side of the bridge, facing the Bessarabian village of Branishtea, the river formed a wide sandy beach, surrounded by a little *padurice* ("little forest"), a wooded area of young silver maples, aspen and willows, ideal for changing clothes or relaxing in the shade in comfort. There, the young sophisticates began bathing, both men and women wearing bathing suits, but *together*. Gradually, everyone came to bathe in the new area hitherto frowned upon as indecent; but not before the unthinkable happened.

One unmarried woman became pregnant. Counting on their fingers, the rumor machines in town whispered that the date coincided with the early-summer swimming season when bathing started in the *padurice*. The girl happened to be of a poor working-class family. The town was agog, for this was unheard of in a rabbunish shtetl, a town where the revered Stefanester *Rebbé* resided. Not only the girl and her family but the entire shtetl suffered intolerable disgrace. Of such stuff was shtetl life achurning.

The Purim ball was a yearly event. It provided excitement for weeks prior to the affair and topics for gossip when it was over. The main purpose was raising funds for Zionist causes. The décor was white and blue, the Zionist colors. It was planned by the students and held under the auspices of the Jewish community, usually in the Jewish school hall. Everyone attended and everyone participated in some measure. Responsibilities were assigned to all; matrons were asked to contribute baked goods or handicrafts for the bazaar. Youngsters were recruited to fetch and carry and help with simpler work. Under competent supervision, white and blue paper chains, by the mile, were prepared to decorate the hall and give it a festive appearance. Young girls, ready with Jewish National Fund blue-and-white tin boxes, pinned blue and white ribbons on men's lapels, inviting contributions.

One was expected to come dressed in a costume, although this was not compulsory. Ingenuity and talents were taxed in devising original costumes in the hope of capturing the evening's first prize.

On the day of the ball, a girl and boy, accompanied by the bagel vendor carrying his huge wicker basket, made the rounds, from door to door, to collect the articles donated for the bazaar. Most donations consisted of handicrafts and home-baked goods. For the housewives, the contribution of baked goods to the bazaar was one more opportunity to show off her culinary talents. For everyone it was an occasion to dress up, enjoy an evening of dancing and have a jolly good time. At about eleven PM the bazaar articles were auctioned off. The cakes and pastries donated by the cordon-bleu ladies were set aside to be raffled off, the name of the donor properly acknowledged. This was followed by the judging for the best costumes. At midnight, the masks were removed, the prizes distributed and the *pièce de résistance* of the evening, crowning the "Queen of the Ball", began. In order not to offend the contestants, the selection was based on a system of bidding, whereby the young men sponsored one of their favorite girls and bid for her. One respondent related that an engagement was almost broken off when the fiancé had failed to win this title for his bride-to-be. The evening ended with the singing of "Hatikva" ("Hope"), now the Israeli National anthem and at the time the acknowledged national hymn of Zionism.

Stefanesti was an important landmark on the circuit of itinerant theater companies and the town eagerly awaited these events. There were the occasional one-night stands of Romanian reviews, featuring some well-known Romanian actor, such as *Tanase*. The main theater entertainment was provided by the travelling Yiddish theater. Comedies and light melodramas were favored; but serious dramas were also part of the repertory. "Shmendrik", the hero of A. Goldfadden's play, which gave the synonym for gullible, Motké Gonnif. The two Kunie Lemls, Hotzmir and Zeitzmir, were characters in plays whose names enriched the shtetl vocabulary. The couplets and love songs of the Yiddish stage echoed in the shtetl and became part of its folklore: "Shmendrik is a cknacker...." People's emotions were stirred by dramas of a high caliber such as Jacob Gordin's *Mirele Efros*, often compared to *King Lear*, where the perennial conflicts between generations were dramatically presented. And always, the favorite Biblical themes: *Shulamis* ("Salomée"), *Akeydas Yitzhak* ("The Sacrifice of Isaac"), keeping audiences at the edge of their chairs.

The circus came to town once a year and provided the usual entertainment; clowns, acrobats, monkeys and bears and ladies on horseback, with the familiar background music. For children the circus held never ending fascination, which they translated into their own shows, charging a button or a candy entrance fee. From time to time fairs would come to town and set up on the *maidan* or in the center of town and for a brief spell, fill the town night with bright lights and exciting smells and noises. The merry-go-rounds, vertiginous swings, girls with bodies of snakes, shooting galleries, a virtual miniature Coney Island miraculously sprang up and as miraculously vanished, leaving the shtetl all the more desolate when the hoopla folded.

Movies never made it big in Stefanesti. Two abortive attempts ended in failure. The town was not able to support a permanent movie house. A certain Mr. Barditza, a Romanian tavern owner, brought films for children and at five *lei* per child, opened for them the magic world, for an hour, but only on Saturday and Sunday afternoons. These were mostly silent films, Mickey Mouse, Laurel and Hardy, (which translated as *Stan si Bran*), and other such. A scratchy gramophone competed with the audience when – as often happened – the film broke and the hall remained in frightening darkness. Adults enjoyed the marvels of cinema only during their trips to the big city.

The year-end *serbare*, the festival at the end of the school year, put on by the kindergarten and the public school, was one event well-attended by parents and relatives who provided an ever-enthusiastic audience. Children recited little poems, acted in plays and danced dressed in elaborate crêpe-paper costumes, created with ingenuity by the teachers. At the end of each child's performance on stage, the little star was pelted with candy bars by his adoring parents and kin. This was beginning to get out of hand, as parents began a marathon as to the size of the chocolate bars they threw on stage. Inevitable complications arose when the wrong child picked up a package destined for another and refused to hand it back.

One form of local entertainment, which appealed to the intelligentsia, was the *process literar* ("literary trial"). The *process literar* was a mock trial based on a well-known fictional character. It was the professionals and the leading intellectuals in the community who were invited to serve as judge, jury and lawyers for each side of the case. King Lear, Shylock and other Shakespearean characters were favorites. *The Lady or the Tiger* by Frank R. Stockton, had been selected as a topic and became memorable, for the verdict, as intended by the novel's author, left the public in suspense and the conflict unresolved.

Public participation during these events was animated. These sessions served not only to make life in the shtetl less tedious, but broadened the otherwise limited opportunity for intellectual stimulus in the shtetl. This form of audience participation opened new vistas for understanding the characters and often helped redefine or reinterpret one's own feelings and attitudes.

Young people were discovering new interests. The *aparat fotografic* ("camera") was a novelty and for the more affluent taking pictures was as close to a hobby as one could imagine in the shtetl. It also served to enhance the status of the owner and win him popularity within his peer group. Taking group pictures gave zip to any gathering of young people on an otherwise dull day.

Similarly, owning a bicycle was an unprecedented status symbol. There were only four or five young men (not one girl) with a bicycle. These boys enjoyed special popularity among their peers, granting the treat of a ride around the block as a special favor. For girls, the bicycle had been declared unladylike. Modesty dictated it, since girls wore only skirts and the bicycle presented technical problems. It also elicited the controversy of riding on the Sabbath, a dispute that resulted in heated debates and a realignment of opinions along generation lines.

To sum up, leisure, like everything else in the Romanian shtetl, was taken in its stride. Too busy with *parnusseh* ("earning a living") and plodding through life as God willed it, leisure, in our sense of the term, was esteemed a desirable side effect rather than an aim in itself.

This attitude is best reflected in the way the shtetl regarded such professions as *klezmer* ("musicians") or *actiorn* ("actors"). These occupations carried a whiff of frivolity, a lack of serious pursuit, and, above all, some artificiality — a cardinal sin in the shtetl. It was also intrinsically related to the attitude towards work: "What is it good for" summed up the concern for *tachless* ("ultimate aim"). For the average individual, the Sabbath and religious festivals provided all the leisure they wished for.

2. Games

Play, defined as "unproductive activity", is an important aspect of any culture. It is instinctive, yet culturally controlled and directed into socially approved channels. We refer to organized play as "games".

Children use play to acquire skills, to learn to communicate with their peers and to master various aspects of the culture into which they are born. As a social phenomenon, games have been studied for a better understanding of cultural traits as well as in studies of personality development.

For the Romanian shtetl, the period between the two wars was a period of transition when Yiddish *mamme lushn* ("mother tongue"), was being inched out of daily use in favor of Romanian and Hebrew. In this respect, as in so many others, the merchant class was leading the way, while the working class trailed behind. While the latter continued to use Yiddish exclusively, the former was rapidly changing; the parents continued using Yiddish among themselves but began speaking Romanian to their children. With the advent of compulsory Romanian education and the intensive Zionist current that brought Hebrew into the kindergarten and primary grades, children's games, too, were subject to this change. The revival of Hebrew as the language of identification with one's roots was encouraged outside the classroom by the teachers, under whose supervision children learned

Hebrew songs, rhymes and games. At the same time, they spoke and played only in Romanian. Few Yiddish rhymes were recalled by the respondents interviewed. In this respect the Romanian shtetl differs from the reports in literature of the Polish shtetl, where Yiddish had not been uprooted and children continued using Yiddish in their games.

A distinction must here be made between a voluntary recreation we call "a game" and an "amusement", technically referred to as a "pastime". While a pastime or amusement suggests an activity that passes the time, games must include some rules as criteria of winning and losing and some elements of competition. Amusements may evolve into games when two or more players are involved and the element of contest is included. Many amusements were originally based on acquiring skills.

Depending on the framework within which they have been compiled, games have been variously classified according to age groups, physical activities, social activities, games of chance, of skill, of mental activity, games involving dramatizing and so on.

One of the ubiquitous pastimes of children was collecting. Children collected odds and ends; boys collected buttons and marbles, which they used in games; little girls collected shiny foil-paper candy wrappers and any colorful bits of cloth, which they used in their games with dolls. Photographs of actors (found in chocolate bars) were collected and traded. High-school children collected and pressed plants in their *herbar* ("herbarium"), for which they were marked in the botany class. For the zoology class they collected insects and butterflies, which they classified according to species and mounted in glass cases. It would have been difficult to draw a line between compulsory work for school and amusement.

On the borderline between game and amusement, one may list *etl-betl* ("cat's cradle"); the hoop for boys; ball playing at all ages; *chechn* ("jacks") and skipping.

Of all the play objects, the most popular by far was the ball, in all its sizes. Regardless of size or material it was favored by boys and girls of all ages. Ball playing was an outdoor game. While boys played *oina*, soccer and other team games, girls preferred the rubber bouncing ball and liked to play in loosely formed groups, the emphasis being on acquiring skills and in competition, rather than in teamwork.

Whether bouncing a ball on the ground or against a handy wall, in marathon competitions or devising pitching and catching games, girls played with balls up to their teens, singing and reciting rhymes while learning skills. Tossing the ball in the air and waiting for it to return, various *figuri* ("movements") were performed with the hands, legs or body, thus learning co-ordination at the same time. Counting rhymes were popular: "Una doua iaca ploua, trei patru, hai la teatru" ("one two there's the rain, three four, come to the theatre").

Oina was a boys' game similar to baseball though less structured, with flexible rules and an indefinite number of players. Any empty lot served. The ball was homemade out of rags, tightly wound around a small stone. Any sturdy stick was used as a bat. It was considered less prestigious than the game called *futbal* ("football"), a form of European soccer. Boys usually graduated from playing *oina* to football.

Futbal ("soccer,") was the élite ball game, played exclusively by boys. Most of the students, members of the sports club Maccabi, played football. It was played by two opposing teams of eleven players each, only outdoors and consequently only during the summer, on a field reserved for this purpose. The field was divided into two halves, with a goal at each end, and with each player occupying an assigned spot on the field, each with specific duties. The two goalkeepers protected the goals; the others pursued the intention of directing the ball into the opposing team's net, while the opposing team did their utmost to prevent it. All the terms used were English, borrowed from soccer, though given a Romanized spelling and pronunciation. The goalkeeper was *golistul*, the two halfbacks were called "bec", which in Romanian means "light bulb", and conveyed to all and sundry the notion that they were an indispensable shining light upon the playing field. Being a "foot" ball game, it was forbidden to touch the ball with the hands; this was a penalty called "hands", which sounded like *hanz* in Romanian, and was frequently heard in shouts from all sides, as were the "out", (pronounced *hout*) and "corner", shouted to the menaced umpire.

The ball used was a round, cowhide soccer ball with an inflatable rubber tire inside, made to withstand kicks of the hefty boys' boots. The local Maccabi team played serious matches, competing with other neighboring shtetl teams. One of the more enterprising young men assigned himself sports reporter and transmitted the local and neighboring events and scores to the national sports journal. Girls were interested in the game only to the extent to which the players represented a romantic interest for them. They cheered and applauded on the sidelines in a somewhat unorganized manner, as did the married men, too old to participate. There was never any question of charging or paying for these games. The idea would have seemed inconceivable in the shtetl.

Ping-Pong was introduced during the early 1930s and played at the

Maccabi clubhouse. A number of young students improvised the table and net and played the game in their own backyard. It was assiduously played by both girls and boys.

Etl-betl ("cat's cradle") was played with a string, about twenty inches long. It required two players and was favored by girls from eight to thirteen; boys considered it a waste of time. There were no rules and no specific element of win or lose. The skill consisted in originality of patterns formed and the ability to sustain the "taking over" of each hand from one player to the other.

In the shtetl, with a minimal traffic problem, little boys liked to drive their hoops along the streets, and especially in the public garden during the summer months. The well-to-do had shiny, lacquered wooden hoops and sticks, which they propelled and manoeuvered with skill; the less fortunate used any metal barrel hoop and any handy tree branch, with no less enjoyment or skill. This was not a girls' pastime.

Chechn ("jacks"), also called *arcishi* (in Romanian, the small bones of the lamb's joints), was played both indoors and out by school children, but was mainly considered a boys' game, although little girls played it as well. It was played with five pebbles of equal size, or with the lamb joints. The players kneeled or sat on the ground, choosing a flat surface, and each player took turns, until he missed by dropping the pebble. The five pebbles were cast on the ground. One was picked up to be used for tossing in the air, while the others were picked up, first one by one, then in twos and three at one time, and finally, all four pebbles had to be picked up in one scoop while the one tossed in the air was on its way down. Boys sometimes added the element of gamble to the game by playing for a prize; girls seemed to enjoy the game for its own sake.

Like ball-playing, skipping was a universally popular children's pastime, accompanied by counting rhymes and songs. It was a girls' game, harbinger of spring weather, and played either alone, to acquire the skill, or as a contest game.

Saritura ("jumping") or hopscotch was a girls' game, played outdoors in the spring and summer. Two or more players participated, taking turns.

A pattern diagram was scratched on the ground with a stick or traced with chalk. It consisted of a rectangle divided into eight chambers and topped by a rounded dome, called *casa* (house), at the far end. Each square was numbered from one to eight; number nine was the *casa*. A small sliver of glass, not larger than one inch square, was tossed into each successive square. It was retrieved by jumping into each square in turn, first hopping in with both feet

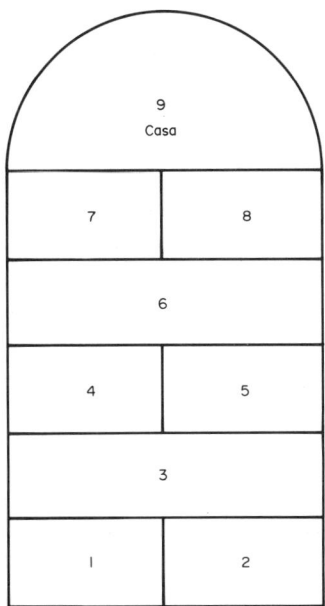

FIG. 14. Saritura — game (hop scotch).

then skipping on one foot, balancing to pick up the glass and returning in the inverse sequence through each square.

The skill consisted both in the ability to aim the piece of glass without missing or touching the margins and in balancing and jumping. Falling or missing a square was "out". This game was played by girls through the primary grades. It lost its interest once the skills were acquired.

Games of strategy may be classified into games of phyiscal participation and games of intellectual strategy. The cat ("pisica"), reminiscent of musical chairs, is known to children under many variants. It was played by girls up to about twelve-years-old; boys were sometimes admitted to complete a team. Five players — four mice and one cat — formed the team. Each mouse took its place at an imaginary square corner, with the cat in the center. The distance between the players was determined by stretching out the arms so that a player touched fingers with a partner in each direction; players exchanged places with partners during the game. The purpose of the game was for the cat to replace one of the mice by pouncing on the empty place; in turn, the mice watchfully exchanged places only when the cat's back was turned. The mouse who lost its place became the next cat.

A similar game played in Poland, was called *Baknbroyt** in which the "it" in the center "goes begging" to each corner. This is an interesting and subtle difference between the Polish and the Romanian shtetl, where begging was too demeaning to be considered worthy of re-enactment in a game.

Metaphorically this game illustrates the deeply implanted cultural belief in the concept of "limited good"† often encountered in European peasant societies, whereby it was held that there was only a limited amount of anything worthwhile and therefore not enough to go around. It instilled an element of envy rather than co-operation, strains of which often appeared in the shtetl personality.

Drop the hankie was a popular game with girls and boys of kindergarten through grade-school age. Any number of players were accepted. They formed a circle and one player walked around the outside of the circle dropping a handkerchief behind one of the players in the circle and running off around the circle. The one at whose feet it fell had to pick it up and at once chase the player, who tried to reach the vacated spot. If he failed to reach the place on time and was caught, he was out. The game was repeated by the player at whose feet the hankie had been dropped. The game ended when all players were out.

Paiul ("the straw") was a game similar to drawing lots. It was played by grade-school girls and had the advantage of being played both indoors and out. Any number could play. Counting out rhymes, one player went to hide while another one was similarly selected to distribute the straw. The players lined up in a row, holding out their palms. The player with the straw, or a small twig, which he held pressed between the palms, made believe to drop the straw in each player's hands, while dropping it only into the hands of one. The one who had been hiding came out and had to guess who had the straw. If he guessed, he was the one to distribute the next straw. If he did not guess, he was out.

Hide and seek had many variants, from the early peek-a-boo (called *cu-cu*) of the toddlers to the pre-teens, when ingenuity and complicated counting-out rhymes were included.

In the same category may be included the various blind man's buff games, where children tried to catch one of the players, while blindfolded, and had to guess their identity.

Tzurca was a local game played outdoors by both girls and boys

---

* *The Shtetl Book* — D & D Roskies, Ktav Publishing House Inc., 1975.
† *Peasant Society*, Little Brown Series in Anthropology; Ed. Jack M. Potter, p. 303, M. Foster, "A Reader".

of grade-school age. *Tzurca* is the Romanian for "a stick sharpened at both ends". The game was played with two sticks, one larger than the other. The small stick was about ten inches long and the larger one about twenty. Two players sufficed, although more would sometimes take turns.

A circle about four feet in diameter was drawn on the ground. Player number one, standing in the center of the circle, threw the small stick by using the larger one as a bat or racket. Player number two marked the spot where it fell and measured the distance from that spot to the circumference, using the *tzurca* ("small stick") as measurement, and recording this as "points" for player number one. The farther it fell the more points for the thrower in the circle. Standing on the spot where the *tzurca* fell, player number two tried to throw the *tzurca* back into the circle, while player number one tried to fend it off with his stick and threw it back out. If it fell into the circle, player number two yelled "tzurca" and won his place inside the circle, while player number one was out. Each time player number one succeeded in throwing back the *tzurca*, the distance was duly measured and added up in his favor.

As an illustration of the ingenuity and adaptability of children's games, where local materials were put to use instead of sophisticated manufactured objects, the game of *tzurca* is perfect. It is reminiscent of the primitive yet effective boomerang of the Australian aborigines. It fostered the skills of throwing, co-ordination and gauging distances. Like other such games, once the skill was mastered the players lost interest in the game.

Beginning with kindergarten and during primary grades, children learned Hebrew songs and games, usually under the supervision of the Hebrew teacher. One dramatization of social activities was the game called *Inei ba ha m'chaçheyfah* ("Here comes the witch"). Boys and girls played together and any number could play. The supervisor selected one child to be the prince or princess and one to be the witch. Both waited on the side for their cue. The children formed a circle, holding hands, and sang "Inei ben a melech ba" ("Here comes the king's son") as the child taking the role approached and began skipping in and out of the circle. As the witch approached, the children began singing "Inei ba ha m'chaçheyfah" ("Here comes the witch"), whereupon the witch tried to catch the prince. The circle of children tried to prevent her from catching the prince by surrounding him or letting him out of the circle to escape. The game ended when the prince was caught and two other players took turns.

We have here a symbol of the conflict between good and evil with the magic protective qualities of the circle against evil.

Games of role-taking were adapted to familiar local situations, giving free rein to the children's creative imaginations. These were, in fact, little plays in which the children took on the roles of the adults in their immediate environment. One respondent recalled that, as a five-year-old, he played with his friends a game they called "electrician" (a recent occupation in town, where electricity had recently been installed). Since the local electrician had a reputation of a simpleton, something of a *shlemiel*, the little boys refused to take on this role and fought to avoid it.

Little girls, starting from nursery school and through grade school, played house, imitating social rituals, tea parties, marriages, taking on the roles of mothers, aunts, dressing up in adult clothes and performing all household chores in miniature, while improvising or using toys.

Guessing games, riddles and intellectual games in general were popular. The emphasis on intellectual activity and disparagement of physical prowess was directly proportional to the social standing of the parents.

The game called "geography" made use of knowledge acquired at school. On the Sabbath it was played orally, while during the week pencil and paper were used. For the latter, each player wrote down as many geographic names as possible beginning with one specified letter within a limited period of time. The one who wrote down the most names was the winner. Orally, the players had to give a proper name beginning with the last letter of the last-mentioned name. For instance: Londo<u>n</u>, <u>N</u>aple<u>s</u>, <u>S</u>pain and so on. Sometimes this game was played with names of history. These games stimulated interest and curiosity and were an encouragement for intellectual pursuits.

Chess, or *shah*, as it was called, was the prestige game of intellectual challenge. It was esteemed to sharpen the mind. Although a number of girls learned to play, it was considered a man's game. Many of the middle-aged couples had learned to play chess during their engagement and courtship, no doubt as much for the interest in the game as for the opportunity to spend the time together.

Tablé ("backgammon") was popular with boys and girls of twelve and older. It shared, with chess, a high prestige. Occasionally, it was played for small stakes. For the younger generation it was becoming what cards and dominoes had been for their parents' generation.

Damé ("checkers") was a popular game played across generation lines. Rabbi Nahum of Stefanesti compared checkers to life; you take one step in order to gain two; you must not take two steps

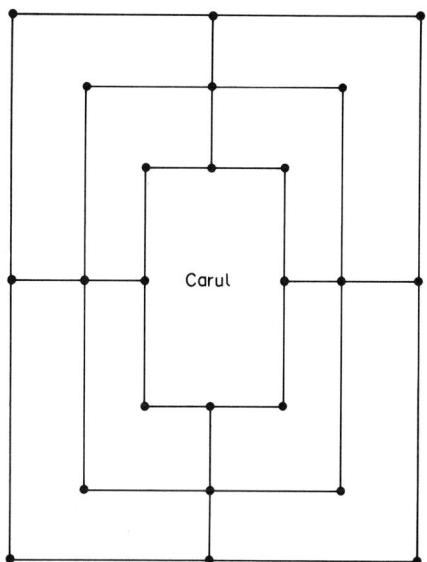

FIG. 15. *Carul*, a popular Romanian shtetl board game played with grain of corn and beans.

at once; you may only go up, once you've reached the top you may go wherever you like.* This bit of philosophy appealed to the shtetl.

Dominoes was a game once popular and still played by the very young and the older generation. The latter played dominoes, which they called *blonch* at the café house, sometimes for small stakes.

Carul ("the wagon") was a local variant of other board games. It was played across generation lines, by all social strata. Two players, each using nine grains of a distinctive color and shape (for example corn and beans) played on a game board where the simple diagram was easily drawn. The diagram consisted of three concentric rectangles with dots marking the corners and halfway points of each of the sides. These dots were joined by straight lines, which, together with the sides of the three rectangles, indicated the possible moves.

Each player started with nine grains, which he took turns to place on the board. The purpose of the game was, first, to place all grains on the board so as to make sets of three in a row, called *car*, and second, to prevent the opponent from obtaining *cars* by obstructing his moves and trying to eat the opponent's grains. After placing all the nine grains, the players began moving them on the board in order

---

* *Encyclopedia Judaica*, Vol. 7, p. 305.

to obtain as many *cars* as possible. As in checkers, if one of the opponent's grains was in the way, one could jump over it and eat it, that is, remove it from the board. Each grain, therefore, had to be strategically protected. The game ended when one had all his grains placed in formation of three or when one remained with only two grains. Like chess and checkers, this was a game of strategy. It also indicates the ingenuity of inventing games with simple means.

Tombola or *lotto* was a game similar to *bingo*, played on printed cards. It was played for small stakes during the long winter evenings at family gatherings. Children were often permitted to participate. Together with the well-known *dreidl* it was traditionally played during Hanukah and Purim.

Every festival had its own traditional children's games, devised and played with any objects, readily available. At Passover, for instance, children liked to play a game with walnuts: a wooden board, about thirty inches long, was placed slanting against a wall. A cuplike hole was dug in the ground at a distance of about one foot from the slanted board. The object of the game was for each player to drop a walnut along the slanted board into the hole in the ground, rolling it from the top. The player who missed lost his walnut. Two or more players could participate.

Another variant of this game was for one player to put down his walnut, which the opponent tried to hit with another walnut by rolling it down the board.

Both of these games evoke echoes of the sophisticated games with which we are familiar. In the shtetl, these were exclusively children's games, beneath the dignity of any self-respecting adult, or even adolescent. The element of gambling in general was mistrusted and gamblers were regarded with more than a little suspicion. All games of chance, even when there was an element of dexterity involved, were associated with loafing, a *leidig geyer* ("worthless character") was no compliment. Billiard players fell into this category, as did most addicted card players. This was regarded as debauchery and was shunned.

Popici ("bowling", "ninepins") was a game played outdoors, usually associated with taverns. It was considered a goyish game, not worthy of a serious-minded Jew.

Adolescent boys and girls began to meet accidentally on purpose. Kissing games were surreptitiously played, with the knowledge that parental disapproval was imminent. *Gajuri* ("pledges") were preceded by a preamble of collecting forfeits with the ultimate purpose of the sender and recipient repairing to a secluded corner for redeeming the pledged object.

One local game where kissing was not involved but where innuendoes provided a certain titillation for the young players was called the "question game". For this game, a previously prepared notebook with questions and answers was used. Questions were listed and numbered on one page; on another page were listed various activities, also identified by numbers. Each player was asked one question, to answer which he picked a number. Reading the answer corresponding to the chosen number resulted in incongruous or embarrassingly suggestive answers, which caused great merriment.

A perusal of the games played in the Romanian shtetl by adults as well as by children reveals two interesting facts. First, games and leisure in general were regarded as primarily the domain of children, not befitting adults; these were frivolous preoccupations.

The second interesting fact emerging from a look at shtetl games is the ingenuity with which the most common objects were transformed by imagination and used as props, be it the children's use of sticks in *tzurca* or adults' use of corn kernels and beans for the game "carul". It demonstrates that complicated, manufactured objects have only snob appeal and are not essential to the intrinsic pleasure derived from playing the game.

Parlour game: who, where, with whom, what, when ...

	1	2	3	4
Name-for girls	Dora	Sophie	Clara	Eva
Name-for boys	Jack	David	Julius	Paul
Where will you meet?	Who knows?	Who knows?	At a party	At a party
What will you dream of?	Of me	Of money	He will kiss you	Of the one you love
What is your sweetheart thinking of now?	To marry you	To betray you	To marry you	To kiss you
Whom do you love?	A poet	A Gypsy	Your neighbor	A tailor
What do people think of you?	You're ugly	Clever	Good scholar	You're a flirt
What do people like in you?	Your figure	Education	The lies you tell	Your manners
How will you make your fortune?	Reading	Marriage	Love	Laughing
What will you be – occupation?	A dancer	To eat	A gossip	A big joke
What do you like most?	To eat	To kiss	To sing	To skate
Where will you live?	Montreal	Botosani	Bucharest	Paris
What will your husband be?	An Officer	A dentist	A teacher	A thief
What will you do most in the future?	Kiss	Play with you	Make love	Travel
What animal do you look like?	A kitten	A duck	A monkey	A horse
Are you in love?	Yes	You were	You're too old	No
What don't you like?	A jealous person	To study	False friends	To flirt

The content of these questions illustrates the preoccupations of boys and girls in their early teens, in the shtetl.

CHAPTER X
Songs

Many of the shtetl's songs, including some of the most beloved Yiddish ones, are the works of well-known poets and date from the nineteenth century. Such is the case of "A Brivole der Mammen" by S. Shmulewitz, or "Of'n Pripichick" by M. Warshawski, both renowned poets of Polish origin. The popularity of these songs entitles them to be considered as true folksongs, for they express in a concrete way the ethos of the shtetl. Like all folk manifestations, the popular shtetl songs embody, often unconsciously, the characteristic spirit of the society that produced them. That is why they survived.

It must also be emphasized that songs are one of the most potent means of perpetuating and reinforcing the accepted values, by instilling them at an early age and by giving or withholding social sanction. They speak of universal emotions with which we can all identify and reveal the specific ways in which a particular society chooses to solve its problems. Through them, we glimpse into the soul of a culture.

The Latin spirit of the host country, so different from the Slavic world of the Pale of Settlement, had a decided influence on the development of the Romanian shtetl. Romanian songs, in spite of often conflicting values, played an important role.

As Zionism expanded and as modern Hebrew was being taught in schools, it was inevitable that new, frequently nationalistic Hebrew songs would revive the old yearning for the Holy Land. The abstract, esoteric love for Jerusalem was paralleled by the new movement of return to the land. This was the core of the *Echalutz* ("young pioneers") movement. Their presence in the shtetl, where they completed the *hachsharah* ("pioneer training"), was a ready source of Hebrew songs, which left its own mark on the Romanian shtetl.

One category of songs that remained intact from Poland were the *hasidic* songs, all based on religious themes, (the glory of God, the rebbé, the Sabbath, the Torah or Jerusalem), expressing with ecstasy their love for Judaism and tradition. The *zemirot* ("songs" or "religious hymns") that Jews carried with them throughout the centuries as part of the religious tradition have been composed as far back as the ninth century and preserved, though melodies varied.

These are true folk songs. In the Romanian shtetl, the term *zmires* referred specifically to the table hymns sung after Sabbath meals.

The fact that the Romanian shtetl, although not exactly opulent, was comparatively prosperous, is reflected in the Yiddish songs with which it tended to identify. Thus, a song such as "Bulbes" ("potatoes"), — where poverty is graphically translated by the monotonous diet of potatoes, — though known, was not one of the favorites. The *bon-vivant* love for a hearty meal and a *shpritz* or a *gleizele vein* ("a little glass of wine") was more in tune with their own way of life. Disseminated by the itinerant Yiddish theater, comic songs such as "Dos beste machl far dem bachl is herring mit kartofles" ("The best dish for the tummy is herring with potatoes") were regarded with derision, as part of life elsewhere. "Koylen a herring far Shabbes" ("Killing, ritually a herring for Sabbath") was one way of summing up the poverty of those whose main dish *for Shabbes* was the lowly herring, decidedly not a festive food. *Mamaliga*, ("corn bread") on the other hand, the staple food of the Romanian peasant though just as lowly, was closer to home.

The lullabies beloved in the Romanian shtetl were, as most of the Yiddish songs, originally from Poland. They expressed with tenderness and love the mother's aspirations for her little ones, her hopes and fears and reverence for learning. Some obviously of a more recent date, were inspired by the concept of inegality, such as: "Break the shackles of poverty."

Though migration to the *Goldene Medine* (the "golden land"), America, was not as heavy from the Romanian shtetl, the pain of parting was a current topic. Sentimental tear-jerker songs such as "A brivele der mammen" ("A little letter to your mother") speak in moving terms of these feelings and the impatience with which the mother awaits her son's letter from afar. Other songs on the same theme present differing views of America. "Die Griene Cousine" ("The immigrant cousin") refers to the pretty young newcomer cousin, courted by the old timer, whom she rebuffs. The marvels of America, where white bread was, (unbelievable as it seemed), daily fare, were less appreciated in the Romanian shtetl where, for most, white bread was not unattainable.

On the other hand, the "doina", the beautiful melancholy Romanian folksong, became part of the Romanian shtetl storehouse. It occasionally brought values alien to the shtetl, as in one *doina* where the peasant mother, no doubt loving and much harassed, leaves the baby to cry among the haystack while she goes about her work in the field, where the Jewish mother, among cares and worries, sings her baby to sleep with promises of the treasures to be found in the *Torah*.

Musicologists and folksingers, have published excellent collections of Yiddish songs. Included here are only the ones most popular in the Romanian shtetl, recognized by the respondents. In some cases, words in the Romanian version differed according to local idiom.

Folksongs in the three languages, Yiddish, Hebrew and Romanian, existed side by side, the latter two, popular mainly among the younger generation. The classification within each language has been made according to topic.

Hasidic Songs

The rebbé or tzadig (saintly man) was the central charismatic figure. Each rebbé had his own following of hasidim who virtually worshipped at his feet. Classified according to theme, there are songs in praise of the Sabbath, of Jerusalem, of the rebbé and throughout, glorifying the One and Only God. Following are a few examples:

Oy, oy, ashreynu, ma tov halkeynu,	Oy, oy, how blessed is our lot
Yim ha nouem goyruleinu	How pleasant is our fate,
Yim ha youffé, youffé irishuseinu	How beautiful is our heritage

Some of the songs were sung while dancing the "hora", a circle dance, with the arms interlocked on each other's shoulders. "Hava nagyla", the popular Israeli hora, was composed at the court of the Rebbé of Sadagura, father of the rebbé of Stefanesti:

Hava, nagyla hava, nagyla v'yishmecha,	Let us be joyful, let us dance
Hava neranenu, hava neranenu, hava neranenu, ve yismecha	Let us be happy
Uru achim ve nisameyach, uruachim b'nisameach	Come brothers, let us be happy
Uru achim, uru achim, v'nisameyach...	Come brothers, let us be happy

Yiddish

Ven eich vel zugn lechudoydy	When I will say come on groom
Vet yir zugn chiri-biri-bim	You will say, chiri-biri-bim
Ven ech vel zugn likras halah	When I will say go to your bride
Vet yir zugn chiri-biri-bim	You will say chiri-biri-bim
Lechudoydy, chiri-biri-bim	Come on groom, chiri-biri-bim
Likras kalah,	Go to your bride,
Chiri-biri-bim	Chiri-biri-bim .....

Some of the songs were frivolous and some songs showed more than a passing interest in the "rebbetzin", the rebbé's wife:

Oy, oy der rebbé geyt,	Oy, oy, there goes the rebbé
Oy, oy der rebbé geyt,	Oy, oy, there goes the rebbé
Oy, die rebbetzin,	Oy, the rebbé's wife
Oy is dus a rebbetzin,	Is she ever a rebbetzin
Vi zi geyt, vi zi shteyt,	How she walks, how she stands,
Aza yor oyf mir.	May I have such a year.

Sha shtill mach nisht keyn geridder	Quiet, still, don't make a rumpus
Der rebbé geyt shoyn tantzn vidder	The rebbé is going to dance again
Sha shtill mach nisht keyn gevald	Quiet, still, don't make such a noise
Der rebbé geyt shoyn tantzn balt	The rebbé will be dancing soon
Un as der rebbé tantzt	And when the rebbé dances
Tantzn doch die vent	The walls dance along with him
Lo mir alle, alle plyesken mit die hent	Let us all clap hands together

Lullabies

As attested by the numerous Slavic words found in Yiddish lullabies, they no doubt originated in Poland and are part of a common heritage. These tender songs express in soothing rhythms the mother's hopes for her baby. More than any other folksongs, the lullaby reflects the spirit of Yiddishkeit, the perrenial love for learning and the reverence for the Torah. Every Jewish mother was convinced that she was rocking in her arms a future great man of letters. "Rojinkes mit Mandlen" (raisins and almonds) was one of the well-known songs believed by many to be part of the folklore but which was composed by Abraham Goldfaden (1840–1908)

Unter Gittele's vigeole	Under Gittele's cradle
Shteyt a klein vais tzigele	Stands a little white kid
Dus tzigele is geforn handln	The little goat went off to trade
Rojinkes mid mandlen	With raisins and almonds
Vus is die beste schoyre	What is the best trade of all?
Gittele's chosn vet lernen toyre	Gittele's bridegroom will study Torah
Toyre vet der chosn lernen	Torah he will learn
Lernen vet er gur kesseider	At all times

Atché patché kichalech	Atché patché little cakes
Der tatica vet koyfn shichalech	Daddy will buy little shoes
Shichalech vet der tatica koyfn	Little shoes will daddy buy
In heyder arein vet dus kind loyfn	To school will the little one run
Loyfn vet er in dem cheyder	He will run straight to school
Lernen vet er dort kesseyder	And there will learn all the time
Dort kesseyder tzvey dray shires	There he will learn two, three lines

Der tate mit der mamme veln hern gitte psires	Father and mother will have good news
Gitte psires un hoyche treyst	Good news and reassuring feelings
Der tatteh mit der mammem veln hubn gitte gest	Daddy and mommy will receive good guests

When asked what songs they recalled, all respondents without exception mentioned "Of'n Pripitchik" as the best known folksong. This song was written and composed by a well-known Polish poet Mark Warshawski at the end of the nineteenth century.

Of'n pripitshik, brent a fayerl	On the hearth, there burns a little fire
Un in shtyib is heys	And the house is warm
Un der rebbé lernt mit die kindelech	And the rebbé teaches the little ones
Dem alef beys	The alef bet (alphabet)
Zugt che kinderlech, gedenkt che tayere	Repeat children, remember dear ones
Vus ir lernt do	What you're learning here
Zogt chet noch a mohl un tacke noch a mol	Say then again and once again
Kometz alef ou	Kometz alef reads ou
Lernt kinderlech mit groys cheysek	Learn dear children with great desire
Azoy sug ich aych un	This I am telling you
Ver s.vet giher kennen lernen	The one who will learn best
Der bakimt a fun	Will receive a flag (reward).
Az ir vet kinderlech elter vern	When you children will grow older
Vet ir alleyn farshteyn	You will understand
Vi fiel in die oysyes lign trern	How many tears lie in these letters
Und vi fiel gevein	And how many sobs
Az yir vet kinderlech dem goles shlepn	As you little ones, are burdened by diaspora
Oysgemytchet zein	And you will be tired and worn
Zolt yir fin die oysies koyech sheppen	Find strength in these letters
Kykt in zey arain	As you look into a book (find solace)

Lullaby	*Lullaby*
Shluf mein kind	Sleep my child
Shluf vider ruig zein	Sleep again, quietly
Die nacht is shtill	The night is still
Und die levune sheint	And the moon shines
Oyf dem hyml glantzn shtern	Stars are shimmering in the heavens
Kik nisht kind mein of meine trern	Don't look, my child, at my tears
Shluf mein kind	Sleep my child
Shluf vider ruig ein	Sleep again quietly
Der tate vet shoyn mer nit kimmen	Your father will not return
Men hot im fin heim avek genemen	He was taken away from home
Of die gassn im geshlept	Off the streets he had been dragged off
Of dem eshafod gekept	He was beheaded on the scaffold
Zenen mir gebleibn kind alein	We, my child, now remained alone

A brooding solicitude for their children's future and a note of self pity crept into some lullabies when Socialist ideals reached the shtetl. (Jewish maids were rare in the shtetl, where most servant girls were gentiles. The following lullaby was sung by a Jewish servant girl from Branishtea, a village across the Prut river, in Bessarabia).

Shlof mein kind, mein tayer haysl	Sleep my child, my dearest life
Lyu, lyu, lyulinké	Lyu, lyu, lyulinké
Mach shoyn tzy dayne tayere eygelech	Close your darling little eyes
Lyu, lyu, lyulinké	Lyu ......
Und ven dyi velst vern gresser	And when you will grow up
Zug mir mein kind tzi	Promise me, my child
Velst tzeraisn dayné shlesser	That you will break your shackles
Lyu, lyulyulinké	Lyu ......
Velst tzeraisn dayne shlesser	That you will break away your shackles
Fun dayne hent und fyis	From your hands and feet
S'is besser tzu ryien tzvishn die toyte	For it is better to rest among the dead
Vin eyder tzu leybn myis	Rather than live enslaved (an ugly life)

Children's rhymes (Yiddish)

Nursery rhymes as such were not part of the Romanian shtetl lore. Children were beginning to learn Romanian and Hebrew rhymes and songs. Some nonsense rhymes seem to be local and even part of specific family lore. The reference to the tall Germans and to their "short clothes" is an interesting comment on the shtetl impression of foreigners. A "Datch" (derived from Deutch, i.e. German) was the name conferred on any outlandish stranger.

Yitzik, pyitzik, nudl tash	Yitzik pyitzik needle purse
Gey in kloyster, ganve a flash	Go to a church and steal a flask
Gey aroys und kik dich oys	Go outside and look around
Und kim arein und zug nisht oys	And come back and don't say a word.

This rhyme goes against several shtetl values: going into a church was in itself esteemed an unforgivable sin; stealing was not only not advocated but severely punished. It reflects contempt for any other religion.

Biribimchik, biribimchik, picupanu	Biribimchik, biribimchik picupanu
La soldat, la soldat	Soldier, soldier
Dray tuller a royte kyi	Three dollars a red cow
Nem a shtrik un bind zi tzi	Take a cord and tie her up
Nem a shtekn un shlog z'azoy	Take a stick and beat her thus
Biz zi't shrayen oy, oy, oy,	Till she'll cry, oy, oy, oy

Ovinu meylech	Our father our king
Dus hartz is mir freylech	My heart is full of joy
Freilech zol mir zein	Let us all be joyful
Trinken vel mir vain	And drink wine
Vain veln mir trinken	Wine we will drink
Kreplech veln mir essn	Kreplech (ravioli) we will eat
Un in unzer libn Got	And our beloved God, we will
Veln mir keymon nit fargessn	Never forget
Of dem oychn bargh	On the high hill
Un of dem grinem gruz	And on the green grass
Shteyen a pur dachn	Stand a couple of Germans
Mit die longe batchn	With long whips
Hoyche menner zennen zey	Tall men they surely are
Kertze kleyder geyen zey	Short clothes they surely wear
Gey nor a bisele vater	Go on a little farther
Bagegn a kyi mit an atter	You will see a cow with an udder
Die kyi vil deh shlugn	The cow wants to hurt you
Gey tzum poretz klugn	Go complain to the master
Der puritz is nisht do inderheim	The master's not at home
Nor dus hintole alein	Only his little dog
Der puretz hakt holtz	The master is chopping wood
Dus hintole lekt shmaltz	The little dog licks chicken fat
Die pritze kimt arein	The master's wife comes in
Der puretz macht vein	The master is making wine

———

Hey, hey hemerl	Hey, hey, little hammer
Kym tzu mir in kemerl	Come to me in my little chamber
Vel ich dir epes vazn	I'll show you something
Shicholech fin azn	Shoes made of iron
Shicholech fin gold	Shoes made of gold
Kim tzu mir abold	Come to me soon

Love Songs

Love has always been an inspiration for songs. In spite of the fact that Romanian songs were becoming increasingly popular, old Yiddish favorites continued to be part of the repertory when young people gathered in informal glee sessions. "Reizele", "Tumbalalayka", "Margaritkelech", were often heard at the youth clubs. (These songs are to be found in most Yiddish collections and need not be reproduced here.) Yiddish repertory theatres left behind couplets often at odds with the values prevalent in the shtetl.

Dayn mamme ker doch meinen	Your mother no doubt supposes
Az dyi velst nemen nodn	That you will take a big dowry
Und mit dem nodn velst dyi vern raich, oy, oy	And with the dowry you'll become rich

Got ken dir helfn	God can help you
Dem nodn zolst faliern	To lose all your dowry
Und mit a koptzn zolst die vern glaich	And wind up poor like a pauper

Oy, oy dus fingerl	Oy, oy, that wedding band
Oy, oy dus fingerl	Oy, oy, that wedding band
Kom git men dus ba yaich a pack	As soon as they catch you with it
Hopt men eich arein in sack	You're trapped in the sack
Pavolié, yir dreyt sich mehr nisht oys	Slowly now, you can't get out again!

Shein vi die levune	Lovely like the moon
Lachtig vi die shtern	Bright like all the stars
Fun hyml a matune	From heaven a gift
Host di mir tzigeshigt	You sent down to me

Wedding Songs

The custom of having a professional jester called a *badchen* at weddings and to bewail the bride (*baveinen die kallé*) was disappearing in the Romanian shtetl. Echoes of the past however remained in many songs. To marry off children and see them settled, *derleibn tzu zeir chuppah* (to live to see them under the wedding canopy) was a most cherished wish. Marrying off the youngest child especially a girl *die mezinké* was the greatest wish of all. *Oysgybn die mezinké* (to marry off the youngest daughter) had come to mean showing off one's abilities with an undertone of "letting one's hair down".

At azoy, at azoy macht men chassene kinder	That's the way, one marries off one's children
Mit a sloy angemachts	With a jarful of jam,
Kikt nor un Got's vinder	Just see God's wonders

A humorous twist to this song was the following version:

At azoy, at azoy, nart men up a chusn	That is the way one hoodwinks a bridegroom
Me zugt im tzy a zack nodn	Promise him a sackful of dowry
Me git im nisht a groshn	Give him just a penny

Another ditty originating from the itinerant theatres was:

Hot a Yid a vabole	Has the Jew a little wife
Hot er groyse tzures	Is she a pack of troubles
Hot a Yid a vabole,	Has the Jew a little wife
Toygt zie of kapores	She is good for nothing

Songs of Parting

Of all the songs on this topic "A brivole der Mammen" (A little letter to your mother) was the most beloved. Like many other songs this tearjerker was believed to be a true folksong. It was written by S. Shmulewitz, inspired by the frequent partings when people left for America.

Mein kind mein kroyn	My child, my crown
Dyi furst avek	You are leaving now
In tiefe vaite lender	To distant far off lands
Dich beit mit trern un mit shrek	With tears and fears
Dein troye liebe mamme	Your loving mother begs you
A brivole der mammen	A little letter to your mother
Zolst dyi nisht ferzammen	Please do not delay too long
Shreib geshvind, mein tayer kind	Write with speed, my dearest child
Shenk yir die nekamme	Give her this comfort
Die mamme velt dein brivole leinen	Your mother will read your letter
Und zi velt azoy genezn	And will be so delighted
Dyi heilst yir shmertz, yir bitter hartz	Her pains will heal, her embittered heart be soothed
Derkvik yir die neshome	Refresh her soul

Street vendors may have inspired melancholy songs such as "Kupitie bublichkie" (buy my bagels) or "koyftchet papirossn" (buy cigarettes) but the Romanian shtetl vendors' cries were far more prosaic. There is no doubt that these songs were of Slavic origin, since most of the words are Slavic.

Oy koyftchet, koyftchet papirosn,	Buy, please buy my cigarettes
Trikene fun reign nisht bagossn	Dry ones, not soaked by the rain
Koyftchet, koyftchet be nemones	Buy please buy and trust me
Hot of a yoysem rachmones	Have compassion on an orphan
Ratevet fun reygn un gefar	Please save me from rain and distress
Der tatte in malchome hot faloyrn zeine hent	Father in war lost both his hands
Die mamme far yissirm dertrogn ot nisht gekent	Mother found the torment unbearable
Koyftchet, koyftchet be nemones	Buy please, buy and trust me
Hot of a yoysem rachmones	Have compassion on an orphan
Ratevet fun reygn un gefar	Please save me from rain and from distress

Bagels (yeast dough rings) that delicacy transplanted to America was a shtetl specialty and *heyse bagels* (hot bagels) was a familiar shtetl sound. The bagel vendor's song, unlike that of the cigarette vendor was not as melancholy, but rather a lively, lilting one.

Oy koyftchet beygolech	Buy little bagels
Kupitie bublichkie	Buy little bagels
Oy koyftchet beygolech	Buy little bagels
Tzvey far a lei	Two for one lei (Romanian currency)

Dissolute life was never glorified. References to excessive drinking or other vices were treated with contempt or irony but never glamorized. Wine was a condiment to life but it was not "yiddish" to drink too much. Moderation was always advocated.

Oy, oy, shicker is a goy	Oy, oy, drunk is the Gentile
shicker is er, trinker miz er	Drunk he is, for drink he must
Vail er is a goy	Because he is a Gentile (not a Jew)

Lo'mir ale'n einem	Let us all together,
Nisht sheymen sich far keinem	Not be ashamed of anyone
Lo'mir ale'neinem freilech zein,	Let us all together be gay
Lo'mir ale freilech zein,	Let us all be joyful, gay
Trinken vein,	Drink some wine,
Lo'mir ale'neinem freilech zein.	together let all be gay

One of the most popular Yiddish songs was "Lo mir sich yiberbetn" ("Let's make up our quarrel") of which a variety of verses existed;

Lo mir sich yiberbetn, yiberbetn	Let us make up ...
Hob of mir rachmones — repeat	Have pity on; me
Lo mir sich yiberbetn	Let's make up
Ich ob dich lieb sekounes	I love you so
Lo mir sich yiberbetn, yiberbetn	Let us make up
Shtey nisht by der tier	Don't stand at the door
Lo mir sich yiberbetn	Let's make up
Vel mir trinken bier	And we will drink some beer
Lo mir sich yiberbetn	Let us make up
Ich beit dir zei mir moychl	Please forgive me
Lo mir sich yiberbetn,	Let us make up
Gib of mir a shmeychl	Give me a smile
Lo mir sich yiberbetn ...	Let us make up
Yich vel zein dein chossn	I want to be your bridegroom
Lo mir sich yiberbetn	Let us make up
Vet zein simche ve sussn	It will be such a pleasure
Lo mir sich yiberbetn ...	Let us make up
Los die mamme vissn	Let your mother know
Lo mir sich yiberbetn	Let us make up
Lo mir sich zukishn	And let us kiss each other
Lo mir sich yiberbetn	Let us make up
Royte pommerontzn	Red oranges
Lo mir sich yiberbetn,	Let us make up
Lo mir geyen tantzn	Let us go dancing

Children were taught not to carry grudges and after a quarrel to make up. As a truce, they sang while hooking together each other's little finger of one hand:

Righiole, righiole roygess	Righiole, righiole roygess
Intz zenen gevorn broygess	We were quarreling
Righiole, righiole righ	Righiole, righiole righ
Intz zemen gevorn krigh	We have now made up
Vus ich vel hubn vell ich dir gibn	Whatever I will have, I will give you
Vus dy velst hubn velst dyi mir gibn.	Whatever you will have, you will give me

Working men and women used to sing at their workbench; the following is a typical tailor's song:

Zitzn zitz ich mir a fis iber a fis	I am sitting one leg over the other
Veil mein arbeyt is mir tziker zis	'Cause my work is so sweet to me
Yich ney und ney a gantze voch	I sew and sew all the week long
Un ney mir oys a Parizer loch	And sew me here a Paris-fashion hole!
Tzien tzi ich mir die farshtrigen	I pull and pull the bastings out
Und ich es mir die mammelige	And eat my mamaliga (Corn bread)
Shabbes gey ich mir aroys vi in possig shteyt	Saturday I go out in style (as ordained in the sacred books)
In die eygene b'godim vus ich ob geneyt	Wearing the clothes I've sewn myself

Another version of this song no doubt originated in Lithuania since the last verse rhymes better with the Litvak pronunciation (*breyt*) rather than the Romanian (*broyt*).

Atazoy neyt a shnayder	This is the way a tailor sews
Atazoy neyt er git	This is how he sews so well
Er neyt un neyt a gantze voch	He sews and sews the whole week long
Fardint a para mit a loch	And earns a para (coin) with a hole
A shnayder neyt un neyt un neyt	A tailor sews and sews and sews
Un hot kadoches nit kein broyt	And gets malaria instead of bread

Mrs. Ernestine Rottenberg offered this Yiddish song, suggesting that the "sickiole" ("the little booth") symbolized Judaism and the Jewish people.

A sickiole a kleine	A little booth
Fun breitolech gemeine	Made of cheap slats and boards
Hob ich mir mit tzores gemacht	I built for myself in woe
Gedekt hob ich dem dach	I covered the roof
Mit a bintole schach	With bundles of reeds
Und ich zitz mir in sichiole ba nacht	And sit in it alone at night
Dos ershte gericht	The first thing you must know
Mit a troerik geshicht	With sad countenance
Romt mir meine mutter harein	My mother whispered to me

Zie shtelt sich avek	She stood there
Un sugt mir mit shreck	And said with fright in her voice
Az der vint vet dos sickole unvorfn	That the wind may blow away this booth
Zey nisht kein naar	Don't be a fool
Hob nisht kein tzaar	Don't be so mournful
Der vint vet dos sickiole nit imvorfn	The wind will not blow away your booth
Vie fiel vintn es brimmen	No matter how many winds will blow
Vie fiel sturmen es kimmen	How many storms will appear
Dos yiddishe sichiole shteyt shtoltz	The Jewish little booth remains standing proud

Hebrew Songs

Hebrew was introduced at the nursery school level by teaching little songs as accompaniment to games and dances. It was also a potent vehicle for conveying and imprinting cultural values.

Madua a olam kolkach affuah	Why is the world so upside down?
Ma she lemala lo le mata	What should be up is down
Ma she lemata lo le mala	What should be down is up
Ma she shachor ve lo lavan	What should be black and not white
Ma she lavan ve lo shahor	What should be white and not black

The same values appear repeatedly in most songs: respect for learning and the wish of continuity through offspring. The greatest aspirations parents had was to see their children successful in life as the following little song taught to kindergarten children illustrates:

Yizké l'irot baniim	Let us be worthy to have sons
Baniim ou banot	Sons and daughters
Oskyim ba torah	Successful in learning Torah
U be avoda	And in their work

There is no doubt that the Protestant work ethic was deeply ingrained in shtetl values. To work was as natural as waking up in the morning, eating at noon and sleeping at night:

Boker, boker, boker iney ba	Morning, morning, here comes the morning
Boker ba l'avoda, boker ba l'avoda	Moring comes, let's go to work
Boker iney ba	Here comes the morning
Tzarayim, tzarayim, tzarayim inei ba	Mid-day, mid-day, here comes mid-day
Tzarayim ba l'ahila, tzarayim ba l'ahila	Mid-day, comes, let's go to eat
Tzarayim iney ba	mid-day is here

Erev, erev, erev, iney ba	Evening, evening, here comes evening
Erev ba le sheyna, erev ba le sheyna	Evening comes, let's go to sleep
Erev iney ba.	Evening is here.

And, as a corollary, the sadness brought about by lack of work during the 1930's *criza* (depression) felt less in the shtetl, but well understood:

Hevrey'a, hevrey'a ma lasot b'li avoda	Friends, friends, what's to do without work
Eifo, v'eifo, v'eifo leavod?	Where, oh where, where to find work?
Cand toata lumea casca gura (change to Romanian)	When everyone idles about
Si Basheul striga urah	And the Basheu (stream) yells hurrah!
Si comertul merge prost	And business is so bad
Nu mai este tot ce-a fost.	It's not the way it used to be

Youth clubs of various political orientations, each had their own arsenal of Hebrew songs, often martial tunes with nationalistic lyrics. At Betar, the Revisionist youth club, young people marched and waved the blue and white Zionist flag glorifying Jabotinsky and Trumpeldor, their heroes.

Kumu, kumu haverim	Stand up, stand up friends
Kumu, kumu bachurim,	Stand up, stand up young boys
Kadima mizracha,	Forward to the East
Mizracha kadima	To the East, forward
Bardu, bardu, bardu ba derech	Make room, make room on the road
Bardu chaverim Yivrim tzofim,	Make room, friends, young Jews,
Tel-Chai!	Tel-Chai! (revisionist greeting)

Be mizrach artzeinu, anu olchim yahad	Eastward to our land, we are going together
Jabotinsky majhigenu, tzofim, eidat, eidat	Jabotinsky is our leader, let's go
Anahnu b'rit Trumpeldor,	We're of the covenant of Trumpeldor,
Anahnu b'rit Trumpeldor, tzofim, eidat, eidat.	Young friends, let's go . . .

Saleynu al shichmeinu	With sacks on our shoulders
Rasheynu bahurim	Young boys
Mi ktzot ha eretz ba-nu,	From every corner of the land
Mi'ktzot ha a Gallil	We come from the Gallilee
Mi Yehuda, mi Yehuda mi shomrot	From Yehuda, from the watchtowers
Mi ha Emek, mi ha Emek ba Gallil	From the Emek in Gallilee
Pa nu derech lanu, ba Gallil itanu	Make room for us, come to Gallilee with us
Ah, ah, ah ma tov, ah a Gallily	Ah, ah, how good it is, how good In Gallilee

The *halutzim* (pioneers) working in the shtetl prior to leaving for Palestine, were a source of Hebrew songs which became part of shtetl repertory.

Am Israel am Israel hay,	Israel is alive,
Am hay, Israel hay, . . . Am Israel hay;	The people is alive, Israel is alive . . .

Some were sung in both Hebrew and Romanian on the same melody:

Bein a harim, bein a suarim	Between valleys, between hills
Misua rokevet	The train is winding
U mi kol a bahurim (bahurot) otah (otha)	From among all the boys (girls)
Ani oev (oevet)	I love you best

or in Romanian, more of the same:

Intre vai si intre dealuri	Between valleys, between hills
Trece o carutza	Goes a horse and wagon
Si din toate fetele	And among all the young girls
Tu esti mai dragutza	You are the prettiest

The Hebrew calendar served as marking post in the Romanian shtetl and each festival came equipped with its own ceremonial and songs. Some, such as the ballads sung during the Passover Seder, were true folk songs, dating back into history and incorporated into the evening ritual. Thus, "Had Gadya" (One kid), "Ehad Mi Iodea" (Who Knows One) have become part of the family sing song after the Passover meal.

Most holy days were somber commemorations of sad historical events. Purim, and especially Simchat Torah however had their own merry songs, geared especially for the children.

Purim, when children dressed up like the mummers *mascatii* and went from door to door, they sang little ditties and received cookies or pennies:

Aint is Pyrem, morgn is oys	Today is Purim, tomorrow is not
Gibts mir a pare un varfts mich aroys	Give me a penny and throw me out

Haynt is Pyrem,	Today is Purim
S'is der yomtov groys	'Tis a great feastday
Kimtz zingt die lieder	Come, let's sing some songs
Geyn fyn hoys tzu hoys	Going from house to house

On the day Moses received the Torah on; Mount Sinai, celebrated on Simchat Torah, children as well as adults sang the glory of the event:

Simchu na simchu na	Let us rejoice
Simchas Torah	In the joy of Torah
Simchu na simchu	Rejoice ye brothers
Na Yismechi acheinu	Who love the Torah
B'simchas ha Torah	

All community events ended with the singing of "Hatikva" (Hope) the hymn which has now become the national anthem of the state of Israel. In the Romanian shtetl it was sung as a national anthem long before the existence of the state of Israel, standing up in reverence.

Romanian Songs

The building of the Jewish–Romanian school at the turn of the century and legislation of compulsory Romanian education, made inevitable inroads into Yiddish life in the Romanian shtetl. Having earlier changed from Cyrillic to the Latin alphabet, Romania had embarked on a campaign of Romanization. Where until then any language but Yiddish and Hebrew, referred to as the sacred language, had been taboo, learning Romanian in public school raised its prestige while demeaning the prestige of Yiddish.

Many songs and ballads were taught in school but many were diffused via the maids, (peasant girls from surrounding villages), who sang their people's songs.

The *doina* is a typical Romanian folksong. It is the generic name of a specific genre of songs. In melancholy, even depressing moods, the doina speaks of "dor" (yearning, longing) and spans all possible topics. There are *doinas* of love, lullabies, longing for the homeland or loneliness and grief.

De cand eram inca mic	Since I was still knee high
Doina stiu si doina zic	Doina I know and doina'I say
Of . . . of . . .	Of . . . of . . .
Caci Romanu cat traeste	For the Romanian, his life long
Tot cu doina se mandreste	The doina he will show off
Boii mei cand aud doina	When my oxen hear a doina
Are tarina si moina	They plow the fields and thawing furrows
Eu de'aud o copilita	When I hear a young girl
Cantand doina'n poenita	Sing a doina in the glade
Ma duc iute s'o gasesc	I rush there to find her
Si de doina sa' soptesc	And whisper to her about the doina

Dorul bade, de la tine	Longing comes from you to me
Peste vai si dealuri vine	Over valleys and over hills
De nu-l poate opri nimeni;	There's no power to halt it
Nici cioban cu fluerul,	Neither shepherd with his flute,
Nici popa cu cintecul	Nor the priest with his chant,
Numai eu cu sufletul.	Only I can, with my soul

Doina, doina cantec dulce	Doina, doina, sweet song,
Cand te'aud eu nu m'asi mai duce	When I hear you, I don't feel like leaving
Doina, doina, cant cu foc	Doina, doina, fiery song
Cand te'aud, eu stau pe loc.	When I hear you, I stand still

"Cavalul" (Mrs. T. Grisaru recalled this: "The Flute")

Si cavalul tot s'aude	And the flute sounds are heard
De departe trist si vag	In the distance, sad and vague
De departe tot rasuna	In the distance still they echo
Doina unui dor pribeag	The doina of a wandering longing.
Pe carari, uliti pierdute	Along paths, lost byways
Umblam lenesh visator	Walking lazily, in a dream
Ma opream s'ascult in vale	I stopped to listen (as) from the valley
Unda limpede de izvor.	Sparkling sounds reached from the brook

Romanian lullaby; (recalled by Mrs. D. Mitescu)

Hai odor, hai pasarica,	Come my treasure, come little birdie
Dormi, o dormi, fara de frica,	Sleep, O sleep, don't be afraid
Sa te'alinte mosh cuminte	May the old man Sleep caress you
Si sa-ti cante'ncetinel	May he sing you quietly
Mugur, mugur, mugurel.	Flower bud, bud, little bud
Ingerii vin tiptil si'alene	Angels come on tiptoe, lazy
Sa te mangaie pe gene	To caress you on the lashes
Si mi-ti leagan' dulce leagan	And to rock you in your cradle
Fraged trupusor de crin	Tender little lily body
Ca s'adormi frumos si lin.	So you may sleep peacefully, soft
Ce tresari? Nu'i nimeni, nimeni	Why the startle? There's no one,
Liniste si intunecime	No one but stillness in the dark
Doar Zefirul, musafirul	It's only Zephyr, the visitor
Cel sagalnic si pribeag	Mirthful and wandering
A trecut pe langa prag.	Who skipped in o'er the doorstep
Si-a trimes o gaza mica	And look he sent a lady-bug
Sa'ti aduc'o scrisorica	To bring you a little message
Si sa'ti spuna noapte buna	And to say to you good night
Ca'i si el satul de drum	'Cause he too is tired of roaming
Merge sa se culce'acum.	And is going to sleep now

Romanian children's songs

Children chanted Romanian rhymes while playing ball games, skipping or playing hide and seek. These are mostly nonsense rhymes, often using counting numbers in the game.

Una doua, iaca ploua	One two, there, it's raining
Trei patru hai la teatru	Three four, come to the theatre
Cinci shase, hai la masa	Five six, come to the table
Shapte opt, ai mancat un caine copt	Seven eight, you ate a cooked dog
Noua zece, un pahar cu apa rece	Nine ten, a glass of cold water
Cioc boc, treci la loc,	Chok, boc, take your place
Esti un mare dobitoc.	You're a big oaf (animal)
Mielc, mielc, codobelc	Snail, snail, without a veil
Scoate coarne boieresti	Stick out horns like an ox
Si te du la balta	And go down to the pond
Si bea apa calda	And drink warm water
Si te du la Dunare	And go down the Dunare (Danube)
Si bea apa tulbure	And drink the muddy water
Ala mala portocala	Ala mala, orange
Iesi Ghorghita la portita	Go Ghiorghita to the gate
Ca te-asteapta Talion	There waits for you Talion
Talion fecior de domn	Talion, son of a gentleman
Cu caruta Radului	With Radu's wagon
Cu carul imparatului	With the emperor's horses
Dorobanz clanz.	Dorobantz-klantz (name of a regiment-klantz)
Sade Turcul pe saltea	The Turk sits on the mattress
Si comanda o cafea	And orders a coffee
O cafea amara	A bitter coffee
Si pe usa'afara	And out you go
Cafeluta'i cu caimac	The little coffee's with thick foam
Hopai tzupai si'un gandac	Hop, tzop, and a bug
La un popa a fost un caine	There was a priest who had a dog
Si pe acela l'a iubit	And he loved him very much
Si-a inghitit un os de peste	And he swallowed a fish bone
Si pe urma a murit	And then he died
Si pe groapa lui a fost scris ca ...	And on his grave it was written that ...
La un popa a fost un caine ...	There was a priest, who had a dog ...
and so on	and so on

In the Romanian nursery school as well as in the first grade of primary school, classes began with warming up calisthenics to the following song:

Luati seama bine	Pay attention well
In picioare drept	On your feet, stand straight
Ochii toti la mine	Eyes all look at me
Mainile la piept	Hands folded on your chest
Luati seama bine	Pay attention well
Dupa cum v'am spus	As I said before
Ochii toti la mine	Eyes all look at me
Mainile in sus	Hands stretched above the head
Un doi trei un doi trei	One two three, one two three
Un doi trei, asa copii	One two three, children, look at me
Luati seama bine, uit'asa frumos	Pay attention well, nicely just like this
Ochii toti la mine	Eyes all look at me
Mainile in jos	Hands and arms straight down

Folk dancing was part of school curriculum and in the Romanian school it occupied an important place in the daily program.

Alunelu, alunelu, hai la joc	Little peanut, little peanut, come to dance
Sa ne fie, sa na fie, cu noroc	May this be for good luck
Cine hora o s'o joace	He who will dance the hora
Mare, mare se va face	Will grow big, so big
Cine n'o juca de fel	He who will not dance at all
Sa ramaie mititel	Will remain a little one

"Ana Lugojana"	"Ana from Lugj"
Ca n!am venit la voi la sura	'Cause I didn't come down to your barn
Ana Lugojana	Ana Lugojana
Sa ma uit pe sub caciula	To peek around from under my hat
Ana Lugojana	Ana Lugojana
Ci'am venit sa joc c'o fata	I came to dance with a girl
Ana Lugojana	Ana Lugojana
Sa ma pomeneasc!odata	So she'll remember me some day
Ana Lugojana	Ana Lugojana
Asa se joaca pe la noi	This is the way we dance where I come from
Uit'asa doi cate doi	This way, look, two by two
Uite, uit'asa	Look, look here, like this

"Trandafir de la Moldava"

Trandafir de la Moldova	Rose from Moldova (the northern province)
Te'asi iubi dar nu'ti stiu vorba	I'd love you but don't know your dialect
Lunca, lunca, lunca'i lata	The meadow, meadow, meadow's wide
Te-asi iubi da-mi esti cumnata	I'd love you but you're my sister-in-law

Trandafir de pe cetate	Rose from the fortress
Spune'i memei sanatate	Wish your mother good health
Lunca, lunca, lunca'i lata	The meadow, meadow, meadow's wide
Te-asi iubi da-mi esti cumnata	I'd love you but you're my sister-in-law

"Colo'n Gradinita"

Colo'n gradinita, sub bolta de vita	Down in the little garden, under the vine'arch
Vin fetito, vin sa te sarut	Come little girl, let me kiss you
Amorul meu e mare, far'asemanare	My love is great, without compare
Vin fetito, vin sa te sarut	Come little girl, let me kiss you
Oh, si mai am inca un singur dor,	Oh, I have one more longing, to marry you
Cu tine eu vreau sa ma'nsor	Near you, it's always good ...
Langa tine' vesnic bine ...	

"In fanul de curand cosit"

In fanul de curand cosit	In the freshly mown hay
Gandind la tine'am adormit	Thinking of you, I fell asleep
Si de miros imbalsamat	And swimming in its balsam fragrance
Ce vis frumos eu am visat	What a lovely dream I dreamed
Mi se parea ca's flori de fan	It seemed to me among the hay blooms
Stam aplecat la caldu'ti san	I was reclining on your warm bosom
Si iti juram ca te iubesc	And I was swearing to you my love
Ca pentru tine doar traesc	That I live only for your sake

"Rodica"

Purtand cofita cu apa rece	Carrying the wooden pail with cold water
Pe ai sai umeri, albi rotunjori	On her, white, well shaped shoulders
Juna Rodica voioasa trece	Youthful Rodica, merrily passes
Pe langa junii semanatori	Near the young sowers, (seeding grain)
Ei cu grabire ii sar'in cale	They quickly hurry toward her
Zicand Rodico Floare de crin	Saying: "Rodica, you lily flower"
In plin sa'ti mearga vrerile tale	May your wishes be fulfilled
Precum tu drago, ne iesi cu plin	As you, darling, meet us with full (pail of water)
S'ajungi mireasa, s'ajungi cariasa	May you become a bride, and be a queen,
Calea sa'ti fie numai cu flori	Your road always be strewn with flowers
Si casa casa, si masa masa,	Your home, a home, your table proper
Si sanu'ti leagan de pruncusori	Your bosom cradle for little babes

All peoples are proud of their heritage and find their language superior to all other languages. Romanians are no exception.

Mult e dulce si frumoasa	How sweet and beautiful
Limba ce'o vorbim	Is the language we speak
Alta limb'armonioasa	Another tongue as harmonious
Ca ea nu gasim	We can find nowhere

Salta inima'n placere	The heart skips with delight
Cand o ascultam	When we hear her sounds
Si pe buze'aduce miere	And on the lips we taste sweet honey
Cand o cuvantam	When we say each word
Romanasul o iubeste	The Romanian loves it
Ca sufletul sau	As much as his own soul
O, vorbiti, scrieti Romaneste	Do speak and write Romanian
Pentru Dumnezeu.	For the Good Lord's sake

Romanasului ii place	The Romanian loves being
Sus la munte, sus la munte la izvor	Up the mountains, in the mountains at a spring
Liber si sa fie'n pace	Free and to be left in peace
Al naturei, al naturei domnitor.	There to reign as nature's own prince
Sa'si traiasca'n fericire	To live in happiness
Libertate si iubire	Live in freedom and in love
Timpul iute, timpul iute trecator.	Flying, speeding, fleeting time

---

When the two provinces Moldova and Muntenia were united, many songs fostered the spirit of unity in the newly formed country.

Hai sa dam mana cu mana	Let us stretch and shake hands
Cei cu inima Romana	Those with a Romanian heart
Sa'nvartim hora fratiei	Let us dance the brotherly hora
Pe pamantul Romaniei	On the Romanian soil
Iarba rea din holde piara	May weeds perish from the fields
Piara dusmanii din tara	May the enemies perish from the land
Si'ntre noi sa nu mai fie	And between us, may there be
Decat flori si harmonie	Only flowers and harmony
Mai Muntene, mai vecine	Hey there "Muntene", hey neighbor
Vino sa te prinzi cu mine	Come put your arms on my shoulders
Sa'nvartim hora fratiei	Let us dance the brotherly hora
Pe pamantul Romaniei	On the Romanian soil

George Enesco's "Romanian Rhapsody" was inspired by folksongs. The popular lyrics of the well known rhapsody are as follows:

Am un leu si vreau sa'l beau,	I have a leu (cent) and want to drink it up
Tra la la la la	Tra la la la la
Nici acela nu'i al meu,	Even this one's not my own
Tra la la la la la.	Tra la la la la
In ciuda barbatului	Just to spite my husband
Am sa beau al dracului	I'll drink and to the devil
Tra la la la la la	Tra la la la la
Tra la la la la la	Tra la la la la

Another few stanzas sung to the rhapsody melody:

Vezi morarul alb ca varul	See the miller, white like slake-lime
Sacu'n spate, nu se'abate	With a sack on his back, keeps on going
Iar Maritza, moraritza	While Maritza, the miller's wife
Nu'i mai tace din guritza	Her little mouth won't stop talking

---

While tippling in the saloon, the peasants entertained one another with:

Cine nu bea vinu tot	Whoever doesn't drink up the wine
Sa'l sarute matza n bot	Let the cat kiss him on the snout
Bea, bea vinu'i dulce	Drink, drink, the wine is sweet
Cine'l bea nu se mai duce	Whoever drinks it will never leave

Nature was an important theme in Romanian songs and each season inspired a variety of folksongs.

"Autumn"

A ruginit frunza din vil	Rusty is the leaf in vineyards
Si randunelele'au plecat	And the swallows have left
Pustii sunt pajuri si campii	Deserted are meadows and fields
Pustii sunt holdele din sat	Deserted are the village pastures
Tra la, la la la . . .	Tra la, la la la . . .

"Spring"

Infloresc gradienel ceru'i ca oglinda	Gardens are in bloom, the sky mirror like
Prin livezi albinele, si'au pornit colinda	In orchards, bees are out with their carols
Canta ciocarliile, himn de veselie	Larks are singing hymns of joy
Fluturii cu miile joaca pe campie	Butterflies dance on the meadows
Joaca fete si baeti hora'n batatura	Boys and girls dance the hora
Vai dece n'am zece vieti	Why don't I have ten lives
Sa te cant natura.	To sing of you, nature

"The Turtledove"

Dece mai zbori o turturica	Why are you still flying, little turtledove
Nu vezi ca ziua s'a sfarsit	Don't you see that the day is done
Intoarce te la cuib mai iute	Come back to your nest, quickly,
La cuibul tau cel linistit	To your peaceful nest

Te'nalta iar in zbor voios		Float up again in joyous flight	
Despica zarea mai vartos	refrain	Split the horizon faster still	
Sa nu te prinda uliul furios		Let not the furious hawk catch you	
Dece nu mai vi pe la fereastra		Why don't you come again to our window	
Sa-ti iei grauntele de mei?		To pick again your millet grains?	
Cand sti ca pe langa casa noastra		You know full well that round our house	
Poci fara grija sa le iei		You can get them without fear ...	
Refrain		Refrain	

As in all peasant communities, Romanian villagers were neighborly, pitching in to help one another with the farm chores. The "sezatoare" (working bee) was a gathering where neighbors helped, while singing and being entertained with riddles, songs and folktales. These songs found théir way to the shtetl. Some were taught in the Romanian school.

Cat e lumea pe sub soare	In the whole world under the sun
Bade badisor,	There's no better place than
Nu'i bine ca'n sezatoare	At a sezatoare (working bee)
Bade badisor!	Uncle mine, dear uncle!
Ca e joc si e cantare	For there's games and there is singing
Dorule, dorule	Yearning, yearning
Si mai uiti de suparari	And you forget some of your troubles
Dorule, dor.	Longing, longing.

"Foaie verde" (green leaf) is part of the Romanian folksong idiom. Many folksongs include this phrase as a refrain. These are true folksongs, some melancholy, other satirical, ironical and changing to fit the situation.

Foae verde si'o lalea		Green leaf and a tulip	
Harnica'i nevasta mea		How hardworking is my wife	
Se scoala de dimineata		She wakes up early in the morning	
Pan'la pranz abia se'ncalta		Takes till noon to put on her shoes	
Nici nu coase nici nu tese		Neither sewing, nor weaving	
Tra la la la la la	refrain	Tra la la ...	
Nai mult trica decat face,		More she spoils than she fixes	
Tra la la ...		Tra la la ...	
Foae verde si'un dulau		Green leaf and a hound dog	
Harnic e barbatul meu		Hardworking is my husband	
Se scoala de dimineata		Wakes up early in the morning	
Pan'la pranz abia se'ncalta		Takes till noon to put on his shoes	
Refrain; Nici nu coase		Neither sowing nor reaping	
Foae verde de cimpoi		Green leaf and a bagpipe	
Harnici suntem amandoi		Hard working we are both	
Ne iubim ne potrivim		We love one another, we're a match	
La lucru ne prapadim.		At work, we're lost (a riot).	

Two Yiddish songs: "Die Soche" ("The Plow") and "Der Mai Lied" ("The May Song") are interesting because they differ from the traditional popular shtetl songs and especially because of the difficulties encountered in finding them in their entirety.

Since Jews were urban dwellers for so many centuries, prohibited from owning land, farming was not a typical Jewish occupation and nature played a marginal role in shtetl life. Yet, "Die Soche" extolls farm life as compared to town living and the "Mai Lied" is a veritable ode to nature. On another plane, both these ballads telescope the shtetl ethos albeit naively.

Among the songs my mother used to sing there were two songs, the melodies of which lingered in my mind and only a few stanzas played stubbornly with my memory. "Die Soche" ("The Plow"), I was able to locate in a collection of Yiddish songs, though only a few verses were reproduced, while I distinctly recalled a lengthy ballad with amusing allusions to the trials and tribulations of city life as compared to the idealized life on the farm. After much research I learned that this ballad was written by the Polish–Yiddish folkpoet Eliachum Zunzer in the mid-eighteenhundreds.

As for the "Mai Lied" ("The May Song") it remained a mystery which eluded all avenues of research. No one seemed to have heard of it or recognized the (admittedly feeble) rendition of the tune I was able to supply. The lilting melody evoked in my mind's eye lovely scenes of springtime, of life awakening, drawn with picturesque — though sometimes too sentimental — metaphors.

Both were ultimately found in an old notebook, dating from 1909.

"Die Soche" idealizes life on the farm. The farmer doesn't need to worry about the tax collector, or feeding an extra child in the family; his wife needs no servants and the only time she indulges in trips is on Friday when she goes to the market. His daughter is no problem as is the city girl, for the father finds for her a suitable husband, gives her two goats as dowry and she lives happily with her husband. It is only at the end of this idyllic picture of worry-free life on the farm, that we learn that this is the life awaiting the "colonists" the Zionists who will go to settle in Palestine. Remembering that this was the time of the First Zionist Congress and of Theodor Hertzl, it all becomes understandable. It is given here as an interesting catalogue of shtetl social values.

"Die Soche" ("The Plow")

In der soche	In the plow
Ligt dos mozl broche	Lies the luck, the blessing
Das varé glick fun lebn	Truly, life's chances
Kein zach mir nit feilt	Nothing do I need
Es kumt der fryi morgen	Comes the early morning
Ich darf nit layen, borgen	I need not loan nor borrow
Der moyech darf mir nit zorgen	My mind need not have cares
Of tog oyznes gelt	To fulfill the day's debts
Es is ungegreyt of winter	There is prepared for winter
A magazin a gezinter	A larder full and hefty
Ich zey und shnayd ganz minter	I plant and reap quite wakeful
Frei in Gottes velt	Free in God's own world
Fun die raiche	Among the wealthy
Ver ken sich tzu mir glaychen	Who can compare with me?
Ver leibt noch ruig, gluklich	Who lies so free and happy
Vie ich bay mir in feld?	Like me on my own land?
Git nor Gott dem regen	Let God only give the rains
Fiele ich gluck und zegen	I feel lucky and plant
Ich fier shoyn snopes vegen	I carry carloads of sheafs
Far der ganzer velt	For the entire world
Ich tie die lait ernern	I feed everybody
Sefers, komissionern	Book-keepers, middlemen
Ich darf nit trachtn klern	I need not think nor worry
Un kosher is mein gelt	And kosher is my money (not tainted)
Fun der modé	About styles
Veis ich nit avode	I certainly know nothing
Vie in shtot ferleibtmen	The way they live in cities
Mehr vie men fardint	Spending more than they earn
A shtroy hut in shvité	A straw hat (I wear)
Trug ich up a shmité	Up to the next fallow (season)
Und mit der selber hitté	And with the same hat
Geyt men oys gezunt	I go out in good health
Der serp is mein casirer	The scythe is my cashier (bank teller)
Der hun mein raportierer	The rooster my weatherman
Die zin is mein zeit firer	The sun is my timekeeper
Der focher is der vint	My fan is the wind
Der kremer	The shopkeeper
Must borgen, redn, nemen	Must borrow, convince and take
Und tumed conkorirn	And always in competition
In alem szolen prozent	Paying interest on everything
Fin vechslen und termemen	Drafts and deadlines
Darf der moirech, die zinen	He must keep in his mind
In krum kent ir gefinen	In his shop you'll find
Heshboinem file vent	Walls full of bills (accounts)
Ich darf nisht concurirn	I don't have to compete
Kein vechslen regulieren	Nor settle drafts

Songs 197

Kein vechslen regulieren	No book-keeping of accounts
Mein bank senen die hint	My dogs are my bank (protection)
Fin shtaier die aghenten	Expenses for agents
Die tayere patenten	Costly patents
Az ersht der ban dernizentin	...
Legt men in hoys arayn	Go into the house
Der shenker	The saloon keeper
Must dulden yedes shvenker	Must endure every drunk
Fun yedem misn shikker	From every ugly lush
Falt die drusl ein	...
Ich bin fun ales frayer	I am free of all this
Bilet kost nicht kein dreier	A ticket costs not a thrypence
Der schnaps cos kimt in shayer	The glass of schnaps
Bleibt gur und ganzlich mein	Remains entirely mine
Meinde dame,	My wife,
Zie braught keine ame	She needs no maid servant
Keine dienst keine bonne	No char woman no nursemaid
Kein fresser of dem kopf	No glutton in the house (on our head)
Zie darf kein hut, kein feder	She needs no hat, no feather
Zie shpartziert nisht keseyder	No constant promenading
Zie furt nisht in die beyder	She doesn't travel to spas
Sadn Frayteg tzum marki	Except perhaps Friday to the market
Kein putz, kein balmasirten	No dress-up, no masked balls
Alein in hoys a virtin	Alone in house, she's a housekeeper
In dem feld a hirtin	On the field industrious
Und zie is gezunt und shtark	And she is in perfect health
Mit yorn,	As years go by
Mir vert a kind geboyrn	Another child is born
Vert gresser mein achnosse	My wealth is increasing
Ich koyf noch a shtik herd	I buy another piece of land
In shtot a kind vos merer	In town with each added child
Vert dem father shverer	The father's burden is heavier
Er must zein a dernerer	He must be the breadwinner
Of dem holz a shtrik	Around the neck, a rope
Bey mir es vacsen kinder	In my place, the more children
Vert mein harbeit linder	The lighter is my labor
Und yedes kind bazinder	And each child separately
Is far mir a glick	Is for me more luck
Mein meidl	My daughter,
Neyech of a prost kleidl	I sew for her a plain dress
Und ty mit yir a shiddech	And arrange a match for her
Un tziring und un gelt	Without jewels or money
Zeyt nor in shtot die kalles	Just see in town the brides
Zey shteyen prost ba dolles	They're as poor as church mice
Zey ramen oys fun der shtib alles	They clean everything out of the house
Vos is nor faran	Whatever they can find

Mir ist leicht tzo krign	For me it's easy to find
A chosn dovk'a hign	A bridegroom, in fact, a local boy
Nodn gib ich tzvey tzign	Dowry I give them two goats
Und zie leibt glicklich mit ir man	And she lives happily with her spouse
Benchn zol nor Got	May God bless
Die menchen	The people
Velche stitzen Zion	Who help along (assist) Zion
Tzurik dus land banait	To renew the old land
Bench nor Got dem Riter	May God bless the rider (the watchman)
Der kolonie bashitzer	The protector of the colonies
Die arbeiter stizer	Who supports the workers
Fin der gantzer velt	From the entire world
Ven fin die kolonien	When from the colonies
Veln vern milionen	Will become millions (will increase)
Velt Zion ersht dermonen	Then Zion will remember
Ale groise lait	All these great men

"Der Mai Lied" ("The May Song")

 This song is not presented here for its literary excellence; nor are anthropomorphic analogies a rare technique in literature. The interest derives mainly from the topic, rare in Yiddish poetry so far as can be ascertained and particularly from the enchanting canvas presented to us, where analogies of social and natural phenomena are so charmingly intertwined. Through lyrical metaphor, the bard (wherever he was) invites us, first to take note, then to assist at the preparations for a very important event: the arrival of Spring, when the bridegroom, Spring comes to wed and claim Nature, his bride. We are urged to attune all our senses to what is happening: "Open your eyes, and listen . . .".

 Everything alive and breathing participates: birds compose melodies, grasshoppers dance and cavort and the month of May is "the young cavalier who dances with Nature vis-a-vis". What emerges besides the image of pastoral reawakening is a virtual catalogue of customs and mores seen through the eyes of a specific culture: that of the shtetl. For the occasion, the bride is dressed in her finery, her gown embroidered with colorful birds, bees and butterflies. Fresh blossoms push up their little heads through the grass and mother nature grooms them and washes their little mouths with dewdrops in anticipation of the great event. The poet must be forgiven a momentary mixed metaphor where the erstwhile bride is suddenly called "mother nature". Call it poetic licence.

 The graphic imagery is unfolded before our eyes as the bare, craggy tree puts on a new green coat and then mingles with the other guests. But note please, he is mingling with the other "machetunem", the all important personages at the wedding.

Like any proper lady the moon immerses herself in the calm pool. Again, the suggestive term: "toivlt sich" is no coincidence; it is a deliberate reference to the all important ritual bath which confers a special aura of sanctity on those who participate in it.

Wedding bells are heard in the distance and we are gently reminded that a wedding gift is in order. It is suggested that composing a song would be appropriate for the occasion. The bird-orchestra musicians have arrived, each with its own instrument, and the ladies clap their hands to the rhythm, as guests do at all proper shtetl weddings.

The bridegroom arrives amid fanfares and "the sun and the moon are the interfirers". The *yiches* is impeccable as at any shtetl wedding. The ceremony proceeds and again, according to custom, the bridegroom "bedecks" the bride with a green veil. The moon showers the bride with little stars; all is now ready for the *chuppa*, the wedding canopy. The wedding canopy is supported by the four poles, love, hope, compassion and joy. What better formula for marital happiness?

The wedding ring is the all important symbol of the union, the true pivot on which hinges the entire world, we are told. The Heavens are the *kessibe blat-* (the marriage contract) and God Himself reads this binding document, written with letters encrusted with the stars above.

Inferred here is the importance of the family within the whole structural plan of nature writ large; the wedding-band as pivot on which everything else in the world depends, the ingredients of: love, hope, compassion and joy. These were shtetl values.

With both hindsight and foresight, the marriage contract stipulates that, should the bridegroom ever tire of his bride, who will inevitably lose her youth and freshness, he will not be able to live without her and will return to her at the proper time. This was the shtetl formula for happiness.

"Der Mai Lied"

Menchen shteyt oyf ganz frie	People, wake up early morn,
Ervacht fun ayer geleger	Get out of your beds
Zeit die sheine armonie	See the lovely harmony
Mit dem naturlichen zeger	With the clockwork of nature
Beimolech raushen, feigiolech zingen	Saplings murmur, little birds sing
Melodien jirmen feigolech arlerley	Birds chirping melodies of all sorts
Eisriklech tantzen und shpringen	Grasshoppers dance and skip around
Und tzum tact halt tzi der salovey	And the nightingale taps the rhythm in tune

Menchen macht aych frei	People, make yourselves free
Gibt yiber ayere gedanken gur	Surrender your thoughts
Tzu dem Mai, dem zissen Mai	To May, the sweet month of May
Die kroyn fun der heiliger Natur	The crown of hallowed nature
Efnt dus fenzterl und tyi a blick	Open the window and catch a glimpse
Vi shein die natur is ungetun	How lovely nature is dressed up
Feigl zingen sheine shtik	Birds are singing lovely tunes
Und der Mai tantzt in mittn kun	And the month of May dances in the midst
Betracht nor arum dir, kik nor und hear	Consider only, look around and hear
Ofen git die oygn und kik dich tzi	Open wide your eyes and look closely
Vie der Mai, der younger cavalier	How May, the young cavalier
Mit der Natur tantzn vis-a-vis	Dances with Nature, vis-a-vis
Shnayder, nemt aich nor tzum hartz	Tailors, please take this to heart
Und neyt kein Shabbes shtoch	And don't sew a stitch on the Sabbath
Macht nicht lang, nicht kertz	Don't make the clothes too long or too short
Und loz by eich nit zein long die voch	And let the week not be too long for you
Lernt aych fun dem Mai	Please take a lesson from the month of May
Firt siech off oyf zaine manieren	Take heed of his ways and manners
Er is oych a shneider yingh by der natur	He too is a tailor, for Nature
Kikt nor zoy sheyn der mantl light of yim	Behold how well the coat fits him
Aza shein geney, zol ich ubn aza yor!	Such lovely stitching, may I have so good a year!
Feigolech, fligolech, vie auch die bien	Little birds, little flies, and the bees too
Auf dem brek fun dem mantl oysgeshtikt	Are embroidered on the edging of the coat
Dos vais, dos royt, dos green	This white, this red, that green
Yedes shtipt dos piskiole und pikt	Each stretches its tiny beak and picks
Bleimolech grezlen oys zeire heyrolech	Little flowers push up among the grass
Die mamme, die Natur ferkemt zei zer shein	Mother nature combs their hair so neat
Tropn rosae falt auf zey vie die perolech	Dew drops fall on them like little pearls
Und shvenkt zei aus die piskolech sehr rein	And rinses out their tiny mouths, so clean
Zeyt nor ich beit aich vos is dos?	Look here please, what's this about?
Ein alter boym naked un a blot	An old tree, naked without one leaf
Der May nemt im shoin die mus	May takes his measurements soon
Und neyt yim oyf a gryinem hallot	And sews for him a green overcoat
Gyib nor a zind dem alten shturmak	Behold please that craggy old stick
Er hot shoyin gur an ander ponem	He's taken on quite a new face
Er bakimt shoin oyich a bisl farb in der back	He has a little color in his cheeks
Und dreit zich zvishn alle machetunem	And mingles with all the *machetunem*

Zeyt nor dort in tiefen tul	Look down there in the deep glen
Vie green grusen ist durich aus bedekt	The green grasses everywhere unfurl
Passen sich sheifolech un a tzul	Countless sheep are grazing there
Yedes shtipt dos zingole und lekt	Each one pushes out its tongue and licks
Der pastech mit zein faifole	The shepherd with his little flute
Geyt noch zey und shpielt mit grois gefiel	Follows them and plays with deep feeling
Sein liebe liebes lied	His lovely song of love
Ein sheinem tzishpiel antfert yim der salovei	The nightingale replies in unison
Und sein gelibte geit im noch sein shlit	And his beloved follows in his steps
Der morgen shtern treit aroys	The morning star has just stepped out
Auf dem breitn blauen himml	Upon the bright blue heaven
Shteyt oyf menchen, rift aroys	Wake up people and call out
Die zin ervacht shoyn fin ihr drimml	The sun too is awakening from her nap
Die himlische keinign shteyt oyf fun ihr bet	The heavenly queen wakes up from her bed
Tzu regirn mit die greslen dem antign tog	To reign over the grass blades today
Yedes gresel ziet tzu ir vi a magnet	Each blade of grass she attracts like a magnet
Die royz dreit sich balt ous in ihr krug	The rose too will soon turn about on the stem
Vi nemt men menchn mit yideien	Where can one find men with ideas
Vos er hat shoyn ales betracht	Who have already contemplated all
Loz er mir gibben tzo fershteyen	Let him make me understand
Vos soyden sich die bletolech ba nacht?	What secrets whisper little leaves at night?
B'shaas die l'vone toyvlt sich in tiefen taich	While the moon cleanses herself in the deep lake
Vos far a broche macht zie derbay	What sort of benediction does she pronounce?
Vos viklt sich die Natur in a grinem shahl	Why does Nature wrap around her a green shawl
Ven zie heibt sich un, sich rechtn of dem Mai	As she prepares herself to greet the month of May?
Varft avek damen, mamzellen	Ladies, mademoiselles,
Fargenigen fun zilber und gold	Throw away pleasures of silver and gold
Treyt nor byte, ariber die shvelln	Step over the threshold if you please
Spatziert oys der shtot in tieffen vald	And take a stroll out of town, into the woods
Zeit nor die sheine royz	See please the beautiful rose
Zie trogt kein brilliantn	She wears no precious stones
Zie is ich gleib, fil shenner fun eich	She is, I believe prettier than you all
Zi lacht oys ayere perl und diamantn	She laughs at your pearls and diamonds
Und complimenten hopt zie mer fin aich	And receives more compliments than you

Geyt nor vaiter mit dem trit	Please go further, one more step
Vet yhr hern fun a chassene a klong	You will hear bells of a wedding
Macht nor yedes a naie lied	Compose please each of you a new song
Und dos vet zein ayer drushe geshonk	And that will be your wedding gift
Der Mai mit der Natur hobn hosene in a gitter shoo	The Month of May and Nature are wed with good luck
Pliesket alle dammen mit die hent	All ladies, clap with your hands
Die klesmer, feigeln sind shoin fun lang do	The musicians, the birds have long since arrived
Yedes halt in moul sein instrument	Each one holding in his mouth an instrument
Rei, rei, rei, rei, der chosn gheyt	Rah, rah, rah, rah, here comes the groom
A sheiner und a yunger cavalier	A young and handsome cavalier
Die zin mit der l'vone shteyen greyt	The sun and the moon are waiting ready
Far interfieren gekimen aheir	Here come to be the *interfirers*
Der chosn varft arof of ir a grinem decktiech	The bridegroom throws on her a green veil
M'derkent nisht oib si is a mohl shvarz geven	No hint that she was ever black
Die l'vone bavarft sie mit shterndlech	The moon sprinkles her with stardust
Men heibt shoyn un tzu der chuppeh tzu gehn	They're beginning to go to the *chuppa* already
Liebe, offnung, gefyil und freud	Love, hope, deep feeling and joy
Sind far der chuppeh die fier shtekens	Are the four posts of the wedding canopy
Die licht ist far a dek geshpreyt	Bright light is spread out like a bedspread
Mizrach, Maaref, Zufen, Tarom, die ecken	With east, west, north and south, the four corners
Der mitelpunct die Natur is a kedishe-fingerl	The pivot of Nature is the wedding ring
Der Mai habt dos oyf in der liftn	The month of May lifts it up in the air
Auf dem fingerl dreyt sich aus die ganze velt	Upon this ring the entire world is turning
Auf dem ist himmel und herde tzenoyf gekumen	The aim for which heaven and earth came together
Der hymmel is dos kessibe blat	The Heavens are the *kessibe* (marriage contract)
Die oysies senen die shtern	The letters are the stars
Die kessibe leint der alter Got	The contract is read by the Ancient God
As dos porfolg zol nisht tzisheyt vern	That this couple may not ever be parted
Und ven er vet afile farvarfn	And even if he will no longer
Oyf dem vaybele a minchein	Find his little wife as attractive
Un ven fun yir antloyfn ganz vayt	And will run away from her, quite far
Zol er sich un ihr nisht kennen bageyn	May he not be able to live without her
Un zol tzerig kimmen tzu der rachter tzait	And return to her at the proper time

CHAPTER XI
Ethos

1. Morality

The term "ethos" has been referred to as the conscience of a people. It is the manner in which a particular society views the world ("Weltanschauung"), the way it perceives itself, including the moral ideals it upholds. It is expressed in the norms by which the individuals of the society live.

Ethos, not to be confused with "ethics", (though both derive from the Greek word meaning "custom,") is much more inclusive, focusing on ideals rather than on the actual implementation of these ideals. Both deal with the intangibles of human values viewed from different aspects. There is an inevitable overlapping between the two constructs, the difference being one of perspective.

In discussing the ethos of the Romanian shtetl the emphasis will be primarily on the ways in which it differed from the larger eastern European cultural complex, of which it was a part. An attempt will be made to indicate where the Romanian shtetl may be situated on the continuum between the ultra traditional shtetl of the Pale, at one extreme, and the larger urban Jewish communities, at the other.

A brief summary will be given on how the Romanian shtetl regarded the various western cultures, comprised in the term "strainatatea" ("abroad" or "foreign lands"), since this, too, is an aspect of the shtetl's world view.

How did the Romanian shtetl view itself? Jewish communities everywhere learned to incorporate elements that reflected the neighboring non-Jewish cultures. For reasons already mentioned, this process was more pervasive in the Romanian shtetl. The term "assimilirt" ("assimilated") was frequently referred to. It implied a betrayal of ancestral heritage and was spoken of with reproof and condemnation. But, while the shtetl regarded the *hasidim* as fanatics and outmoded, it clung to its faith and traditions and would not have admitted that it was *assimilirt*. This was a term reserved for the city Jews, and especially for the Jews in western countries.

From a historical perspective, the two great movements of the past, the enlightenment of the *Haskala* and the religious revival of *Hasidism*, both left their impact on the Romanian shtetl. The upsurge of Zionism brought about a series of conflicting views and values. Instead of the traditional inward-looking view, a new openness appeared. The shtetl found itself somewhat precariously balanced between the two currents: on the one hand, the tradition-oriented but constraining Jewish world, which offered a confined form of security; and, on the other, the wish to gain acceptance, to become part of the broader world, to escape. This was prompted more than anything else by the hope of assuring for their children a security they had been denied and that they continued to crave.

In accepting the replacement of Yiddish with Romanian as the spoken language, the shtetl had taken a decisive and irreversible step on the road to acculturation. The attitude towards religion and the entire social structure, may have changed gears but did not change direction.

Linguistic behavior patterns express correspondingly different values. The individual's position on the cultural continuum in the shtetl was predictable by his position on the linguistic continuum. His skill in using the language of a second culture symbolized his status in the society. It was therefore possible to place any given individual on a scale in terms of the language he used and the level at which he functioned.

Each successive generation spoke a better, purer Romanian. An intensive and deliberate effort was made to speak Romanian without any tell-tale Yiddish accent. This was no doubt a common phenomenon wherever Jews willingly adopted the language of the host country. To speak Romanian without a Jewish accent was a sign of good breeding, whereas the Jewish inflections were esteemed vulgar, apt to elicit derision. As previously pointed out, the kinship terms used distinguished the social classes. In most middle-class families, the parents conversed in Yiddish with each other but always spoke Romanian to the children. Children learned Yiddish only through speaking to the grandparents or listening to adult conversations. *Mamme lushn* ("mother tongue") Yiddish was replaced with Romanian in one generation.

Self-improvement was an intrinsic aspect of shtetl ethos and speaking a pure Romanian was seen as self-improvement, as was learning in general. But whereas traditionally it was the men who were entrusted with study, the new current involved women as well. Men were still supposed to study the sacred writings, but increasingly channelled all efforts into entering the professions. *Litérè* ("arts and letters"), literature and modern languages became the woman's domain.

Contact with the larger cities, whose inhabitants tended to look down on the shtetl, made shtetl residents fully aware of their own disadvantages regarding possibilities for improvement. Items of luxury such as better quality in furniture, silverware and china were sought after, though still looked upon as extravagances. The strict necessities of life having been taken care of, efforts were made to improve the immediate surroundings.

Prohibited by Judaic tenets, painting and sculpture did not have any place in shtetl life. Church icons seen during religious processions were not regarded as works of art but instead were associated with religious symbolism and, when not ridiculed as pagan idolatry, were ignored. Even a furtive glance at an icon or a religious statue was considered sinful. Aesthetic needs were fulfilled at a different level by embellishing utilitarian objects and by needlework and embroidery.

Evil was envisaged as punishment for sins. "I must have committed some grave sin to be so punished" was fervently believed, inferring that the fault was entirely one's own. The inevitable result was self-blame and guilt.

Guilt was enshrined at every level in the shtetl ethos. Parents did not hesitate to point out to their children what sacrifices they had made or spell out their expectations. "You will regret this when I am gone" was one of those self-fulfilling prophecies that left a legacy of guilt. One felt guilty for breaking any of the six hundred and thirteen *mitzvot*.

Two concepts permeating the entire social fabric were the ideas of self-discipline and self-restraint. From observance of strict hygenic rules to adherence to dietary laws, the underlying principle was mastery of oneself and, as a corollary, of personal responsibility. The postponement of momentary pleasures for increased future good was stressed explicitly and by subtle implications. Temperance and self-control were basic virtues. Comparisons with animals were often brought as arguments to instill self-restraint.

Self-control in itself was regarded as a form of personal growth. By setting limitations for oneself, one created the feeling of mastery over any given situation. One acquired the decision-making power of choice in limited areas, and, by implication (or illusion), it extended to other areas of life. Immediate gratification was *goyish* ("not Jewish"); delaying gratification was Jewish and, by definition, right.

Hospitality, enshrined through Biblical writings, was institutionalized in the traditional *oyrech for Sabbath*. The *oyrech* ("guest") was selected from among the poor mendicants at the synagogue and invited home for the Sabbath meals by the prosperous members of the congregation. It was a charitable act. In daily comportment, too, hospitality was a virtue. It was, however, extended only to one's equals. The Romanian expression when someone dropped in during mealtime was: "Poftim la masa" ("Please join us at the table"). This was not to be taken literally, however, as the rhyming retort shows: "But bring your own food." On the other hand, there was always room in any home for an out-of-town relative, visiting for several weeks. This was concomitant with the degree of kinship or friendship. "When there is room in the heart, you find room in the house."

In *Dynamics of Benefice** the author states that gift-giving in the shtetl went only downward, from the well-to-do to the needy. This was not the case in the Romanian shtetl. The Romanian saying "To the rich, even the devil brings cakes" would suggest that the rich were rewarded with gifts by their social inferiors. The added dimension in this case was the tacit possibility of a form of bribery — where favors were expected in return as the saying "put an egg to obtain two" suggests. Gifts were generally exchanged among equals and only on special occasions, such as when leaving or returning from trips, at births and weddings. Children received gifts from their elders on their birthdays, holy days or simply as a show of love.

Downward giving was regarded as charity, and was institutionalized. It was considered more worthy to give to those in need without waiting to be asked and to give as discreetly as possible. Charity was not devoid of a whiff of self interest, since by giving charity one stored up merits in Heaven and would be rewarded tenfold. On the other hand, the professional beggar, the *shnorer* (beggar) was a contemptible figure in the shtetl. They developed a veritable talent for asking, which most people found humiliating to submit to and detestable in others.

Generosity was a virtue, in theory. The concept of "limited good"[†] and the belief that all desired things in life existed in limited quantities, hampered free sharing or giving without some personal gain.

The shtetl accepted the proposition that there was not enough to go around and consequently one's good fortune was at the expense of another's loss. Envy, though fervently denied by all, was not unknown, especially towards one's equals, as the wish, "May we not envy one another," suggests.

Giving to the needy was charity, institutionalized through synagogue donations such as the Passover *moschitten* ("charity") and the

---

* Natalie Joffe, *Dynamics of Benefice*; Socal Forces, Vol. 27, 1949, p. 348.
† M. Foster, *Peasant Society*, A Reader, p. 303, *Op. Cit.*

charity for the departed, *yisker gelt*, given to insure repose for the soul. This illustrates the interdependence of cultural patterns where social needs are fulfilled by tending to the emotional needs of the individual.

The institution of *gimeles chessed* ("friendly loan") was established to avoid asking for favors which was humiliating and put one in an inferior position. The relationship between borrower and lender was thus one of reciprocity and interdependence and the one in need was not regarded as incompetent, assured that he, too, might have the opportunity to reciprocate in the future.

Egalitarian principles were not part of shtetl values; children owed deference to their parents, youth respected old age, students respected teachers and the wife owed obedience to her husband. All people had their role and the expectation was that their turn would come to elicit respect from their inferiors. The entire social structure was based on the accepted reality that people were different and that each had his role to play. The fallacy of the principle of equality was taken for granted. It was summed up in one favorite Romanian fable, where dogs seeking equality within the animal kingdom conclude that what they really wanted was equality with the lions, not with the insignificant lap dog.

The hierarchical view of the world was acknowledged, since there did not seem to be any evidence to the contrary. This was an authoritarian society where social stratification was undisputed, where ranking was part of every aspect of life and each member of society was aware of his own standing. The question of ascribed versus achieved status may have been debatable, but no one denied the reality that some were more equal than others. It was on this vulnerable point that Marxism was able to attack the tradition-oriented shtetl values.

Imported through neighboring Bessarabia, where Jews still spoke Russian, and were therefore more amenable to the propaganda, Russian style Communism infiltrated among the young idealists. Where religious beliefs were the raison d'être of the shtetl, "Communist godlessness" was a dangerous menace; "free love" was seen as a direct threat to marriage and the family and economic determinism, a meaningless phrase for the self employed individualists, did appeal to the naive young. The older generation as well as the Romanian officialdom viewed these simmerings with alarm. Midnight arrests of ring-leaders and their converts stemmed the tide for a time; the war and subsequent contact with reality, did the rest.

In a small community where daily, face to face encounters make posing artificiality impossible, one is judged, weighed and measured by one's peers. Reputations, based on past experience, once established, were difficult to forget. Labels stuck. Nicknames, often painfully cruel, testified to this. By the same token, self praise was shunned as was any form of hypocrisy, which was easily detected. No one is able to wear a mask at all times.

A bekuveder Yid (a dignified Jew) dressed properly (meaning neat and clean in somber tones) and showed moderation in every respect. The "seven years from home", that is, background and the home environment were credited for dignified behavior in adults.

Derech eretz, may be translated as "respect for one's elders". The term is more suggestive however; the mot-à-mot translation is "the way of the land" implies a respect for the accepted manner of doing things and a respect for tradition. It summed up the concept of accepted and expected behavior. One showed *derech-eretz* in standing up before an older person, or using the respectful pronoun, as well as in observing the Sabbath. Any breach of conformity was attributed to ill manners, befitting only a *grobyon* or a *grobber yingh* (a roughneck).

Arrogance and aloofness were not appreciated while modesty was highly prized. Posing or behaving above one's standing was ridiculed, and scoffed at.

Should anyone attempt to behave in a manner considered by others as above his assigned standing, he was greeted with "Nu Graff (Count) Pototsky!" ("No less") and immediately cut down to size. Ridicule was a potent, frequently used weapon. There was acceptance and pride in the "local boy makes good", but one had to win recognition from the outside world before being accepted by the shtetl. This may be interpreted as a feeling of low self esteem in which they held themselves, reflected in the reluctance to admit that one of them was worthy.

In theory, truthfulness, honesty and sincerity were virtues upheld in the shtetl in practice, expediency and realism prevailed. Not surprisingly, society protected itself by underscoring honesty and proving that dishonesty did not pay in the end. As in any small community, public opinion and social sanctions were potent deterrents for any anti-social behavior. Many proverbs buttress this. Trust was important in the functioning of society and any breach was easily discernible.

Interpersonal relationships were of two distinct types. With those one considered as social equals they were close, warm and outgoing. Across social class or age barriers, the relations were reserved and polite. The respectful pronoun *yir* ("thou") was used for older persons or those of a higher social standing. A *per tu* or *per dyi* (for which there is no equivalent in English) relationship was reserved only for close friends and immediate family of the same age group. Parents, aunts and uncles were addressed with the respectful plural pronoun *yir*.

The first-name basis was not customary. A man was addressed by his family name prefixed by *Domnu* ("mister") or the Yiddish *Arb* or *Reb* ("sir") using the first name or the family name, depending on the person's social standing. Working-class persons were usually addressed by their first names, whereas they addressed a merchant or shopkeeper by his family name. A woman was called *Doamna* (or "madam".) A single woman was addressed with the prefix *Domnisoara* ("miss"). Servants addressed their employers simply with *Domnu* and *Doamna*.

Friendships were established along age lines, often within the extended-family circles and always among social equals. Parents discouraged any close friendships with children of families they estimated on a lower social level, and, conversely, encouraged relations with equals or those one notch above. Friendships were based on compatibility, common interests, affection. To be *afurisit* (literally, "cursed") was a term applied to those individuals who held themselves aloof from the community. They were regarded with suspicion.

Once established, friendships were maintained throughout the years, based on reciprocal loyalty and a strict code of ethics, with mutual moral support and expectations of genuine understanding. Men formed lasting friendships during their years of military service. The generation of the First World War, maintained relations of friendship even when circumstances disrupted normal expectations. Among the young, personal confidences were exchanged, especially concerning the opposite sex.

Physical proximity was not stigmatized; walking *bratz la bratz* ("arm in arm") with a friend of the same sex was commonplace. Conversely, no such permissiveness was allowed between members of the opposite sex. Only engaged couples were granted such intimacies as holding hands or walking arm in arm in public. In general, showing affection in public was not acceptable.

Babies and young children were hugged, kissed and caressed in public by parents and relatives or friends. It was not uncommon for well-meaning strangers to kiss babies. One way of showing affection for young children was a pinch on the plump cheek.

Kissing a lady's hand was a genteel gesture practised by gentlemen, who bowed, doffed their hats and touched the lady's hand with their lips. This custom, practised by the upper-class Romanians, was borrowed from the west, as the accompanying greeting *sarut mana*

("I kiss the hand") or the German equivalent *Küss die haende* would suggest. It is interesting to note that the Romanian peasantry practised this custom in quite a different context. The peasants, both men and women, kissed the hands of their social superiors, but not those of their equals. This was no doubt a relic of feudal times, in the not-too-distant past, when the landless peasants were indeed subservient to their masters and had to kneel and kiss the hand of the *boyer* ("landowner" or "nobleman").

Jews, who did not kneel even to their God, considered any kneeling a form of self-abasement; kissing a lady's hand, however, was regarded as good manners.

The emotional bond between parents and children was one of those values deeply embedded in the shtetl ethos, to a point where it was taken for granted. Parental love and concern for their children was as natural as breathing. Parents saw their personal fulfillment through the success of their children; no effort was insurmountable, no sacrifice too great to achieve this end. This was a child-oriented culture and proud of it:

> *Iské l'irot baniim, baniim ou banot*
> *Oskiim ba Torah, ou be avodah.*
>
> "Let us be worthy to see our sons and daughters
> Successful in Torah and in work."

This little song, taught in nursery school, sums up parental attitudes.

Many parents deliberately accepted assimilation with the sole intent of sparing their children the hurt they had known. Nazi Germany proved them wrong. When parents in Israel were asked why they had uprooted themselves and left comparatively successful lives, the unanimous reply was: "For the sake of our children's future; we didn't want for them the hardships we had experienced."

Children, in turn, owed respect and felt indebted to their parents. It was not a burden, but rather a responsibility, that they, in turn, would expect of their children. To disobey a parent was a guilt-laden act. No son or daughter, for instance, would have placed a parent in an institution to be cared for by strangers under any circumstances.

The image of the shtetl has often been one of overcrowded, dilapidated or slovenly surroundings. Yet one of the prime virtues in the Romanian shtetl was being a *gospodar or gospodina* ("good manager"). This referred to the manner in which the home was conducted and maintained. Keeping the house neat and orderly at all times was the wife's domain. The term *shlimezolnitze* ("bad housekeeper") was an insulting epithet. The *gospodar* was supposed to provide the wherewithal, look after household repairs and insure food supplies. Though interchangeable, the responsibilities were specified for husband and wife. Being a *gospodar* had little to do with financial means, since there were both good and bad housekeepers at all levels.

Thrift was a virtue of necessity. Clothing as well as household articles were expected to last, often for a lifetime, and waste was downright sinful. One did not throw out anything that still had some good use in it. This applied to food, as well. A piece of bread was picked up off the floor, wiped and kissed. (The same was true of any book or sacred writing). Clothing was handed down from parents to children and so on, down the line to the youngest. This suggested the anecdote that when the father or the oldest son chose the cloth for a suit or an overcoat, the youngest child examined the reverse side, convinced that by the time it would reach him, that would be the right side. Women remodeled dresses, combined and transformed to be *la moda* ("in style").

Savings and frugality did not include food. The Romanian shtetl appreciated and enjoyed a hearty meal and a *shpritz* ("wine with soda water"). The Sabbath meal was never skimped on. One saved on many other items but not on the quality or quantity of food. The line between thrift and stinginess was often difficult to tread. As in other respects, individuals were spotted and judged accordingly. Neither the spendthrift *mana sparta* ("cracked hand") nor the avaricious, fared too well; moderation, as in other matters, was the ideal to strive for.

Privacy was one value conspicuous by its complete absence in the shtetl. There is no equivalent term in either language to translate our concept — and consequently the need — for privacy. The term *privata* in Romanian refers to the toilet, and carries connotations appropriate to such circumstances. Not only among the poor, who were of necessity living in overcrowded conditions, but among the relatively affluent, privacy was unknown. Judging by the respondents, there was no awareness of any duress in this respect. The feeling of togetherness compensated for any possible physical discomforts. It was rather the feeling of loneliness that was dreaded and avoided. On the other hand, judging by the number of expressions meaning "bother" ("dilln", "hack nisht"), one may surmise that there were circumstances when one should have appreciated some privacy.

The shtetl held the undisputed view that intellectual work was superior to manual labor. Businessmen were held superior to other men by virtue of their working with their head. Brain versus brawn was the basic cleavage within the social structure. Intellectual activity received the higher prestige and the shtetl rewarded men of thought rather than men of action. In the shtetl of old, this was reinforced by many other structural elements, such as the husband's spending his time in study while the wife (or her father) carried the burden of the family. This was not the case in the Romanian shtetl, where the husband was the breadwinner. Nevertheless, the prestige of learning remained; it was directed into more contemporary channels, where the rewards of economic success accrued.

Jews have often been accused of cowardice. The shtetl was aware of this, if somewhat perplexed at the accusation, since the concept of cowardice, as of bravery, depended on interpretation. In the shtetl, courage, the sense of fearlessness in battle, was academic, since Jews were treated as foreigners in the land of their birth and were not given the opportunity of proving themselves. Bravery was extolled in Biblical heroes, but for the shtetl, this was a moot question.

Jews had a reputation for shrewdness and were believed to fall short of the mark regarding honesty. The shtetl itself, however, did not hold this self-image; it attributed these undesirable characteristics to individuals. As is so often the case, it was the outsiders, in this case the Bessarabians, who were referred to as "horse thieves", although individuals were recognized as upright and dignified.

Fighting, in the sense of fisticuffs, was Goyish: "Jews don't fight", was the frequent admonition. Parents did not encourage children to settle disagreements by fighting. The Romanians themselves did not place courage on the top of the list of virtues as may be surmised from "flight may be shameful, but it is healthful!" Bullies were hooligans. Bravery in battle, though extolled in poetry, was not one of the outstanding qualities of the Romanian peasant.

On the other hand, the indomitable clinging to ancestral traditions, in spite of life threatening dangers, would certainly merit the term "courage".

Attitudes towards sex may be summed up as Victorian, with some qualifications. The shtetl did not regard itself as deprived or oppressed in this respect. As in everything else, the Bible was the fundamental source for moral guidance, from bringing up children to every subsequent stage in life. Self-restraint was the essential principle; postponement of immediate pleasure for the more lasting future satisfactions were constantly reiterated. Temperance and moderation were virtues, while excesses of any sort were goyish and hence outside the confines of shtetl values.

Sex was taboo as a topic of conversation in polite society and doubly so in the presence of children. It was considered vulgar.

Children were not given any instructions on the subject and learned haphazardly from peers.

Sexuality, however, was recognized as a basic need. Judaism does not subscribe to asceticism or abstinence for its own sake. The community regarded celibacy as calamitous to the individual and a danger to the community. This was one of the reasons early marriages were advocated. There was no stigma attached to the sex act, and no concept of original sin. Legitimate relations and enjoyment within the bounds of marriage were not only approved, but marital sex was a positive *mitzva* ("good deed"). It was only outside the confines of marriage that sex became sinful and a danger to the community as a disrupting factor. Looked at from this point of view, the interdependence of structural elements instituted for the effective functioning of the community and for the benefit of the majority of its members becomes evident.

As admonished in the Bible, masturbation was declared a sin. It was taboo. The Romanian term *onanie*, named after the Biblical character Onan who "spilled the seed on the ground" and was condemned to perish, was used as a supporting argument. The guilt feeling instilled was intensified by warnings of the irreparable harm resulting from this vice. Children lived in fear of becoming blind or losing their potency as a consequence.

The double standard was accepted without question. Men were different; they had different needs and *vive la différence* was the prevailing sentiment. Abstinence was believed to be more trying to men than to women. Ideally, it was preferable for both boys and girls to marry young and abstain till marriage. But, whereas a girl's virginity was an unconditional must, for the boy it was rather an ought. Depending on his age at marriage, a man was permitted certain indiscretions, as long as he showed prudence. The fear of venereal diseases was one of the major deterrents. It was tacitly accepted that at the age of twenty-one, when men were called for compulsory military service, it would have been unreasonable to expect them to remain abstinent. Young men were often incited by their peers to prove their virility. The prevailing attitude was that sexual activity in men was an expression of manliness, while in women it was unforgivable. Women were tainted, they were damaged goods to be disposed of at bargain basement prices. The bloodstained bedsheet of the bridal bed, though not any longer in practice, was accepted as need for the proof of the bride's virginity at marriage.

One of the respondents said: "There were girls who did and girls who did not play around, the boys played with those who did but married those who not; why should he have secondhand goods?

And how could he know that she won't cheat on him afterwards, too? She did it before! That's the way it was."

There were no unwed mothers or children for adoption. (Adoption was only practised within the family circle, in case of misfortunes, or — the sole case of an unwed mother in the shtetl — brought up by the mother's parents). A *mamzer* ("bastard") was an insulting epithet, which, nevertheless, popular wisdom transformed into a compliment, in the sense of "sharp" or "canny".

The attitude of the shtetl towards the host culture was both anomalous and ambiguous. It was anomalous because although a tolerated minority, it considered itself superior. Yet it wished to be accepted. This feeling of superiority was engendered by their unswerving faith, their conviction of their own intellectual superiority reinforced by their reverence for the Bible. The Romanian peasant, in turn, regarded the Jews with some awe and respected them for what they considered intellectual superiority. It was well known that the Jews formed the middle class in Romania, where eight-five per cent of the population were peasants.

The shtetl attitude towards the peasants differed from that held towards the upper-class Romanians. While individual peasants were recognized as shrewd, upstanding and hard-working, the culture as a whole was regarded as rude, primitive and illiterate by comparison to their own. The shtetl considered its own religious rituals as right and just, whereas the observances of the gentiles were viewed as primitive and held up to ridicule as childish.

Vi ba die goyim ("like the gentiles") expressed anything not befitting a Jew. Bright colors and excessive adornments, such as glass beads, were goyish. Shtetl values were the antithesis of the values of non-Jews. Whistling was not Jewish; *a sheigetz faift* ("a gentile boy whistles"). Brawling was goyish. Walking around barefoot, like the *shikses* (like "gentile girls") was demeaning for a Jewish person. These sentiments were summed up with *A goy blabt a goy* ("a gentile remains a gentile"). Where Jews extolled temperance and self-restraint, gentiles were prone to excess. *Shiker is a goy* ("Drunk is a gentile").

The shtetl considered family life sacrosanct. Wife-beating, for instance, or marital infidelity, were atrocities that rarely occurred in the shtetl. When they did, as occasionally happened, the perpetrators were shunned. The Romanian peasant said: "The unswept house is like the unbeaten wife," implying that it was commonplace.

The upper-class Romanians were regarded with admiration, and their approval and acceptance was sought. Their mannerisms, their accent and, inevitably, their values were imitated.

This need to emulate the upper-class Romanians was based on a desire to improve one's social standing in the hope that by acquiring these new manners one would be less prone to hurtful discriminations.

Attitudes towards urban centers, too, were fraught with ambiguities. On the one hand, they admired the higher living standard, regarded *case peste case si trancalai fara cai* ("one house on top of the other and horseless carriages") with awe and envied the stylish clothes. On the other hand, "God made the shtetl and the devil made the big cities." Debauchery, perversions and shameless corruption were associated with the big city. The big city reciprocated by regarding the shtetl as Hicktown, though many big-city dwellers or their parents came from those very small towns.

With the mass of Jews in Poland and Lithuania, the Romanian shtetl maintained a loose contact. Lithuania, once the center of learning of the eastern European Jews, was part of Soviet Russia. The center of learning shifted to Poland, where the *yeshivot* ("centers of Hebrew higher learning") were situated. Only those studying to be ordained as rabbis travelled and studied in Poland or in some of the newly formed centers of learning in Bucovina or Bessarabia. The Romanian shtetl regarded these centers with respect but channelled their own energies and interests into secular studies.

The Polish Jews consequently tended to regard the Romanian shtetl as uncultured in Yiddish, lackadaisical about religion and even assimilated, which was only a matter of relativity, and which the shtetl vehemently denied.

Foreign ways were always regarded as worthy of imitation. This was, in the shtetl mind, civilization with a capital C. This is where the shtetl gave tacit proof of its feelings of self-doubt and of inferiority.

It was *strainatatea* ("foreign lands") that elicited the highest adulation. This meant the west — and the farther west — the greater the prestige. Immediate neighbors such as Bulgaria, Yugoslavia, Greece and Hungary were placed on an equal footing with the Romanians; Poland and the USSR were lands tainted with bitter atavistic memories and therefore *hors concours*.

The closest and best-known to the shtetl were Vienna and Berlin. Before the First World War, the boundless admiration for the *Deutche Culture* was expressed in such homely sayings as: "Vi Got in Berlin" ("Like God in Berlin"), implying that it was paradise on earth. The shtetl image of a German as rendered in one children's rhyme was: "Hoiche menner zenen zey, Kertze kleider geyen zey." ("Tall men, wearing short clothes"), referring to the fact that the Germans were probably the first foreigners seen in the shtetl wearing the short jackets rather than the kaftan type coats of the period. The language was considered superior to their own lowly Yiddish, (an offshoot of German). Yet, given the similarity of the two languages, there was a feeling of kinship, although, admittedly, one of poor relation. During the First World War, Jews enjoyed the status of *dolmetch* ("interpreters") on the battlefront, by virtue of their supposed knowledge of German. This had given rise to many humorous anecdotes, relating how Jews used Hebrew words, convinced that they spoke German. Genteel young ladies studied German and began using German words to replace those of Slavic origin. Schiller, Goethe, Heine were household names; Mendelssohn and especially Hertzl were products of that culture, which in itself was sufficient proof of Germany's superiority. Furthermore, Vienna and Berlin were world centers for medicine as well as music and held in highest regard. All this ended with the advent of the Nazis and their atrocities.

Incredible as it may seem in retrospect, the shtetl heard of the concentration-camp atrocities but, frozen by terror, refused to believe. Only as the horror struck closer to home did they begin to look, in despair, for escape.

France enjoyed a unique relationship with Romania. The Romanian ruling classes – mainly educated in France – were eager to establish and maintain close ties with France, based on their common Latin origins. France was the big brother, revered and emulated. By definition, everything French was superior. France invented elegance and *savoir faire*; French mannerisms and terms of politeness became part of the Romanian language; the shtetl was not far behind. French was being taught in high schools from the first grade (our fifth grade) and, together with German, was the language of the élite. Balzac, Flaubert, Daudet, Emile Zola, all were read and discussed in the intellectual circles of the shtetl, Napoleon was the hero who brought *Liberté, Egalité, Fraternité* to Europe; the "Marseillaise" was more meaningful to the shtetl than the Romanian national anthem. The shtetl spoke of Leon Blum as if he were one of theirs.

Wealthy Jews sent their daughters to convents run by French nuns. There were few shtetl families able to afford the extravagance, but those who went returned with an aura of refinement that they carried with them throughout life. One eighty-year-old lady who went to Notre Dame de Sion did not fail to mention it and insisted on speaking French, seventy years later. The shtetl was as enamored of France and everything French, as were the upper-class Romanians. Speaking French was the hallmark of elegance and distinction in itself.

This high regard for France was immeasurably enhanced by the aid received from the *Alliance Internationale Israelite*, with whose aid the Scoala-Israelito-Romana-Narcisse-Leven had been built in Stefanesti, as in many other small Jewish towns of eastern Europe. It is not surprising that France represented culture, generosity and tolerance in the shtetl mind. France was as close to the ideal as the shtetl imagination was able to conceive.

It was the Jewish students who were the important agents of acculturation. Barred from Romanian universities, they went to study abroad, mainly in France or Italy. They brought back to the shtetl values that often clashed with the traditional shtetl values, which, though not totally accepted, had considerable influence on the local mores. The average French Jews, of whom little was known, enjoyed the same aura of superiority as their co-citizens.

So far as the shtetl evaluation was concerned, England was somewhere in the stratosphere. It was not only an island looming great on the horizon, the greatest political power on the world scene; it was the beacon of civilization, democracy incarnate. The English were spoken of with awe, as if they were all lords. For the shtetl there did not seem to be any poor Englishmen; the image the shtetl had formed did not include the working man, though his existence was suspected. The Englishman was an upright, trustworthy, industrious individual, the epitome of what the shtetl conceived as a civilized person. For was it not Lord Balfour who had given the Jews the much-coveted Balfour Declaration? There were many conflicting gray areas in these views, to be sure, but then, the shtetl had probably never seen a real live Englishman. Everything they knew had come down to them on hearsay. The rare individuals who had visited London were themselves esteemed too superior to be asked direct questions and did not disclose any details.

Unlike French and German, English was not taught in Romanian high schools at all. Commercial high schools taught elementary English in the upper grades, since it was known that English was essential in the world of commerce (yet another accolade). English books were read in translation and Shakespearean plays were well known, discussed and debated at local literary trials. *Hamlet, King Lear, The Merchant of Venice* were part of the well-known repertory.

Everyone knew that the best woollen cloth came from England; the English played golf and wore *pantaloni galofei* ("golf pants") and tweed sports jackets or bowler hats and always carried an umbrella. "To an Englishman his word was his bond" appealed to the shtetl as did "To the Englishman, his home is his castle." Democracy was invented in England, as diplomacy had been in France. England was the most tolerant land; proof: Marx had written his *Das Capital* in London; almost everyone knew that much. It all added up to an exalted image of an incomparable people.

Except for Disraeli and the Rothchilds, life for Jews in England was a mystery to shtetl Jews. The Jews, too, were thought of as lords for to have had the good fortune of breathing English air sufficed to imbue all Englishmen with qualities of excellence.

America was in a class by itself. It was somewhere over the Atlantic Ocean, referred to as *iber dem potikl* ("over the little puddle"). Somehow vaguely, it was known that there was Brazil and Argentina in the south, and then there was America. Canada was generously included as part of America, for in the shtetl mind there was no difference to speak of. Ultimately, there was New York, pronounced "Névyork", where, as everyone knew, the streets were paved with gold, but also tainted with vices.

The mere mention of the word evoked a paradise on earth, but a paradise that one could hope to attain, in spite of apparently unsurmountable obstacles. Although farther in miles it was closer in spirit to the shtetl. There was a lifeline between the shtetl and *die goldene medine* ("the golden land"), a lifeline made of an endless chain of its own kith and kin, which breathed hope. Mothers sang lullabies about the marvels of America where one ate white bread and chicken soup every day of the week. And although in the Romanian shtetl these were not rarities, America was still *Amerike gonnif* ("America, thief"), where the impossible became commonplace. No one knew exactly what those who had left the shtetl were doing in America, how they earned their living or how they lived; all they knew was that the parcels of clothing arriving from there were of unparalleled quality. "Er scrippet mitder tier und macht gelt" ("he makes the door squeak and earns money") implied the multitude of weird occupations and money-making schemes available in that unimaginable land.

The fact that many of those who had been poor and considered failures in the shtetl had become successful in America, and that those who were successful in the shtetl did not venture outside, made it all the more unbelievable. It was also known that many former respectable individuals were unable to make it in the same golden land. The shtetl knew from personal experience that some ran away to America, fugitives from the law, and that over there "one had to have seven eyes" not to be swindled by the con artists on the loose. For many years, those well established, with high local prestige, hesitated to leave their homes looking for adventures. By the time Hitler and the Iron Guard came to power it was too late.

And then there were the gypsies who invaded the shtetl during the summer months. They arrived in town on a few rickety carts, drawn by scrawny mules, and set up camp in their tattered, smoke- and grime-embedded tents, either on the *maidan* ("open market-place") or at the outskirts of town, just before the flour mill and the vineyards. For the local authorities they were not a welcome sight.

In appearance they resembled the East Indians, dark-skinned, handsome, of medium height. They spoke only a few words of Romanian; their own language, which sounded like jabbering, may have been similar to Hindi. They were a colorful lot. The men wore brown or green corduroy pants with open-necked shirts, which may have been white at one time but tended to be a dirty gray. Their unkempt, unruly black mop of hair reached to their shoulders and mingled with similarly unruly black beards. Their battered felt hats looked as if they had been picked out of the dump heap. To the shtetl they looked like savages.

They were tinkers by trade and used to repair the copper and enamel pots and pans for the shtetl and village housewives. They sometimes walked about town with a copper or brass cauldron on their heads, looking for customers, for these copper cauldrons were important household utensils, highly sought after for the preparation of preserves.

Their young women were often strikingly beautiful, with flashing bright black eyes, white teeth and a come-hither glance. They wore brightly printed peasant-style skirts (with patches of various scraps of mismatched prints) reaching to the ankles, and peasant blouses. They always wore strands of beads, some turquoise, coral, Venetian glass and coins; large dangling earrings in their pierced ears competed with the two or three long braids, into which they plaited brightly colored bits of ribbon, and coins collected throughout the various lands of their wanderings. The blouse, more often than not, had a critical button missing in the front, and with their firm, provocative breasts bobbing as they sauntered about town, they were a difficult sight to ignore.

The old worn out gypsy women, their faces shrivelled into prunes, were known for their fortune-telling talents. They walked around with a *ghioc* ("cowry shell") and a pack of cards, begging to tell your fortune.

Their children, boys and girls alike, walked around naked or wearing some makeshift patched-up cotton shirt, either too large or too small for the skinny little bodies, expert at begging for food. For a candy or a penny, they would do a dance in the dust, turning cartwheels, jumping around and whining a ditty while strumming their dirty little fingers on their lips:

"Hai la ripu ripu
Gheorghe si Dumitru."
"Hai la ripu rai
Gheorghe si Mihai."

This meaningless rhyme performed, they tried to kiss the hands or feet of the onlookers, and begged for the reward. The older boys took to performing on the streets, and sang through a piece of tissue paper stretched on a comb.

The gypsies' social structure could only be guessed at, since they were kept away from the local communities both by the Jews and by the Gentiles. Their leader, or elder, was referred to as the *bulibasha*, strangely recalling the Hebrew *baal a bays* ("house owner"), who seemed to have the authority and decision-making powers over the *chatra* ("tribe"). Their moral standards, so far as the shtetl was concerned, were loose. Whether individual nuclear families existed or monogamy was rigorously practised was not ascertained. Nor was their religion explicitly known. Their moral and ethical values did not measure up to those of the shtetl or of the surrounding villagers. The Romanians accused gypsies of being chicken thieves and worse. There were rumors that gypsies liked to steal little children and take them away with them, and stories were told with warning to children to keep away from gypsies. In the shtetl, they did not enjoy a higher reputation. As customers, they were not welcome in the stores, since they "could steal the white of your eye".

On the socioeconomic scale, the gypsies were placed on the lowest rung, a condition apparently still prevalent in Romania.

The shtetl considered itself culturally superior to the backward peasantry. As Ruth Benedict reported in what is probably one of her earliest studies: "(The Jews) ... were regarded by the peasants as 'living off the peasants' the way the boyers and urban population did in general."* This view was not unanimously shared. It was the authorities who continued to propagate this. A description of Jews in Iassy the capital of Moldova, one century earlier may give a brief glimpse of the attitude of Romanians towards the Jews.

"Strada Mare" (Broadway) as the streets were called ... all you could see were the Jewish shops with iron shutters closed up at night, mostly one storey houses, the owners living in the back yard in other small

---

* Ruth Benedict, *Op Cit.*, p. 20.

houses, together with their "balabuste" (housewives) with their children and their helpers, in the same smell of garlic, in the same mess. These small shops were mostly all groceries with a string of dried figs between two rows of candles and a fistful of almonds between a lemon and an orange. Sometimes the helper slept on the push-cart outside, to watch even at night, the owner's goods, God forbid for a ruffian thief!

"At the right there was the line, Podul-Rosh (the Jewish neighborhood) at the corner of which a well kept, rambling green house, belonging to the Jew banker Michel Daniel . . . p. 241."

"All these smothered by countless 'dugheni jidovesti' (Jewish little shops) such as harnessmakers, blacksmiths, groceries, notions, all crammed with saloons run by ritual slaughters of the filthiest, with the ever present jars of brandy at the window among strings of dried figs. p. 244 . . ."

"Stealthily, straining through the crowded streets on covered wagons pulled by two or four shrivelled up nags, shoved in ten to twenty souls of Jidani from seven months to seventy years on one wagon, through Broadway they didn't mind a whip or two (from the Gentiles) but were they ever furious when some sassy Christian would count them pointing the finger; this forebode that one of them would surely die on the way. 'Why should the infidel cause life destruction with a finger?', 'so that there will be one less of you', they were told."*

This seems to have been the way upper-class Romanians of the nineteenth century looked upon the Jews. The excerpt was first written in the nineteenth century and reprinted, in 1941, by the Iron Guard Government.

The polite Romanian term for Jews was *Evrei*, derived from "Hebrews". *Jidani*, on the other hand, directly traceable to the Slavic *Jid*, was derived from "Judah" ("the traitor") and, by analogy, Christ killer, all of which were conveniently heaped on the contemporary Jews. It was an insulting term used by Gentiles when speaking about Jews in the latters' absence.

In spite of the deeply instilled and undeniable hate mongering, the local peasants and the few Romanians in the shtetl did make clear distinctions between the merchants they respected and those they had learned to mistrust. Expressions such as *da'i ca'i Jidan*, ("let him have, he's a Jew") or *Jidani's de vina* ("it's the Jews' fault") or again *Jidani la Palestina* ("Jews go to Palestine") were views and feelings fostered and carefully nurtured by those whose vested interests it was to maintain this animosity and hatred and to have a ready available scapegoat on whom to blame their own incapacities.

The Jews retaliated with the same attitude of condescension: *Goyisher kop* ("head of a Goy", implying inferiority) or *Vulech*!

---

* *Trecute Vieti de Doame si Domnite*, G. Gane. Edit. Ziarul Universul, S. A. Bucuresti, 1941.

followed by often unsavory epithets. (Wallachia was the ancient name for Romania.) *A badie Gheorghe* ("uncle George"), too, was used in the sense of ignorant, uncouth person. Individuals, however, as is so often the case, were known and respected for their admirable qualities, on a man-to-man basis.

2. Nicknames

Nicknames are part of any small community where contact inevitably creates sportive familiarity and brings out the folk sense of humor. Nicknames are sometimes given in contempt, but often are simply obvious identifications added to the name.

In Stefanesti it was said by one wit that one could "build a whole human body by using the nicknames in town". For instance: there was Mendl *kop* ("the head"), because his head was proportionately larger than average; Yankl *gorgl* indicated that his Adam's apple was too visible; Shome *pipick* referred to the oversized abdomen; Strul *gângâ* ("stammer") stated a fact, cruel as it was, as did Shmil *nonie* ("big-nose"). One unfortunate enough to have too visible a hernia was called *die kille* ("the hernia"). Body size was often added to the name: Berl *der longer* ("the tall one"), using "the longer" rather than the *hoycher* ("the tall one"), as a form of irony.

Personal characteristics gave obvious nicknames, such as red hair giving: the "red one" or "the black one", if the complexion happened to be somewhat darker. A person whose face had been scalded was der *upgebritter* ("the burned one"). A child with a small red birthmark on the lip was nicknamed *vamerpl* ("little berry").

Personality defects were picked up and stuck to the name: one slow-moving person was *Shome-momelige* ("the mushy one"). Another one was called Iankl *doarme* ("Iankl is asleep") because this excuse had been used too often to explain his absence from the store.

Molke *spodik* ("Molke the gossip") revealed the reputation this woman seemed to have for gossip, otherwise referred to as *plotkemachern* ("rumor-mongering"). A simpleton was *a lom-baseiser* ("a sheep").

Occupations often gave cause for nicknames: the upholsterer's habit of saying *kniak* with each bang of his hammer was *toblitzierer kniak* ("the tapestry man, bango"). Haym *dotzer* was so called for some forgotten reason — dotzer is the key button with which children play the game of buttons.

Pincu *gata* was the unfortunate nickname of one citizen. The embarrassing origin, commemorated very private circumstances: it seems that husband and wife, she tall like a stringbean and he short and shrivelled, were out for a walk, when nature called and they stopped at the appropriate establishment at a friend's backyard. While the husband was busy inside, the wife was waiting for him outside. Losing patience, the wife called to her husband: "Pincu, gata?" ("Pincu, are you ready?") To which, the man, still busy and in the throes of efforts, replied in tones and modulations that left little room for the imagination: "Inco'oleaca" (the colloquial for "a little longer"). And so the shtetl knew him as "Pincu gata" to a point where his real name was all but forgotten.

Max *opay* acquired his nickname when, under his wedding canopy, while breaking the traditional glass, he innocently called out "Opay!", pleased with himself, but a most inappropriate remark given the dignified occasion. ("Opay" is the onomatopoeic term often used when children accomplish a feat deserving applause, such as jumping or catching a ball, not unlike our "Oops! a daisy!" This nickname has a sequel. The *gabbai* at the synagogue had to call the gentleman in question to read the *Torah*. Admit the solemnity of the moment, with the *Torah* scroll ready and the congregation waiting, the red faced *gabbai* could momentarily not recall the man's full name; all he was able to remember was "Max *Opay*", certainly not an adequate appellation at any time, least of all in front of the *umed* (the reading lectern in the synagogue). To the consternation of the congregation, who knew the *gabbai* as an impeccably serious person, the latter burst out laughing and was unable to continue the service, which had to be taken over by someone else for that occasion.

3. Proverbs

Popular wisdom gleaned through the ages is expressed simply and directly in proverbs, sayings and maxims. These are the true poetry of a people and, like poetry, they have meter, rhyme and rhythm. In content, they cover the whole range of human experience. Yiddish, long considered a mongrel tongue, has been recognized as a language in its own right, with a picturesque vocabularly and rich literature.

The Romanian shtetl, heir to Yiddish folk wisdom, has availed itself of the Romanian cultural heritage as well, and it is not surprising to find many popular aphorisms based on the peasants' shrewd observations. Similarities and differences in attitudes are illustrated in many proverbs dealing with the same topic.

Many sayings are based on anecdotes, which, like Biblical or literary quotations, evoke meaning only for those familiar with the source, in which case they are a form of shorthand, succinctly summing up a situation. If they had been over used and have become hackneyed clichés, it is only because of their aptness. Many are untranslatable or require circumlocution in order to transmit the various shades of meaning and cultural underpinnings implied.

Each culture treasures these gems, for they declare what is right or wrong, true or false, proper or improper, according to that particular culture. It is a built-in mechanism to assure that the authority of custom, transmitted from one generation to the next, will remain unchallenged. With imagination, irony and wit, they provide guidelines for each succeeding generation.

Yiddish is a pithy language with graftings from every language with which it came into contact throughout the centuries. The Yiddish spoken in the Romanian shtetl had incorporated many Romanian words, sometimes appending to them Yiddish endings, a fact often held up to ridicule by both Yiddish and Romanian purists, but which contributed to the dynamic vitality of this little known subgroup.

The following is by no means an exhaustive list of Romanian shtetl sayings. It is an attempt to illustrate, with concrete examples, how the shtetl defined itself.

Rhyme and meter are part of folk idiom. In the Romanian shtetl, rhyme was spontaneously contrived at the drop of a hat. Any word that did not seem to be relevant to the basic issue was immediately dismissed by the simple device of adding a prefix and turning it into a rhyme. Thus, the word "rhyme" (to take an example), if it presented no interest to the question at hand, would become: "rhyme-shyme" — "who cares?" As important was the expressive shrug of the shoulder and wave of the hand, followed by "Ich veis vus?" ("What do I know?").

Anything irrelevant was: "Shtram-gram, mach mir a letnik" ("Shtram-rhyme, make me a loose coat").

The mechanism of scaling a word up or down by means of a prefix or suffix (common to many languages) enriched the vocabulary. For instance, someone who eats is an *esser*, an eater, but someone who overeats, is a *fresser*, an epithet that conjures the image of a rather uncouth person.

By adding the ending "ole" to any word, it became a diminutive, while the ending "oy" borrowed from Romanian, implied an inordinate enlargement. Thus, *meydl* ("girl") became *meydole* ("little girl"), while *moyd* carried the meaning of large, and also clumsy or awkward. The Russian suffix "nick" was often used such as in *nudnick* ("one who pesters"). A diminutive of a name, when applied to an adult, carried a derogatory dimension. For instance, "Yankl" (a common masculine name) became "Yanokle" when used for a child; when applied to an adult, it implied some questionable quality.

All unsophisticated cultures excel in the use of exclamations or voluble expletives. Shtetl language abounded in them. Here are some: "Oy, vey mir" ("Woe is me"). "Alevay" ("Wish it were so"). "Pypoy-ponafidl" or "Py-hah" ("Really, now!")

Many Romanian folk songs begin with the idiomatic phrase *foaie verde* ("green leaf"). When used verbatim in Yiddish, the phrase acquired an entirely different sense: "Faoie verde pisteh dillechts" ("Green leaf, waste and bother"), intimating "so what?" or "who cares?". Another way of questioning the relevance of a remark was: "Nu, will there be anything for the Jews?" ("How relevant is it?"). In Yiddish, this is summed up in one simple word: *tachles*. The importance of "relevance" to shtetl culture is undeniable, and another frequently heard word was *yicker*, again meaning the most important, or relevant.

Judging by the number of expressions referring to being disturbed or being bothered by someone, this must have been important in shtetl interpersonal relations. "Dillechts" is an offshoot of the verb "dilln" ("to disturb or pester"). It is the root of a series of diverse expressions, all meaning "Don't bother me" or "Don't disturb me".

    dill mir nisht dem spodik   don't bother my bonnet
    dill mir nisht die kardike   don't bother my tight fitting short overcoat
    dill mir nisht dem piddl   don't bother my box

In the same vein were: "hack mir nisht a tchainik" (don't bang a teakettle), "hack mir nisht a kop" (don't bang my head). A rather vulgar expression, rarely heard in polite society was: "Gey mir in bud arein" ("Got to the communal bathhouse"). The "mir" (for "me") is used as emphasis.

"Farchiode mir nisht dem kop" ("Don't suffocate my head") had a similar meaning. *Chod* is Russian for "smoke".

As a preamble to anything undesirable; "Holileh, hosveshulem, hos-vehos", meaning, roughly, "God forbid", was uttered in one breath or used one phrase at a time, as circumstances dictated.

For something exceptional: "Azoins vi azelechts" ("Something like this or like that"); and an emphatic negation was "Veisech vus" ("Do I know what?").

"Epes bomblet sich mir in kop" ("There is something dangling in my head") meant that there was something one half remembered.

"Secunes nefushes" or "interfering with life itself" was used with reference to a grave danger, to be avoided.

Picturesque imagery was part of the daily vocabulary, used to communicate the message or sum up the gist of a situation. It added color to the simplest remark. A woman busy working in the kitchen was said to "ratn of dem fartech" ("horseback riding on her apron"). Someone who insisted in believing an absurdity was said to "sich einredn a kind in bouch" ("to have talked himself into being pregnant"). If someone dressed or did something unbecoming, he was told, "Se past vi a chazer oiringlech" ("It fits like earrings on a pig"), immediately conjuring the ridiculous image of dangling earrings on a muddy pig. Speaking nonsense was expressed in Romanian as "green horses on the walls," while in Yiddish it was "shtissem". "Hint trugn gantze kep" ("dogs carried away entire heads") implied abundance at a feast, where even dogs were overfed.

"To make a mosquito into a horse" was the Romanian's way of saying that it was a gross exaggeration, while developing a lengthy philosophical irrelevance, was to expound the theory of the matches."

Where the devil weaned his children" or "at the devil's mother's" implied an inaccessible, far away Godforsaken place.

"Like the cat looking into a calendar" more than conveyed someone's ignorance, while the same idea was hinted at by the Yiddish: "Vi a hun in bney Udem" ("Like a hen among the sons of Adam").

"Pulling the cat by the tail" or "He plays the Jew's harp" suggested a failure or someone unsuccessful at his work.

A humorous (though vulgar) analogy for someone who seemed to be aimlessly wandering about was: "Like a flatulence in fish broth."

"Er gibt nisht avek a zack borsht far dir" ("He won't give away a sackful of borsht for you") conveyed the meaning that someone thought very highly of you, in spite of the dubious image of a dripping sack of beet broth.

"Colac peste pupaza" ("a fancy bun on top of a partridge") intimated that it was simply too much — "as if that was not enough".

"He took his nose for a walk" was said of someone who was insolent.

"Er hot nisht kein zitz fleysh" ("He has no sitting muscles or padding on his backside") was said of an impatient person who didn't sit still too long.

"An ox has a long tongue but he cannot speak" was an adage used when one preferred not to say anything or give further explanations.

"Git is ba a chozer a ur" ("From a pig, obtaining even one hair is an achievement") was said when a donation was squeezed out of a reluctant giver or a notoriously avaricious person.

"A meyvy, vi a kotz of eyvn" ("Understands as much as a cat is an expert on yeast"). (Yeast was used, here, mainly for its rhyme value).

"Like a calf at the new gate" was said of someone looking lost or waiting sheepishly. The implication is that a calf would not recognize its home when a new gate was placed there.

"To string a clothesline through the land" was a Romanian figure of speech often used in fairy tales and in daily parlance, to mean "to broadcast".

"A carload of years" expressed a very long time, while a minuscule amount was "not as much as black under a fingernail".

"A gragger noch Pyrem" ("a noisemaker after Purim") signified anything out of place or arriving too late, while "die tzveite tog yomtov" ("the second set of festival days") indicated a superfluous interference or uninvited comment. Also used in the same sense was "the fifth wheel to a wagon".

"Shlugn Kapures", a rite of redemption whereby a chicken was sacrificed to expiate for one's sins, was often referred to in sayings and expressions:

"A sheyne, reyne, kapureh" ("A beautiful, clean, redemption") meant "good riddance".

"Toigh of kapures" ("worthless") was also a frequently used expression, as was:

"A kapure far" ("May this be sacrificed as a redemption.").

"A fink fin dem Gehenem" ("a spark from hell") referred to someone of quick wit or sparkling intelligence.

"Kvell vi a pryeshké" ("swell like dough pastry") expressed satisfaction and pleasure derived from success of loved ones.

"To give water to the mill" meant to provide added arguments against one's better judgment.

"The wolf changes his hair, but not his habits" indicated unreliability of superficial changes and suggested mistrust in such changes.

"Yearning for blackberries, one will eat the leaves" hints at accepting second best when longing for the real thing.

"From a distance like a rose, tastes of bitter from up close" was said of anyone who looked better from the distance than at close range.

"He feels himself with the fly on his fur hat" was used when someone was known to feel guilty or self conscious.

"Er veist nisht vin ein und vin ous" ("He does't know when to be in and when out") summed up someone's questionable judgment.

"In the house of a hanged one, rope should not be mentioned" referred to tactless or undiplomatic remarks.

"Caught between the hammer and the anvil" suggested an impasse or a difficult choice.

The expression "Shyist a Terk un rietz sich up" ("Shoots a Turk and takes a rest") applied when someone did not seem to be overworking. The phrase was meaningful only to those familiar with the anecdote on which it was based: A shtetl mother was giving advice to her son, leaving to fight the Turks. She told him: "My son, don't work too hard in the wars; shoot a Turk and take a rest, shoot another Turk and rest up some more."

The *boydem*, the loft or attic, was an important part of the shtetl house. Many analogies refer to the *boydem*. "Of dem boydem is an yirid" ("There is a bazaar in the loft") meant "What will you be telling me next?". "Lost zich oys a boydem" was used as "It turned out that there was nothing worthwhile there." "Lach dich oys of'n boydem" ("Go laugh yourself out in the loft") suggested that someone was not in a laughing mood.

To borrow trouble, the Romanian saying was: "You tie up your head when it doesn't hurt," while in Yiddish it was "With a healthy head in a sick bed!"

Irony was a device frequently used to make a point. There seems to have been a propensity for using the opposite of what was meant and for a touch of light ridicule or humor. "A fainer tachshid" ("a fine darling") was said of a decidedly undesirable character, as was the Romanian "poama buna" ("good fruit").

A wedding gift was a *drushé geshonok*. When the mother-in-law was included in a young couple's ménage, she was referred to as a "drushé geshank".

"Bleib noch nisht gezint, ich fur noch nisht avek" ("Don't remain in good health yet, I am not ready to leave") needs no elaboration.

With irony, but also with tenderness, the importance of the wedding day, (some distant future date was frequently alluded to, especially with little girls. "Se vet sich oys heiln bis tzu der chassene" ("It will surely heal before your wedding day — don't worry") was a comforting remark for a minor scratch.

Or, "S'vet nisht shotn tzum shiddech" ("It won't affect the marriage match"), indicating an insignificant problem of little consequence.

"A chasurn, die kalle's tsi sheyn" ("a shortcoming, the bride is too beautiful") mockingly pointed out unjustified complaints, referring to obvious assets.

Anything absurd or nonsensical was "nisht geshtoygn, nisht gefloygn" ("neither climbing, nor flying — but up in the air just the same").

"Burech à bo" ("Blessed be the one who arrived") was a rather formal greeting when a guest arrived. In popular parlance, if anyone not quite welcome showed up unexpectedly, he may have been greeted with the ironical "burech à bo, bisteh do" ("There you are, and who, pray, sent for you?").

Should a notoriously mischievous or undesirable person appear, the somewhat uncharitable greeting was "A riech in mine gost arein" ("May the devil get into my uninvited guest").

Anyone who seemed to take seriously trifling matters was asked: "Are they playing the game of buttons with the country?"

Vasilacké was a typical clown's name; the expression "instead of Vasilacké" suggested that someone was a mere figurehead.

"Tzegeit sich Yidenes, vi zoltz in vasser" ("Melt away, old women, like salt in water") was said to a group of busybodies obstructing the roadway.

The shtetl mother's concern for her offspring has become proverbial. The *American Yiddishe mamme* lives up to the reputation of her shtetl forebears. She would constantly wish to put herself between any hurt and her child. This is not unique in itself; what is unusual is her articulating it: "Mir far dier" ("May it happen to me instead of you"). With this, she constantly consoled her child in pain. To the little girl, the mother used to say: "mir far dier, un far dein shviger's shnier, und far dein chusn's kalleh, und far deine beindolech alle." ("May it happen to me instead of you – and for your mother-in-law's daughter-in-law, and your bridegroom's bride, and for every little bone in your body"). This was not mere lip service, it was a genuinely felt sentiment.

In the same vein was the oft-heard wish, "May I have upkimmen (atonement) for my children, with my suffering."

"Yedes heirole, a perole" ("Every little hair, a precious pearl") indicated a fastidious concern for minute details, or tender, loving, care.

"You don't escape whatever you fear most" would suggest an inate understanding and appreciation of the importance and influence of self programming.

"The unswept house awaits guests" implied that one was often caught unprepared, at the worst possible moment.

"Nemen die fis of die pleitzes" ("to take one's feet on one's back") meant to run fast or disappear.

"To feed the berry straight into the mouth," meaning to spoon feed or patiently explain, implied someone slow to understand.

"Er ot farkocht a kasha" ("he cooked up a kasha") or "shoyn farkocht a gitteh kasha" ("already cooked up a good mess") intimated a mixup or concoction from which it was difficult to extricate oneself.

A nincompoop or oaf had many titles conferred upon him. He

was: *a shlemiel, a Kunie leml, a Lom baseyser, a lémishké, a geghiole mée*, while *a schlack* or *a shlakitura* was a mean, nasty person.

"Vi der balabos holt dus hintl, azoy hold dus hintl dus gonze gezindl" ("As the master treats the little dog, so does the little dog treat the entire household"). The inference here is that the head of the household sets the standards by which the household behaves.

"Fish begins to smell foul from the head down" was the equivalent saying expressing the belief that the leader sets the tone.

In a small community where reputations were earned and based on past experience, artificial behavior was shunned. Truth and sincerity were highly prized. Both languages abound in examples:

"A nochgemachte machsheyfe is arger vi a geboirene" ("An artificial witch is worse than a true-born one") ridiculed anyone who tried too hard to be what he was not.

"Hilm und erd ot geshvoyrn as gurnisht zol nist geyn faloyrn" ("Earth and heaven vowed that nothing should ever be lost"). This referred to the importance of truth and that lying was not worthwhile. It was also said that truth will come up like oil on water.

In Romanian, the same idea was expressed: "Whatever in the pantry, is also outside," implying that underhanded methods were not trustworthy. This was again repeated in "Whoever knows me will buy me, who doesn't, will sell me." Or, "Either speak according to your national costume or dress according to your manner of speech." Incongruous behavior or misleading statements were not tolerated.

To be caught "with the small *occa*" (a weight measure) referred to a dishonest use of weights — cheating.

"The earthen jug doesn't go to the fountain too often." Chances were that by taking an earthen jug instead of a less breakable wooden one to the well, one would break it sooner or later. This, too, was a warning against cheating or lying.

"To steal one's hat" implied willful self-deception, also to be avoided.

"Many see but few know" referred to the fact that only those who understood a situation well were able to appreciate it fully.

"Man sanctifies the place, not the place the man" was a basic Romanian philosophy that the shtetl found congruent with its own world view. It said simply that a man must be judged on his own merits rather than on superficialities.

"Gold sheint oys der blotteh" ("Gold will shine through mud"), that is, true qualities of excellence will ultimately prevail. By the same token, "to show the brass on the surface" indicated that the thin veneer is easily rubbed off, in manners and character, as well as any false front or pretence.

"Az men hot nemunes, gibt men nemunes" ("If one is honest himself, one has confidence in others") states succinctly that one judges others by oneself.

One respondent remarked that "in America being aggressive was a quality, while in the shtetl, being *obraznic* (Cheeky) was uncouth".

A braggart was shunned. Jokingly he would be asked whether he had bad neighbors.

In Romanian the saying went: "Self-praise doesn't smell good."

"Yi anuve ob ich, yi kein gelt kost mich nisht" ("I derive satisfaction and it doesn't cost me anything") applied to a situation where one enjoyed a revenge without any effort on one's part.

In spite of the avowed preference for honesty, there were situations when one had to put on a front. "A knap in beckl, und gey vayter" ("A pinch in the cheek and keep going") is understood only in the light of the stereotyped image of good health of the shtetl, where pink cheeks were a sign of health, hence desirable. To pinch one's cheeks in order to bring color to the face, one tried to hide any personal malaise from the public's prying eyes.

Lest these sayings conjure the image of a purely utopian society where only integrity was upheld, let us look at some less high-minded sayings, which enjoyed as great a popularity. "Az me shmirt, furt men" ("If you grease the axle you travel") implied that in life, too, oiling the wheels gives a smoother ride.

"Leigh an éy s'zol aroys tzvey" ("To put an egg, to get two"), a concept based on the habit of putting an egg under the hen to stimulate laying another, acknowledged that gift giving was not always a purely disinterested matter.

Co-operation and mutual assistance were important: "One hand washes the other, and both wash the face." Although reminiscent of "you scratch my back, I'll scratch yours", there is a difference of principle between the two attitudes, since the Romanian proverb does not infer any sly or self-seeking motives, but is a simple expedient.

"Whoever digs a grave for another, will fall into it himself" pointed out the danger of harming others or of making false accusations, lest they backfire, being the implication, not devoid of selfish motives.

"When two quarrel, the third one wins" sounds the warning against the futility of quarreling rather than settling differences in an amicable way. On the other hand, it was well-known that "a sweet word brings more" and in Yiddish, it was said: "A git vort, macht a breit ort" ("A good word makes a wide place").

A note of caution was sounded against taking advantage of one's position of power: "One must stand up when the *Rebbé* passed by but the *Rebbé* must be wise enough not to pass by too often."

"Arup fun der madreighe" ("down from the high standing") was said with compassion about anyone who was losing or had lost a high social standing.

Moral values were inculcated with graphic examples: "Whoever steals an egg today, will steal an ox tomorrow." The principle, rather than the issue, was emphasized.

"The barking dog doesn't bite" was the Romanian proverb, and again: "The quiet cat scratches viciously," that is, beware of the sweet, quiet person; you may have unpleasant surprises.

In Yiddish, too, the equivalent was "a shtill vasserl grupt tief" ("a still water runs deep").

"Arup fun dem marki" ("down from the market") indicates with finality that something was ended.

"I don't want your honey, don't give me your sting", is self-explanatory.

"Er nemt vi a blind ferd" ("He takes like a blind horse") inferred someone too eager to accept whatever was offered to him.

When the answer was well known in advance, one asked mockingly: "Ketzole, vilst pitter?" ("Kitten, do you want some butter?".

Prudence rather than daring was advocated: "Don't give the sparrow in your hand for two on the fence," implying that the only thing to be trusted was concrete proof: "What's in the hand, is not a lie."

It was wise to "stretch yourself only as far as your blanket allows or suffer the consequences". The philosophy of "buy now, pay later" was unknown.

"Who sows the wind will gather the tempest," of Biblical renown was often quoted when stressing the responsibility for one's actions.

Personal responsibility is the theme for "gebencht zenen die hent vus helfn zich alein," ("Blessed are the hands that can help themselves"), and the peasant's view: "The owner's eyes fatten the cattle."

As a corollary, caution was advocated: "Don't say hop, until you've jumped." Sayings such as "beat the iron while it's hot" would suggest taking advantage of an opportunity rather than launching into the unknown.

Excessive caution, however, was shrugged off with "The wet one is not afraid of the rain," in other words, once wet, what else can happen?

"If you've burned yourself with hot borsht, you'll blow into yogourt" was repeated in the proverb: "Lock the stable after the horse was stolen."

Belief in "fate" was inate to the shtetl and both the optimist and the pessimist found justification. The Romanian rhyme said: "Where it's good, it's not for me, where it's bad, hop, there I be." Yiddish wit summed it up picturesquely: "Ven die toybe moyd geyt tantzn, geyen die klezmer pishn." ("When the deaf girl goes to dance, the fiddlers take their break for nature's call").

The *shlimazl* ("luckless one") was said to always have his buttered bread fall "with the butter downward".

The Romanian population, forced to submission by a series of tyrannical rulers, preferred prudence to bravery, especially when life was at stake. "Flight is shameful, but it is healthful" and quoting from a popular poem: "The saber will not sever the bowed head."

"Gefalene schoyre heibt sich" ("Fallen goods will rise again") sounded an optimistic note, based on the merchants' experience, but sometimes addressed to a fall both literal and figurative.

"One never knows from where the hare will jump out," meaning that one may hope for a pleasant surprise.

The optimist in the shtetl was said to see the bagel, while the pessimist saw the hole.

Hospitality and generosity were highly prized: "a krankn freigt men a gezintn gibt men" ("You ask a sick person; to a healthy person you give without asking") applied to a guest who was asked whether he would like to have a drink or a fruit.

A visitor was said to "come for a while and see for a mile", thus summing up the visitor's power of observation, or perhaps first impressions.

"Leibn a shvern vogn is gring tzu fis tzu geyn" ("Near a heavy wagon it is easier to walk along") inferred advantages to be derived from associations with important persons or large establishments.

Any deliberate obstruction was "to put sticks in the spokes of the wheels".

Past experience had taught that a small object was able to endanger or obstruct important situations: "The small stump overturns the large wagon."

Troublemakers were known by reputation and held up for ridicule. In Romanian they were said to "look for a knot in the rushes" (where there are no knots to be found), or to be "Tarae brau" ("dragging the peasant woven girdle"). This referred to someone who would deliberately look for a fight by provoking anyone who stepped on his girdle.

Absurd analogies were rebutted with "Ven mein bobbé hot reider, furt zie" ("If my grandmother had wheels, she'd be a conveyance").

Grandmothers were the butt of many remarks: "Dertzeil der

bobbé" ("Tell it to your grandmother") implied that only your grandmother would believe. In Romanian this became "Tell it to the dumb one," who presumably would not be able to reply even if he did not believe.

"Farzorgt der bobbé or indernuch" ("Assure the grandmother's future") referred to a somewhat unnecessary concern, considering the grandmother's age.

"Derlegn der bobbé's yirishé" ("to lose grandmother's inheritance") — since grandmothers did not presumably have too much, the matter was insignificant.

Someone who, after being helpful, undid it all with a wrong gesture, was compared to a cow, who, after giving a bucketful of milk, spilled it with one kick.

A deplorable situation was summed up with "Farviest is Parreh gevorn in Myitzrayim" ("afflicted was Pharaoh in Egypt") — "Too bad it reached this stage."

"Ich veis nisht fin kein pisser un fin kein hullem" ("I haven't the vaguest notion").

Physiological sensations were often metaphorically appealed to, as in: " 'S mir gevorn kiel bam hartz" (My heart froze), Finster far die oygn, ("Dark in front of the eyes"). The same expression was translated to Romanian "To see green stars."

"A white liver" expressed someone who kept his cool. The same idea was conveyed by "Arn tzitzl un a goll" ("someone without a gall bladder").

"Fargissn dus blit" ("to spill blood") or embarrass someone, was an unforgivable sin.

"Vi a toytn bankes" ("as helpful as cupping is to a dead man") summed up futility. The same idea was conveyed by "Se helft krachtzn" ("It helps as much as whining helps pain").

"Er zitst of der heibershter bonk un shreyt, heys" ("He sits on the upper bench in the steam bath and cries, it's hot") referred to someone who complained but did nothing to avoid the problem.

"Dus im un vet er meinen s'is barn eingemachts" ("Give him garbage and he'll believe it's pear marmalade") graphically described one who in his ignorance was ready to accept anything without questioning.

Someone seemingly unaware of being in a bad situation was said to be as comfortable as "a worm in a jar of horseradish".

"Er is gur arangefaln in a shmaltzgryb" ("He fell into a hole full of chicken fats") summed up the epitome of good fortune.

To express despair, the Romanian was ready to "take the world on his head", while in Yiddish, one said: "dropet zich of die gleiche vent" ("climbing the straight walls").

"Zich geyn glichn of'n ayz" ("to go slide on the ice") implied someone who had it too good and was going out of his way to find trouble. The same idea was conveyed by "mit a gezintn kop, in a krankn bet" ("with a healthy head, in a sick bed").

The oft maligned mother-in-law and her relationship with her son's wife was the butt of many jokes and aphorisms. The diplomatic mother-in-law would scold her own daughter within earshot of the son's wife: "Zug der tochter, meint die shnier" ("Tell the daughter when you mean the daughter-in-law"). This bit of diplomatic hinting was part of shtetl philosophy.

The Romanian slovenly daughter-in-law, on the other hand, was said to clean only "where the mother-in-law can see".

"Varfn dem get far die fis" ("to throw the divorce in front of the feet") implied: "don't threaten me" or "Don't use blackmail on me."

"Like the daughter-in-law in the dishes" was the Romanian expression referring to a clumsy person, sure to do some damage.

Social-class distinctions were a formidable force in the shtetl. One associated exclusively with one's social equals, as prescribed by one's *yichus*. It is not surprising to find countless sayings specifying and supporting this.

"Tell me with whom you associate and I will tell you who you are" or "If you push yourself in the chaff, you will be eaten by the pigs." The clear lesson gathered from this was that one's prestige was affected by those one associated with. Another proverb, found in many cultures, was "From a dog's tail, you won't make a silk sieve."

Yiches was a family qualification and it was well-known that both good and bad qualities ran in families, hence, "The apple doesn't fall too far from the tree."

"Se shteyt dir nisht un?" ("What's the matter, it is beneath you?") applied both in its direct connotation of comparative equality and in the mocking sense when it was taken to mean, "Is this not good enough for you?"

Shtetl Jews as well as Romanian peasants were a proud lot, sensitive to their standing in the community. Much as big-city living enjoyed prestige, the saying was "Rather than the last in the city, better head man in my village."

"Vi tzvei is er der dritter" ("Where two people meet, he is the third") implied a busybody who mixed into everyone's affairs and didn't wait to be invited.

The gypsies were the lowest men on the totem pole. Many references allude to their lowly standing and uncouth manner. "When the gypsy became emperor, first his own father he hung" denotes the ruthlessness and lack of consideration of those who were themselves of lowly origin.

"The gypsy drowns just as he is about to touch shore" was said of someone foolish enough to give up just as he was in sight of his goal.

"First I want to become an officer, then I'll try for a fireman" referred to the gypsy's lack of discriminating judgment regarding rank, since he considered the fireman status superior to that of an officer (presumably because the fireman's uniform was more impressive than that of the officer).

"Tontzn of tzvei hossenes" ("dancing on two weddings at once") expressed the impossibility of being in two places at the same time or being involved in too many things at once. In a much more graphic manner, this became "mit ein toches of tzvei irridem" ("One cannot sit with one behind in two marketplaces at the same time").

When referring to the core of an issue that seemed to be overlooked, the saying was: "A pintole iber dem gontzn kepole" ("A small dot, covering the whole head"), implying neither more nor less but the most important.

"To put the dot on the 'i' ", on the other hand, referred to being specific.

"A coat for foul weather" was used in the sense of "playing second fiddle," a role much resented by everyone.

German was considered far more prestigious than the lowly Yiddish. Speaking German added distinction but was also resented and ridiculed: "Plitzim ret der Datch" ("Suddenly, he speaks German") was an accusation of putting on airs, unforgivable in the shtetl. The same idea was expressed in: "Noble geyt die velt tzu grunde" ("Nobly does the universe disintegrate"), sometimes accompanied by "py, poy, ponafidl".

"A nar tur men kein halbe arbeit nisht vazn" ("To a fool one should not show an unfinished work") referred to the supposed lack of imagination of a simple person, who was unable to visualize the completed work, and would, presumably criticize it, for lack of understanding.

"With lard at the heart" was the unlikely expression used about someone whose self-confidence bespoke his affluence.

"Where goes the thousand, currency bill, there goes the hundred" was an expression used by a lavish spender who didn't try to scrimp on anything.

Trying hard to be of help, the Romanian said, "I turned myself into a row boat and a foot bridge."

Someone who was difficult to classify, and who didn't seem to belong, was: "neither dog nor grayhound."

"Der eibishter fin dem shteisl" ("the upper part of the pestle"), that is, the most important, used in a mocking sense.

"Ich gib dir a patch redsty datch" ("I will slap you so hard you'll speak German"), inferred a whack that would produce confusion in one's head.

The concept of "beauty" is a function of many parameters. "Beauty" is culturally defined: "Alba, grasa si frumoasa" ("white, stout and beautiful") were the attributes of beauty in the shtetl. Being *fardart* ("dried up") or *fardronjet* ("more of the same") was synonymous with sickly or ill-fed and, therefore, presumably, poor. A double chin was a sign of pulchritude, although *sich goydern vi a hindig* ("to show one's double chin like a turkey") was a sign of arrogance and not tolerated in the shtetl.

Talking too much without concrete results was referred to as "to beat water in the churn". Anyone talking too much was reminded that "any empty barrel made more noise than a full one".

Women were reputed for having *nine moos reid* ("nine measures of words") with which, according to legend, they had been blessed. But the Talmudic saying was: "The Lord gave man two ears and one mouth, so that he may listen twice as much as he talked." In general, "speech was silver, silence was golden". *Gura bogata* ("a rich mouth") in Romanian, oddly enough, meant someone who spoke out of turn and said more than was called for.

If someone was rudely interrupted or prevented from saying something, the remark would have been: "Farpatch mir nisht dos moul" ("Don't slap my mouth").

"Yeder leibt sich ba anondern in freidn" ("Everyone believes that the other person is happier") implied that one may envy others, unaware of the serious problems they may have.

"Az me ken nisht arriber, mus min arinter" ("If you can't step over, you must bend under"), indicated a willingness to compromise.

"Oder se helft nisht ober me darf nisht" ("Either it doesn't help, or one shouldn't try") injected a note of futility.

"To put salt on his tail" was said of someone who disappeared without a trace.

"Expensive at the chaff and cheap at the flour" was said of one who was generous with small things and stingy with big items.

"Az se mult sich nisht in deroisn, mult sich in shtib" ("If things don't go well outside, there is activity inside") referred to marital conflicts arising when financial problems appeared from the outside.

The cavalier manner of dispensing advice, especially that someone else bear the brunt of a burden, was resented: "Inter yenem's urm is gringh a maché tzu trugn" ("It is easy to have a boil on someone else's underarm").

To be used as a guinea pig aroused resentment: "Of yenem's burd is git zich tzu lernen shern" ("It is easy to practice shaving on someone else's beard.")

"Mit yenem's hent is gringh koyln tzu sharn" ("With someone else's hands it is easy to spread live coals") expressed the same resentment.

Ideals were there to strive for but reality was a fact of life and the shtetl was pragmatic: "Der zotter gleibt nisht dem hingerign" ("The sated one doesn't believe the hungry").

"Einer vein der borsht is'im bitter, anonderer as die perl zenen tzi shitter" ("One cries the borsht is too bitter, another that the pearls are too loosely strung") was the way popular wisdom summed up the blatant inequalities and problems in the shtetl.

"The dog with money is called Mister Dog" or "Of gelt shteyt die velt" ("The world rests on money") or the quote from a popular song: "gelt is kalechik se kulket sich avek" ("Money is round, it rolls away fast") give us an idea of shtetl pragmatism, in spite of a certain disdain toward the newly rich and the continuous reverence for learning and knowledge.

"To the rich, even the devil brings *colaci* – (fancy rolls)" was the cynical acknowledgement that the wealthy are lucky in everything.

Excessive praise was mistrusted: "To the highly praised tree, don't go with an empty sack" lest you be disappointed.

"Kleine kinder, kleine tzures, groyse kinder, groyse tzures" ("Small children, small worries, grown-up children, big worries"). This often heard truism expressed not only the constant concern of the shtetl parents for their children's welfare but also emphasized the fact that parents of grown-up children often faced more serious and complex problems.

"Ich darf dos, vi a loch in kop" ("I need this, like a hole in the head") is self-explanatory.

Although individuals were judged on their own merits, the shtetl tended to be condescending towards their Goyim neighbors. "A fainer Goy" or a "kliger Goy" carried a note of surprise. More common were remarks such as: "gey dertzeil dem Goy a vitz" ("Go tell a joke to a Gentile"), suggesting some doubt as to his ability to grasp the finer points of a joke. The Romanian, in turn, felt the same way about the gypsy: "Does the gypsy know what saffron is?"

Resting on past glory was questioned: "Sheyn gevein un gelt gehot macht nisht oys" ("Was beautiful once and had money once, doesn't count"). The implication is that there was not much consolation in past assets; it was the present that mattered, not the past.

"After the war, many braves show up" implies that there are usually more critics after the fact than willing workers when needed.

Respect for learning was summed up in "The book makes a better man as grafting makes a better fruit tree." This analogy, with a more familiar milieu for the farmer shows that, in theory, at least, learning was regarded with respect by the Romanian peasants as well. For the shtetl, this was a simple fact of life, which needed no elaboration. It was summed up in "Torah is chochma" ("In the Bible there is wisdom").

The absurdity and tyranny of fashion was bluntly put: "Why wear boils on your head, old woman? Well, if it's in style, what else can I do?".

The Yiddish expression for something out of style was "fin Mnishkes tzeitn" ("from the times of Mnishkes").

Many warnings were sounded against being gullible: "With a swallow you will not have spring" or "Not all that flies is to be eaten," that is, don't believe all you are told.

Many proverbs advocated the Protestant ethnic of work, thrift, savings, which seems to have been arrived at in many cultures. "The one who wakes up early will reach farther" or "The lazy one runs more and the stingy one spends more," suggesting that carelessness results in unnecessary effort or loss. This is repeated in: "Haste spoils the work." A spendthrift was said to have "a cracked hand", conjuring the image of a hand through which money slipped out.

"Oats wasted on geese" suggested misplaced advice, or waste of effort bound to be unappreciated, since oats were usually fed to horses, while geese were able to feed by scratching.

"You don't look a gift horse in the mouth" was as true in the shtetl as among the Romanian peasants or anywhere else.

The Romanian way of saying that something was unbelievable was: "Your mind would stand still."

Concern with trifles, when important matters were at stake, was expressed: "The old woman is combing her hair while the village is in flames."

"Geshtorbn, bagrubn, of yener velt vi geffinen" ("Died, buried, on the other world, like found anew") was a quaint expression used as: "Finished, now let's forget it and let's go on from here."

The expression "he lost his *lefteria*" was used in the sense of someone who was a great disappointment. In Greek *elefteria* means "freedom". It is interesting to ponder just how this change in meaning occurred.

"Vi in pussig shteyt" ("As it is written in the Codified Decisions Tome") meant to do something properly, in the accepted manner.

"Ich'ob mich badingen mit zein kopdarenish" ("I made a contact with his own head-shrinking") was another one of those expressions frequently used in the sense of "It's not my problem any longer, let him worry."

To aggravate a situation already in bad shape was: "to pour salt on a wound."

"Water flows, the stones remain" referred to the truism that some things are transitory while others are permanent.

"Noyeh mit sibn grazn" ("Noyeh with seven mistakes") was used to indicate an ignorant person.

"Tzu zingen un tzu zugn" ("to sing and to say") conveyed a pack of trouble.

"Besser mit a klign tzu derleign, vi mit a nar tzu fardinen" ("It is better to lose an argument with an intelligent person than to win with a fool").

"One raven does not gouge another's eyes" implied that those of a kind don't hurt one another, or don't take advantage of one another.

To tell someone "a gantze megillah" indicated that it was a long endless story. It was derived from the lengthy "megillas Esther" of *Purim*.

Anything mismatched was *Yukl mit Faivish*, two comic characters, like Laurel and Hardy; anything that did not fit or was out of place. In Romanian this was expressed with "like the nut against the wall".

"An antik" (used in the sense of a rare, valuable article) was used in its positive sense; depending on the tone of voice, it could become an insulting epithet.

To reprimand someone, there were a wealth of metaphors and hyperboles. "A shvartzn sof" ("a black end") or a "shaloteh" ("salad") derived from the Romanian for "salad", *salata*. To elaborate, one added "with oil and vinegar", which implied that the person had *oysgelost dus hartz* ("really let himself go"). The Yiddish equivalent was "to give someone a *bavash*" ("to wash thoroughly").

Someone in a bad mood looked "like a rained on turkey" (wet).

"After a storm, comes good weather" was the optimistic consolation.

Some folk preferred to see less of one another: "not too often is nicer."

"I've lived my life, I've eaten my share of malai" (corn fritters) implied that a person had reached a stage in life when they felt that they've had all the excitement and mundane matters were of little consequence.

"Alein is die neshume rein" ("Alone one's soul is clean") implied a preference for remaining uninvolved.

Food was a focus of interest in the shtetl. It is not surprising to find many aphorisms referring to food, or using food as analogies. Chicken fat, and especially the cracklings, were a special delicacy, associated with festive occasions: "a gedile mit grivn" ("a joyful occasion with cracklings") referred to any gay, happy time. Like so many other expressions, this was also used ironically, when there seemed to be little reason for rejoicing.

Kasha was the poor man's daily food, eaten with milk, or with chicken fat, or in soups. "Vasser tzu der kasha" ("water to the kasha") was said of one who did not earn too much, that is, earned enough to buy water to eat with *kasha*. This was also expressed by the saying that "he needed only ninety nine cents to the hundred".

"Lozt zich nisht shpayen in der kasha" ("He doesn't let anyone spit in his kasha") implied someone who had acquired the reputation of not letting anyone get away with anything. It was based on the story of a very poor family where one of the children would spit into his brother's plate in order to prevent the brother from eating his food. When the brother prevented this and objected loudly, the family accused him of being uncharitable.

"Loz meins ibergeyn" ("Let my share overflow") implied an attitude of self-denial for the sake of obtaining approval.

Cheese was an important part of shtetl diet. "Araingeshtipt dem gentzn keys in ein varenek" ("stuffed the whole cheese in one varenek" — (a ravioli-like dish stuffed with cheese), implied questionable judgment and unequal distribution.

"Iaca branza" ("there, I found some cheese") was more than a hint that there was less than one expected.

The Romanian saying "Brother with brother, but the cheese is with money," although used in the shtetl, was somewhat alien to the accepted values. To the family-oriented shtetl mentality, where brothers were indeed expected to share, asking a brother to pay was unbrotherly.

Much more in keeping with shtetl values was the saying "From blood, you don't make water," that is, family ties are strong.

"Se farloift die die tzingh in toches?" ("Is your tongue running away to your behind?") was an uncouth remark when one tasted food impatiently, before the others.

Jam, like any sweet, was a luxury reserved for special occasions. When someone was sick a teaspoon of cherry or strawberry jam was offered as a special treat to perk up a dull appetite. "Of nisht tzu bedarfn" ("May it not be needed") was the euphemistic way of referring to the fact that it may have been destined for convalescing.

"Er ligt in der erd und bakt beygl" ("He is buried in the ground and bakes bagels") was said of one who was poor, working wretchedly and earning a pittance.

"In der herd ligt er und mit a fiss varft er" ("He is half buried but still keeps kicking") suggested perseverence or persistence.

The familiar "rotten apple spoils all the good ones" had its counterpart in Romanian as well.

Alcoholism was not a shtetl problem. The rare alcoholic was regarded with contempt, but also with some compassion. References to drunkenness are not complimentary: "Vus ba'nichtern of der lingh, is ba'shikern of der tzing" ("What is on the lungs of the sober is on the tongue of a drunk") more than hinted at the danger of uninhibited behavior of the inebriated.

"A drunk wakes up, but once a fool, always a fool" denoted some tolerance for a drunk but avowed contempt for a fool. The Romanian said: "With a fool, have nothing to do, either in the seams or the sleeves," conveying the same idea.

"A gontz yor shicker, nor Simchas Toyre nichter" ("The whole year drunk, only on *Simchas Torah* sober") was said of someone who was out of step.

"Moyshe kapoyer" ("Moses, backwards") referred to someone who did things upside down, out of step with the usually acceptable conduct.

"Oysgibn die mezinkeh" ("Marrying off the youngest daughter") showed that one was capable of achieving and doing it with a flourish; the proverb has cultural overtones. When the youngest daughter was married off (at last!) the joy of the parents was unsurpassed.

"Me leibt un me lacht" ("They live and they laugh") expressed having a great time.

A poor person showing unjustified joy was told: "Frei dich koptzn, drek is volvl" ("Enjoy yourself, poor man, dirt is cheap"). (Using scatological terms was decidedly not done in the shtetl, and only heard among the lower classes.)

"In" jokes were common. "Shmil nar, hot zein veibt nisht derkent" ("Shmil, the fool, didn't recognize his own wife"), was frequently quoted, based on local lore Shmil, an old man was told that he need not travel all day to get to the next town, that the train — instead of his nag and wagon — would take him there effortlessly;

all he had to do, he was told, was to buy a ticket, sit down on a bench and in no time he would arrive at his destination. He went to the train station, bought a ticket, sat down on a bench and promptly fell asleep. When he awoke, convinced that he was in the next town, he picked up his bundle and walked out of the station. To his amazement, he saw, across the road, a woman who looked exactly like his wife. "Well," he said to himself, "if I didn't know that I traveled all night, I'd swear that I was at home and that was my own wife walking there." Hence, anyone surprised by the obvious was *Shmil nar*.

As in any small community, *plotkes* "gossip" was a quasi accepted pastime. Shunned for the inference of malice, it was indulged in, often with relish. Those known for their talents in this domain were *plotke-machers*, *intrigants*, *a spodik* or *a koch-lefl* ("a mixing spoon"). Concern with other people's business was not at all appreciated; such persons were known by many unflattering names. Coined by a shtetl wit, it was referred to as the *IPA*, or *Yiddische Plotkes Agentur* (Jewish Gossip Agency). It was part of shtetl life.

Romanian folk wisdom concluded that one could not prevent idle gossip: "Gren leaf, orach-herb (lboda), the world's mouth is free (sloboda)."

This tolerance was also expressed in: "As many huts, so many customs."

Observing that all people had their own problems, the Yiddish truism was: "Aldinks in einem, is nishtdo ba keynem" ("No one has everything"), implying that everyone has their own problems. This was reinforced by the graphic image of the saying that if everyone hung out their *pekl tzures* ("bundle of worries") on a clothesline, everyone would run to get their own bundle of troubles back rather than those of their neighbors.

Fighting or loud bickering in public was relegated to the lowest of the low, especially when relatives or close friends were concerned. This was enunciated in the renowned aphorism: "Dirty linen is washed only in the family."

Elementary observation taught that "sickness comes with the wagonload and leaves by the gramload".

"When the cat is away the mice play on the table" referred to the need for vigilance necessary to maintain order.

"Die zelbe Yenteh, nor ondersh farshleyert" ("The same Yenteh, but with a different veil") vividly pictures the ploy of presenting the same old idea in a camouflaged way. During the First World War, when shortages of food reduced the daily diet to a constant fare of beans, the saying went: "Seven kinds of meals, all made with beans."

"Er lekt a bein" ("He licks a bone") referred to those who enjoyed advantages from associating with the affluent.

A cynical remark often repeated was: "Those who handle honey inevitably catch a lick of the fingers."

"Er scrippet mit der tier un is batzult" ("He is paid for making the door squeak") was the shtetl opinion about the weird occupations one found in America.

To an obviously absurd question, the repartee was: "Vi nemen narunem schlesser?" ("And where do fools get locks?").

"To set fire to one's hair" was said when one touched inadvertently on an explosive question.

"The smaller the business, the greater the worry" was an observation gleaned from daily experience.

"Foch mit der neshumeh" ("To fan oneself with one's breath") signified that one was out of breath; breathlessness brought about by anxiety.

"Honik lekt er nisht" ("Honey he doesn't lick — by any means") implied an unpleasant situation in which one found oneself, perhaps unexpectedly.

"Lo'mich meich kennen alein farzorgn" ("Let me be able to settle my own worries first") or "Ich hob im fin long farzorgt" ("His affairs I've settled long ago") implied a preference for minding one's own business.

"When does the pauper rejoice?" The reply was: "When he finds something he had lost," thus summing up the rare possibilities for rejoicing available to a pauper.

"Se helft vi kaduches tzum toches" ("It helps, like dysentry to the derrière") was a most uncouth saying, heard only among the lower class, who nevertheless displayed a rich sense of humor and, like the Cockney, did not miss an opportunity to use an appropriate rhyme.

"Rabt sich oys a shmateh" ("A rag is being rubbed to shreds"). This bit of shorthand is better understood in the context of a society where thrift was a virtue and everything was used up, to the utmost. By analogy with a worn rag, someone who, to everyone's surprise, developed unforeseen qualities, was paid a compliment.

"Er lacht mit grimmenish" or "mit yarshenkies" ("He laughs with a stomach ache") was said of one who put on a Pagliacci-like front for the world but cried inwardly. The same masking of one's feelings was expressed in "Toteh dyi lachts, az vei'tsu dain gelachter" ("Father, you're laughing, woe to your laughter").

"Ich volt oych gelacht, ven der nar iz nisht meiner" ("I, too, would laugh if the fool were not my own" implied the inability of remaining indifferent to a ridiculous situation when one had a personal stake in the problem.

"Eyidl gepatzket" ("delicately splashed and splattered") was said with irony about one who put on airs.

"Ich vell mich koylen mit a shtik papier" ("I will cut my throat with a piece of paper") showed utter indifference to a threat.

An ugly or repulsive person was "A farzeyenish" ("shrivelled, shrunken") or "a shenern dergrupt men" ("one dug up from the ground is better looking") or "a farshlepte krenki" ("a dragged-in disease"). In Romanian it was: "Like death on vacation."

Daily speech was replete with references to the fatherly, All Mighty and just God. "Got git dus kelt noch die kleider" ("God gives the cold weather according to the clothes") inferred both an order in the Universe and a complete trust in God.

"Az Got vill shyist a beyzem" ("If God wills it, a broom too can shoot") summed up the unquestioned power of God.

"Az Got vill vern fin malles hasroynem, un fin hasroynem malles" ("If God wills, defects become qualities and qualities become defects") was used when the unlikely happened, especially in a marriage, where the couple seemed to disprove the popular consensus.

"Got shlugn nisht mit tzvey shtekeness" ("God does not hit with two sticks at once") expressed the conviction that divine judgment was compensating.

"Loz zich Got zorgn" ("Let God do the worrying") is one more saying that denotes the complete trust in God.

"Der Eibishter zitzt oyvn und purt hintn" ("The One Above sits up there and matches couples down below") was based on the conviction that God was interested in everyone's welfare and that marriages were made in Heaven.

"Er ot git gedovnt" ("He certainly prayed well") implying that he was lucky. The saying expressed the belief in the efficacy of prayer, yet with an undertone of doubt.

"Shlug dich arim mit Got" ("Go fight with God") expressed the futility of complaining. It was one of the rare sayings, hinting at God's indifference.

Much more frequent was the remark "Got is a futer" ("God is a father"), implying that one need not worry too much about the future.

"Dray tug unter Lespitz" ("It happened three days before Lespezi") (a town) was said of an unlikely occurrence.

"Kop in der vant" ("with the head against a wall") expressed contempt and indifference to irresponsible behavior with inevitable dire consequences.

Wasting time rehashing an issue was "Men mult, gemullen meil" ("Ready-ground flour is being reground").

If in the course of a conversation someone sneezed, it was taken as proof that whatever was being said was true. If the cat sneezed its veracity was questioned. "Die katz hot genossn" ("The cat sneezed") therefore, was said when a statement was somewhat doubtfully received.

A small amount of anything was "a shmek tobeke" ("a smell – or pinch – of tobacco").

"A mamme is a mitter, a totteh is a maskvitter" ("A mother is a womb, a father is intransigent"), epitomized the mother's intrinsic importance. It was used especially with reference to a mother's forgiveness, unquestioned love and devotion.

"Folg mich a gong" ("Do this for me please") was used in two senses, depending on the tone of voice. Directly, it was used to ask someone to go fetch something. Ironically, the same statement implied it was asking too much.

"Veimen vet nisht toign, zol im aroys die oygn" ("Whom it doesn't suit, may his eyes pop out") was the indifferent reply to criticism of one's behavior or choice of clothing. It implied disregard for public opinion, a strong control agent in the shtetl.

"Tzi shteln a benkiole" ("to put a little chair close by") to add fuel to a fire, especially by divulging incriminating facts.

"Er is Got die neshume shildig" ("He is a naive innocent"). He owes his soul to God.

"Kik is un, und mool is oys" ("Look at it and do a portrait"), usually a loving exclamation about a beautiful child.

"Kleipt sich, vi a nosse shmatteh t'zum toches" ("sticks like a wet rag to the backside") was a picturesque image of saying that one was trying too hard to be friendly.

"Ich faif of zey" ("I am whistling on them") or I couldn't care less.

"Man is made of iron" expressed the feeling that man can endure stress beyond imagination. On the other hand, "Eizener moyeh" or "eizener kop" implied a highly intelligent person, someone with an iron mind or an iron head. Quipped one wit: "No wonder he is so rusty!"

"Pavolie mit'n dishl" ("Slowly with the shaft") meant: not so fast, there! It was used in the sense of "You may find it more difficult than you think."

Historical events are recalled in several sayings. Romania had been under Turkish domination and, earlier, in the path of invading Turkish and Tartar hordes; hence, when someone was rushing away in too great a hurry, he was told: "The Turks or Tartars aren't coming yet." And again, "Interesul poarta fesul" (self interest wears the fez) showed the cynicism of a subjugated people who knew that decision-making came from Constantinople.

"What a man does to himself, the devil won't do to him" reinforced a feeling of self guilt, also implying a sense of responsibility.

"Escaped like through the needle's eye" was said to one who barely made it.

"Dos gontz kekiole koon" referred to a notorious clique or coterie.

"Me vet mir shteln a goldene m'tzeive?" ("Will they give me a golden monument when I'm gone?") was a justification for not making an unreasonable or unnecessary effort.

"Ifter, pifter, parnuse ot er?" ("Ifter, pifter, but does he make a living?"). This saying ridiculed the ignorant who did not known that *ifter* meant "dead" in Hebrew, while at the same time illustrated the importance that "parnuse", making a living, had in the shtetl world view.

"A pogrom is a pogrom" refers to an anecdote telling of a husband who, during a pogrom, was trying to fight and protect his wife from being raped, to which his apparently not too reluctant wife replied: "Never mind, a pogrom is a pogrom."

Commenting that one did not look too well was considered a goyish compliment. Similarly, speaking of death or illness without first saying the protective formula "Nisht du gedacht" ("May it not happen here") was also goyish. "Beat the saddle to teach the mare" bespeaks folk diplomacy. "Ba nacht zennen alle keyen shvartz" ("At night all cows look black") would indicate that in some cases, differences did not matter too much.

"The appetite comes while eating" as well as "Hunger is the best cook" were truths gleaned from daily observations.

"You cannot make love by force" implied the assumption that, in any relationship, reciprocity was essential.

"The needle is small but sews expensive garments" pointed out the importance of superficially small or insignificant matters.

"One nail pries out the other" says basically that it takes one to know one.

"Az tzvey zugn shicker, geyit men sich leyign shlufn" ("If two persons say you're drunk, better go lie down") implied respect for the opinion of the majority.

"Meliché, meluché" ("One's kingdom consists in one's trade or profession.") This Hebrew shorthand went somewhat against the grain of shtetl values regarding manual labor. Though often quoted, it was advocated for others but not for oneself.

"A good road and a well-beaten path to you" expressed disdain and disapproval for someone's behavior. Yiddish expressed the same disdain with the remark "Have a good sledding road."

4. Curses

Curses were considered uncharitable and most uncouth. Their use was inversely proportional to the social standing of the individual. Just as blessings pertained to the well being, health and success in life, curses invoked ill health, misfortune, poverty and so on. Here are some examples:

A shvartzer, vister, finsterer hulem
of zein kop, vus s'ot sich mir gehulemt
die nacht, yene nacht un ale nacht fin
a gantz yor, zol nor tzu zein kop ousegyn!

A black, hopeless, tenebrous nightmare
on his head, what I dreamt this night,
last night and all the nights of the whole year,
may it end up on his head!

or

A shvartze leid of zein kop, of zeine
hent un fis, un of zein lab un leibn

A black affliction on his head, on his
hands and feet and his whole body and life!

This pronounced in one breath by a furious woman, was a sight to behold. Other curses pertained directly to specific diseases:

A kaduches zol im trefn	The dysentery should find him
A kaduches zol im hopn	The dysentery should catch him
A krenk of zein kop	A disease on his head
Er zol nor tzepicket vern	May he only burst (shatter)
A halerie zol zein of zein kop	May a cholera be on his head
Anemen a misa meshunah	Drop dead
Gelamt zol er vern	May be become paralyzed

Any of these, or the entire litany was poured out in one gushing jet.

It is interesting to make a brief comparison between Yiddish and Romanian curses or swear words. Swear words are not merely superficially voiced words; they touch and express profound cultural values and pinpoint vulnerable areas and preoccupations of a culture. Yiddish curses and swear words almost all refer to matters of health and disease or to fertility, evidently important to the culture. In Romanian, on the other hand, swear words have either a religious content or refer to sexual organs and activities. This is not the case with Yiddish, since it is commanded not to use the Lord's name in vain and any reference to sacred objects was taken as sacrilege. Sex was accepted as a normal function, provided it was contained within the boundaries of the family; hence it was devoid of the usual connotations. To say "A riech in zein totn's totn's totn' . . ." ("a devil in his father's father's father . . .") seemed to produce the equivalent emotional relief that the Romanian obtained from sending the enemy "on a reverse obstetric voyage". For collective enemies, referred to as *soine Yisroel* ("enemies of Israel"), the formula when hearing or pronouncing the name was *Yimach shemoy* ("May his name be damned").

The common Romanian swear phrase was *Dute la dracu* ("Go to the devil"). In Yiddish, the immediate equivalent was *gey in der herd* ("Go into the earth"), without other details.

The comparative terms for an illegitimate child are also revealing. In English, "bastard" is decidedly insulting; the Yiddish *mamzer* on the other hand, is one of those terms that may be used both in a derogatory sense and sometimes with a tinge of admiration, depending on the tone and content. A *mamzer* is a clever fellow, perhaps because these individuals (though rare in the shtetl) had to learn early in life to fend for themselves. In Romanian, *copil din flori* ("a child from flowers") is much more indulgent and, though not fully accepted, was tolerated.

Conclusions

The Romanian shtetl was a microcosm where, as in any small community, social phenomena were easily identifiable and where the drama of life, though played on a smaller stage, was none the less intense. Every element of a culture phenomenon was to be found duplicated in the shtetl culture as it is in every culture known to history or ethnography.

The point has been made early in this study that although the Romanian shtetl is part of the larger east European Jewish culture complex (as listed in the *HUMAN RESOURCES AREA FILES* — an index of cultural traits of all known cultures*) there are sufficient differences to warrant specific attention. As well, there is a dearth of reference material regarding the Romanian shtetl. Both these points prompted this study.

Cultural characteristics within a given society are not a jumble of haphazard traits. In spite of superficial appearances parts are not interchangeable, any more than parts of a wristwatch would fit into a grandfather clock, though both serve the same function. For a society to survive, its institutions must be well integrated and each trait must fit into a well defined place and fulfill a specific function.

In the course of history, cultures have borrowed traits from neighboring peoples with whom they came in contact. Just as individuals under hypnosis can only be persuaded to perform those tasks which they would do of their own accord, a culture will select only those traits compatible with its own basic values and reject those it deems inimical to its wellbeing. The shtetl was no exception in this respect. Throughout the centuries the shtetl borrowed only those customs which fitted its own accepted principles. It is this selectivity which resulted in the differences between the Romanian shtetl and its slavic counterpart.

In this brief study of the Romanian shtetl an attempt has been

---

* G. P. Murdock — Yale University *HUMAN RESOURCES AREA FILES* an index.

made to show how the interdependence of cultural patterns functioned to preserve the Judaic traditional values yet adapted itself to the Latin culture of the host country. The institution of dowering daughters and mate selection by parents fitted in with the specific socio-economic structural patterns of the shtetl, where by enlarging the family circle one was assured of a network of trustworthy reciprocity and a measure of security in the midst of an otherwise alien world.

The Romanian shtetl was part of the larger east European Jewish culture to which it belonged by virtue of a common religion and language. Yiddish, the language of the shtetl has several distinguishable dialects: Litvak, Russian, Gallitzian (Southern Poland), Hungarian and Romanian. The Romanian Yiddish is distinctly different in accent, intonation and especially in the pronunciation of vowels. The vocabulary of the Romanian shtetl had inevitably incorporated Romanian terms and by the (often amusing) mechanism of giving Yiddish words a Romanian ending or vice versa, achieved a uniqueness all its own. The differences are not, however, wide enough to prevent communication between these groups.

With the building of the Scoala Israelito Romana at the turn of the century, a movement to replace Yiddish was rapidly gaining momentum. Within the brief period of one generation, Yiddish was relegated to the status of a second class language used only by the older generation. The better-educated youth of a post First World War period prided themselves on their inability to speak Yiddish and in the purity of their Romanian accent. It was as if they were trying to dissociate themselves from the denigrated Yiddish language and the culture it represented in the hope of eliciting respect. It is not surprising therefore to find few Romanian Jews writing in Yiddish.

The task of discussing so vast and well documented a topic as the shtetl religion within the scope of this study was, of necessity, limited to superficial descriptions. What emerged from this rapid glimpse at shtetl religion was the importance assigned to the child in the religious ceremonies of the Romanian shtetl. It was this emphasis on children's participation which contributed to the maintenance of traditions throughout the ages. Deep roots were planted in the past and continuity for the future assured.

Though a small community, the shtetl was not, as is often believed, a homogeneous society. Social stratification was rigid without having any formal structure of casts or social class. One simply did not associate with those esteemed below one's own social standing. This stratification was reflected in every aspect of life: the neighborhood, the type of housing, size of the family, health care, education, aspirations and, in general, the life style of the family. All were determined by and were in turn the index of "yichus", the family status.

The family was the basic unit upon which the community was solidly founded and within which the individual developed. It was within the family that traditions were transmitted. Mutual interdependence based on rights and obligations were the cement which bound the family into a cohesive whole. Those unwilling to fulfill their responsibilities forfeited the privileges as well and they usually left town. Family ties were such in the Romanian shtetl that when emigrating to America it was as a family unit rather than break up the family even temporarily.

We only have to look at the image of God as "the Heavenly Father" to see that this was a paternalistic society. Though the father was the dominant figure in the family, his primary concerns were family oriented and the family itself was child oriented. Assuring a good future for their children, i.e. a suitable match and a trade for the son and dowry for daughters, was not only an obligation, it was the parent's purpose in life. To see the children under the wedding canopy or as the song said "Let us be worthy to see our sons and daughters succeed in Torah and in work" was the most cherished parental wish.

Though male dominated, the role of the wife and mother was not ignored. Her work was highly valued by her family as well as by society. Ideally the wife owed obedience and respect to her husband who, however, was repeatedly enjoined to respect his wife. The wife was the queen of the household. It was, furthermore, by virtue of the wife's piety that the husband gained entrance to Paradise, for it was the wife and mother who was entrusted with maintaining the Judaic traditions within the home and above all with instilling the proper values in the future generations. The extent to which spouses lived up to this ideal type was one more index of the social standing of the family. In practice this was a matter of individual behavior, often respected more in the breach than in practice.

The Romanian shtetl was a true enclave of private enterprise. The shtetl Jew was an independent spirit who believed in private property and preferred to deal with God without any intermediaries in his religion as well as in his business. He prized his independence above a sense of security. Working for someone else was considered demeaning even when wages were superior to potential profits. Every worker was his own master. Self reliance and hard work were highly valued virtues.

The concept of personal responsibility and self reliance runs like a leitmotif throughout shtetl values. Excess was shunned, moderation cultivated and encouraged. This concept of personal responsibility and of moderation in all things, the postponement of immediate gratification for a better future good, was constantly appealed to when establishing the barriers between shtetl values and the outside world. Anything undesirable was stamped "goyish", not Jewish and hence by definition objectionable.

Sex was recognized as a healthy human need, provided it was confined within marriages. The double standard allowed leeway for the single male, while the female was guarded and virginity highly prized. This too fitted in with the importance given to blood lineages and insistence upon the laws of inheritance. Celibacy was not condoned since single persons were regarded as a threat to the cohesiveness of the rest of the community. There were no children born out of wedlock though wagging tongues sometimes spoke of the first child in a marriage being somewhat premature.

Although divorce was relatively easy to obtain, it was a rare occurrence in the Romanian shtetl where the entire family suffered embarrassment.

The shtetl was a rigidly endogamous society where marriage outside the religious group was a tragedy for the entire family. Those who dared break this rule were obliged to leave town. This, too, fitted in with the cultural patterns since Judaism was not a proselitizing religion, and the loss of an individual member or the dilution of the tennets presented a threat to the cohesion of the entire group.

In a world where the book was a symbol of the divine and where mothers sang lullabies telling how sweet the study of Torah was, it is not surprising to find a reverence for intellectual pursuits and a disdain for manual labor.

There was an assumption that one who earned his livelihood by manual labor was not capable of intellectual pursuits and consequently, inferior. The other side of the coin was that intellectual activity conferred status and dignity and was one of the determining parameters of social stratification. Since many of the ancient sages were known to have been artisans, this attitude was often left in a haze of ambiguities.

Although anti-Semitism was a fact in Romania, the Romanian national character influenced the expression of anti-Semitism. The shtetl Jews lived and dealt with the peasant population for whom the Jews did not present a competitive threat since the Jews did not own or cultivate land. It was the ruling classes and the Orthodox Church which fomented anti-Semitic outbursts for their own vested interests.

Zionism, the movement advocating the return to Palestine as a solution for the Jewish question, was making inroads in the Romanian shtetl. Though Zionism stirred sentiments of longing for a better life, conditions in the Romanian shtetl were not sufficiently abject to foster migrations. In most small towns only a handful of young people were idealistic enough to join the Echalutz (pioneer) movement for return to Palestine. For most shtetl Jews the support for Zionism was expressed in donations to the Jewish National Fund for the purpose of reclaiming land in Palestine. These donations were as much a matter of prestige reflecting one's standing in the community as a purely patriotic act.

Hasidism, the eighteenth century revivalist religious movement, said to have resulted as a rebellion of the simple folk against the abstract intellectualism of their leaders, was represented by the rabbinic court. Stefanesti, the shtetl used here as a model, was the seat of a well known and revered rebbé. This gave the shtetl a unique distinction it shared only with a handful of other such towns. The rebbé's court was a independent unit in the shtetl, attracting hasidic followers from distant places. The local merchants who tended to regard the hangers on at the court — though not the rebbé himself — as fanatics, did not as a rule participate in the ultra religious life at the rebbé's court. They kept to themselves, somewhat aloof, though not adverse to the fame the rebbé's court conferred on their shtetl and enjoying the financial advantages they gleaned from the visitors to the rebbé's court.

A well integrated society is reflected in the functioning of its institutions with a minimum of conflict or friction. In spite of many inevitable shortcomings, using these criteria as a litmus test, the Romanian shtetl presented a well integrated society. Alcoholism was not a problem; drinking wine was part of every religious ceremony and in moderation, drinking among friends was part of the social life.

Symptoms of social upheaval such as suicides, divorces, delinquencies or crimes were almost unknown. Most conflicts were solved within the confines of the Jewish community by arbitrators or by the rabbi (the rov). There was little need for policing. It was the mechanism of social sanction rather than complex external laws that controlled aberrant behavior in the shtetl. Romanian authorities were resorted to only in extreme cases.

This was the Romanian shtetl, Stefanesti, an example of so many other such small Jewish towns of northern Romania. Stefanesti was bombed out of existence and the inhabitants dispersed to the proverbial four corners of the earth.

It is perhaps a concrete proof of the well integrated society of the shtetl to note that an inordinately large number of former shtetl inhabitants were successful in whatever endeavor they undertook to pursue.

The shtetl culture disappeared as did most of the Jewish communities of eastern Europe but it left a legacy of reverence for learning, a spirit of self reliance and a gift of resourcefulness which the citizens willingly shared with their new surroundings.

Glossary

	H	– Hebrew
	R	– Romanian
	Y	– Yiddish
	YH	– Yiddish and Hebrew

Actior	Y	Actor
Afurisit	R	Anti-social, literally cursed
Agunah	H	Woman unable to marry for lack of proof of divorce or husband's death
Ajutor de primar	R	Assistant to the mayor
Alifie	R	Ointment
Alyiah	H	Being called to read the Torah in synagogue
Aparate	R	Sports equipment for gymnastics
Aphikomen	H	Half of the middle matzo used during Seder ceremony
Aranjama'	R	Home furniture provided by bride's parents as dowry
Arun-Kodesh	H	Holy Ark where Torahs are stored in synagogue
Armata	R	Military service
Ashkenazim	H	German or eastern European Jews – Older Hebrew pronunciation (Modern Hebrew pronunciation was called Sephardit)
Astrachan	R	Sheepskin from newborn lamb
Asimilirt	Y	Assimilated
Azil	Y	Shelter (used in the sense of old people's home)
Azoy	Y	Tusly, or really!
Bacalaureat	R	High School Matriculation, – in value closer to a B.A.
Bacanie	R	Grocery store
Badchen	Y	Jester at Jewish weddings in past
Bakshish	R	Bribe
Balaboos	Y	Proprietor – fem. balabosteh, plural – balabotem
Balabotish	Y	Upstanding, decent
Balgule	Y	Carter
Bankes	Y	Cups, for cupping, – R. Venutze
Bar-Mitzvah	H	Rite of passage; ceremony at age thirteen when boys become adults
Bedekn die Kalleh	Y	Ceremony whereby bridegroom covers bride's face with veil before wedding
Beigel (bagel)	Y	Baked dough rings sprinkled with sesame or poppy seeds

Glossary 257

Beigheolech	Y	Diminutive for beigel — Romanian shtetl — cheese rolled pastry
Bekuved	Y	Respectable
Bench	Y	Benediction, to bless
Berlach	Y	Burdock weed burrs — boys threw at girls' hair on Tishe b'av
Beteala-x Biberon	R	Tinsel, threads of silver-like or gold-like metal used as trimming with bridal veil. Also called "peteala"
Biberon	R	Baby's milk bottle
Bilbl	Y	False accusations
Bimma	H	Center platform in synagogue where Torah is read
Birja — Birjar	Y	Coach — Coachman
Bli-neider	H	Without presumptions
Blonch	Y	Dominoes
Bly-gissern	Y	Diviner with melted lead (female)
Bobskie mitlen	Y	Old wives' remedies
Bocitoare	R	Professional weeping women at Romanian funerals
Bodega	R	Bar-restaurant serving charcoal-broiled steaks, etc.
Boidem	Y	Loft, attic
Bonditza	R	Sleeveless vest made of sheepskin
Borsht	Y	Beet soup
Borshtenitze	Y	Woman who sold borsht
Boxer	Y	Carob pod — St. John's bread (eaten on Hamishuser)
Boyer (Boyar)	R	Landowner, Romanian nobleman
Branza	R	Salted cheese made with sheep milk
Bratz la Bratz	Y	Walking arm in arm
Bris	H	Circumcision Brit-Milla-ceremony at birth of male child. Covenant
Bubbeh	Y	Midwife
Bulibasha	R	Leader of Gypsy caravan
Bursa	R	Stock exchange
Carul	R	Table top game played with beans and corn-kernels
Cafenea	R	Coffee house
Catrintza	R	Peasant skirt of woven wool, usually black
Catzaveica	R	Tight fitting overgarment worn by Romanian peasants
Chehn	Y	Children's game played with pebbles (jacks)
Cinsti (a cinsti)	R	To do honor, when peasants transacted a deal, they drank in each other's honor
Cerealist	R	Grain dealer
Cofeterie	R	Pastry shop — Tea room
Cojoc —	R	Sheepskin coat worn with fur inward
Cojocar	R	Furrier
Coloneale	R	Grocery — specialty shop of imported foods
Coldere	Y	Quilt, usually made of satin, filled with raw wool
Commitet	Y	Jewish Community Board of Governors
Comis	Y	Apprentice salesman (pronounced Koomis)
Condici	R	Ledgers
Crivatz	R	Strong north-eastern wind blowing in winter
Curea	R	Leather belt
Cursa	R	Daily bus line

Cushmar	R	Furrier specializing in fur hats
Damé	R	Checkers
Datch	Y	German
Davenen	H	To pray
Derech eretz	H	Way of the land — has come to mean respect for one's elders
Descanta	R	Antidote to casting a spell
Docar	R	Two wheeler
Dracul	R	The devil (from dragon)
Doina	R	Romanian melancholy folk tune
Dolméch	Y	Interpreter
Domn-doamna	R	Mister — Mrs.
Domisoara	R	Miss — young lady
Drushé geshank	Y	Wedding present
Dulceatza	R	Jam
Dyi	Y	You — used when addressing equals or social inferiors
Eidler man	Y	Refined person
Erev	H	Eve (as erev yomtov-eve before a holy day)
Esther Tannes	Y	Fasting day; day before Purim
Etl-betl	Y	Game (cat's cradle)
Evreii	R	Jews
Fardart	Y	Dried-up
Farkikt	Y	Pregnant woman who supposedly imprinted on foetus whatever she had stared-at during pregnancy
Fardronjet	Y	Shrivelled up
Fartuch	Y	Apron
Farzesseneh	Y	Old maid
Feidern	Y	Feathers
Felcher	Y	Apprentice medic or paramedic
Fierzuggern	Y	The woman who read prayers out loud in women's sector in synagogue, for those unable to read themselves
Fleishik	Y	Dietary law pertaining to meat
Flocht — flochton	Y	Long side curls, derogatory
Fludn	Y	Layered honey cake with walnuts and honey
Fondante	R	Soft center candies
Freilechs	Y	Gay music — lively
Gabbay (gobbé)	Y	Chairman of board of synagogue, also Tsaddik's secretary
Gan a yeladim	H	Kindergarten
Gaj — gajuri	R	Pledge — game similar to "Post Office"
Galantar- Galanterie	R	Showcase Haberdashery shop
Galoshn	Y	Rubbers — rubber boots
Gefilte-Fish	Y	Fish dumplings
Gessl	Y	Small street
Gimeles Heysed	H	Good will loan
Gitter sheliech	Y	A good messenger

Goldene medine	Y	Golden land, i.e. America
Gospodar	R	Good messenger of a home fem. – gospodina
Gospodaria	R	Household
Got	Y	God
Goy – plur. Goym	Y	Gentile, non-Jew
Goyish	Y	Not Jewish, derogatory implications
Gradinita	R	Nursery school
Graf	Y	From Polish, "count" as in Graf Pototsky
Gradina Publica	R	Public gardens
Gonnif	Y	Thief
Ghyoc	R	Conch shell used by Gypsies to read future
Gyt Shabbes	Y	Sabbath greeting
Gyte voch	Y	A good week – greeting at end of Sabbath
Gyt Yomtov	Y	Holiday greeting
Haggadah	H	The story of Exodus read during Passover ceremony
Haknassat Kallah	H	Society for helping poor brides with dowry
Hakuffas (hakkafot)	H	Ceremonial procession with Torah scrolls at Simchat-Torah
Hala	R	Meat market
Hallah	Y	White bread eaten on Sabbath and holy days
Halutz	H	Young pioneer
Hahambasha	R	From Turkish. The representative of Jewish community during Turkish rule.
Hachsharah		Pioneer Training camp for emigrating to Palestine
Hasid	Y	Follower of hasidism and of a rebbé
Hasidism	R	Ultra religious sect – religious revivalist movement
Hatikva	H	Hope – Zionist national anthem
Hazuka	H	Right by precedent – claim based on possession (Tenure)
Hevre-kadisha	H	Burial society
Holemoyd	Y	Half holy days, the four days between the first and second set of holy days at Passover and Succoth
Honeke gelt	Y	Money given to children at Hanukkah
Hosseneh	Y	Wedding
Hoyf	Y	Rebbé's Court, residence of Hasidic rebbé
Hremzlech	Y	Sweet matzo-meal dumplings fried in chicken fat and honey, eaten on Passover
Humentashn	Y	Three-cornered cookies filled with walnuts and honey or with prune marmalade, eaten during Purim to remember Hamman's three-cornered hat
Hummetz	H	Anything leavened or fermented unfit to be used on Passover
Heyder	Y	Elementary religious Jewish school
Huppah	Y	Wedding canopy – marriage ceremony
Hussn	Y	Bridegroom
Hussn-sot	Y	Groom's relatives at wedding
Ibergeshept	Y	Overflow
Icré	R	Fish roe (carp and pike caviar)
In "particular"	R	Studies with private tutors in towns where there was no high school

Interfirer	Y	Sponsors at wedding (one couple for bride and one for groom)
Intrevedere	R	Viewing of prospective bride and groom
Jidan	R	Jew (derogatory)
Judetz	R	District. There were seventy two districts in Romania
Kaddish	H	Prayer for dead — son's mourning prayer after death of parents
Kaftan	Y	Long satin robe worn by hasidim
Kalleh	Y	Bride
Kalleh's sot	Y	Bride's relatives at wedding
Kanchik	Y	Leather whip
Kappures (kaparot)	H	Scape goat, ransom to expiate one's sins
Kardiké	Y	Sleeveless overgarment
Kasha	Y	Buckwheat
Kasher	H	To sterilize utensils for use during Passover
Keren Kayemet	H	Jewish National Fund
Keren Hayessod	H	Jewish National Fund
Kest	Y	Room and board promised by bride's parents to couple as agreed in marriage contract
Ketuba (Ksibbeh)	H	Marriage contract
Kiddush	H	Benediction over wine
Kiffert	Y	Hope chest
Kisea	Y	Jam bowl
Kishif	Y	Black magic
Klezmer	Y	Musicians
Kleibn	Y	Gather (kleibn naches — gather joy from children)
Kloys	Y	Rebbés private synagogue
Knishes	Y	Baked dough patties filled with kasha or with mashed potatoes
Kniakn-kern	Y	Eating pumpkin seeds or sunflower seeds
Koylen	Y	Ritual slaughtering of fowl or animals
Krim	Y	Crooked, lame
Krishma leinen	Y	Ritual of reading prayer at bedside of newborn male child "Kriat Shema" (Hear Oh Israel)
Kvitl		Receipt used for slaughtering fowl — tax for Jewish community; also written request handed to rebbé by supplicants
Kvosnetzé	Y	Pickled apple
Kygl	Y	Sweet noodle or potato pudding with raisins and jam, cinnamon, etc.
Kympet tzetl	Y	Lying-in amulet placed in room, after birth
Latkes	Y	Pancakes made with potatoes or with matzo meal
Latrina	R	W.C. (outhouse)
Leidig geyer	Y	Ne'er do well — without steady occupation
Levaye	Y	Funeral procession
Leu (plur. lei)	R	Romanian currency
Litere	R	Studies in Arts, Philosophy
Logofat	R	Chancellor
Luft mench	Y	One who seems to live on thin air

Glossary

Luftsgesheft	Y	Flighty business, without visible means
Lulav	H	Palm branches used for Sukkot ritual
Lushn koydesh	H	The sacred language i.e. Hebrew
Maccabi	H	Sports club
Machetunem	Y	Plural "in laws"
Machteinesteh	Y	Female in laws
Maftir	H	Reader of last portion of Torah in synagogue
Mahala	R	Outskirts of town
Mahitn	Y	Male in law
Mahloykeh	H	Revolt
Mahzar	H	Prayer book
Malai	R	Dish of baked corn meal, with eggs and milk
Mamaliga	R	Staple food of Romanian peasants made of cornmeal, — polenta
Mamme lushn	YH	Mother tongue
Manufactura	R	Dry goods store
Martzishor	R	Charms exchanged on March 1st
Maskierteh	Y	Masked persons
Matzos	H	Unleavened bread
Maydan	R	Market place
Mazel tov	H	Good luck. Congratulations
Megilas Esther	H	The scroll of Esther read the day before Purim and on Purim
Merarie	R	Fruit store
Meshures	H	Servant
Meshiech (Messiah)	Y	Messiah
Mezinnek	Y	Youngest child, mezinké — fem.
Mezuzah	H	Parchment scroll with verses from Torah, placed on doorstep of Jewish homes
Milechick or Milechdick	Y	Utensils of foods pertaining to milk (fleishig, for meat)
Mikvah	H	Ritual pool for ablutions — ritual bath house
Minyan	H	Quorum required for communal prayer, ten male adult Jews
Misa Meshunah	H	"A strange death" curse to mean a sudden fit, apoplexy (anemén a misa meshunah) — drop dead
Mitbeyeh	Y	Coin blessed by rebbé, worn as a charm
Mitzva	H	Good, pious deed
M'nishkes tzeitn	Y	Expression denoting something out of style
Moda	R	Style
Mode Ani	H	Morning prayer "I stand before Thee ..."
Mohel	H	Circumciser
Momzer	Y	Bastard
Mopl	Y	Miscarriage
More Judaico	R	From Latin — Oath taken by Jews; humiliating, demeaning
Mos hittn	H	Charity donated during Passover to support poor in the community
M'vaker choyle zein	Y	(Bikur Holim) Visiting the sick, esteemed a good deed

Naches	Y	Comfort, pleasure, joy
Negidem	Y	Wealthy
Negustor	R	Merchant
Nehoré	Y	The evil eye
Ne'ilah	H	Closing of gates of Heaven, last service on Day of Atonement
Ner-tamid	H	Everlasting light
Niddah	H	Menstruating woman
Nepot	R	Nephew
Nodn	Y	Dowry
Numerus Clausus	R	Latin — Anti-Semitic discriminatory law whereby admittance to faculties was on a percentage-of-population basis
Oina	R	Ball game played with rag ball and stick
Olam a ba (Oilemobe)	H	World to come, meaning changed to: "have compassion"
Opinci	R	Home made cowhide footwear, worn by Romanian peasants
Onanie	R	Masturbation
Oyfrifechts	Y	Calling bridegroom to read the Torah on Sabbath before wedding
Oyrech pl. orchim	H	Guest, inviting a pauper for the Sabbath meal
Oyvn	Y	Large wood burning stove built into room — for cooking and heating
Padurice	R	Small wooded area
Pale of Settlement	—	The 25 provinces of Tzarist Russia where Jews were allowed to settle
Parnusseh	Y	Livelihood, earning a living
Partida	R	A partnership, used as in a marriage match
Pavolie	Y	Slowly there! (probably of Slavic origin)
Peckl	Y	Bundle, package
Peyes	Y	Side curls worn by Hasidic men
Pidyan ha ben	H	Ceremony whereby after four weeks from birth, the father redeems a first-born son from "service to the Temple" by paying a sum of money to a Kohen
Pishké	Y	Box
Plita	R	Built-in cooking stove
Plemenek	Y	From Slavic Nephew
Plemenetze	Y	From Slavic Niece
Prefect Prefectura	R	Chief of a district. District administration
Privata	R	Toilet
Pocinog	R	First sale of the day or week
Pogrom	Y	Anti-Semitic massacre of Jews (mostly in the Ukraine)
Ponchikl	Y	Cookie made with honey-dough in the shape of an "S". (Local idiom)
Poskenen	H	To interpret — the rov's interpreting the law (as in poskenen shalles — answering questions)
Pripichik	H	Probably Slavic — hearth, fireplace or oven
Ptiu, ptiu, ptiu	Y	Spitting sounds to ward off evil

Glossary 263

Rabbi (Rov)	Y	Spiritual leader of Jewish community. (There was only one in a shtetl)
Rabbunish	Y	Pertaining to the rebbé
Rackiu	R	Bourbon, brandy
Rahat	R	Turkish-delight (sweet used in baking cakes and pastries)
Raspantie	R	Crossroads — Center of town
'Reb	Y	Mister
Rebbé	Y	Hasidic rabbi, also master or teacher
Rebbeh	Y	Used in this book as "teacher of young children" as distinct from the Hasidic rebbé
Rebbetzn	Y	Wife of rabbi, or rebbé
Riech	Y	The devil (from rouach, spirit)
Robinet	R	Fawcet
Rola	R	Baking oven built into the "plita oven"
Rollé	R	Corrugated wrought iron shutters
Rosh hodesh	H	First day of the month
Saftea	R	First sale of the day, week or of newly started bundle
Saritura	R	Hop skotch, children's game (jump)
Sarvern	Y	Caterer (female)
Seder	H	Passover celebration. (Actually meaning "in order")
Serbare	R	Celebration
Seuda shelishit or Sholeshides	H	Communal meal taken at the synagogue on Saturday night. (The third meal of the Sabbath)
Sfardit	H	Modern pronunciation of Hebrew in contrast to old style "Ashkenaz"
Shabbat (Shobbes)	H	Saturday — holiest day after Day of Atonement. Virtually considered God's gift to mankind, as a day of rest.
Shachthouse	Y	Slaughter house — where ritual slaughtering takes place
Shachtn	Y	Ritual slaughter of fowl or animals
Shadchan	Y	Matchmaker
Shadchenteh fem.	Y	Matchmaker
Shadchuness	Y	Matchmaking
Shalleh	H	Question (as in "what a question!") or the rov's interpretation of a ritual question
Shammas	Y	Sexton, beadle (Janitor of synagogue)
Shatra (chatra)	R	Gypsy nomadic colony
Shechinna	H	Divine presence — (on a bride, during Sabbath)
Sheppn naches	Y	Enjoy, gather pleasure
Shes	R	Flat field (used for playing ball in shtetl)
Sheygetz	Y	Gentile boy
Shiddech	Y	Marriage match
Shikse	Y	Gentile girl
Shivah	H	The seven mourning days following burial of relative
Shlemiel	Y	Bumbling slow witted
Shlepper	Y	One who drags (pulls in) by force, lowly character
Shlepperké	Y	Fem. of shlepper, used to mean slovenly
Shlimazl	Y	Luckless one

Shloshim	H	The thirty days of less intensive mourning following shivah
Shlugn kappures	Y	Ritual of using hen or rooster as scapegoat to expiate one's sins, (day before Day of Atonement)
Shmaltz	Y	Fats, usually chicken or goose fat
Shmier	Y	To spread, or lubricate, used as "to bribe"
Schnaps	Y	Brandy
Shnorer	Y	Professional beggar
Shofar	H	Ram's horn
Sholchemones	Y	In Hebrew, "Mishloah-monos". Custom of exchanging food with friends and relatives on Purim
Sholem aleichem	H	Peace to you, a common greeting
Sholeshides	H	Communal meal taken at the synagogue on Saturday night
Shoychet	YH	Ritual slaughterer
Shprits	Y	A glass of wine with soda water added to it — typical shtetl table drink
Shtoch	Y	Stitch — sharp pain in one side
Shtraml	Y	Fur trimmed hat worn by hasidic Jews
Shul	Y	Synagogue (Romanian Yiddish pronunciation was "Shyll")
Shyrayim	H	Leftovers on plate of rebbé over which followers fought in the belief that they partook of blessed food
Sicha pl. sichot	H	Meeting, gathering
Simches-Torah	H	Rejoicing with the Torah
Soba	R	Wood burning furnace (stove) built into wall
Sondek	H	Person who holds infant boy during circumcision ceremony
Strand	R	Beach
Strainatate	R	Abroad
Tachrichem	Y	Shroud
Tablou	R	Scene, painting
Tachles	Y	Purpose, goal
Tallis	Y	Four cornered, tasseled shawl, worn by Jews during prayer "tallis kattan" is a ritual undergarment with fringes, worn by orthodox Jews
Tannik	Y	"Tannik shepn" to derive great pleasure
Tapet	R	Stencil, pattern painted on walls of room
Tashlich	H	"Thou shall cast all sins" ceremony of "casting" sins into water and begin the new year afresh
Tatica	R	Daddy
Tchollent or cholent	Y	Baked dish of meat with potatoes and carrots, prepared for Sabbath meal in order to avoid lighting a fire
Tefillin	H	Phylacteries, small leather cases containing passages from Scripture, worn on forehead and arm by male Jews during morning prayer
Tehinna	H	Women's prayer book
Tenoyim	H	Engagement
Tickern	Y	Woman bath attendant

Glossary

Titrat	R	One with a title, meaning a professional such as Doctor, lawyer
Tobletzirer	Y	Upholsterer
Torah	H	Body of traditional Jewish teachings, Pentateuch, scroll for reading the Law in synagogue
Transha	R	To settle a marriage match
Treyf	H	Forbidden, non kosher according to Jewish dietary laws. Defiled
Trufanda	R	First fresh fruit of the season
Tuches	Y	Rear end (of person)
Tzaddek	H	Pious, saintly man
Tzap (de bere)	R	Beer mug
Tzeduka	H	Charity
Tzigganner	Y	Gypsies
Tzimmes	Y	Sweet stewed vegetables served as dessert — carrots, beans, chickpeas
Tsurca	R	Outdoor children's game played with two sticks
Tzures	Y	Worries
Umed	Y	Reading table in synagogue
Unkikechts	Y	Formal meeting of prospective couple (viewing)
Upgeshmissene oyshane	Y	Like a beaten bunch of willow twigs (used in rite of "beating Hosannas")
Upshprachn	Y	To remove evil eye. To counteract effect of evil eye
Visinata	R	Cherry brandy
Vulech	Y	Romanian from Wallachia (Romania) Term commonly used when referring to Gentiles
Yeshiva	H	Center of Hebrew higher learning
Yenteh	Y	Busy body. Also a woman's given name
Yichus	Y	Inherited status based on ancestral prestige, learning, wealth and family respectability
Yicker	Y	Essential, most important
Yid	Y	Jew
Yiddish	Y	Jewish language. The vernacular spoken by east European Jews
Yinger tzutzig	Y	Adolescent, "whipper-snapper"
Yir	Y	You — second person plural, used when addressing superior
Yisker	H	Prayer for remembrance of the dead
Yisker gelt	H	Charity donated in the name of departed
Yivreh	Y	Bible studies in Hebrew
Yomtoyvn	H	Holy days
Yortzeit	Y	Observance of anniversary of a death
Yukw mit Faivish	Y	Mismatched
Zece Mai	R	Tenth of May, Romanian national holiday
Zemirot	H	Songs, religious hymns sung after Sabbath meals
Zchyis	Y	Merit
Zestre	R	Trousseau
Zivvig	Y	Match fated in Heaven (forty days before birth, marriage partner is decreed in Heaven)

Zoyché	H	To be worthy in the eyes of God. . . .
Zugerkeh or Fierzuggern (in Romanian Yiddish)	Y	Woman who read the prayer in women's section, for those unable to read themselves

Appendix I

From *Alef Bet* pp. 134
by Victor Rusu

Translated from Romanian
by G. Sternberg

Not few were the homes where only one photograph was to be found: that of the revered rebbé Mathtiahu Friedman of the renowned Ruzhin dynasty. His hasidim used to say about him that he had the mind of an old man and the soul of an innocent child and that his entire life was in fact one huge, tremendous awaiting for the Messiah. So great was his yearning and so convinced was he of the imminent coming, that if he happened to fall asleep for a few moments, day or night, the sage with the soul of a child never failed to remind his servant to wake him up immediately should the Much Awaited One arrive at that very moment.

How did the photograph of this most revered teacher come to adorn the humblest abodes in the shtetl? Surely the sage never crossed the threshold of a photographer's studio, nor did he allow his countenance to be caught on film. It happened however that once, when the rebbé was leaving his house of prayer, someone furtively turned the camera and in a fraction of a second, fixed his image on film. As I said, the revered rebbé had not learned of the existence of this photograph. Furthermore, the hasidim whose good fortune it had been to live close to him used to say that the Master never even glanced into a mirror to see his own face.

On that somber and gloomy Thursday afternoon when in the shtetl the shattering news which announced the end of the venerable rebbé spread, the printer copied the photograph on a zinc plate and hurriedly printed several hundred post-cards. Hoskiola the paper-boy, burst out with them onto the shtetl streets and everyone yanked them out of his hands, to the very last one, paying twice and even three times the price. Since then, the huge eyes, sheer kindness and wisdom of the famous rebbé brightened the sad and crowded little dwellings of the poorest shtetl sons.

Appendix II

Exhumation of the Remains of the Tzadig from Stefanesti

From an article in *Revista Cultului Mozaic No. 13*, 194, Nov. 1962

Rebbé Avram Mathtiahu Friedman of sainted memory, whose father Rebbé Nahum was the son of the great rebbé Israel Rijiner, reigned in Stefanesti (Jud. Botosani) for over seventy years. Faithful flocked to his court, not only from the towns and cities in Moldova but from afar and even from foreign lands. Thousands came to ask for his counsel and blessing. He died at the age of ninety six in 1933 and his mausoleum in Stefanesti attracted pilgrims who came to honor his memory.

On the 23rd of October 1968 the body of the saintly tzadig (the just one) was exhumed in order to fulfill the ancient custom of entrusting the earthly remains to the sacred soil of Israel.

Chief Rabbi Dr. Moses Rosen of Romania officiated at the services and gave guidance for the proper proceedings, in the presence of representatives of many communities, and many non Jews, from Stefanesti and the surrounding towns.

A special coffin was prepared to receive the remains. In an emotion filled moment hundreds of faithful bent over the coffin to ask the traditional "Mehilla" (forgiveness) and weeping took leave of their tzadig.

After exhumation the coffin was taken to the kloys (the synagogue of rebbé's court) where the late rebbé used to raise his prayers to the Almighty. Along the road from the cemetery the faithful intoned Psalms and at the kloys the religious ceremony of "yisker" was pronounced.

Dr. Rabbi Moses Rosen and other officials carried on their shoulders the coffin which was subsequently sent to Bucharest. On October 24th, 1962 the coffin arrived at the synagogue *MALBIM* in Bucharest where a great many faithful gathered to take their leave of the venerable rebbé. On the same day the remains of the Stefanester rebbé arrived by plane in Israel, where a multitude received it with all honors befitting the occasion.

Appendix III

THE JEWISH MINORITY IN ROMANIA: Correspondence with the Romanian Government Respecting the Grievances of the Jews — London 1927 THE JOINT FOREIGN COMMITTEE OF THE BOARD OF DEPUTIES OF BRITISH JEWS AND THE ANGLO JEWISH ASS.N. Lucien Wolf, Secretary;

Memorandum on the Anti-Semitic movement in Romania; p. 48 December 4, 1926

The Romanian Minister of Interior, Mr. Goga has contributed a sum of 20.000 lei to the publication fund of the Anti-semitic students' movement which was used for the purpose of issuing publication agitating for enforcement of numerous clausus against Jews. The report states that an announcement of the contribution was made to the Students' Congress at Iassy by M. Danulescu.

p. 51. Attitudes of the Church: March 19, 1926: The Patriarch of the Orthodox Church Dr. Miron Cristia delivers himself of a violent outburst against the "alien elements". The spiritual father of 14 million Romanians demands that justice be restored and all contracts which have been made with aliens elements be revised.

April 12, 1927: On March 29th a group of students armed with heavy sticks attacked in his laboratory Professor Rascanu of Iassy University with whose attitude toward the Anti-semitic movement they were dissatisfied. In order to frighten them, Professor Rascanu had to fire a revolver in the air. The academic staff of the university has now sent to the Minister of Education the following address:

"Sir,

For a long period of time the normal activity of our university has been disturbed by a number of students who by means of agitations, strikes and acts of violence try to solve public problems which are neither within the scope of academic interests nor are capable of being solved by the University. This state of things which leads to sad results in so far as the culture and education of our youth are concerned, forms an obvious danger for the future of this country. Unfortunately, heretofore, no serious steps whatever have been taken for the remedy of this situation and things have now come to such a pass that relations between professors and students, instead of being of collaboration in the research for an ideal of culture and progress, are of such a nature that some students show not the least sign of respect for their teachers when they come in contact with each other. This lack of consideration is proof of anarchic spirit and of a total lack of education, which gives the impression that professors and students belong to two enemy camps. It must be clear to everybody that in such circumstances academic activities cannot follow a normal course.

Furthermore, of late in consequence of certain events on which we will not insist, since they are only too well known, those students who are causing the disturbances have become convinced that anything is permitted to them in this country without fear of punishment. In the name of a principle which they interpret as they do, they consider that they can attack the liberty of others without fear of legal sanctions, that they can use any means they like without fear of consequences and an attitude which constitutes a danger for the present and even more so for the future when the young people who grow up in such a state of mind will be called upon to govern this country.

This anarchic situation must come to an end. Those who indulge in disturbances believe that the university is there solely to manufacture degrees giving rights in the state; that the professors are obliged to pass them at examinations without regard to knowledge and preparation, that they may IMPOSE BY SHEER FORCE a certain viewpoint on political and social issues. A number of students believe themselves entitled to solve within the university problems which are within the jurisdiction of other organs and institutions in the state. The immediate consequence is that time valuable for study is being wasted in sterile agitations and the Romanian element enters society and the life struggle in disturbing state of ignorance and unpreparedness.

The disturbances of academic life have gone from bad to worse and now the point has been reached when the professors are in the sad necessity of defending their lives and their institutes with weapons in hand, to defend them against destruction by whom? By those young people for whom with heavy sacrifices they have been created by the state. The recent case when Professor Rascanu was attacked in his own Institute by a group of students . . . and desperately forced to defend his life and institute with the revolver, is not an isolated case and it reveals the evil which is rotting deeply the foundations of academic life.

The authorities concerned are incapable of keeping order; this is evident and it is not to be wondered that professors are forced to have recourse to such means of self defence. This state of affairs must come to an end and it is in the first place the duty of professors to take measures. All those professors who desire to see the progress of this high educational institution must consider severe and effective means for putting an end to this situation. The professors have the means of clearing the university of all those elements which indulge in sterile agitation, harmful to the activity of the University. Acting within the framework of the law regulations, stringently applied, it is possible to weed out all the disturbing elements within a short time. To that end all professors who desire order should work in agreement for the execution of the measures proposed. The perennial love and kindness hitherto displayed by the professor towards students who disturb order within the university have not produced desired results. Moreover, sir, the solving of this problem depends a good deal on your attitude. The students must not find encouragement in their mistaken ways anywhere, neither from authorities nor public opinion. You, sir, by the position you occupy are in a position to intervene with full authority so that they should take severe steps for the maintenance of order and that they should no longer adopt attitudes intended as encouragement of these anarchic activities and by the place which you personally occupy in our public life, you could enlighten and influence public opinion so that it should no longer offer moral and material support to agitators who are harming our country and our culture.

We therefore beg of you sir, that together with us, your colleagues, anxious to restore order in the University, you should consider the means best suited for helping us in the task we have herewith undertaken."

Signed: A. Cardish, C. Otin, I. Botez, Eng. Horovanu, Dr. Giaconu, A. Philippide,

A. Ibraileanu, Dr. Anghel D. Tanasescu, S. Procopiu, V. Buteanu, N. Costachescu, V. Pascu, P. Andrei, A. Popovici, S. Sinilevici, V. Miller, Dr. A. Slatineaun, Dr. P. Glasescu, Mihai Ralea, Dr. Ciuca, Dr. Hortolomei, I. Constantinescu, I. Simionescu, Tr. Bratu, Dr. Enescu, Dr. Mironescu, I. Minea, Th. Ionescu, Dr. V. Rascanu, Dr. Stefanescu-Galatzi, C. Popovici, Dr. Parhon, Dr. Ionescu Mahaesti, Alex Myller, Zaharescu-Caraiman

Adevarul; April 12, 1927.

Appendix IV

From *Sanatatea si Viata Fericita*, No. 17–18, November 1933, p. 418
Excerpt from *Buletinul Demographic al Romaniei*

The number of deaths for the entire country 32.772, i.e. 21.5 per 1000 of inhabitants: 27.292 (22.1 per 1000) for rural area, 5.480 (18.9 per 1000) for urban area. The provinces with a higher rate were Oltenia, Dobrogea, Moldova, Basarabia and Banat.

Mortality varies from 29.1 per 1000 in Jud. Durostor to 14.5 per 1000 in Jud. Brasov.

Both mortality and natality are higher in the Old Kingdom than in the country as a whole.

Mortality is higher in villages than in cities and especially for infants under one year.

Natural excedent (surplus). Over the entire country, during April an increase of 27.007 souls have been registered, that is 13.8 per thousand distributed as follows: 20.304 (16.5 per 1000) in rural, 701 (2.5 per 1000) in urban areas.

In the entire country there were 995 still births, 5.565 marriages and 550 divorces were registered.

Infant mortality records 9.130 deaths among those less than one-year-old, i.e. 17% live births and 27.9% out of the total number of deaths.

Deaths; Causes: Generally speaking sanitary conditions are improved as of April 1933 as compared with the same month the previous year.

Calculated on a yearly basis mortality per 100.000 decreased from 2.464 to 2.151 deaths. The most marked decreases have been in scarlet fever, flue, T.B. pneumonia, septicemie, puerperal fever, childhood diseases and accidents.

In rural areas there is an increase in deaths from: rheumatism, whooping cough and malaria. It must be remarked that small pox has disappeared. Suicides increased slightly in villages although the rate is four times greater in the cities than in villages.

Causes for deaths as of April are:
Respiratory 7.088 of which 5.653 pneumonia   Enteritis   1.707
Senility   6.179   Nervous system   1.366
Infantile   6.103, of which 5.631 congenital debility   Nephritis   844
Infectious   4.754, of which 3.398 T.B.   Violent deaths   720
Circulatory   1.960   Of these, suicides   159
Cancer and other tumors 656   homicides   96
Pelagra   250   accidents   465
Septicemias and puerperal fevers 90.   Alcoholism poisoning 32

Appendix V

A random sample of the topics dealt with between 1916 and 1938.

June 1916

About co-education; Are women capable of following University studies?
(This article discusses points of view in: England, (Cambridge Univ. G. H. Darwin-Germany, Dr. Winkel; Austria; Belgium–))
Alcoholism – consequences
Headaches, About the gums and oral hygiene
Replies, advice, suggestions
One short story –

April 1925

Health for Society:
    Alcoholism
Health for Youth:
    Medical advice for the over 18-year-olds
    If your skin is oily
Health for Women:
    Childbirth without pain – Dr. Sigma
    Anemia
Health for Children:
    How to protect the child when the mother has a cold
    If a child was bitten by a dog
Household:
    How to prevent uremia
    Hygienic advice for asthma sufferers
    Illustrated medical vocabulary
Artistic and Literary Health:
    Virility among the women of Genius – Sapho, George Sand
    Fiction – Why many women don't know true happiness

November 1929

Social Health:
    The chemistry of thought
    Women who fall in love with their doctors
Health for Youth:
    Physical culture (Official) is dangerous for youth
    What the ancients believed about moderation: Epictet, Seneca, Cicero–Socrates–Plato–Hipocrates

Health for Women:
    Why women should not smoke
    Letters to a mother by Dr. Sigma
Health for the Child:
    Excessive attention ruins the child
    Dangers of discharge from the ears
Household:
    Hypertrophy of the prostate — diagram
    First aid in case of asphixiation
    The function of nitrogen in nutrition
Artistic and Literary:
    Mama — poem
    Who is Katie Kolvitz? examples of her work
    Novel — The white rose

January 1932

Social:
    The happiness of living a healthy and moral life
    Medicine and religion
    Advice for our times by André Maurois
Youth:
    The tragedy of a young syphilitic
    Winter sports
Women:
    New surgery to rejuvenate women
    Black coffee and pregnant women
    Chapped lips
Children:
    Letter XI to a mother
    Nursing babies with cow's milk
    What to think when a child has a tummy ache
Health for All:
    Nutritive value of eggs
    Tonsils and general disease
    For the diabetics
Artistic and Literary:
    Jesus healing the sick
    Verses
    Popular beliefs; The stars and Medicine
    Maurice Chevalier and his mother

June 1932

Social:
    Dignified and undignified aging
    Crime in all phases, sin, war, mobs, alcohol, erotism, heredity
Youth:
    Youth and crime
    Fighting against timidity
Women:
    Divorce due to gonorrhoea
    Diet contributes to beauty

Children:
  And crime
  Constipation
  Diagrams
Health for All:
  How to avoid arthereoschlerosis
  The mother's page — Love your child

July–August 1933

Social:
  Modernism
  What is Psychotherapy?
Youth:
  About the sex hormones?
  What is stuttering?
  Aphorisms about love and marriage
Women:
  After the honeymoon
  Grey hair
Children:
  Dyphtheria
  Infants during the hot months of summer
For All:
  Salt as a therapeutic nutrient
  Climate cure for T.B.
  Healing powers of mineral waters in Romania
  Blood transfusions
Artistic:
  Love and jealosy
Literary:
  Baths in antiquity

Titles of topics in the popular health journal *Sanatatea si Viata Fericita.*

Health and the Happy Life

June 1932 Issue dedicated to "Crime"

Dignified and undignified old age
The War against Crime — Hunger as a factor in crime
The Press and criminality
A sinful life provokes crime
War as a factor in crime
Mob crimes
Alcohol and Crime
Erotism and Crime
Heredity and Crime
Children and Crime
A few words about constipation — a diagram of the internal organs of the body
What does low blood pressure mean? How to avoid Artereosclerosis.

March 1933

Depts: Social, Health
  Ciclotomy
  How Infections have been conquered
  How patients used to be examined
  The Jubilee of the Microscope
  Ten years from the death of Roentgen
Youth Health:
  Letter addressed to a mother by Dr. W. Stekel Trans; Dr. Sigma
  Should sexual diseases be considered shameful
  Spiritual dewdrops
  Why should the husband be older than the wife?
  Why smoke?
Health for Women:
  The woman and make-up
  Puberty and menstruation
  Don't be embarrassed to wear glasses
  Don't tire your eyes!
Health for Children:
  Near the child's cradle
  Constipation and the newborn infant — breastfed
  Cleaning the child's ears
  Children with a dry cough
Health for All:
  Icter
  Fishoil
  Tapeworms
  How T.B. begins
  Pulmonary gangrene
  For those who have the common cold
  What is bronchoctazy?
Health; Artistic and Literary:
  The evolution of medicine in the past and now

Article from *Sanatatea si Viata Fericita*, March 1933, p. 48, by Liviu Munteanu. Translated from *Revue d'Hygiène et de Medecine Sociale* by Dr. M. Schachter Nancy

Hygienic Precepts among the Ancient Hebrews

According to the Bible, the rules of hygiene were given by God himself, the greatest of doctors, and their disobedience attracts heavy punishment. It is interesting to note that the ancient Hebrews considered illnesses as being provoked by the sins committed against God. This idea explains why they did not believe in good and evil spirits which are in a constant war with one another, a belief frequently found among peoples of antiquity.

Whoever followed faithfully the rules of hygiene was protected from illness, enjoyed a long life on earth. This promise of a long life and not a future life is often mentioned in the Bible and in the Talmud.

This is how the Jews put into practice some of the hygiene problems:
Palestine being a relatively dry land, supplying the large cities with water was a most important problem; this was resolved by constructing reservoirs, huge

bodies of water. It was well known that these reservoirs had to be well protected from dust and dirt. Many Talmud chapters speak of the efforts made by authorities to assure the high quality and purity of the water. It seems that the learned, planners of the cities knew that unclean water provokes disease and epidemics.

All factories, tanneries, limestone burning ovens, all industries today known as unhealthy, had to be installed at a specific distance from the cities. Without exaggeration, we may consider the Jews as the first people who had the modern understanding regarding urban hygiene.

Still in the same area of thought, we must mention that the Jews had a very strict regulation regarding the burial of dead. It is known that incineration, the burning of cadavers was forbidden in antiquity as it is today. The Talmud ordains rigorously that inhumation be made as soon as possible after death to avoid the possibility of infection.

Exceptions to this strict rule were permitted only when there was some doubt about the cessation of life, cases of "apparent death" being known and cited in the Talmud.

Ritual bath houses were very numerous in Palestinian cities and much frequented. The Jews were familiar with the hygiene of the house and of the street. In front of each house there was a patch of land and the inhabitants tried to have a little garden around the house. It is precisely known that the streets were paved, especially the large ones such as Jerusalem and Antioch.

Regarding the provision of meat for the cities, the Jews were the first to understand that this food had to be well controlled before consumption. Not only the meat of large animals was thus examined but that of the birds as well. Meat from sick cattle had to be incinerated immediately even when the cattle was presupposed to be cured. Similarly the meat of animals found sick after being killed or those found to have abnormal internal organs, had to be burned. We will insist upon this point since it is well known by hygienists that the Jews were the first people in the world who organized what is today understood as veterinary control of the abatoires.

First of all, every community had to have a butcher, with veterinary medical knowledge (the shochet) who judged whether the meat was adequate for consumption according to ritual kashrut. The butcher had to control whether the animal was in a perfect state of health. He had to pass a series of practical and theoretical examinations in front of a commissions of rabbis, experts in this matter.

The organs and especially the lungs were examined with the greatest attention. The Jews believed that in the lungs were found not only the animal's soul but as well, the place of origin of many diseases which might pass on to man through the consumed meat.

It seems that they were not too sure — which is perhaps exaggerated — but they suspected that the lung diseases of the animals were transmittable to man via the meat. The Talmud discusses this question and establishes precise rules, which have been faithfully followed.

In a recent study by Dr. Loir, former director of the Pasteur Inst. from Tunis, it is mentioned among other things: "The Jews understood perhaps before the great Villemin (French doctor 1827–1892) that animal T.B. may be passed on to man via the meat." It may be said that the Jews, without knowing about T.B. of the animals and the other lung diseases, such as periphenomony of the horned animals, suspected that they can be transmitted to man.

The killed animals found sick were burned far from town together with offal. We must also mention here that the blood from slaughter houses was carefully buried. If this was not possible, it was at least covered with ashes, sawdust or pebbles and gravel.

The milk of sick animals was also forbidden. Eggs with blood drops (fecundated) were also thrown away.

Military garrisons were obliged to respect strictly the cleanliness rules. Faecies had to be as far as possible, the cleanliness of food observed closely. Religious prescriptions were strictly respected as much as in the cities. War booty had to be "cleansed" before being given as food.

Corporal cleanliness was considered of great importance. Besides the ritual public baths found in all cities, religion obliged Jews to wash their hands several times a day, according to circumstances. In the morning, the first thing was to wash the hands before even taking one step; objects touched with unwashed hands were "unclean" and unusable. It was not allowed to wash the face in the same water that the hands had been washed. This had to be thrown out where people do not pass during the daytime. Washing of hands was stipulated before saying prayers, after sexual relations, after finishing "natural necessities" etc. It was not allowed to drink from a stranger's cup. Cut nails, hair etc. had to be burned.

From the hygienic point of view the sexual relations were studied in great detail by the Talmudists. The scope of the sex act is God's commandment: the reproduction of the species. Not to fulfill this divine commandment is a sin. Thus, according to the laws of Moses, a marriage could be broken if the woman was sterile. Prostitution was punishable by death. Especially the priests were enjoined to respect faithfully the healthy sexual life. Sexual perversions of all kinds, such as masturbation, homosexuality were punished by death. For health reasons were also forbidden marriages of close relatives to a certain degree. A man who had discharge was considered unclean as was the menstruating woman. They had to live away from their family. It seems that gonorrhea was known by the Jews (priests) who had medical knowledge. The Talmud advises men not to marry women from families known to have hereditary diseases. Abuse of alcohol intake is forbidden. The rabbis and other clergy were removed in case of such offence.

The doctor was then, as now, very much honoured by the Jews. All religious prescriptions are immediately put aside when healing a patient is at stake. Thus for instance, it was allowed to prepare medicines during holy days, the sick person was dispensed from fasting, the doctor had the complete freedom to save life, the religious obstacles not considered sufficient cause to prevent him from exercising his skills.

It seems that skin diseases gave much concern to the priests as they did later on to the learned Talmudists. The Bible as well as the Talmud speak in great detail about these diseases. The priest's duty was to examine all uncleanliness of the skin which suggested a disease and if the man was a carrier of a skin disorder, he had to be isolated for a specific time fixed by the priest. His clothing was burned or at any rate disinfected. It is not known whether this applied only to leprosy or to all skin diseases.

Epidemics were announced with drumbeats all over town and sanitary measures were taken for the protection of the people. Against diphtheria, blood letting was used and against moskito bites known to bring malaria, gauze sheets were used.

The child occupied a place of honour in the framework of the old Jewish culture and enjoyed a particular attention. Ill treatment of children was almost unknown and if a parent beat his child he was reprimanded by the community.

The child was considered as a gift from God and punishing him, a sin. The pregnant woman enjoyed the same privileged position. The mother was obliged to nurse her child herself and infanticide was unknown and punishable by death. The same fate awaited the woman who aborted. The child sick from birth had to be looked after by his parents and cured. We see here a great difference between these principles and the all too eugenic views of the Spartans. While nursing, the woman was not obliged to fast or keep other religious precepts. Furthermore, a woman who lost her husband while she was nursing was not permitted to remarry before two years so that she should be able to look after the child. By contrast, a man who remained widowed was able to remarry before the prescribed time if he had to look after an infant who needed care.

The scholar too was esteemed and the schools were quite hygienic and large. The Talmud describes the gardens to be found around schools. Unfortunately, today things are not quite the same. The students received besides booklearning education in citizenship but were protected from any sexual relations too early. Also as a hygienic measure, children were not supposed to sleep together, not even children of the same sex.

Joyfulness, cheerfulness was recommended as a stimulant for life, anger as well as sadness being considered a sin. Maimonides, a Jewish doctor from Cordoba in the XIth. century insists on this point as well as to live in the open air, to do exercise, things which bring good humor and health. More than 8 hrs. sleep was considered unhealthy.

We must also mention that non-Jewish hygienists have recognized the hygienic value of circumcision which avoids a series of diseases such as "fimoze, parafimoze balanite etc." The custom of having the rabbi suck the incision which was considered unhygienic is not practiced any longer.

It was not possible to tell everything about the Hygiene of the ancient Hebrews in this article, but we succeeded — we hope — to show in general outline that hygiene existed among the Jews of antiquity. Dr. M. Schachter (Nancy).

From *Revue d'Hygiène et de médecine sociales*. Translated by Liviu Munteanu.

Bibliography

Aleichem, Sholem, *The Bewitched Tailor*, Foreign Languages Publ. House Moscow, U.S.S.R.
Aleichem, Sholem, *The Great Fair*, The Noonday Press, N.Y., 1955.
Aleichem, Sholem, *Adventures of Mottel the Cantor's Son*, Collier MacMillan, 1961.
Aleichem, Sholem, *Thé Tevye Stories and Others*, Pocket Book Inc., 1965.
Barnow, V., *Culture and Personality*, The Dorsey Press, 1963.
Baron, J. L. (ed), *A Treasury of Jewish Quotations*, The Crown Publ. Inc., 1956.
Beatie, John, *Other Cultures*, Rutledge Paperback, 1964.
Belshaw, Cyril S., *The Conditions of Social Performance*, Shocken Books, 1970.
Bellow, Saul (ed), *Great Jewish Short Stories*, Dell Books, 1963.
Benedict, Ruth, *Rumanian Culture and Behavior*, Institute for Inter Cultural Studies N.Y., (mimeographed manuscript).
Benedict, Ruth, *Patterns of Culture*, Mentor Books, N.Y., 1950.
Bettelheim, Bruno, *Children of the Dream*, Collier MacMillan, 1969.
Beinenstok, Theodor, "Social Life and Authority in the Eastern European Jewish Shtetl", *Southwestern Journal of Anthropology* No. 6, pp. 238-54.
Browne, L., *The Wisdom of Israel*, Random House Inc., 1956.
Brunvand, J. H., *The Study of American Folklore*, W. W. Norton and Co. Inc., N.Y., 1978.
Chagnon, Napoleon A., *Yanomamo, The Fierce People*, Holt Rinehart and Winston, 1968.
Cohen, Israel, *The Jews in Rumania*, (Repr. from the *Nineteenth Century and After*), 1938.
Cotter, Manascu, *Comunitatea din Tirgul Stefanesti*, Revista Cultului Mozaic, Nov. 1st, 1972, No. 286.
Davidowicz, Lucy, *The Golden Tradition*, Holt Rinehart and Winston, 1967.
Eiden, Ben M., *Jewish Customs and Ceremonies*, Hebrew Publishing Co., 1941.
Freedman, J. D., *On The Concept of the Kindred*, Journal of the Royal Anthropology Institute, No. 91, pp. 192-200.
Fried, Morton H. (ed), *Readings in Anthropology*, Vol. II, Thomas Y. Crowell Co., N.Y., 1968.
Friedl, Ernestine, *Vasilika a Village in Modern Greece*, Holt Rinehart, Winston Inc.,
Gane, C., *Trecute Vieti de Doamne si Domnite*, Editura Ziarului Universul S.A., Bucuresti-Roumania, 1941.
Gaster, Theodor, *Festivals of the Jewish Year*, Wm. Sloan Associates Publ. N.Y., 1952.
Giurescu, Constantin C. and Dinu C., *Istoria Romanilor*, Editura Stiintifica Bucurest, 1974.

Gluckman, Max and Fred Egan, *The Relevance of Models For Social Anthropology*, Tavistock Publishers.
Goldschmidt, Walter, "Social Class and the Dynamics of Status in America", *American Anthropologist*, Vol. 57, pp. 1209–17, 1957.
Goldschmidt, Walter and Robert Edgerton, "A Picture Technique for the Study of Values", *American Anthropologist*, Vol. 63, 1961.
Goldschmidt, Walter and Robert Edgerton, *Exploring The Ways of Mankind*, Holt Rinehart and Winston, 1960.
Gottschalk, Louis, Klyde Kluckhohn and Robert Angel, *The Use of Personal Documents in History, Anthropology and Sociology*, Social Science Research Council, N.Y.
Graetz, H., *History of the Jews*, Jewish Publications Society of America, 1898.
Graysel, Solomon, *A History of the Jews*, Jewish Publications Society of America, 1953.
Grey, Alan, *Class and Personality in Society*, Atherton Press, N.Y., 1969.
Hagen, Everet E., *On The Theory of Social Change*, Dorsey Press, 1962.
Halaey, A. H., "Genetics, Social Structure and Intelligence", *Br. J. Soc.*, Vol. 9, 1958.
Hebb, D. O., *The Socialization of the Child*, Readings in Social Psych., Holt Reinhart and Winston Inc., 1958.
Henry, Jules, *Culture Against Man*, Vintage Books, N.Y., 1965.
Herskovits, M. J., "The Significance of the Study of Acculturation", *American Anthropology No. 39*, pp. 259–264, 1937.
Herskovits, Melville, *Cultural Dynamics*, Alfred A. Knopf, N.Y., 1976.
Howe, Irving and Eliezer Greenberg, *A Treasury of Yiddish Stories*, Viking Press, 1954.
Hsu, Francis L. K., *Kinship and Culture*, Aldine Publ. Chicago, Ill.
Jaffe, James, *The American Jews*, Paperback Library, 1969.
Joffe, Natalie, "Dynamics of Benefice Among Eastern European Jews", *Social Forces*, Vol. 27, pp. 238–247, 1949.
Kardiner, Abram, *The Individual and His Society*, Columbia University Press, N.Y., 1939.
Kardiner, Abram, *Sex and Morality*, Charter Books, Bobbs Merrill, 1962.
Kluckhohn, Florence, *Variations in Value Orientation*, Row Peterson and Co., Evanston, Ill.
Koestler, A., *The Thirteenth Tribe*, Pan Books Picador, 1976.
Kroebr, A. L., *Configurations of Culture Growth*, University of California Press, 1944.
Landes, Ruth and Mark Zborowski, "Hypothesis Concerning Eastern European Family", *Journal of Psychiatry*, Vol. 13, pp. 447–464, 1950.
Langness, L. L., *The Life History in Anthropological Science*, Holt Rinehart Winston Inc., 1965.
Levitats, Isaac, *The Jewish Community in Russia, Econ. and Public Law*, No. 1, 1943.
Lewis, Oscar, *Tepotzlan, Village in Mexico*, Holt Rinehart and Winston Inc., 1960.
Linton, Ralph, *Acculturation in Seven American Indian Tribes*, Appleton Century, N.Y., 1940.
Lowie, Robert, *Social Organization*, Holt Rinehart and Winston Inc., 1960.
Lynd, Robert S. and Helen M. Lynd, *Middletown in Transition*, Harcourt Brace and World Inc., 1937.
McGill, Norman and A. Chance, "Acculturation, Self Identification and Personality Adjustment", *American Anthropologist*, Vol. 67, 1966.

Mead, Margaret, *Columbia University Research in Contemporary Cultures*, Carnegie Press, 1951.
Mead, Margaret, *New Lives for Old*, New York, William Morrow Co., 1956.
Mead, Margaret, *Continuities in Cultural Evolution*, Yale University Press, 1964.
Meites, Irving, *The Marriage Broker*, P. Putnam's Sons, New York, 1960.
Meltzer, Milton, *World of Our Fathers*, Dell Publishing Co., 1974.
Mendole Mocher Sforim, *Fiske the Lame* (in Romanian), 1935.
Merton, Robert K., *Social Theory and Social Structure*, Glencoe, Ill., 1957.
Miner, Horace, *St. Denis, A French Canadian Parish*, University of Chicago Press, 1939.
Miner, Horace, "The Folk Urban Continuum", *American Soc. Review*, Vol. 17, No. 5, 1952.
Mlotek, Eleanor G., *Mir Trogn a Gesang*, Waldon Press Inc., 1977.
Murdock, G. P., *Social Structure*, The MacMillan Col. New York, 1960.
Orlansky, H., "Infant Care and Personality", *Psychological Bulletin* XLVI.
Pan, Anton, *De La Lume Adunate si'Napoi La Lume Date* Proverbs, (From the folk gathered and back to the folk returned.)
Radin, Paul, *The World of Primitive Man*, E. P. Dutton, New York, 1971.
Redfield, R., *A Village That Chose Progress Chan Kom Revisited*, University of Chicago Press, 1950.
Redfield, R., *The Little Community*, University of Chicago Press, 1971.
Riggs, James S., *A History of the Jewish People*, D. D. London Smith Elder and Co., 1900.
Rosenthal, Celia Stopnicka, "Deviations and Social Change in Jewish Community of Small Polish Town", *American Journal of Sociology*, Vol. 60, 1960.
Roskies, Diane K. and David G., *The Shtetl Book*, Ktav Publishing House Inc., 1975.
Rosten, L., *The Joys of Yiddish*, Pocket Books, New York, 1970.
Roth, Cecil, *History of The Jews*, Schocken Books, 1961.
Rubin, Ruth, *Voices Of A People*, Jewish Publication Society of America, Philadelphia, Pa., 1979.
Rubin, Ruth, *A Treasury of Jewish Folk Songs*, Schocken Books.
Rusu, Victor, *Alef Bet*, Federatia Comunitatilor Evreiesti din Romania Bucuresti, 1976.
Schwartz, Leo W., *Memoirs of My People* (3d), Schocken Books, 1963.
Siegel, R., M. and S. Strassfeld (ed), *The Jewish Catalog*, The Jewish Publication Society of America, Philadelphia, Pa., 1980.
Singer, Isaac B., *The Slave*, Avon Books, 1962.
Steinberg, Milton, *Basic Judaism*, Harbrace Modern Classics, 1947.
Strauss, Claude Lévi, *The Elementary Structures of Kinship*, Beacon Press, 1969.
Tax, Sol (ed), *Anthropology Today*, Phoenix Books, University of Chicago Press, 1962.
Trachtenberg, Joshua, *Jewish Magic and Superstitions*, Atheneum College Ed., Temple Book, 1979.
Zborowski, Mark, *Children of the Covenant*, Social Forces No. 4 XXIX, p. 351–364, 1951.
Zborowski, Mark and Eliz. Herzog, *Life is With People*, Schocken, 1952.

Marele Dictionar Geografic Al Romaniei (Biblioteca Nationala – Bucuresti).
Encyclopedia Judaica
Revista Cultului Mozaic: Nos. 194, 11/1/68 – No. 215, 226, 242, 284, Nov. 1, 1972, No. 286.
Yvo Bleter I. Kara, *Yiddish Business Letters from Moldavia, 1829–1842*, Vol. 44, 1973, pp. 74–106, 190, 9/1/68, p. 4.

Index

Abraham Matathias 118
address
    modes of 208–9
administrative structure
    Romania 41–5
adolescence 130–2
adultery 73
Alexander Ypsilanti, *Prince* 32
Alliance Israelite Universelle 33–4, 133, 216
alias
    auctioning 94–5
amulets 82–3
anti-semitism 29–30, 34, 37–40, 220–1
Antonescu, *General* Ion 28
apprentices 52–3
Aron-Kodesh 116
arranged marriages 140–3
artisans 54–60
assimilation 29, 203
Atzeret 99

Ba'al Shem Tov 118, 122
baby teeth
    loss 130
baccalaureat 135, 137–8
backgammon 168
bagel vendor 60
bakers 56
Bal Mascat 105
Balfour, A. J., *1st Earl* 36–7, 134
Balfour Declaration 36–7
ball games 162–4
Bar Mitzvah 131
barbers 58
    leeches 81
bargaining 53
bath, communal 60
battered children 129–30
bears
    dancing 156
beggars 60, 206
Benedict, Ruth 220
Benjamin of Tuleda 31
Berlach 111
Berlin 215
Bessarabia 11–12

Betar
    youth movement 139
Bialik, H. N. 134
Bickel, Solomon 32
bicycles 160–1
Binder, Hayim and Charlotta 14–15
birth 124–9
blacksmiths 59
bleeding
    leeches 81
blind man's buff 166
bly gissern 59, 81–3
borshtenitze 59
Botosani 10, 32
boys
    adolescence 130–2
breast feeding 128, 129
bricklayers 58
bris 125
Buber, Martin 122
building trade 58
bus route
    Stefanesti 11
butchers 57

cabinetmakers 58
cafenea 15, 153
cameras 160
cantor 115
Carol I, *King of Romania* 27–8
Carol II, *King of Romania* 28, 38
carpenters 58
carters 59
carul
    game 169–70
cat
    game 165–6
cat's cradle 162, 164
cemetries 151
cemetry-plot sales 42
cerealists 50, 153
charity 206–7
charms 82–3, 119
chazn 115
chechn
    game 162, 164
chedder 133

284 Index

chess 168
Chevre Kadisha 148
chicken dealers 57
childbirth 126
children 72
   naming 127
   parents and 210
   pastimes 162
   rearing 129-30
   rhymes 18-9, 178-9
childrens' songs
   Romanian 189-90
china shops 50
chollent 91-2
chumetz 107
chuppa 144
cinema 159-60
circumcision 70, 125
citizenship
   Jews 37
cleaning
   Passover 107
climate
   Romania 24-5
coachmen 59
cobblers 54, 56
Codreanu, C. Z. 37
coffee-house
   Stefanesti 15
cohens 94-5
coins
   mitbeyes 119
collecting
   pastime 162
comis 52-3
committee
   shtetl 41-5
communal bath 60
communism 138, 207
concerts
   public gardens 156
conformity 208
cooking stoves 20
coopers 58
corporal punishment 72, 129-30
Cotter, Manascu 31
Council for Jewish Minority Rights 37
craftsmen 54-60
Crimen Gessl 14
cupping 79
curriculum
   schools 134
cursa 11
curses 248-9
Cuza, A. C. 28, 38
Cuza, A. I. 27

Daci 26
dancing bears 156
death 87, 147-51
debt 48
dentists 4, 46
devil 87
dignity 208
diminutives 127
discipline
   schools 135
district nurse 76
divorce 73-4
doctors 46-7, 77-9
doina
   folk song 187
double standard 213
dowries 141, 142
Dragos Voda 27
draughts 168-9
draymen 59
dressmakers 55
drop-out
   high school 137
Dynamics of benefice, The 206

education 132-8
   compulsory 133
   discrimination 39-40, 137-8
   girls 137
   high school 136-7
Eliachum Zunzer 195
Enesco, George 192
engagement 142
England 217-18
English language 217
epidemics 78
Eretz Israel 34, 35
Esther 103-4
etl-betl
   game 162, 164
evil 87, 205
evil eye 82
extended family 63, 69

family 7-8, 62-74
family roles
   terminology 63-5
family size 63
fanaticism
   hasidim 123
Farmacia 45-6
fasting 96-7
father
   roles 65-6
felcher 80-1

Ferdinand, *King of Romania* 28
festivals 93-112
    school 160
Fiddler on the roof 5
first born sons 128
fishmongers 56, 57
Fiske the Lame 60
flour mills 52
folk dancing 190-1
folk medicine 80-4
food 57, 211
football 155-6, 163
Foster, M. 166n, 206
France 216-17
Friday evening meal 91
Friedman, Abraham Matathias 118
friendships 209
frugality 211
fruit stores 56, 57-8
funerals 148-50
furriers 55-6

games 161-72
    role-playing 168
Gane, G. 221n
Gaster, Theodor 97n, 99, 100, 109, 110
Germany
    admiration for 215-6
gift-giving 206
gimeles chessed 48, 207
girls
    adolescence 130-2
    education 137
gobbé 112-14
God 85-93
godfather 70
Goga, Octavian 28, 38
Goldfaden, Abraham 176
Gordonia
    youth movement 139
grain dealers 50, 153
gramophone records 155
Grigore Ghica, *Prince* 31
Groza, Petru 28
guilt 205
gymnastics 155-6
gypsies 219-20

Hachscharah 39
Haggadah 109
haggling 53
Hahambasha 31
hairstyles 73
Halutzim 39
Hamishusner B'Shevat 103

hand kissing 209-10
Hanukah 101-3
hardware shops 50
hasidic songs 175
hasidim 119, 121-3
hasidism 204
Haskalah 34, 204
havdalah 92
health 75-84
Hebrew 161
    songs 184-7
    teaching 133
Hebrew names
    changing 127
Hertzog, Elizabeth 1
Herzl, Theodor 35, 134
Hibbad Zion 34
hide and seek 166
high school education 136-7
Holy Ark 116
hop-scotch 164-5
hospital 76
hospitality 205-6
houses
    Stefanesti 16-24
Hovevey Zion 34
Hoyche shyll 113, 114, 115-17
hoyf
    Rebbe's court 119
Human Resources Area Files 250
humentash 104
husbands
    roles 65-6

Iassy 11, 77
ice-cream parlours 156
infant mortality 77-8, 128
inns 52
intellectual work
    prestige 211-12
intellectuals
    Jewish 34
interfirers 69, 143-5
Iron Guard 28
Israel of Ruzhin 118

jacks 162, 164
Jewish Party 39
Jewish students 217
    university entrance 137-8
Jews
    Romanian 29-40
Joffe, Natalie 206
journalism
    Romanian Jewish 36
Judenstaat, Das 35

286 Index

kaddish   67, 87, 125, 149–50
Kardiner, A.   62
ketubba   145–6
Khazars   31–2
kindergartens   132
kinship   69–70
kinship terminology   63–5
kissing
    hand   209–10
kitchens
    Stefanesti   20
knackn kern   154–5
Koestler, Arthur   31
Kol Nidrey   97
kopl   90
krishma-leinen   126–7
kvotter   70

Lahovari, G. I.   27n
Landes, Ruth   66n
League of National Christian Defence   39
leeches
    bleeding   81
Leg boymer   110
leisure   152–61
levayeh   149
Leven, Narcisse   34
levites   94–5
Life is with people   1
Lilith   82
literary trial   160
local government
    Romania   41–5
lotto   170
love songs
    Yiddish   179–80
lullabies   174
    Romanian   188
    Yiddish   176–8

Maccabi
    sports club   139
machetonem   63, 69
Mai Lied, Der   198–202
Marie, *Queen*   28
marital fidelity   73
marriage   139–46
marriage brokers   71
marriage contract   145–6
marriages
    arranged   70–1, 140–3
mascattii   105
maskierteh   105
masturbation   213
matzo baking   43

meat   57
medicine   46–7, 75–80
    folk   80–4
Megilas Esther   103–4
Menahem Nahum   118
merar   58
merchants   48–54
Michael, *King of Romania*   28–9
midwives   83–4, 126
milk dealers   57
milk teeth   130
Miner, Horace   148
mishpocha   63, 69
mitbeyes   119
modes of address   208–9
mohel   125
Moldova   10–11, 26–7
morality   203–222
more Judaico oath   33
morning prayer   88–90
mother–daughter hostility   67
mother–son bond   66–7
Murdock, G. P.   250n

naming
    children   127
National Anthem
    Romanian   27
newspapers   155
    Romanian and Yiddish   36
nicknames   222–3
nuclear family   62–3
numerus clausus   39, 46
nursery schools   132

oath, more Judaico   33
oina
    game   163
old age   146–7
old wives' remedies   75

paiul
    game   166
Pale of Settlement   2–3
Palestine
    mandate   37
parents
    children and   210
parlour games   171
Partidul Evreesc   39
Passover   106–10
pastimes
    children   162
paupers   60–1

peasants 29-30, 220
    shtetl attitudes to 214
Peretz, I. L. 134, 153
personal relationships 208-9
Phanariot regime 27
pharmacists 45-6
photographers 50
photography 160
phylacteries 89-90
piano lessons 155
pioneers 39
pisica
    game 165-6
play 161
plita 20
plumbing
    Stefanesti 18, 23
porters 59
Potop's ice-cream parlour 156
prayer 88-90
pregnancy 124-5
printers 50
privacy 211
process literar 160
professionals
    shtetl 45-7
property rights
    Jews 38
proverbs 223-48
Prut, River 9, 157-8
public gardens 156
public nurse 76
pumpkin seeds 154-5
Purim 103-6
Purim Ball 105, 158-9

quiltmakers 59

Raspantie 15
reading 154, 155
rebbé 92-3
Rebbés court
    Stefanesti 118-21
religion 85-93
restaurants 52
rhymes
    children 18-19, 178-9
ritual slaughtering
    tax 42
role-playing
    games 168
Romania
    administrative structure 41-5
    climate 24-5
    history 26-9

Parliament 39
Romania's Scapegoat 32
Romanian citizenship
    Jews 37
Romanian language 26, 133, 161, 204
Romanian Rhapsody 192
Romanians
    shtetl attitudes to 214-15
roofers 58
Rosh chodesh 90-1
Rosh Hashanah 94, 95
Roskies, D. and D. 166n
Rosten, L. 149n
Rottenberg, Ernestine 183
rov 92-3
rural lands
    ownership 38
Russia
    Pale of Settlement 2-3
Rusu, Victor 120

Salon Binder 14-15
Sanatatea 75, 77, 78, 80
sanitation agent 76
saritura
    game 164-5
saving 211
scapegoats 95-6
schochet 42
school tax 42
school uniforms 136-7
schools
    festivals 160
Scoala Israelito-Romana Narcisse Leven
        34, 133, 217
seder 108-9
self-control 205
selling methods 52-3
serbare 160
sex
    attitudes to 71, 132, 212-14
Sforim, Mendele Mocher 60, 154
Shabbat Shuva 94-5
Shabbés goy 91
Shabbés meal 91
shadchen 71, 140-1
Shalom Aleichem 5, 153
shammes 115
Shavout 110-11
Shemini-Atzeret 99
shiva 150
shlugn kappures 95-6
Shmulewitz, S. 173
shoe shops 50
shoemakers 54, 56
shopkeepers 48-54

shops
 Stefanesti 14
shroud
 burial 148-9
shtetlech 250-5
 defined 1
 government 41-5
 Romanian 3-7, 9
Shyll 112-17
siblings
 relationships 68
Simchas Torah 99-101, 121
skipping 162
soba 20
Soche, Die 196-8
social standing 208-9
social stratification
 shtetl 43-5
Sokolow, N. 36
sondek 70
songs 173-4
 hasidic 175
 Hebrew 184-7
 Romanian 187-94
 Yiddish 175-84, 195-202
sons
 first-born 128
 importance of 125
spells
 midwives 83-4
spring cleaning
 Passover 107
status 7, 44-5, 49
Stefanesti 4-5
 layout 12-16
 rabbinic shtetl 118-23
 site 9-10
stepfathers 70
Stephen the Great, *Prince* 27
stepmothers 70
stoves, wood-burning 20
straw, the
 game 166
students
 Jewish 217
Succot 97-9
sunflower seeds 154-5
swaddling clothes 78-9, 128-9
swimming 157-8
Synagogue 112-17

table 168
tachrichen 148-9
tailors 55
Taschlich 95
taverns 50-2
taxation
 shtetl 42
tea rooms 156
teachers 47
tension equilibrium
 family 66-7
Tevye the Milkman 5
theatre companies 159
Thirteenth Tribe, The 31
thrift 211
tinkers 219
Tishe B'av 111
tombola 170
tombstones 151
Torah
 reading 100
town
 shtetl attitudes to 215
town crier 59-60
Trajan, *Emperor of Rome* 26, 30
tzadik 118
Tzurca
 game 166-7

uniforms
 school 136-7
United States 218
Uniunea Evreilor Pamanteni 39
university entrance
 Jewish students 137-8
upholsterers 59

Vasile Tziganer 156
vegetables 57
Versailles Treaty 37
Vienna 215
violin lessons 155
vitamins 78

wagonners 59
Warshawski, Mark 173, 177
watchmakers 50
water supply
 Stefanesti 18, 23
wedding canopy 144
wedding songs 180
weddings 143-6
Weizmann, Chaim 36
wheelwrights 59
wife beating 73
wigs 73
wives
 roles 65-6

women's hall
    Hoyche shyll   117
work
    leisure and   152
    working songs   183-4
World Zionist Organization   35

yarmulké   90
yichu   49
yichus   7, 44-5
Yiddish
    Romanian   32-3

Yom kippur   96-7
Yomtoyva   93-101
Yorga, N.   32
youth clubs   138-9
Yukl's Cofeteria   156

Zborowski, Mark   1, 66n
Zece Mai   27
Zionism   34-5, 39, 134
    youth clubs   138-9
Zionist Congress, first   35
Zumser, Eliakum   142